THE ESSENTIAL T. E. LAWRENCE

Malcolm Brown is co-author of *A Touch of Genius: The Life of T. E. Lawrence*, and editor of *The Letters of T. E. Lawrence* (published in Oxford paperbacks).

THE ESSENTIAL
T. E. LAWRENCE

Selected with a Preface by
DAVID GARNETT

Oxford   New York
OXFORD UNIVERSITY PRESS
1992

Oxford University Press, Walton Street, Oxford OX2 6DP

Oxford New York Toronto
Delhi Bombay Calcutta Madras Karachi
Petaling Jaya Singapore Hong Kong Tokyo
Nairobi Dar es Salaam Cape Town
Melbourne Auckland
and associated companies in
Berlin Ibadan

Oxford is a trade mark of Oxford University Press

First published 1951 by Jonathan Cape
First issued as an Oxford University Press paperback 1992

British Library Cataloguing in Publication Data
Data available
ISBN 0–19–282962–9

Library of Congress Cataloging in Publication Data
Lawrence, T. E. (Thomas Edward), 1888–1935. [Selections. 1992]
The essential T. E. Lawrence / selected with a preface by David Garnet.
p. cm.
Originally published: London: J. Cape, 1965. With new introd.
Includes index.
1. Lawrence, T. E. (Thomas Edward). 1888–1935. 2. Soldiers—Great
Britain—Biography. 3. Great Britain. Army—Biography. 4. World
War, 1914–1918—Campaigns—Middle East. 5. middle East-
-History—20th century. I. Garnett, David, 1892–ロ II. Title.
940.4'15'092 dc20 D56804.L32 1992
[B]
ISBN 0–19–282962–9 (pbk.)

Printed in Great Britain by
Biddles Ltd.
Guildford and King's Lynn

CONTENTS

PUBLISHER'S NOTE

The secret report dated 10th July 1917 (pp. 119–22) is incorrectly ascribed to the *Arab Bulletin*. It is to be found in the Public Record Office, Kew, Richmond, Surrey, reference FO 882/16 folios 246–9.

INTRODUCTION

by Malcolm Brown

The Essential T. E. Lawrence fulfils the dual role of being both an anthology and an autobiography; not only does it contain a judicious and wide-ranging selection of Lawrence's writings, it also offers us the story of his life. It begins with the eloquent letters of the young adventurer from Oxford, eagerly expanding his horizons beyond Britain to France and subsequently to the Middle East; it ends with the fatal telegram thirty years later which preceded his last, unfinished motor-cycle ride from Bovington Camp to Clouds Hill. In between we meet Lawrence as archaeologist, intelligence officer, soldier-in-the-field, polemicist, diplomat, and as Tank Corps or RAF serviceman under the aliases first of Ross and then of Shaw. Reading the book we experience again the dramatic twists — the exaltations and the troughs — of his remarkable career.

In fact we do so twice, in that we are also offered by way of programme note a fourteen-page 'Patchwork Portrait', compiled from *T. E. Lawrence by His Friends*, the volume of memoirs which his younger brother, A. W. Lawrence, published in 1937 in lieu of an official biography. This may be a relatively short book — and in paperback virtually a pocketable one — but it certainly gives generous measure.

It dates, however, from 1951, and the question must be asked: if an *Essential T. E. Lawrence* were to be compiled today, over forty years on, how would it differ from this present volume?

It would doubtless find space for some of the rich official documentation relating to the Arab Revolt which did not emerge from a fifty-year embargo until 1968 — though the editor, David Garnett, was able to reprint a number of reports from the *Arab Bulletin*, the secret Middle Eastern Intelligence digest produced in Cairo from 1916 onwards to which Lawrence was a leading contributor. It would certainly include some of the 300 or more letters written to his principal correspondent from 1924 onwards, Mrs George Bernard Shaw — known to all Lawrence students as 'Charlotte Shaw'. (Their absence, it should be noted, was due not to any lack of awareness or turpitude on the part of the editor, but to the firm refusal of the original recipient to divulge.) It would also probably find space for some of Lawrence's franker, less inhibited letters — to Robert Graves, for example, or E. M. Forster —

which are more acceptable in print today than they would have been in the 1950s. Yet despite all this, the book, I believe, still stands, indeed it more than holds its own, and if it were the only Lawrence publication available it would give a by no means inadequate impression of him both as man and writer.

An *Essential Lawrence* produced in the 1990s, however, would certainly be somewhat more defensive in its editorial tone. Quoting the admiring tribute of Sheikh Hamoudi, comrade of Lawrence's archaeological years, at the beginning of his 'Patchwork Portrait', Garnett commented (p. 13): 'Whatever more we can discover in the pages of analysis and self-analysis which follow in this book, that verdict given by a man belonging to an earlier and nobler age will stand. It cannot be reversed, but only supplemented.'

No editor would make such a claim today. In 1955, four years after this book first appeared, Richard Aldington's debunking attack, *Lawrence of Arabia: a Biographical Enquiry*, was published, causing a literary, indeed almost a national sensation. (The title under which it came out in France, *Lawrence L'Imposteur*, can be taken as giving a fair indication of its general drift; indeed its message went before it, in that the French edition was published ahead of the British one, in 1954.) It brought cries of protest from what became known, disparagingly, as the 'Lawrence Bureau', while producing smiles of pleasure on the faces of those who had found Lawrence's virtual icon status rather more than they could take. Overnight it turned his reputation into a battleground on which defenders and detractors have clashed ever since. It was also in Aldington's book that the hitherto well-kept secret that Lawrence was illegitimate, and that the name by which he became famous was the invention of his runaway parents, was given general currency. When subsequent revelations showed that in the latter part of his life he had submitted himself to ritual beatings (seen as masochism by some, as medieval flagellation by others), the resultant debate about his personality and proclivities raised more clamour than the debate about his achievements. Lawrence the guerrilla leader gave way to Lawrence the case history. It came to seem far more important to argue as to whether he was a homosexual than whether he was a hero. There have been some notable, and largely successful, attempts to get the balance right in more recent years, but once a major reputation has been destabilized there is no possibility of a complete restoration. The court-case, as it were, becomes permanent. No sooner has one advocate sat down than another stands up to make a counter-claim. The jury will never be allowed to retire.

One might go on to argue that it is perhaps just as well that there is no chance of ever arriving at an agreed verdict on the character and achievements of T. E. Lawrence. An unquestioned reputation can very easily turn into a dead one. Figures who rise above all controversy are all too often lost in the clouds. Certainly no such fate awaits 'Lawrence of Arabia' for the foreseeable future. It is this continuing, indeed increasing interest — for example, Lawrence is now a cult figure in Japan — which justifies the republication of this present book.

The Essential T. E. Lawrence was not a book on its own, but one of a distinguished series of literary anthologies which appeared under the Jonathan Cape imprint between 1947 and 1951, all of them bearing the same keynote adjective. The other authors purveyed to the public in this way — in an attractive uniform format and at an affordable price — were Ernest Hemingway, James Joyce, Samuel Butler, Richard Jefferies, Mary Webb, Neville Cardus, and (by courtesy of Joel Chandler Harris), Uncle Remus. After the wartime years, in which books had been slim, austere, and printed on paper arguably more suitable for the bathroom, the volumes of the *Essential* series were sumptuous indeed. Moreover, at a time when rationing was still in force and virtually everything was in short supply, eyebrows were not too readily raised at the thought that the essence of a writer's work might be crammed into one companionable volume. On the contrary, such compilations were seen as highly palatable and had a powerful appeal. They were a kind of wine-tasting *in extenso*, giving the reader enough to become positively acquainted with a writer rather than merely nod at him, while the title carried the clear implication that what was on offer was an authoritative as opposed to a facile or random selection. In other words, these were serious guides to a writer's territory, not merely a handful of short cuts. The claim of the prospectus for the series was that 'in each of these volumes the generous samples of the author's best work are so representative that the reader can assess the author's qualities and decide for himself whether he wishes to read the complete works'.

The reviews of *The Essential T. E. Lawrence* show that by and large this policy seems to have worked. It is true that one reviewer attacked it hip and thigh, stating that 'there is something annoying in the title of this collection and in the idea behind it. The essential T. E. Lawrence is to be found in the entirety of *The Seven Pillars of Wisdom*, in his collection of letters, and, perhaps, when it appears, in *The Mint* — not in a paste and scissors job which cuts him up into snippets.' But that reviewer was writing in *Time* magazine (10 December 1951) after the publication of the American edition — in the relative prosperity of the United States, not in frugal Britain. *Time*'s compatriot journal *The New Yorker* (5 January 1952) was, by contrast, positively benign, stating:

> The object of the work is to explain and portray Lawrence in his own words, with a little assistance from outside commentators. If this aim has not been completely realized, the book is nevertheless the clearest picture of him yet achieved.

On this side of the Atlantic, there seems to have been little or no criticism on account of the book's method of presentation. The overall reaction was one of gratitude for what was offered rather than carping at what was not. And in so far as the publishers hoped that the critics might help to create an appetite for more they could hardly have been better served. At this time *The Mint* — Lawrence's documentary account of low life in the RAF (referred to in the *Time* quotation above) — had not appeared in public print. *The Essential T. E. Lawrence* was the vehicle of first publication of substantial extracts from it, and some reviewers fell on them as though they had spotted the advance guard of a masterpiece. For example, William Scawen, writing in *The Adelphi* (27 April 1951), quoted one particular extract at considerable length (from pp. 242–3) and then exclaimed:

> This is one of eight selections from *The Mint*. They show that it may be one of the great books of our time . . . So formidable are the passages from *The Mint* that they lead to the realisation that Lawrence was as remarkable as a writer as he was as a man of action . . .

He concluded his review with the affirmation:

> So in this volume of selections David Garnett has performed a real service and the most important part of that service is to show that *The Mint* should be published.

It duly appeared four years later, in 1955, though in a chastened version; the unexpurgated text was not published until 1973.

If Scawen welcomed the book for its literary interest, other reviewers welcomed it because it allowed them to think again, while still under the shadow of the then recent war, about Lawrence the desert soldier — the best known guerrilla tactician of the previous war. Stories of unconventional forces making mayhem behind enemy lines were much in vogue in the late 40s and 50s as a stream of 'now it can be told' books poured from the presses and Lawrence was seen as their honourable predecessor. Indeed, he was hailed as the role model of his kind — justifiably, in that among those with whom he is now bracketed as practitioners of this style of warfare, such as Mao Tse-Tung, Che Guevara, and Ho Chi–Minh, as well as notable British examples like Wavell and Stirling, he is undoubtedly senior man. The reviewer in *The Times Literary Supplement* (1 June 1951), under the title 'The Solitary Warrior', stated:

> The present moment is a particularly propitious one for a new selection of the writings of T. E. Lawrence to make its appearance. Guerrilla tactics played, on the whole, a much larger part in the Second World War than in the first: and in the past five years we have had numerous opportunities of studying the exploits of a 'Popski' in the Western Desert, an Orde Wingate in Palestine and Burma, of commandos and frogmen and paratroopers whose very existence to the men of 1914–18, trapped in the miry insatiable inferno of the Somme, would have seemed an overwrought fancy, the figment of some super-Wellsian romance. . . . [W]herever they operated — those small bands of happy fanatics who, with knives in teeth and blackened faces, scaled enemy-held coastlines, swam beneath rivers or dropped from the innocent clouds — all shared in their lesser or greater degree the mantle of T. E. Lawrence. . . .

A parallel reaction was that of V. S. Pritchett, in a long and eloquent review in the 'Books in General' feature in the *New Statesman* (28 April 1951). *Maquis* stories, yarns of underground resistance in the occupied countries, were also highly popular in these post-war years and Pritchett saw links in this area also. Describing Lawrence as 'a new and prophetic prototype', he stated:

> He stands, rather flamboyantly guilty, at the beginning of a new age to which the conflicts of *The Seven Pillars* were to become soberly familiar. In everything, from the hold-ups, the executions, the intrigue and the tortures to the final nihilism, he was the first guinea-pig of the underground.

Pritchett is particularly stimulating and incisive in his scrutiny of *Seven Pillars of Wisdom*. These are his most important paragraphs:

> The theme of *The Seven Pillars* seems to be ecstasy, guilt and suffering. In action, that means the satisfaction of the well-laid mine, the provision for the tribesmen of timely loot, excitement and slaughter;

it means blood-guilt; and it means the martyrdom of leadership —
having to shoot a man oneself in order to prevent a blood-feud —
and a curious moment like the one when, after a massacre, Lawrence
went round and arranged the dead in more seemly positions. The
self-questionings have the rhetorical touch — later Lawrence criti-
cised the 'foppishness' of his mind — but the manner he adopted,
one feels, was simply his device for screwing the last ounce out of
sensibility, or a kind of flagellation . . . .

The pages on self-surrender, obedience and abasement are, in their
way, religious and, indeed, were observed among believers in a warlike religion. The final desire is for physical solitude. Lawrence could
not bear to be touched, unless, one supposes, he was hurt . . .

Throughout a swift, masterly narrative, packed with action, character and personal emotion, we have the extraordinary spectacle of a
brain working the whole time. It is as if we could see the campaign
thought by thought. The close texture of genius in action has never
been so livingly done by an active man. . . .

This is serious analysis, of the man, the book, and the situation, with
almost a prophetic glimpse of aspects of Lawrence of which Pritchett at
that time could not possibly be aware. Indeed, in virtually all the original reviewers of this book, there is a tendency which I find greatly re-
freshing to accept Lawrence as what he surely was, a serious contributor
both to war and literature, without the queasy doubts and disclaimers
which some later commentators seem to consider obligatory whenever
his name is discussed. It is also reassuring to find that the US paperback
edition of *The Essential T. E. Lawrence* published by Viking in 1963 —
i.e. *after* the great Aldington destabilization — carries this comment by
the eminent American critic Irving Howe: 'Lawrence is not yet a name
to be put away in history, a footnote in dust. He continues to arouse
sympathy, outrage, excitement.' Yet there is an important rider to be
added here. It would be ingenuous to imply that Howe was welcoming
Lawrence back untouched and untarnished into the old Valentino
mould. Indeed, in the article from which Viking took its quotation
Howe specifically disclaimed such tired and discredited trappings.★
'Time has mercifully dulled the image he despised yet courted: T. E.
Lawrence is no longer the idol of the twenties, no longer "Lawrence of

★Entitled 'T. E. Lawrence: The Problem of Heroism', Irving Howe's article was first
published in *The Hudson Review*, Autumn 1962, and reprinted in his book *A World More
Attractive*, New York, Horizon, 1963.

Arabia".' Instead, Howe welcomed a reconstructed, more contemporary Lawrence with whom one could identify, as opposed to the previous Lawrence whom one could only admire from afar — a Lawrence who had, as it were, made the leap from old hero to new man:

> I would suggest that it is this Lawrence — the hero who turns into a bewildered man suffering the aftermath of heroism — who now seems closest to us. Had Lawrence simply returned to the wholesome life of an English gentleman, . . . he would still have been noteworthy. Such a man, however, could hardly have captured the imagination of reflective people as the actual Lawrence did. His wartime record was remarkable, the basis of all that was to come; without it he might have been just another young man afflicted with post-war malaise. But what finally draws one to Lawrence, making him seem not merely an exceptional figure, but a representative man of our century, is his courage and vulnerability in bearing the burden of consciousness. "One used to think that such frames of mind would have perished with the age of religion: and yet here they rise up, purely secular."

The quotation is from Lawrence himself and will be found on page 254; it comes from the third of five deeply moving letters written in 1923 to Lionel Curtis from the army camp at Bovington when he was at his lowest ebb, for all of which Garnett rightly found space in this book.

Significantly it was Howe who labelled Lawrence a 'prince of our disorder', providing the phrase which Professor John E. Mack was to use as the title of his keynote biography — a modern interpretation of outstanding quality and interest — in 1976. All this is not to suggest, however, that the comments made by the reviewers of *The Essential T. E. Lawrence* in 1951–2 were, as it were, the products of an innocent age before Galileo and should therefore be discounted. On the contrary, they emphasize important aspects of Lawrence's achievements acknowledged and appreciated then of which we do well to remind ourselves today.

For the skill and professionalism with which this book was compiled, gratitude must be expressed to David Garnett. Indeed, anyone interested in T. E. Lawrence, whether admirer, sceptic, or general reader, is deeply in his debt.

Garnett's most important legacy is the volume of letters which he edited for Jonathan Cape in 1938; nearly 900 pages long and containing almost 600 letters, it is still much admired and sought after today. In the same year he produced a shorter selection, which, by arrangement with Cape, reappeared in 1941 in a cheap edition in the 'World Books' series produced by the Reprint Society. Long after that pioneering book club faded into history, this popular abridgement was regularly to be seen on the shelves of second-hand bookshops. It must have introduce Lawrence the letter-writer to many readers, among whom — I am pleased to acknowledge — I count myself.

David Garnett also made an effective contribution to *T. E. Lawrence by his Friends* (as also did his father, Edward Garnett, doyen of publishers' readers and Lawrence's prime literary mentor, through whom Lawrence and David had met). In 1962, David Garnett published his translation from the French of one of the strangest, and most moving, studies of T. E. ever to have been written: *338171 T.E.: Lawrence of Arabia*, by the Argentinian writer Victoria Ocampo. In the same year he portrayed Lawrence among a host of other writers in his very readable autobiographical volume, *The Familiar Faces*. In 1979 he touched again on Lawrence (calling him by the name by which he knew him, T. E. Shaw) in a late book of essays about writers he had met and admired, entitled *Great Friends*.

Anyone prefacing a book by or about T. E. Lawrence must always be aware that he was a master of the art of the Introduction himself. It is widely acknowledged that his Introduction to the 1921 Edition of Charles Doughty's *Arabia Deserta* is a model of its kind. (It also, by making the edition a best seller, launched Jonathan Cape as an independent publisher.) Yet, typically, he hated the very idea of such writings, and did all he could to avoid them. In 1923 Edward Garnett asked him to introduce a new edition of *The Twilight of the Gods* by his father, Richard Garnett. 'Introductions are vicious things, and I've sinned once already', he wrote in reply, but gratitude to Edward and admiration for the book itself won him over and his piece duly appeared in a fine printing from The Bodley Head in 1924. In 1930 Edward tried again with regard to a forthcoming book from Cape on the Middle Eastern campaign entitled *Red Dust*. Lawrence's answer was forthright: 'I will not write a foreword, or a back-word, or a middle piece, or any old piece, for anyone or any-thing, I hope. I always say "hope", because I daren't say "never". . . .' He was wise to enter the caveat, because soon after he yielded again, contributing a lively Foreword to Bertram Thomas's account of his crossing of the Empty Quarter, *Arabia Felix*, published by Cape in 1931. He knew, of course, that his mission was not merely to enhance the book's general interest, it was also to sell copies. In the Foreword he could not resist an amused reference to the commercial aspect of his role, beginning his last (highly laudatory) paragraph with the statement: 'I will not say how much I like this book, lest Jonathan C. dig out the odd sentence for his blurb.'

He also knew when to end. '[T]his note grows too long,' he wrote, in the final section of his Introduction to *Arabia Deserta*. 'Those just men who begin at the beginning of books are being delayed by me from reading Doughty'. In the same way this present piece is perhaps in danger of delaying people from reading Lawrence and should therefore be concluded.

MALCOLM BROWN

Postscript: Acknowledgement is made to *T. E. Lawrence: A Bibliography*, by Philip M. O'Brien, St Paul's Bibliographies, 1988, for help in tracing reviews of the original editions of *The Essential T. E. Lawrence*.

PREFACE

T. E. Lawrence's writings consist of *Crusader Castles*, a diary, part of *The Wilderness of Zin*, contributions to *The Arab Bulletin*, *Seven Pillars of Wisdom*, various articles and letters to the press on Arab politics, *The Mint*, some book reviews, translations of various books, including the *Odyssey*, a technical manual on the construction and handling of *The 200 class R.A.F. Seaplane Tender*, and the volume of his letters published after his death. Not one of these was suitable for inclusion here in its entirety; all except the translations are represented. The selection is therefore perforce more scrappy than the other volumes of The Essential Series. I have tried, however, to make a virtue of the scrapbook form by using this opportunity to put together a biography of T. E. Lawrence out of his own writings, making my selection of passages not for their abstract literary merit, but in order to complete the self-portrait.

The selection is preceded by another patchwork selected from the recollections published in *T. E. Lawrence by his Friends*, a collection of essays published after T. E. Lawrence's death by the care of his brother A. W. Lawrence. To all those whom I have quoted I am greatly indebted.

The chief liberty I have taken in making this selection is in interspersing the extracts from *Seven Pillars of Wisdom*, which were written some years later, with passages from *The Arab Bulletin* and letters which were written during the course of the war. My justification is that the unity of *Seven Pillars of Wisdom* was inevitably destroyed by the process of selection and that it was better to present Lawrence's part in the Arab war as one story and not to deal with the same events in widely separated parts of the books. I have also placed the Introduction and Chapter I of *Seven Pillars of Wisdom* at the end, after the capture of Damascus. I have done this because they contain a summing up of his motives and judgments of events and are the lessons learned during the war and the Peace Conference. I wish to thank Professor A. W. Lawrence and Mr. J. H. Nerney for their assistance. The Controller of H.M. Stationery Office has generously given permission for the passages quoted from *The 200 class Royal Air Force Seaplane Tender* to be included here.

DAVID GARNETT

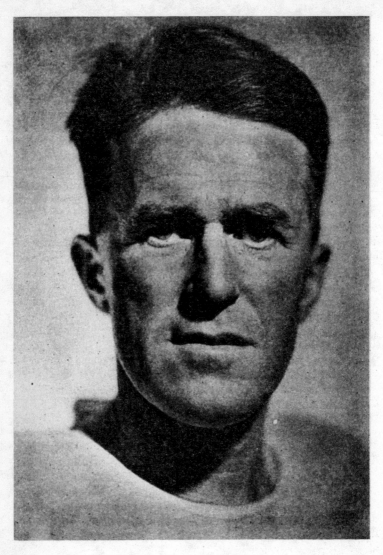

T. E. LAWRENCE

From the photograph by Howard Coster

AFTER he had been told of T. E. Lawrence's death, Sheikh Hamoudi strode up and down a stone-flagged hall in Aleppo, exclaiming in his grief:

'Oh! If only he had died in battle! I have lost my son, but I do not grieve for him as I do for Lawrence . . . I am counted brave, the bravest of my tribe; my heart is iron, but his was steel. A man whose hand was never closed, but open. Tell them . . . Tell them in England what I say. Of manhood the man, in freedom free; a mind without equal; I can see no flaw in him.'

Whatever more we can discover in the pages of analysis and self-analysis which follow in this book, that verdict given by a man belonging to an earlier and nobler age will stand. It cannot be reversed, but only supplemented.

With that in mind, I shall put together in this introduction facts of T. E. Lawrence's life and interpretations of his character, as recorded by his family and friends, in the hopes that such a patchwork portrait will enable the reader to understand more fully the selection of Lawrence's own writings and letters which follow and make up the main body of this book.

Most of these passages are taken from a volume of reminiscences called *T. E. Lawrence by his Friends*, collected and published after his death by the care of his brother, A. W. Lawrence.

Thomas Edward Lawrence was born at Tremadoc, Carnarvonshire, on August 16th, 1888. His father belonged to the Anglo-Irish Protestant landed gentry, his mother was Scottish and partly of Highland crofter descent. Thomas Edward, Ned in the family, was the second of five brothers, the youngest of whom was his junior by nearly twelve years. During Ned's infancy the Lawrences moved about, living in Scotland, Jersey, France and the New Forest and he was eight years old before they settled in Oxford.

'When we were small and shared a large bedroom, he used to tell a story which went on night after night without any end. It was a story of adventure and the successful defence of a tower against numerous foes, and the chief characters were Fizzy-Fuzz, Pompey and Pete — fur animal dolls that my brothers had. Long pieces of rhyme telling of the exploits and achievements were composed by him, and this was before he was nine.' (*M. R. Lawrence, Ned's elder brother*, 'Bob'.) T. E. Lawrence's interest in castles was to last all his life and led to his first visits to the East.

'When he was about five, Ned was able to read the *Standard* news-paper upside down; and in after life he told us he could always read the newspaper of the man opposite him in the train.' (*M. R. Lawrence.*)

He was a precocious child: 'his memory was remarkable, any book he took up he seemed to read at a glance, but he knew it all as I soon found out . . . Lessons were never any trouble to Ned, he won prizes every year . . . In the senior locals in 1906, he was placed first in English language and literature . . . and thirteenth in the first class out of some 10,000 entrants.' (*S. Lawrence, T. E. Lawrence's mother.*)

T. E. Lawrence received a devoutly Christian upbringing. 'He was for many years a constant worshipper at St. Aldate's Church and taught in the Sunday School there twice every Sunday.' (*S. Lawrence.*) 'He was also for two or three years an officer in the St. Aldate's com-pany of the Church Lads Brigade.' (*M. R. Lawrence.*)

Unlike his brother Bob, who became a medical missionary in China, T. E. did not continue in the faith in which he had been brought up. (See p. 23.)

He was clever mechanically. 'Ned was always the one to mend any object, or find out what was wrong with the electric light, etc.' (*M. R. Lawrence.*) Physically he was very strong. 'No tree was too high for him to climb and I never knew him to have a fall.' (*S. Lawrence.*) 'He was good at gymnastics and took part in games in the playground, but cricket and football had no interest for him.' (*M. R. Lawrence.*)

'When out in the playground one day at 11 o'clock, he saw a small boy being bullied by a bigger one; he went to the rescue. They had a struggle and fell and one of the bones in Ned's leg got broken near the ankle; he was wearing boots that day which helped to support it. He walked into the school supporting himself by the wall, and did his mathematics until one o'clock. He told his brothers he had hurt his leg and could not walk home, so they put him on a bicycle and wheeled him back. He never grew much after that — he had grown very fast before (three inches in a year) so evidently the bones were not strong.' (*S. Lawrence.*)

Lawrence 'had never possessed the average boy's interest in natural history and our rambles in the countryside of Oxford had ignored it . . . he inspected my quarries and jurassics but their cliffs and crags spoke no sermon in stones; they were fit material only for scaling. The plantations of St. John's in Bagley and Tubney woods remained just trees . . .' (*C. F. C. Beeson. At Oxford High School with T. E. L.*)

He cared little for animals, but admired their beauty. 'One day a

14

magnificent blue Persian cat appeared on the wall and took up his abode with us ... we found him with the cat on his knees stroking it, and he remarked: "I think this is the most beautiful animal I have ever seen." ' (*M. R. Lawrence.*) Woolley and Lawrence had previously kept a snow leopard as a pet at Jerablus.

Lawrence was from his childhood far more interested in history than in any other subject. This took many forms. He went bicycling all round the south of England, making rubbings of monumental brasses. 'Cut out and pasted on the walls of his bedroom were life-sized figures of knights and priests, with Sir John D'Abernon and Roger de Trumpington, a Crusader, in pride of place. It was no collector's hobby ... The Wallace Collection and the Tower armories became familiar ... Heraldry displayed an alluring field . . .' (*C. F. C. Beeson.*)

While still a small boy he had bought two books on Layard's excavations of Nineveh and knew them almost by heart. Later on 'lectures by Flinders Petrie to the Ashmolean Society renewed an interest in oriental antiquities . . .' In the autumn of 1906 a good deal of rebuilding took place in the heart of the city (Oxford). Lawrence soon discovered that the excavations were bringing to light quantities of early pottery and glass. To ensure that the specimens were carefully dug out and preserved, the workmen were bribed with a few pence apiece . . . This organization was extended to other sites and lasted two or three years. It yielded a fine series of vessels and pottery, glazed ware, blown and moulded bottles, pipes, coins and tokens, etc., mostly fifteenth to seventeenth century work. The cream of the collections was eventually presented to the Ashmolean Museum.' (*C. F. C. Beeson.*) The study of old pottery took Lawrence constantly to the Ashmolean, and it was while arranging the medieval cases there with the Assistant Keeper that he first came in contact with D. G. Hogarth, who had recently become Keeper.

In the summer holidays of 1906, 1907 and 1908, Lawrence bicycled all over France and visited many medieval castles, photographing, drawing and planning them. In the spring of 1907 he visited the principal Welsh castles. He decided to follow up these studies by visiting Syria, in order to find out whether the castles built by the Crusaders had followed the models of western Europe or those of Byzantine military architecture.

As a preparation he took a few lessons in Arabic and visited Charles Montagu Doughty, to whom D. G. Hogarth had given him an introduction. He also obtained, through Lord Curzon, an *Iradé* from the

Turkish Government which proved invaluable. In June 1909, he visited Syria and travelling on foot visited most of the castles of the crusading period. He was attacked, robbed, beaten and left for dead by Kurds at the end of the trip. The results of his research were summed up in the thesis he wrote for his Finals. He took a first class in the Honours School of History in 1910.

'He returned to Oxford full of a love of the silence of the desert places. Noise — the noise of Oxford traffic — was insupportable, and, in the garden of his parents' house in Polstead Road, was built a room, the walls of which were draped to keep out noise.' (*Leonard Green.*) He planned at this time, with Leonard Green, to buy a windmill on a headland washed by the sea, and set up a printing press, binding their books in vellum stained with Tyrian purple. He had brought jars of Murex back for this purpose.

In the summer of 1910, Lawrence was in France studying medieval pottery. He went out to Syria in the winter of·1910, visiting Athens and Constantinople on his way. After Lawrence had been several weeks studying Arabic, he joined D. G. Hogarth in a tour of Palestine and Syria, visiting Nazareth, Damascus and Deraa. In March, Hogarth started excavations at the great mound at Carchemish on the banks of the Euphrates where Lawrence, who took charge of the photography, was to spend the greater part of the next three years. Hogarth was succeeded as head of the dig by Campbell Thompson, who was in turn succeeded by Leonard Woolley, and Lawrence stayed on with each.

In July 1911, when the dig closed, Lawrence set off on a walk to Urfa, during which he was very ill with dysentery, toothache and fever. It is possible that he would have died but for the care of Sheikh Hamoudi. Lawrence had quickly made great friends with the Arabs employed on the dig. The chief of these was the foreman or Hoja, Sheikh Hamoudi, and a houseboy called Sheikh Ahmed, nicknamed Dahoum, or 'Darkness', because of his fair skin. To Miss Fareedeh El Akle, who taught in the American Mission School at Jebail, Dahoum said:

'You ask why we love Lawrence? and who can help loving him? He is our brother, our friend and leader. He is one of us, there is nothing we do he cannot do, and he even excels us in doing it. He takes such an interest in us and cares for our welfare. We respect him and greatly admire his courage and bravery: we love him because he loves us and we would lay down our lives for him.'

At Jerablus — the headquarters of the Carchemish dig — 'Lawrence cast much of his absorbed and discomforting aloofness, together with his visiting clothes and, clad in shorts and a buttonless shirt held together with a gaudy Kurdish belt, looked what he was: a young man of rare power and considerable physical beauty. The belt was fastened on the left hip with a huge bunch of many-coloured tassels, symbol, plain to all Arabs, that he was seeking a wife. I have not seen such gold hair, before nor since — nor such intensely blue eyes.' (*Mrs. Fontana.*)

'. . . his hair was always very long and in wild disorder — he used to say it was too long when it got into his mouth at mealtimes. In the evening he would put on, over his white shirt and shorts, a white and gold embroidered waistcoat and a magnificent cloak of gold and silver thread, a sixty-pound garment which he had picked up cheaply from a thief in the Aleppo market; in the evening too his hair was very carefully brushed: sitting in front of the winter fire reading — generally Homer, or Doughty's poems or Blake — he would look with his sleek head and air of luxury extraordinarily unlike the Lawrence of the day time.

'For while he frankly enjoyed his ability to live more roughly than most people could or would consent to do, and when tramping in Syria would put up with the plainest fare and very little of it, deliberately training himself to do without things, he quite appreciated comfort. He did not smoke, he took wine seldom and spirits never, but he liked good food and had a critical taste in the Arab dishes, which we had at Carchemish, and in Arab coffee he had the judgment of an expert. . . .

'In the actual work he was curiously erratic. From the outset he was excellent with the Arab workmen, in a way he was rather like them, for the fun of the thing appealed to him as much as did its scientific interest . . . Lawrence and Hamoudi would suddenly turn the whole work into a game . . . until with two hundred men running and yelling half a day's output would be accomplished in an hour . . . But another time I might come along from another part of the field and find practically no work being done at all, because Lawrence was sitting with the men round him discussing some point of village custom or clearing up a question of local dialect; and if I groused at all he would grin and ask what anything mattered.' (*Sir Leonard Woolley.*)

The years at Jerablus were adventurous, as Syria was in an extremely disturbed state, owing to the defeat of Turkey in the Balkan War. Lawrence had made friends with Kurdish chieftains who were planning to sack Aleppo and Lawrence and Woolley engaged in smuggling rifles ashore from a British gunboat, to protect the British Consulate, in case such plans were realized.

They were also, for a variety of reasons, on bad terms with the German engineers engaged in building the Baghdad railway. As striking as Lawrence's seriousness and intelligence, was an impish schoolboy humour. D. G. Hogarth summed it up by saying:

'Lawrence was an Arab: a street arab.'

'Once I asked him to write a detailed description of a row of sculptured slabs and he duly handed in a notebook which he said contained all that was wanted; long afterwards, when I came to look at it, I found that each slab was dismissed with a sentence or two which merely made fun of it.' (*Sir Leonard Woolley*.) In January 1914, Woolley and Lawrence were sent by the Palestine Exploration Fund, with a survey party, to explore and survey from Gaza and Beersheba southwards and eastwards to Akaba. Lord Kitchener was anxious to have this area properly mapped and Colonel S. F. Newcombe was in charge of the surveying work, the archaeology being to some extent camouflage.

On the outbreak of war, Lawrence went to the map department of the War Office and brought out an urgently needed map of Sinai.

'Woolley and he had, however, completed in the nick of time the last of the six successive seasons' work, which provided a topographical map of Egypt's eastern approaches . . . In December 1914, he was ordered, in company with Woolley and Newcombe, to Egypt and quickly became the effective link between the Military Intelligence Service and, in due course, the Arab Bureau on the one side and the Survey of Egypt on the other. His appearance ''an extremely youthful, insignificant figure, with well-ruffled light hair, solitary pip on sleeve, minus belt and with peaked cap askew'' prompted wonder as to who this young man was, and astonishment at his impudence. ''Whoever can this extraordinary little pipsqueak be?'' For Lawrence's quiet forcefulness had still to be realized . . . What then were those qualities? On reflection, I think the foundation of all was a rare capacity to regard an operation of any sort objectively, and in the process to get inside the skin of the participants . . . It is idle to pretend he was not ambitious. He was vastly so: but like all men of large calibre, ambitious for achievement rather than recognition . . . The diversity of Lawrence's capacity was so remarkable that one only slowly and sceptically accepted its genuineness.' (*Sir Ernest Dowson, K.B.E., Director-General Survey of Egypt.*)

Lawrence's career during the war is recorded in his own words and need not be recapitulated. But one or two of the opinions of the soldiers with whom he was working cannot be passed over:

'The quickening of Sherif Hussein's family revolt into the movement that poured into Damascus was something that no one else could have achieved, even with unlimited gold: it was a spiritual even more than a physical exploit . . . he had read more and thought more on military history and the military art than probably any Great Commander . . .' (*Field-Marshal Lord Wavell*.)

'Am I the only writer in this book to call him a little monkey, I wonder? And am I the only one to criticize him? If so, I shall be the only one whose account will please him wherever he may be. I am afraid I always thought he was a mischievous little imp and this mischievousness was undoubtedly a flaw in his fine character. Another small failing was the vanity which led him to pose, and tortured the better side of his nature. His attitude to publicity was that of Brer Rabbit to the briar-bush . . . I never knew him hesitate to take a decision, and I would rather have served under him than under any regular soldier I have ever met . . .' (*Sir Hubert Young, K.C.M.G., D.S.O., Indian Army*.)

'It was astonishing to see how that slight Englishman could beat the Arabs at their own game. At camel-riding and shooting, in endurance and courage he was their master . . . He seemed immune to the fiercest heat, more so than the Arabs . . . Many times, when resting after a strenuous march, have I seen him engrossed in a small red book, his constant companion . . .' (*Sergeant Instructor W. H. Brook, D.C.M., 'Stokes' of 'Seven Pillars'*.)

Lawrence left Damascus after its capture and was in Cairo on October 14th, 1918. On October 30th, he reported to the War Office in London. The three years which followed were devoted to trying to gain in the Council Chamber that freedom for Arabs which he seemed to have won by force of arms. In particular he tried to establish Feisal as an independent Arab sovereign in Syria, with the seat of his Government in Damascus. The attempt failed and, in the opinion of the best observers, it was this political failure which profoundly altered Lawrence.

'When I knew him in the spring of 1919, I should have said that he was a man fully in control of his nerves and quite as normal as most of us in his reactions to the world. I agree with you strongly that it was subsequent events which twisted him. I have always thought that the view which attributed his state of mind to the privations and experiences of the war years was wrong.' (*J. M. Keynes — afterwards Lord Keynes — in a letter to David Garnett.*)

Lawrence's mother has described how, after his failure at the Peace Conference, when he returned to Polstead Road, he would sometimes sit the entire morning between breakfast and lunch in the same position, without moving, and with the same expression on his face.

These months, which drew out into years, are unfortunately the worst documented of Lawrence's life. There are numbers of political memoranda, of minutes recording the details of possible political compromises, of letters to the press after the Arab cause seemed lost. There are letters to friends, but there are no intimate revelations, except those in *Seven Pillars of Wisdom* of which the Introduction and Chapter I are the most notable.

To the bitterness of failure and of feeling that he had betrayed the Arabs by false promises, were added other strains. He was engaged in writing *Seven Pillars of Wisdom* and often working for many hours at a stretch without stopping for food or rest. And, in the spring of 1919, when flying in Cairo, he was in an air crash and sustained broken ribs, broken collar bone and mild concussion. One rib, which I believe was broken then, pierced a lung, an injury from which he suffered for the rest of his life. I think also that the fact that his political defeat coincided with his being 'put on the map' by the illustrated lectures of Mr. Lowell Thomas was an added mental torture. These lectures were given at the Royal Opera House, Covent Garden, and at the Albert Hall to audiences totalling over a million people in London alone. Lowell Thomas afterwards toured the world for four years with his travelogue, 'With Allenby in Palestine and Lawrence in Arabia'. Lowell Thomas had been at Akaba . . . 'we never had the slightest difficulty persuading T.E. to pose for Harry Chase's camera . . . Lawrence loved the sensation of wearing his Sherifian regalia. He enjoyed posing for his photographs . . . While I was delivering my illustrated account of his campaign at Covent Garden, Queen's Hall and the Albert Hall, Lawrence came at least five times . . . Whenever he was spotted he would crimson, laugh in confusion, and hurry away with a stammered word of apology . . . I felt that many would have found it difficult to reconcile his modesty with the fact that he frequently came to hear me tell about his campaigns in Asia . . . He had a genius for backing into the limelight.' (*Lowell Thomas.*) It was perhaps as much Lawrence's sense of humour as his vanity which drew him to the lectures.

In 1920, the French bombarded and occupied Damascus and drove out Feisal and, in Iraq, the British were spending millions of pounds in putting down 'rebels' in battles round Baghdad, and hanging Arabs who were still nominally Turkish subjects. But in the spring of 1921 Winston Churchill went to the Colonial Office and decided to reverse this disastrous policy. He offered Lawrence a post and he accepted it.

A conference was held at Cairo with Lawrence, Young and Trenchard as Mr. Churchill's principal advisers. 'Towards the end of the year, things began to go better.. All our measures were implemented one by one. The Army left Iraq; the Air Force was installed in a loop of the Euphrates; Baghdad acclaimed Feisal as King; Abdulla settled down loyally and comfortably in Trans-Jordania. It would not be just to assign the whole credit for the great success which the new policy secured to Lawrence alone. The wonder was that he was able to sink his personality, to bend his imperious will, and pool his knowledge in the common stock. He saw the hope of redeeming in a large measure the promises he had made to the Arab chiefs, and of reestablishing a tolerable measure of peace in these wide regions. In that cause he was capable of becoming — I hazard the word — a humdrum official. The effort was not in vain. His purposes prevailed.

'One day I said to Lawrence: "What would you like to do when all this is smoothed out? The greatest employments are open to you if you care to pursue your new career in the Colonial service." He smiled his bland, beaming, cryptic smile, and said: "In a very few months my work here will be finished. The job is done, and it will last."

' "But what about you?"

' "All you will see of me is a small cloud of dust on the horizon."

'He kept his word. At that time he was, I believe, almost without resources. His salary was £1200 a year, and governorships and great commands were then at my disposal. Nothing availed. As a last resort I sent him out to Trans-Jordania, where sudden difficulties had arisen. He had plenary powers. He used them with his old vigour. He removed officers. He used force. He restored complete tranquillity. Everyone was delighted with the success of his mission; but nothing would persuade him to continue.' (*Winston S. Churchill.*)

Apparently he had felt the strain of the negotiations acutely. 'On one occasion I went to his hut after the last parade of the day and found him in bed. He looked haggard and seemed very depressed. When I sat down he apologized for his state and said he had a touch of fever. He explained, apropos of nothing, that his visit to the Hejaz in 1921 had been almost too much for him and that the mental strain to which he was subjected during the negotiations had been worse than anything he had known during the campaign.' (*Alec Dixon, Corporal in Royal Tank Corps, 1923.*)

Lawrence sent in his resignation from the Colonial Office on July 4th, 1922. Less than two months later, with the help of highly placed officers, he enlisted in the R.A.F. under the alias of John Hume Ross, A/C 2 No. 352087. An authorization for his special enlistment was signed on August 17th, 1922.

Lawrence's experiences as a recruit in the R.A.F. are recorded in the first part of *The Mint*. There is no doubt that life in the ranks imposed further very heavy strains upon him physically and mentally. Not only was he ten years older than most of the recruits, but he suffered from over a score of wounds, including broken ribs which had not been properly set. As a result, physical training was often torture to him, and the experience of living without any privacy in a hut full of men was a violation of his instincts. After training, A/C 2 Ross was posted to the Farnborough School of Photography early in November 1922. Five weeks later he was recognized and his presence given away to the press and the story was splashed over the front page and centre pages of the *Daily Express* on December 27th.

A few days later he was turned out of the R.A.F. For several weeks Lawrence made unavailing efforts to get this decision reversed. He toyed with the idea of becoming a lighthouse keeper, or enlisting in the Irish Free State Army, but early in March he was enabled to enlist in the Royal Tank Corps under the name of T. E. Shaw. A series of letters to Lionel Curtis, included in this volume, show his state of mind. Nevertheless, while in the Tanks, Lawrence made friends with whom he remained in touch for the rest of his life.

'One had but to watch him scrubbing a barrack-room table to realize that no table had been scrubbed just in that way before: he was the most conscientious man I have ever known. Neither could he escape becoming a schoolboy's hero, for he never grew old and he might well have stepped from the pages of Mallory ... T.E.'s unworldliness gave him a tremendous influence over his comrades; they had no time for "good" men and knew nothing of saints, but they knew a man when they saw one and Shaw was their ideal of a man. It is no exaggeration to say that, in his day, Shaw was the most popular man in the camp.' (*Alec Dixon, Corporal R.T.C., 1923.*)

While at Bovington, Lawrence acquired a derelict cottage, Clouds Hill, which he rebuilt and which became his headquarters. He entertained many friends there and it was a great source of happiness to him.

But he disliked the army and, while in it, made several applications to be allowed to rejoin the R.A.F., which were refused.

Finally, he went so far as to hint at suicide in a letter to Edward Garnett. This threat, and the influence of John Buchan, led Mr. Baldwin to order that Lawrence should be allowed to re-enlist in the R.A.F. His transfer was arranged in August 1925, and he was posted to Cadet College, Cranwell. His stay there was extremely happy and he was recovering his normal outlook, when he was sent to India in July 1927, as he wanted to be out of the way when the abridged version of *Seven Pillars of Wisdom* was published under the title of *Revolt in the Desert*. Such a publication had become financially necessary, in order to pay the artists and printers he had employed in the production of the limited edition of *Seven Pillars of Wisdom*. While he was at Karachi 'he made an official application to be excused attending at church parades in the camp . . . he said that he felt almost to the point of being an unbearable restraint upon discipline, the strain of having to sit and listen to sermons with which he could not agree, without being allowed to challenge in argument and request foundation for what was being said, and that, try as he might to change his own outward personality in his new life, it was obviously impossible to alter one's own mentality and he had therefore to bite down constantly upon the affronts of his intelligence, which itched to arise and refute what to him must always be palpable errors . . .' (*W. M. M. Hurley, Squadron-leader, R.A.F., and Adjutant, Karachi.*)

Here perhaps it is the place to ask what was T. E. Lawrence's religion? One of his friends asked him.

'I had long wished to get a statement from him, which would throw light on the spiritual difference I knew there was between us. What was his God? He answered without hesitation, and once more I missed his words, so beautiful was his face. He had a glory and a light shone in his eyes, but more of sunset, than sunrise or midday. What I think I heard in the flow of eloquence, was a record of process without aim or end, creation followed by dissolution, rebirth, and then decay to wonder at and to love. But not a hint of a god and certainly none of the Christian God.' (*Eric Kennington.*) In other words T. E. Lawrence was a rationalist.

'In Karachi T. E. Lawrence worked in the engine repair sheds and if speculation deepened into wonder when our formerly dry and unspirited correspondence took on a touch of the classical and the challenge of logical disputation . . . light only dawned when a private note came from R.A.F. Headquarters, Delhi, telling of the identity of A/C.2 Shaw, the acting clerk . . . One felt from the first and all the time, the pitiful vulnerability, the barrier which was there ready to be shut down at once as the only shield against probes into his privacy.' (*Squadron-leader W. M. M. Hurley.*)

But apparently senior officers disliked his presence in the camp and, in May 1928, Lawrence asked Sir Geoffrey Salmond to post him up-country. He was sent to Miranshah, on the borders of Waziristan. While there, he did much of the translation of the *Odyssey*, which had been commissioned by an American for printing in a de luxe edition by Bruce Rogers. After seven months, the Lawrence legend blazed up in a new and cruder form. The Afghan chiefs revolted against Amanullah, their westernizing King and Labour members of Parliament believed that the Government of India had inspired the revolt and that the presence of Colonel Lawrence on the borders of Afghanistan was connected with it. The rumour that 'the Arch-spy of the world' was behind the revolt was widely published. The Government of India decided that Lawrence should be returned to England and to his great indignation Lawrence was placed on board the S.S. *Rajputana*.

On the ship's arrival at Plymouth, he was got away without reporters being allowed to see him and was posted to a squadron of flying boats at Mount Batten.

The extreme secrecy with which the affair was handled aroused more suspicion and questions were asked in the House, as to why he had been allowed to enlist under a false name. Lawrence decided to try to stop this persecution and rang up Mr. Thurtle and afterwards had tea with him and other Labour members.

The five years which followed were as happy, though less adventurous, as the years at Jerablus. At Mount Batten, Lawrence was on warm terms of friendship with the Commanding Officer, Wing Commander Sydney Smith, and served as his clerk. As such he made many of the arrangements for the Schneider Cup race.

The need of high-speed boats to act as tenders for the flying boats and as rescue launches in case of accident was urgent. 'In the autumn of 1930, an opportunity occurred for his employment to assist in testing out new and more speedy types of experimental boats . . . He was working with me almost continuously from that time until the autumn of 1932, during which period we carried out together a number of tests and trials of speed boats and he contributed many practical ideas and suggestions which were of great benefit to the Service.

'The most happy relationship always existed; his whole-hearted co-operation, untiring efforts and wealth of technical knowledge and determination to help to solve many and varied difficulties that had to be overcome, were remarkable. We spent long hours at sea together taking boats round the coast ... These were far from being joy rides, particularly during the winter months.' (*Flt.-Lieut. W. E. G. Beauforte-Greenwood, Head of Marine Equipment Branch, Air Ministry.*)

Lawrence remained working in the Marine Craft Section until his discharge from the Service in February 1935. During this period he pursued his many interests happily and kept up an immense correspondence with his multitudes of friends, besides seeing them continually. His friends were drawn from all classes of men and women — they included tough 'old sweats' from the Army and R.A.F., two Field-Marshals, a schoolgirl and a very large number of artists and writers, for he had an ardent enthusiasm for the arts unusual in a man of his age. A large proportion of T. E. Lawrence's letters are concerned with the art of writing and with literary criticism. But it was the subject in which, I believe, he was least sure of himself. '... he could accept only unfavourable judgements upon his work. The reason for this attitude I should trace to a fundamental distrust of himself and consequent need of self-justification ... He had I believe a diffident, perhaps weak, core so controlled by his colossal will power that its underlying presence was rarely suspected.' (*A. W. Lawrence.*) Many, perhaps almost all, of his friendships were somewhat one-sided, though many who enjoyed such friendship may not like to acknowledge the fact.

'Most certainly he did not always speak me the truth, though did it matter? One felt safe in his hands. I seldom asked questions because they involved him in answers and though I was frank with him he was never equally frank in return, nor did I resent his refusal to be so. This explains, in part, why he was a great leader of men; he was able to reject intimacy without impairing affection.' (*E. M. Forster.*)

T. E. Lawrence greatly enjoyed riding his big Brough motor cycle and it was thanks to it that he was able to visit so many of his friends during his periods of leave. He was fatally injured on May 13th, 1935, in avoiding two errand boys on pedal bicycles, who were concealed in a dip in the road, when riding it back from Bovington Camp to

THE ESSENTIAL T. E. LAWRENCE

PART I

ARCHAEOLOGY

August 16 1906 [*His eighteenth birthday.*]

My dear Will, Your letter has put me in a fever heat of expectation: but: — what is it you are going to dig up? Your letter bristles with inconsistencies. You think it is a Roman or Celtic camp (the two things are absolutely opposed to each other) and then you proceed to say that it is a mound on some rising ground. If it includes a mound, say 40 feet high, it is a Saxon or Danish fortification, with probably an interment or two on the top; if the mound is 10 feet high or less, and is about 30 feet in diameter, then it is a barrow, as you said in the former part of your description, which has a lamentable lack of exact figures. You next say that you cannot see traces of vallum or fossa, which are both terms to be applied to a Roman camp, and not to a Celtic, Saxon, British, or Danish erection. These last three or four possibly might have *mounds* and *dykes*, but you see no traces of them. If the mound is British it will be closely encircled by its fortifications, (if it ever had any). If the mound is Saxon, the encircling lines of fortification may be half a mile away. The bayonets Florence describes are bronze spearheads, of a very early pattern: they might point either to an encampment or a burial, probably the latter, if no great quantity was found. So far all that you have told me which stands is that the mound is round. If I had further details I could advise you where and how to dig: a camp would not be worth excavating: — you might dig over half a mile of ground and only find a spear head: a burial, if a low mound, should have a trench cut through it, from S.W. to N.E., on the level of the ground. Keep all flints, except the whole mound is flint and gravel, and by all means keep all bones; if you find human bones, do not disturb them, but dig round them, to find if they are male or female, and to recover the whole skeleton if possible: the skull is the most important part to determine the date. Any bronze implements found should not be disturbed at first, but try to trace the haft, which will have shrunk to the thinness of a pencil. You will find this very difficult but the result will repay it. If the mound is small sift the earth you throw out — Frank and Arnie can help in this while you and Bob dig. Work very carefully, so as not to break any tender article: if the mound is large, you should begin in the same way from the top,

[1] Aged 16.

and work down until you are sure the strata have not been disturbed: i.e. if you find pure clay with no admixture of earth, you may be certain that it has not been moved. You may discover the whole mound to be natural (you say it is 'unnatural', most archaeologists use 'artificial') in which case only the upper three feet need be dug supposing it is a large mound. You see I am trying to advise something for every case. In a small barrow 4-8 feet high, the articles would probably not be more than two feet from the body on each side: to search further out is an energetic course which occasionally repays itself, but not as a rule. It might be worth while trying to obtain some of those 'bayonets'. I think they are preserved in the village, unless those preserved are real bayonets, dating from 60-70 years back. They will probably not be so old as the civil war, although it is possible that they might be. I should advise you to find out where they were discovered, and why they dug there, and at what depth they lay. You should be able to draw conclusions from the answers to these questions. Let me know how the matter progresses, and unless it is very light soil, use small spades. Keep an accurate account of your progress, and mark on a plan where each important article is found. You have my best wishes for success. Don't give up at once if you don't find anything. Digging is an excellent exercise.

[In a second letter, on the same subject, to his brother Bob he wrote: 'I will refer to Woolley.' Lawrence had got to know Leonard Woolley through his interest in ancient pottery, at which he had been working in the Ashmolean Museum.

In July Lawrence left the City of Oxford High School for Boys and in August went on a bicycling tour of French castles with his father, taking photographs as he had planned.]

TO HIS MOTHER

Sunday 11 *August* 1907   *Evreux*

Dear Mother, Father is out, and so I am at last writing to you. I would have written before, but was so busy taking photos. etc. at Château Gaillard. Beauvais was a wonderful place, and I left it with great regret for Gisors which was disappointing, (a large castle, but all the towers locked up), from Gisors we came to Petit Andelys. The Château

Gaillard was so magnificent, and the postcards so abominable, that I stopped there an extra day, and did nothing but photograph, from 6.0 A.M. to 7.0. P.M. I took ten altogether, and if all are successful, I will have a wonderful series. I will certainly have to start a book. Some of them were very difficult to take, and the whole day was very hard. I think Pt. Andelys would be a good place to stop at. The hotel is cheap, and very pleasant. The Seine runs near the back door, and the bathing is excellent, from a little wooded island in the centre of the river. There are plenty of hills within sight, and many interesting places. Also the scenery all along the river is exceedingly fine. Long strings of barges pulled by a steam-tug pass the hotel occasionally, and the whole place is over-shadowed by the hills with the ruins of the Château. I have talked so much about this to you that you must know it all by heart, so I had better content myself with saying that its plan is marvellous, the execution wonderful, and the situation perfect. The whole construction bears the unmistakeable stamp of genius. Richard I must have been a far greater man than we usually consider him: he must have been a great strategist and a great engineer, as well as a great man-at-arms. I hope Mr. Jane[1] will emphasize this in his book. It is time Richard had justice done to his talents. From Pt. Andelys we came on here, where there is a fair cathedral, with the most exquisite stained glass, all old, and of a glorious scheme of gold and red. The effect is magnificent, and makes a poor building look splendid. Our further movements are doubtful.

TO HIS MOTHER

26 August 1907   *Mont St. Michel*

Dear Mother, Here I am at last about to spend a night at the Mont. The dream of years is fulfilled. It is a perfect evening; the tide is high and comes some 20 feet up the street. In addition the stars are out most beautifully, and the moon is, they say, just about to rise. The phosphorescence in the water interests me specially: I have only seen it once or twice before, and never so well as tonight. The whole sea, when oars are dipped into it, seems to blaze, for several feet around. I rode

[1] Lawrence coached with L. C. Jane in his last year at the City of Oxford School and as an undergraduate. Mr. Jane has given a short account of Lawrence in Robert Graves's *Lawrence and the Arabs*, p. 16.

here from Dinan getting Frank's p.p.c. in St. Malo on my way ...
With Dinan and the Rance I am entirely in love. The Rue de Jersual
from the old bridge to the 'place' is perfect: the river is most lovely.
Above the town it becomes very quiet and peaceful like the Thames:
lined with aspens and Lombardy poplars. When you add water-lilies,
willows, and an occasional high bank, crowned with a quaint farm-
house or château, you have a fair idea of the characteristics of the
stream. ...

Since I left Father I have had a very wonderful time. It began at
Fougères, which I saw by moonlight and a more exquisite sight I have
seldom seen. That castle is quite above and beyond words. It pollutes
it to mention any but Château Gaillard, Pembroke, and Caerphilly in
the same breath, and I am not sure but that Fougères is the finest of
them all. The Tour des Gobelins is six stories in height, and circular.
It stands on a granite cliff 80 feet high, and in the moonlight had a
marvellous effect. It set off the strength of the Mélusine, a tower near,
with an enormous expanded base. The talus shoots right out like the
Keep of Ch. Gaillard. Beyond the Mélusine, after a hundred yards of
machicolated curtain come Raoul and Yrienne, two wonderful chefs-
d'œuvre of the military architect. They are semicircular bastions,
projecting some 70 feet from the wall, are over 80 feet in diameter, and
more than that in height; neither has a window or projection in the
face and over against them leans the spire of St. Sulpice the most
crooked and the thinnest in Bretagne. I would have given anything to
have been able to sketch or paint these things as I saw them. I really
must return to Fougères soon and do justice to the whole. The neglect
in which it has been left by the Guide-books is abominable.

From Fougères I glided S.E. to Le Mans, to photograph the effigy
of Mrs. Richard I, Berengaria, in the cathedral there. The apse and
nave of the building were splendid: the former especially. From Le
Mans I rode to Saumur via Le Lude a most splendid Renaissance
château, unhappily private. Saumur itself is still in parts as Balzac
painted it in *Eugénie Grandet*, though the main streets have been rebuilt.
The Castle is a military storehouse. I slept that night at Angers. The
Cathedral roofed as it was in domes was a new style for me in architecture. From Angers I rode the next day through Lion d'Angers to
Rennes and so on to St. Malo and Dinard. The vineyards were quaint
but monotonous. At Dinard I tried 5 hotels but all were full. As it
was then 8.0. P.M. I went to the Chaignons. When I spoke and
revealed myself there was a most enthusiastic scene. All yelled Wel-

come at once ... M. Corbel was with them and collapsed when he heard where I had come from. I have given them a topic of conversation for a week — Deux cent cinquante kilomètres, Ah la-la, qu'il est merveilleux. Deux cent cinquante kilomètres.

Next day I went on to Lamballe meaning to go as far as Guingamp. It however began to rain heavily so I stopped and made a careful study of the Rood screen in the church there. Next day I photoed it, and the time taken (3 hours to focus) should ensure a presentable result, better than the vile p.c. I sent you. Next day (by the way the Chaignons and the Lamballe people complimented me on my wonderful French: I have been asked twice since what part of France I came from) I went on to La Hunaudaye, and took 4 photos. In the evening at Dinan I wrote to M. de la Brière asking him to take steps for the preservation of the Château. Nothing like making his society of use. Tomorrow I am going to ride into Granville.

TO HIS MOTHER

29,8,09   *Latakia*

Dear Mother, Another chance for a note, this time hurried. I wrote last from Tripoli. I went thence to Aarka, and then to Kala'at el Hosn, passing one night on a house roof, and the second in the house of an Arab noble, reputed, as I was told next day, of the highest blood; a young man very lively, and rather wild, living in a house like a fortress on the top of a mountain: only approachable on one side, and there a difficult staircase. If you keep this note I can tell you all sorts of amusing things about him later: name Abdul Kerim. He had just bought a Mauser, and blazed at everything with it. His bullets must have caused terror to every villager within a mile around. I think he was a little cracked. Then I got to Hōsn which is I think the finest castle in the world: certainly the most picturesque I have seen — quite marvellous: I stayed 3 days there with the Kaimmakam, the governor: a most-civilized-French-speaking-disciple-of Herbert-Spencer-Free-Masonic-Mahommedan-Young Turk: very comfortable. — He sent an escort with me next day to Safita, a *Norman keep, with original battlements*: The like is not in Europe: *such a find*. Again I slept with Kaimakam & Co. (Co. here means fleas) and next day I went on again with a huge march, to two more castles, & a bed for the night in a threshing floor, on a pile of tibn, chopped straw, listening to the Arabs beating out their Dhurra in the moonlight: they kept it up all night in relays, till about 2 a.m. when they woke me up, & said they were all exhausted, would I keep watch because there were thieves, & I was an Inglezi and had a pistol: I obliged, thinking it was humbug of the usual sort, (every village distrusts its neighbour) but they told me in Tartus next day that there really were not thieves, but *landlords* about! Isn't that charming? These dear people wanted to hide the extent of their harvest. Next day as above I went to Tartus, by another good castle: then struck far inland, (through a country of flint and steel and hand-mills, to Masyad, the chief city of the Assassins country: and then to Kadmus another of that gentry's strongholds, where the 'Old Man of the mountains' himself lived: (I slept in his château[1]) and so to Aleika, to Margat, a castle about as big as Jersey I fancy: one wanted a bicycle to ride round it: to another Banias, to Jebeleh, and here to Latakia, all well.

Monday I want to get off to Sahyun, and then in 4 or 5 days to Antioch, and then to Aleppo in 5. I hope there to hear from you because Bob's going to Germany is in the nature of an experiment: he will have better food than I have — last week only bread, & that bad: this is a considerable town however, with native restaurants. I have got to like leben. No smoking yet, though every man woman and child does. The peasants dry and smoke their own. I will have such difficulty in becoming English again: here I am Arab in habits, and slip in talking from English to French and Arabic unnoticing, yesterday I was 3 hours with an Orleannais, talking French, and he thought at the end I was a compatriot. You may be happy, now all my rough work is finished successfully, and my thesis is *I think assured*. *Iradé*[2] *invaluable*.

TO HIS MOTHER

September 7 1909   *Aleppo*

I wrote to you from Latakia: on the Monday I went from there to Sahyun, perhaps the first castle I have seen in Syria: a splendid keep, of Semi-Norman style, perfect in all respects: towers galore: chapels; a bath (Arabian) and a Mosque: gates most original: and a rock-moat

[1] Demolished by Ibrahim Pasha in 1838!

[2] Lawrence carried an *Iradé* or letter of protection from the Sultan obtained for him by Lord Curzon, then Chancellor of Oxford University.

50 feet across in one part, 90 feet in another, varying from 60-130 feet deep: there's a cutting for you! And in the centre had been left a slender needle of rock, to carry the middle of a drawbridge: it was I think the most sensational thing in castle-building I have seen: the hugely solid keep upstanding on the edge of the gigantic fosse. I wish I was a real artist. There were hundreds of other points of interest in the buildings. I stayed there two days, with the Governor, who was most obliging and then came on here by forced marches, 120 miles in 5 days, which no doubt Bob or Will will laugh at, but not if they had to do it stumbling and staggering over these ghastly roads: it took me 13 hrs. of marching per day, & I had an escort with me (mounted) so I lost no time . . . By the way, I took the escort abused above because I was shot at near Masyad: an ass with an old gun: I suppose he was trying it. At any rate he put in a shot at about 200 yards, which I was able to return rather successfully: for his horse promptly bolted about half a mile: I think it must have been grazed somewhere: at any rate he stopped about 800 yards away to contemplate the scenery, & wonder how on earth a person with nothing but a pistol could shoot so far: & when I put up my sights as high as they would go & plumped a bullet somewhere over his nut he made off like a steeple-chaser: such a distance was far beyond his old muzzle-loader. I'm rather glad that my perseverance in carrying the Mauser has been rewarded, it is rather a load but practically unknown out here. I complained of course to the governor of the district: who was furious, and sent out all his police at once: he agreed with me however that the man simply wanted to frighten me into money-payment: no success for him. I am now of course far beyond any disturbed country, and there is no chance of a repetition of the joke: which is why I tell you. . . .

[On September 22nd Lawrence wrote to his mother to say he was coming home at once for lack of money, in a letter which is full of suppressions of alarming facts. Thus he said that his stomach had never been upset 'I suppose my exercise, etc. (I have walked 1100 miles) is responsible for my health'. He admitted, however, that his feet were in a bad state — and further long walks would be imprudent — besides which he would need a new camera for his had been stolen from a carriage while the coachman was asleep. 'I find an absurd canard in the Aleppo paper of a week ago: my murder near Aintab (where I didn't go) . . . The hotel people received me like a ghost. Mr. Edvard Lovance sounds like me.'

The camera had not been stolen from a carriage but taken when he was 'robbed and rather smashed up', by Kurds who beat him and left him for dead. I believe that in this passage of the Oxford text of *Seven Pillars of Wisdom*, after describing the ghastly flogging he endured at Deraa, Lawrence refers to this incident.

> I struggled to my feet and rocked unsteadily for a moment wondering that it was not all a dream, and myself back five years ago in hospital at Khalfati, where something of the sort had happened to me.

In the Subscribers' edition he altered the wording to 'five years ago, a timid recruit at Khalfati, where something less staining of the sort, had happened'.

Khalfati [Halifeti] is between Aintab and Urfa. If I am correct in my interpretation, it was eight years. Five years would make it 1912. It is quite possible there was such an incident then, but I have found no record of it. The word *recruit*, if meant literally suggests that Lawrence may either have entered the Turkish Army deliberately or have been taken for military service while in Arab dress. I have no other evidence for this supposition.

In the first half of 1910, T. E. Lawrence completed writing his thesis on *Crusader Castles*, which he submitted for his degree.

The thesis has been published since his death, together with his letters written while collecting the material for the thesis, and with photographs which he took to illustrate it (two volumes, Golden Cockerel Press, 1936). The thesis was annotated in later years by T. E. L., with characteristic marginal notes[1] which show his continued interest in the subject. Only short extracts have been chosen which will serve to show the assurance of Lawrence's style and his preoccupation with practical details of war.]

from CRUSADER CASTLES

THE Byzantine curtain-towers are mysteriously inadequate. The Tactica demands that towers be octagonal outside and circular inside: and one of this pattern exists at Dash Borgh in Asia Minor:*

> * Constantinople has lots.

[1] These notes are shown by * † ‡ etc.

but generally there are none such. Occasionally towers are octagonal, inside and out, more often hexagonal: nine-tenths are simply rectangular: in the African fortresses round towers are sometimes used at the angles of the larger places, and very occasionally there is one on the curtain wall. Procopius mentions towers that commence square with a circular superstructure : — and there is one at Dash Borgh, and three or four in Africa. The shallow rectangular shape however is the usual one: the towers have the tiniest walls on the enceinte, often only half the thickness of the curtain, and are hollow to the ground level. There is hardly a Byzantine tower that could not be smashed in with a few blows of a ram.* Their square fronts made attack easy, and mangonel stones found a fair target: also the square shape gave very little flanking fire and was less defensible from the walls.†

Before an earthquake it was most liable to collapse. The only point in its favour‡ was its readiness of construction; that they valued more than the round tower or the polygonal was shown by their placing these at important points. For the rest they seem to have trusted to the weakness in siege craft of the enemies they had to ward against: the Arabs were, till Saladin's§ time contemptible engineers: and the Greeks found that a plain wall without towers was often sufficient to check them.‖

Indeed as a rule loopholes are meant less for firing through than for admitting light: the recesses in which they are placed are seldom made high enough for a long bow, or broad enough for a cross-bow. The archer would be forced to stand back within the tower: and to pass a yard-long arrow or broad quarrell through a slit three inches or less in width is a feat requiring some skill, even if the shot is to be straight ahead. Through such loopholes as those in the garden wall of New College, Oxford, an arc of fire** only 21 yards long at a range of 100 yards is the maximum. Walls generally are†† always defended from the top.

The loops at Safita are evidently intended only to light the chapel, and they do it very badly at that. Those of the hall occupying the first floor are a little broader, but it is hardly possible from them to com-

---

* Not having used a ram myself.
† Being of small projection with a dead centre.
‡ According to Proffessor Lethaby.
§ Good for Saladin.   ‖ Quote examples.
** An efficient arc.   †† Were.

mand the ground near the foot of the tower. The roof on the other hand is flat and unencumbered with fittings, and on the top of each merlon is a recessed socket, for the swinging bar of the shutter that closed the crenellations: this shows that some use was made of it in attacks, but even so the keep of Safita can never have been a very efficient stronghold.★ It would be crowded with a garrison of 200 men and the necessary stores, which must have included water, for the upper floor (evidently meant, by its barred door, as a last resort) has no means of access to the cistern in the foundations.

★ The battlements of Safita are the oldest extant.

TO HIS MOTHER

August 1910   *Le Petit Andelys*

The book I had was *Petit Jehan de Saintré*, a XV Cent. novel of knightly manners — very good: — I have wanted to read it for a long time, but the Union copy was so badly printed that I had not the heart for it. Now I have found (for 1 f. 25) a series quite nicely typed on fairly good paper. So far I have only got 4 volumes, because they are rather much to carry: it is altogether glorious to have found good French books at last. I can read Molière and Racine and Corneille and Voltaire now: — a whole new world. You know, I think, the joy of getting into a strange country in a book: at home when I have shut my door and the town is in bed — and I know that nothing, not even the dawn — can disturb me in my curtains: only the slow crumbling of the coals in the fire: they get so red and throw such splendid glimmerings on the Hypnos and the brasswork. And it is lovely too, after you have been wandering for hours in the forest with Percivale or Sagramors le desirous, to open the door, and from over the Cherwell to look at the sun glowering through the valley-mists. Why does one not like things if there are other people about? Why cannot one make one's books live except in the night, after hours of straining? and you know they have to be your own books too, and you have to read them more than once. I think they take in something of your personality, and your environment also — you know a second hand book sometimes is so much more flesh and blood than a new one —

and it is almost terrible to think that your ideas, yourself in your books, may be giving life to generations of readers after you are forgotten. It is that specially which makes one need good books: books that will be worthy of what you are going to put into them. What would you think of a great sculptor who flung away his gifts on modelling clay or sand? Imagination should be put into the most precious caskets, and that is why one can only live in the future or the past, in Utopia or the Wood beyond the World. Father won't know all this — but if you can get the right book at the right time you taste joys — not only bodily, physical, but spiritual also, which pass one out above and beyond one's miserable self, as it were through a huge air, following the light of another man's thought. And you can never be quite the old self again. You have forgotten a little bit: or rather pushed it out with a little of the inspiration of what is immortal in someone who has gone before you.
                                                                              NED

TO V. W. RICHARDS

le 29 Août [1910]   *Carentan*

For the rest when are you going to get into Northern France? Take someone with you, or go alone to Rheims, and sit down at the base of the sixth pilaster from the West on the South side of the nave aisle, and look up between the fourth and fifth pillars at the third window of the clerestory on the North side of the nave. Take all the direction in at a gulp, and find yourself looking at an altogether adorable mist of orange and red, such a ruby, and such a gold as I have seen nowhere else in glass. And here it is all in a maze of colours, blended to despair, without a suspicion of pattern or form in it. One can imagine saints & angels & medallions and canopies, but without the smallest reason or foundation. It is pure colour, perfect — . I don't suppose there was a piece of glass in it of one colour more than 3 inches square (in a window of 30 feet) and it stained the floor of the nave (there being no chairs) an indescribable blend. The sun only came through it about five o'clock, and the 'purple patch' climbed from the floor up one of the pillars, and faded into grey, but while it lasted I came to myself & abjured presumption & Rossetti saints. We can't do it! or at any rate I can't and you are little more ancient (i.e.

mediaeval). Go also to Lisieux, the most perfect town (all superlatives tonight) of wooden houses in Normandy. Every other house at least is old, & I think two out of three, and they have wooden pillars and brackets, & crochets & corbels, and dormers, and gables, and barge-boards, & ravishing little pillarettes alongside the windows, and gargoyles on the gutters, with carved lintels & side posts, and many-beamed ceilings, and an inn staircase with a roughly squared oak-trunk across its midst, so that all people going up or down had to bow their heads & do obeisance to sir beam, and the irreverent suffered. You know Montaigne used to write up his best-liked saws & instances on his rafters;[1] what do you think of something piquant and to the point, on the business part of the log with which you are going to block your staircase? . . .

Would it bore you (somewhat before Oct 2) to inquire of Hollings what would be the cost of the first edition of Doughty, the *Arabia Deserta*, published by the Cambs. Univ. Press about 20 years back? Also of a copy (now out of print) of the *Wandering Scholar in the Levant* by D. G. Hogarth, one of the best travel books ever written.

[Lawrence took first class honours in history, partly on the strength of his thesis *The Military Architecture of the Crusades* (since published as *Crusader Castles*). D. G. Hogarth recommended him for a demyship at Magdalen College, Oxford, and Lawrence set off for the Carchemish dig, then being begun under Hogarth's leadership, for the British Museum, on the Messageries Maritimes boat *Saghalien*. 'By extraordinary good fortune' the boat kept breaking down. He thus had a day ashore at Naples and another at Athens.]

TO HIS MOTHER

December 1910   *Messageries Maritimes*

. . . I had to go back through the town to reach the Acropolis, and chose therefore to wander into by-streets, that I might come out at the Theseion; and the further I went the stronger became a curious sense of unreality, almost of nightmare. Here was a town full of people

---

[1] These are still to be seen. Lawrence had visited Montaigne the year before; see letter 12.

speaking the same tongue and writing the same character as the old inhabitants of 3000 years before . . . It was all out of Aristophanes or Juvenal, all in keeping, so that it seemed quite natural when I walked up a little hill, and passed under the pillars of the temple. It stands today as perfect as ever it was, with the added beauty of the stains and hollows with which Time has endowed its stones. When you have passed around one of the angles of its cellar[1] wall, you see framed between two pillars the sunlight on the steps of the Propylea and the pediment of the Erectheum. The rock of the Acropolis is very large and high and steep. The quiet was really almost uncanny, as I walked up the shallow valley below Mars Hill, and along the processional way to the gateway of the citadel. There were no boys to bother one, no loud bellows'd leather sellers, only a misty sunlight in which all Attica, Phaleron, Salamis, Eleusis, and the distant Peloponnese lay motionless, 'drowned in deep peace', below the rock platform of the Wingless Victory. To get there I had to climb up the white marble staircase of the Propylea within the entrance gate. There were no porters, no guides, no visitors, and I walked through the doorway of the Parthenon, and on into the inner part of it, without really remembering who or where I was. A heaviness in the air made my eyes swim, and wrapped up my senses: I only knew that I, a stranger, was walking on the floor of the place I had most desired to see, the greatest temple of Athene, the palace of art, and that I was counting her columns, and finding them what I already knew. The building was familiar, not cold as in the drawings, but complex, irregular, alive with curve and subtlety, and perfectly preserved. Every line of the mouldings, every minutest refinement in the sculptures were evident in that light, and inevitable in their place. The Parthenon is the proto-cathedral of the Hellenes. I believe I saw the Erectheum, and I remember coming back to look again at the Propylea, and to stand again beside the Niké Apteros: but then I came down again into the town, and found it modern and a little different. It was as though one had turned from the shades of the ancestors, to mix in the daily vocations of their sons: and so only this about Athens, that there is an intoxication, a power of possession in its ruins, and the memories that inhabit them, which entirely prevents anyone attempting to describe or to estimate them. There will never be a great book on Athens unless it is one by an enemy: no one who knew it could resist its spell, except by a violent attack upon its spirit, and who can attack it now of artists, when

---

[1] i.e. The body of the temple as distinguished from the portico.

43

Tolstoy is dead? He, and he alone, could have uprooted Greek culture in the world. I am coming back by Athens I think next year to stay a little time. For the present I am only confused with it: I do not know how much was Athens, and how much the colouring of my imagination upon it.   N.

[Lawrence reached Syria in January 1911. In Aleppo he sought out the last working maker of chain-mail in order to buy his tools and study his methods on behalf of his friend Mr. C. J. ffoulkes.

The following letter is in answer to Leonard Green's asking advice about lectures which he was giving on the Crusades. It is in marked contrast to the youthful plans for living in a windmill. Lawrence in his answer is concerned with the physical geography of Syria from the point of view of a general conducting a military campaign in it. It shows what an extremely clear grasp he already had of the problems that he and Allenby would have to face seven years later.]

TO LEONARD GREEN

[*Received January 14th*, 1911]   *Jebail, Syria*

What I felt most myself in Syria, put shortly, was the extreme difficulty of the country. Esdraelon, & the plain in which Baalbek lies are the only flat places in it. The coast road is often only 50 yards wide between hills and sea, and these hills you cannot walk or ride over, because they are strewn over with large & small boulders, without an inch of cultivated soil: also numberless small 'wadies' (torrent-beds) deep and precipitous: not to be crossed without a huge scramble. In one day's march, from Lake Huleh to Safed, one ascends & descends 16,000 feet in hills & valleys, often 1,500 feet deep & only 200 yards or so across, and in all the way only a single track path on which one can ride without fear of smashing horses' legs. Make a point that for heavy-armed horse operations in such country are impossible: they can march in single file, but cannot scout, or prepare against surprise: the battle-field of Hattin (near Tiberias) is like a dried larva-flow, or the photograph (only in rock) of the pack-ice of the Arctic seas. Blame the pen and ink not me for this letter's illegibility. Even when there are no mountains or rivers there will be hills & valleys enough, with rock-stretches, to make an impassable tract. You will never, without seeing it, conceive of the difficulty of the country. On the main road from Antioch to Aleppo my escort walked with their horses (after Harim) for nearly four hours: and for a Syrian to fare afoot is much against the grain.

The next point is the rivers: the Jordan is hardly passable except at three points: just below Lake Huleh (Gisr Benat Yakub, to-day: Castle Jacob or le Chastellet in the Crusade authorities) a bridge & ford. Another ford just below lake Tiberias, (near Semakh) and one more (very difficult) near Jericho. The first two were available for or against the Damascenes. From Lake Huleh northwards is a swamp & the river Litani, until the hills get steep enough & high enough to be impassable: and then (very quickly) comes the Orontes, which is nearly always impassable (from Riblah downwards) to Esh Shogr, on the road from Latakia (Laodicea) to Aleppo. There is a ford there, and after a bridge near Antioch (the Iron Bridge). Above Antioch came a large lake, and then very hilly ground from the Kara Su to Alexandretta. So you see W. Syria is pretty well defended. In the early days of the Latin kingdom they held all this, and as well pushed across the Euphrates (via Harim, Tell Bashar, and Biredjik) to Urfa, (Edessa). This was a sort of outpost, which kept apart the Arabs of Mesopotamia and the hills to the north (Kurdistan) from the Arabs of E. Syria (Aleppo, Homs, Damascus) and the Arabians. While the Crusaders held Edessa, which is a tremendous fortress (of Justinian's) they were unassailable except through the Damascus gap, and one opposite Homs (Emesa) extending to Tripoli. This last gap (which I forgot to mention before) is a nearly sea-level pass between Lebanon & the Nozairiyeh hills. It was defended by three tremendous Crusader castles (Crac des chevaliers, in Arabic Kalaat el Hosn; Safita, Chastel blanc in the French authorities; and Aarka, just above Tripoli). These three places made this gap tolerably harmless, except from Arab raids: these were continuous: but only did temporary harm: still they neutralized the force of the county of Tripoli[1] from 1140 onwards. The Damascus gaps were also blocked: the northern one by Banias beyond Huleh, by Hunin, above the lake, by Safed, and by Chastel Jacob, just beside the ford, which last castle only existed a few months. Stevenson in his book points out its importance rather more cheerfully than usual with him. The Southern ford, below Lake Tiberias, was

[1] The Count of Tripoli was one of the great princes of Crusader Syria.

defended by the town of Tiberias by Kaukab el Hawa (one of the Belvoirs, just above Beisan) and by an outpost, el Husn, occasionally held beyond Jordan: it is not marked on any map. The Jericho ford was never very important. There were some little Crusader castles on its Syrian side.

The whole history of the Crusades was a struggle for the possession of these castles: the Arabs were never dispossessed of Aleppo, or of Hamah, or of Homs, or of Damascus, and so they had all possible routes open to them: they had unlimited resources to draw upon, as soon as the Mesopotamians had recovered Urfa (Edessa), which the Crusaders could not hold on account of its isolated position (Euphrates 10 feet deep, 150 yards wide, very rapid, & often flooded, much difficult hill thence to Seruj, & even nearer Edessa) and the shiftiness of the Greek Armenian population, who were allies, at times, but fighting men not at all: more harm than good usually. The native population of Syria very much sympathized with the Arabs, except the Maronite Christians & the Armenians; and news travels amazingly in the East: so that the Latins were more often surprised than not. Any counter stroke in the nature of ambush against the Arabs was impossible, since half their people were spies. Then in the hills above Safita lived the Assassins (Haschishīn) sometimes at war with the Arabs, more often confederate, and linked with them by an Orontes-bridge at Shaizar (Kalaat Seidjar). They could not attack Tripoli because of the 'Gap' castles (see before) and Markab (Margat) a huge fortress north of Tartus (another stronghold): but they could and did hold Antioch in check from the South, while the Aleppines pressed on the Iron Bridge, and the Greeks and Arabs attacked by Alexandretta & Beilan & Bagras (the two last big castles). So Antioch could only just hold its own, and the Tripoli castles, and when Damascus (Noureddin) joined with the north, and added Egypt, Syria was ringed round. The battle of Hattin was lost in an attempt to relieve Tiberias, the second of the great 'gap' fortresses. Banias (the first) was lost about 1150. For most of the occupation the Latin sphere of influence was limited to their castles: the peasantry paid them taxes, & wished for the Mohammedans to come: and come they very often did, to plunder such Christian villages as were left. So far as one can see they spared the Mohammedans. Latin Syria lived on its fleets.

[A letter of January 24th, 1911, shows that the project of starting a private printing press had been discussed with his parents but that he never had contemplated letting it take up all his time.

> You will see I think, that printing is not a business but a craft. We cannot sit down to it for so many hours a day, any more than one could paint a picture on that system. And besides such a scheme would be almost sure to interrupt the *Seven Pillars of Wisdom* or my monumental book on the Crusades.

This original *Seven Pillars of Wisdom* was described by him as:

> a youthful indiscretion book ... It recounted adventures in seven type-cities of the East (Cairo, Baghdad, Damascus, etc.) and arranged their characters into a descending cadence: a moral symphony. It was a queer book, upon whose difficulties I look back with a not ungrateful wryness: and in memory of it I so named the new book.

He burned the manuscript in August 1914.

Towards the end of February, Lawrence accompanied Hogarth and Gregori, Hogarth's Cypriote head-man, by sea to Haifa, where they visited the monastery on Mount Carmel before going on to Damascus by train. On the journey they saw Nazareth, 'no uglier than Basingstoke, or very little', the Yarmuk valley, and the pilgrims' route: 'the great Hajj road. Doughty is the only man who has been down it, and written what he saw'. The mountains were snow-covered, but Deraa was sunny; Hogarth talked Turkish and Greek and French, German and Italian. They reached Damascus late and went on next day to Aleppo.

In March they started work on the great mound at Carchemish, where Lawrence was to spend the greater part of the next three years.]

TO HIS MOTHER

March 31, 1911   *Jerablus*

Excuse this paper, and general appearance of letter. It is being written on the mound, in a dull day of digging, with an empty pen. The pen, by the way is a very distinct comfort out here. Today we are moving great stones: the remains of walls and houses are buried about $\frac{2}{3}$ of their height in fairly clean earth, but the upper few feet are filled up with rubble, and small rocks, with the ashlar masonry and concrete of the late Roman town. Whenever we break fresh ground dozens of these huge blocks have to be moved. Some of them weigh tons, and we have no blasting powder or stone-hammers with us. As a result they have to be hauled, prehistoric fashion, by brute force of men on ropes, helped to a small extent by crowbars. At this moment something over 60 men are tugging away above, each man yelling Yallah[1] as he pulls: the row is tremendous, but the stones usually come away. Two men out of three presume to direct operations, and no one listens to any of them, they just obey Gregori's orders, and their shouting is only to employ their spare breath. Now they are raising the 'talul', the curiously vibrant, resonant wail of the Bedawi. It is a very penetrating, and very distinct cry; you feel in it some kinship with desert life, with ghrazzus[2] and camel-stampedes. (Meanwhile the stone has slipped and fallen back into the trench, and Gregori's Turkish is deserting him. Whenever he is excited he slips back into Greek in a high falsetto voice, that convulses our hoarse-throated men.) To-day is a lovely day, in the shade of the diggings as I am at present: outside it is a little warm, with the usual streaming sunshine everywhere. We have had no rain since we came to Carchemish, but generally sun, with often after midday a gale from the North that drives the workmen off the top of the mound, and tosses up the dust of our diggings and dump-heaps in thick blinding and choking clouds all across the site. If one can struggle up to the top of the mound and hold on one can look over all the plain of the river valley (a very narrow one to the N. wide to the S.) up to Biredjik and down to Tell Ahmar, and over it all the only things to show out of the dust clouds are the hills and the tops of the tells. There might be no river except when a side-shift of the wind splits the clouds, and shows it running brown underneath. It still is not in flood, but is very swift, and cold with the melting snows of the Taurus. We look out for the hill tops above Andiamar every morning and see them each time with more and more lines and black spaces on their white. Before very long I expect the $\frac{3}{4}$ of a mile of river-bed will be one unbroken race of water. That will be the time when our mound looks best, but at all times it is very impressive rising about 100 ft. direct out of the river very steeply as all those North Syrian mounds are. I have taken a photograph or two, and will try a drawing, when I have leisure enough, if ever that will be.

[1] Oh God! = Hurry up!   [2] Raids.

It is not that there is much to do, of course: for most of the day we are not in the least necessary, and in those times I play with the pottery, which Mr. Hogarth has handed over to me as my particular preserve. Our house is half a mile away, and so we cannot all go back there and amuse ourselves, or work as the case may be during digging hours. Somebody must be within call of the diggers and so I am usually down here, with just sufficient interruptions to make writing or sketching not worth while. As soon as these Northern hurricanes stop, however, we intend to give up our house, and camp out on the mound. Then we will have time to do things. At present our evenings are filled up with the odd jobs that might have been done in the day, squeezing and copying inscriptions, writing up pottery and object lists, journals etc. Also it gets cold after sunset, and we go to bed early (about 10 or 11 as a rule), to avoid it. In the matter of food all goes quite easily, except for Haj's quite inadvertently emptying a curry tin into a pilaff! It was like eating peppered flames, and the other two are now crying aloud about their livers! That has so far been our only little hardship. I learnt a little about Syrian food from Miss Holmes'[1] servants, and this has come in usefully, for the Haj is not original, except in the matter of cakes that are half custard and half rubber sponge. Of course he has no oven which makes matters a little complicated. I am now building him one, out of a water jar. My power of sleeping through anything, which I acquired in my little house by aid of late hours and a telephone bell is standing me in excellent stead. I am the only one out of the three who gets any sleep at all at night. Mr. Hogarth is always getting up, to chase cats or rats or birds or mice or dogs. Everything comes in and out of the window holes, and the light sleepers suffer. The only time I woke up was when a cat scratched my face, entirely without provocation so far as I am aware. We are tired of the village bread (the thin cloth-like galettes) and still more of the bread so made out of English flour. The villagers all live on barley-bread, but the Haj tried to use our home flour, and the result was a sheet, not of paper or cloth, but of wash leather or thin indiarubber sheeting. It is very tough and holds water, and most elastic. Mr. Hogarth's teeth refuse to eat it, and so he is brought very low. Thompson[2] can just get through it: I flourish, but the others got tired of seeing that, and have made arrangements with the Commandant of Biredjik to supply us with mule-loads of the soldiers' bread. This is thick, brown, whole-meal stuff, rather like

---

[1] Principal of the American Mission School at Jebail.
[2] R. Campbell Thompson.

the ideal bread of the Limousin, but darker in colour, and without the very slight sourness of the French stuff. By the way 'whole-meal' does not mean that it is like Veda bread, or the English 'whole-meal'. Sometimes we have Euphrates fish: the small ones taste of mud, and are more bony than herrings: and thick bones that choke a cat. The larger ones are much better. Another year we will have a sailing canoe, or something of the sort: it will be splendid to go down the river to Bassorah. This much is being written on the great mound, with the main branch of the river some 200 yards wide at my feet. The men behind, digging in the top of the tell have got down about 10 feet, through an Arab stratum, into a Roman one. This means cement and big stones, and slow work: but they have found a very nice little cup of early Arab ware, probably xith century. At present they are pulling up stones from the bottom of their pit, in a mist of 'Yallah's' and 'Issa's'.[1] The last is curious for they are all nominally Mohammedans. They can do nothing without noise. A man has just put off from the island across the near branch of the river, to swim across to us. Their antics on the inflated skins are more curious than beautiful. The skin itself is goat or sheep: (though a man came across the other day between two wild-boar hides): very perfect vellum in appearance. I hope to buy enough to bind a Xenophon and another book or two, if I can find a new skin, for they have the bad habit of rolling them up tightly when dry, which lines them with cracks. The method of preparation must be most interesting. I cannot pretend to understand it yet, but in some way the skin is taken off whole, but for the head and lower legs, and the hair is stripped from it, and it is cured, without lime, or veget- able stupes and fomentations. I hope to get to know about it: and to get a few of the skins, at 6d each! Worth 5/- in England, you know, if such natural-coloured vellum could be got out of Italy. The legs are tied up with sinew, and the man inflates the skin through the neck, until it is as tight as he can blow it (42 blows, to be very precise in a biggish skin): then they lie down on it, face down, in the water, and paddle across with hands and feet. Being light, the current catches them little. They take their clothes across as well, on their backs. My faculty of making and repairing things has recently demonstrated how to make paint (black and red) for marking antiques, how to render light-tight a dark slide, how to make a camera-obscura, how to re-worm a screw (difficult this without a die), how to refit a plane-table, and replace winding mechanism on a paraffin lamp. Also I have devised a derrick,

[1] Jesus Christ, who is a Moslem prophet.

and a complicated system of human-power jacks (out of poplar poles, and ropes, and Arabs) which have succeeded in setting an Ishtar on her legs again. The Romans or Assyrians had broken her off at the knees, and the men could not shift the slabs back again, with any delicacy: so Mr. Hogarth and myself set to, and with our brains, and the aid of 90 men, put all right again. Before this there had been 120 men playing about with the ropes quite ineffectually. Digging results will appear in *The Times* as soon as Mr. Hogarth gets back. They have been meagre, and not very satisfactory to date: but it is like Pandora's box with Hope always at the bottom: and we are not nearly at that yet. I will send drawings when I have a quiet Sunday. The women here weave very beautiful cloth: and sell it at about 1½d a yard; it is thick and coarse, like grey sacking: the probabilities are that I will bring home a bale: also enough camel-hide to bind my Doughty, when I get him. The book will be necessary, for I must know it by more than library use, if ever I am to do something of the sort. Mr. Hogarth thinks my idea of patronizing the Soleyb, instead of the Arab, promising, both in security, and novelty. They are an interesting people: however no hurry about that, with Carchemish and military architecture and above all the necessary Arabic first. There is one thing I think I will get you to do: this piece of country is all rock, and very hard on one's boots. Will you get down to Gillman, and order another pair of boots, as before, only with slightly thicker soles: nails as before, leather bootlaces. When these are made will you send them to Miss Holmes, and a letter asking her to be good enough to pay the Customs charges, and forward them to the Consul at Aleppo? They cannot be sent direct: as the adventures of my films, still held up somewhere in the country, go to prove. There is no hurry about them: it is only in case I am able to do some walking out here, if we knock off here before the rains. It would be appreciated if Will asked Blackwell's to write to Jean Gillequin, publisher Bould. St. Michel Paris, ordering the 3 volumes of the Rabelais in his 1f.25 collection (*La Renaissance du Livre*) to be sent to me C/o Consul. Aleppo. But not if you think books unnecessary! This letter is only an interim scrawl, to be strengthened by a heavy letter in a week: I hope by then to have heard of Mods. We get weekly post from Biredjik. All very well.   **N.**

[On July 12th he wrote home that he was setting off that afternoon towards Urfa, on foot.

The story of the trip he was undertaking is recorded in a diary which he kept from about July 12th until he embarked for Europe on August 12th. It has been published in *Oriental Assembly*, Williams and Norgate, 1939.]

FROM THE DIARY OF 1911

Monday, July 17: Up about four, but was a long time getting on the road. The tooth rather worse: an abscess and face painfully one-sided. Bought a metallik of bread, and went over to the castle. Town wall is 9 to 10 feet thick.

About 6 started for Harran. No incidents, country everywhere as flat as possible; only huge tells about every two miles; crossed one small stream soon after mid-way. Much mirage: tried to photograph one pool, but failed: nothing shown on the ground-glass. The tower of Harran cathedral was in sight for four hours: all elongated by the mirage, it becked and bobbed in the most fantastic way, now shivering from top to bottom, now bowing to right or left, now a deep curtsey forward. Day very hot and drank five bottles of water between 6 and 2.30: did not stop anywhere on the way.

The people rough and unmannerly, half-Turkish spoken, and dressed in rags; children mostly naked. Many camels. Plain all wet and very fertile. Dhurra, liquorice, barley, and corn. No springs. Afternoon cloudy: was in shade for some moments. Soles of feet very tired. . . .

Tuesday, July 18: Up by daybreak, and round the outside of the castle. The inside I had explored with the Sheikh the afternoon before. Feet very tired, tooth much worse. Side of face all sore and swollen. . . .

Wednesday, July 19: Up about 4, and to the cafe for a time. Got the Sheikh to send if possible and find my telephoto tape: very unwilling, for he wanted me to stay over the day, or permanently in the village. Has offered me two first-class wives in his gift. The women here are extremely free, handling one's clothes and putting their hands in one's pockets quite cheerfully. Also they never pass on without speaking.

Messenger came back without the tape: so Sheikh turned out himself, *et ne trouva rien dans le village*. Then he got on a horse and scoured the country: in about an hour he brought it back. All well! Found it with a Turk, who had taken it from my box while at Bir Yakub. . . .

Sunday, July 23: Feet better: up about 4, paid for khan and went down to ferry: bought two metalliks of bread, and ate it waiting for the boat: saw Shemali, who said there was now no work in all Jerablus: brought a message from Dahoum,[1] to the effect that the Kala'at was sad.

Then set out from Biredjik for Belkis: road up and down the cliffs. At Belkis nothing at all. Road continued Roman, in one place diving through the rock for a few yards. Road very pretty some hour or two after this: wound up a narrow and deep valley full of wood and fruit trees, to Shard'at, a pretty village where I had a row with the Mukhdar: he demanded a tezkereh from me, which I refused: he threatened to imprison me, and I turned and twisted him into knots. Ended by his kissing my hand in tears and promising never to be naughty again. . . .

Friday, July 28:
. . . The Hoja[2] filled me a special water-bottle of water, and gave me great honours and attentions. About 7 p.m. he brought in bread, and fried eggs and khatir (yourt) and iran, and then (refusing to eat with me) went out and closed the door after him: this is the highest politeness I have ever met from an Arab. I was most exceedingly comfortable in his house with my big lamp burning and all things of mine about me, though I did not, of course, unpack my boxes of stores. About 10 p.m. I went on to the roof and slept, very soundly. Had a headache all the evening, but very pleasant to be with these men again. They are more mannerly than the other Arabs. The Hoja very anxious for me to live with him the winter. But the poor man is a most terrible bore conversationally, and sticks to one without end.

Saturday, July 29: Up in time to see the sun rise over the hills of Mesopotamia: very lovely in its colouring as this Carchemish plain always is. Sent off a man to Tell Halesh to the camel-driver to ask why the cement had not come. Found the camel-driver not at home, and no signs of any cement. So just started off for the Kalaat to measure the floor of the palace. Hoja started with me, but my distemper of the past few days increased suddenly, so I went on alone.

[1] Sheikh Ahmed, a boy of remarkable character employed on the Carchemish dig. He had begun to learn to read alone: Lawrence taught him to read and to take photographs and found him a kindred spirit who became his most intimate friend among the Arabs. The nickname Dahoum means Darkness given on account of his fair complexion.

[2] Sheikh Hamoudi, foreman of the Arabs employed in the Carchemish dig. His recollections of Lawrence are quoted on p. 13. Lawrence brought both Dahoum and the Hjoa to Oxford on a visit in July 1913.

Then it developed unexpectedly in a sharp attack of dysentery. I got on to the Kala'at into a lonely place and lay down on my back, from about 8 to 2.30, feeling most weak and ill. About 3 I sat up and tried to dress, but fainted promptly for about an hour, and again then when I made a second try. Under the circumstances I was afraid to go near the edge of the pit with the measuring tape, and so could not work. About 5 p.m. I got to the village, after a very hard walk. Decided to get out a tin of arrowroot, and send a man with letters to-night to bring a carriage from Biredjik. Cannot possibly continue tramp in this condition. Can hardly lift hand to write this. Dreamed when fainting of milk and soda! Sublime Greeting from every man, woman, and child in the district I fancy, but I could not see half of them, so only did a poor best at politeness. Fed on arrowroot and milk about 6 p.m. To bed at 8 on the roof. Slept well.

Sunday, July 30: Spent the day in the Hoja's house, lying on my back. A good deal of internal trouble. Up about 4.30, fed about 6, on arrowroot and milk. Fainted again about 10 o'clock when a little way from the house, and cut my cheek rather badly on a stone. Rested so, with visitors to see me, till 6 p.m. when I fed, again of arrowroot. Dahoum came to see me. Slept about 9.30, badly. Up three or four times in the seven hours, and had headache besides.

Tuesday, August 7:
. . . In evening felt a little better, and got down to dinner all right: there summed up enough irritation to tell my vis-a-vis he was a pig. Tremendous uproar of Levantines (little man a Greek Jew), 8 or 10 of them shrieking together and dancing about. I was the only person at the table who went on eating. Little man speechless with astonishment. Sudden irruption from near table of eleven mighty German railway engineers who told little man they had considered throwing him into the river which ran at the bottom of the garden, and would do it at once if he or his friends said another word. An immediate collapse of the Levantine element, which ate in whispers and melted silently away after the coffee. Landlord amusing, running round the table during the row wringing his hands and calling aloud in Armenian. Slept exceedingly badly, high fever, great sweating and delirium. Worst night have ever had.

TO MRS. RIEDER

Am August 11, 1911   *Hotel Deutscher Hof, Beirut*

... What I wanted for the donkey boy[1] was a history book or a geography which should be readable and yet Arab. I cannot give him such productions as those Miss Holmes uses, since nothing with a taste of 'Frangi'[2] shall enter Jerablus by my means. I have no wish to do more for the boy than give him a chance to help himself: 'education' I have had so much of, & it is such rot: saving your presence! The only stuff worth having is what you work out yourself. With which last heresy please be content a while. I will (probably ...) write from England. Yours sincerely,   T. E. LAWRENCE

TO MRS. RIEDER

Sept 26 [Postmark 1911]   *Oxford Union Society*

... Now about Doughty's other books. *Adam Cast Forth* is on the way. I like it: — but I would never venture to maintain its cause too openly. *I* think it's the best thing he's done: — and no one will ever agree about that, I'm sure. Let's leave it; you will judge for yourself. It is short at all events.

The Cliffs. A patriotic drama: invasion of Britain by aeroplane, & eventual victory of ourselves, chastened into a national frame of mind. I haven't read it: and I don't think I want to: I should be too much afraid of bathos: and the author of *Adam & Arabia* can't afford to fail.

Dawn in Britain. I have read this. If you express a wish, I'll send it by return. It will fill up many blank evenings. Behold an epic in 6 volumes: — a stage from Greece to the North Pole: — a period of 500 years, from the sack of Rome by Brennus, to the siege of Jerusalem, and the departing this life of Joseph of Arimathea.

You'll see that the 'epic' has no unity: there is no hero; plenty of characters: heaps of incidents told all in 'great' style. There is very little in the book which is less than magnificent: but do you want so much magnificence? Just as you like of course. It could well be read

[1] Dahoum.   [2] European.

in sections, for there is little coherence in the whole: you get Cassivelaunus, Caractacus, Boadicea: most Romans: a few Greeks, Tyrians, water nymphs: some *perfect* 'songs', semi-lyrical narratives in blank verse of twenty or thirty pages: these have nothing to do with the book and I mean to print them: they are perfect.

Do you want this book: I would like to send it you; immensely: but I am afraid it will only irritate you: remember Doughty goes his whole way along as he pleases: there is not the least concession to use or custom or authority: he *calls* it an 'epic' and presumably one has to do the same: but it is rather an imaginative history: of course it is meant to glorify things English, which with Doughty means not the Empire and *The Times* and the House of Lords but the language and 'Spenser & Chaucer traditions'. It contains about 33000 lines: all blank verse: — like *Adam*, but more regular....

TO D. G. HOGARTH

Dec. 16. [1911]   *Jerablus*

I hope you got my letter from Aleppo. I set off just after that, taking Haj Wahid with me as an afterthought that there might be buying to be done.

The arrival was a great success. The German works broke up with a yell, and rushed down the path to meet me. The poor engineers looked as though the Jehad[1] had arrived. We put up with the Hoja, and had a most glorious night. All the village dropped in, and I heard all about the Germans; they put on airs — they are ignorant of antikas — not recognizing a Hittite inscription; they know no language — they say sacral mento,[2] and when we ask what they want shut, they only say it again — they drink raki[3] all night, to two mejidies[4] — we work seven days a week — they do no work with their hands, but sit in the tents — we may not smoke: there is no bakshish — we may not speak to them, they say it is adibsis[5] — they cannot swim — they make a bargain and break it — Oh God the pigs, they eat crabs — and tortoises.

---

[1] Holy War against non-Moslems.
[2] Sakrament – German oath.
[3] Levantine brandy distilled from grapes.
[4] Turkish silver dollar, worth about 3s. 6d.
[5] Turkish = edepsiz = impudent.

After this the talk drifted naturally to demons & ginns. The Hoja and the rest told tale after tale, each more ghastly than the last: till all, glancing furtively into the darkness, refused with one voice to go home. So we slept there happily, the Hoja, his wives, his four children, the Haj, Dahum, myself, and fifteen others, in a house about the size of your room. I had a most royal heap of quilts, all wonderful to say, nearly deserted. It was one of the best nights I've had, and yet the Hoja told Thompson there were no local demons: why, one tore in half the brother of Khallaf Khalifa, another stole some halawi from Hassan Agha, another so bereft Hamman of his wits for a year and six months! The great mound is full of them, and all begged me for a few of my experiences.

It's a splendid place, but I suppose I must be serious. There are four or five Germans here: about 20 tents, and mud houses building: everything in between the Kalaat and the village. Their chief told me that the latest (and last) change of plan takes the railway outside the walls, right to the river: not a sod or a stone of the site is to be touched. This is splendid: for unless under direction of one of us I feel sure no stone could have been removed with safety. The bridge is to be S. of the site. I'm sorry though that some beast (or fanatic for the really inspired in art) has bruised the eyes of the basalt charioteers. I have sworn for the offender when discovered flaying alive, and rolling in salt, and then a grill before a slow fire of quotations from Dickens. The chief engineer supports the idea warmly: says he has never seen it done. . . .

[Early in January 1912, Lawrence joined Flinders Petrie's dig at Kafr Ammar in Egypt for a few weeks in order to learn something of the methods of other archaeologists, and two impudent letters show his appreciation of Professor Petrie. That Petrie appreciated Lawrence's qualities is indicated by his suggestion that he should do work at Bahrein.]

TO MRS. RIEDER

[*Postmark* 23.1.12.]   *Kafr Ammar (which is 40 miles S. of Cairo, on the desert)*

. . . No one but I would have achieved a letter at all from a Petrie dig. A Petrie dig is a thing with a flavour of its own: tinned kidneys mingle with mummy-corpses and amulets in the soup: my bed is all gritty with prehistoric alabaster jars of unique types — and my feet at night keep the bread-box from the rats. For ten mornings in succession I have seen the sun rise as I breakfasted, and we come home at nightfall after lunching at the bottom of a 50 foot shaft, to draw pottery silhouettes or string bead-necklaces. In fact if I hadn't malaria to-day I could make a pretty story of it all: — only then I wouldn't have time. To begin with the Professor is the great man of the camp — He's about 5′ 11″ high, white haired, grey bearded, broad and active, with a voice that splits when excited, and a constant feverish speed of speech: he is a man of ideas and systems, from the right way to dig a temple to the only way to clean one's teeth. Also he only is right in all things: all his subs. have to take his number of sugar lumps in their tea, his species of jam with potted tongue, or be dismissed as official bound unprogressists. Further he is easy-tempered, full of humour, and fickle to a degree that makes him delightfully quaint, and a constant source of joy and amusement in his camp. . . .

TO DR. A. G. GIBSON[1]

June 26, [1912]   *Aleppo*

Dear Dr. Gibson, Excuse the apparent fluency of my hand-writing above, but the pen-nib was working crossly, and I flourished it to put an end to its folly.

This place is having a cholera epidemic, and matters will probably get pretty bad with the arrival of the very hot weather at the end of this month. There are now about 40 deaths a day, and nobody is doing anything. I fear that in time we may have cases in our village, since there is much coming and going just now over the 70 miles in between, owing to the making of the Bagdad Railway. There are about 200 people in the village, and it has a lovely spring used for all drinking and washing, but a spring with a flow of about 200 gallons a minute: a very small, but very strong flowing stream.

Can you tell me, very shortly, more or less what to do? I mean in the way of medicines: I have corrosive sublimate in bulk, but not much else. If there is anything very necessary besides, could you be

[1] The Oxford pathologist with whom his brother Bob worked.

good enough to send a little out? You are not trespassing on the domains of any other medical man: you see I am local doctor. I don't like writing and telling my people, because they will only (or Mother will only) go wild with alarm: but my elder brother (Bob) is quite sensible and will pay for what is wanted: they come parcel-post to Aleppo to the British Consul there, which is my address: my brother knows. If the trouble comes I will probably have about 100 cases I suppose: it isn't that so much, as the trying to isolate them that matters. The people here in Aleppo are losing about 90 to 95% of their cases, so one cannot be much worse than that. It seems, however, very little contagious: seldom attacks more than one person in a family.

The town of Biredjik is about 20 miles up the Euphrates, which flows at 5 miles an hour with a stream of 400 yards wide and 15 feet deep. Will this water-supply be tolerably safe?

If there is a case in the village, and one fears the spring is affected (sick people bathe in it always) how long will it take to become clear? it flows very hard as I told you.

Does a cholera germ require much boiling to become dead?

I hope there is a vaccine treatment: I can get that done quite easily for the Arabs do as I want them most charmingly: if there is, please don't forget a squirt! And say how shortly before contagion it can be administered. . . .

[The first Balkan war broke out at the end of September 1912. Lawrence returned to Oxford towards the end of that year. While there he bought a Canadian canoe. Later it was fitted with an outboard motor. Lawrence went for long trips in it down the Euphrates, sending it back overland. On his return to Syria, he remained for a short time at Beyrout and, in February 1913, was occupied in smuggling rifles from a British gunboat into the British Consulate. Lawrence was closely in touch with the Kurds who had hopes of sacking Aleppo. The disturbed state of affairs was due to the defeat of Turkey in the Balkan war.]

TO FLORENCE MESSHAM

April 18, [1913]   *Carchemish*

Dear Florence, This is Friday, and writing day: and I am actually going to write to you. It is a *very* great compliment, for we are particularly busy. We have 200 men this year, but soon we will lose the most of them for harvest. After that perhaps we will have peace again.

We are finding a great deal this year: — great slabs of stone, carved with pictures of rows of foot-soldiers, and men hunting lions, and lions hunting bulls, and all sorts of strange beasts. We have found more this year than we have ever found before. The weather just now is splendid: warm, and sunny, but with a fresh wind, and every now and then a little splash of rain. The Euphrates is in flood, and it is great sport waving about over it in a canoe. We have a railway now, running regularly every day between Jerablus and Aleppo, so that we do get posts sometimes. It is not at all like last year: we are quite over-run with visitors: they are worse than fleas!

There is really nothing else to say! Everything is going on so well that nothing else matters. Yr.   NED

TO V. W. RICHARDS

Dec. 10, 1913   *Carchemish*

Dear Richards, It's quaint, isn't it, to begin again a correspondence which has lapsed for about a twelve-month? but, you know, I'm about as sick of myself and my affairs as one can well be, and it would be a consolation, if not exactly a comfort, to hear something of the sort from you. The fault was in ever coming out to this place, I think, because really ever since knowing it I have felt that (at least for the near future) to talk of settling down to live in a small way anywhere else was beating the air: and so gradually I slipped down, until a few months ago when I found myself an ordinary archaeologist. I fought very hard, at Oxford and after going down, to avoid being labelled: but the insurance people have nailed me down, now.

All this preface is leading up to the main issue — that I cannot print with you when you want me. I have felt it coming for a long time, and have funked it. You know I was in England for a fortnight this summer, and actually found myself one afternoon in Liverpool St. coming up to you . . . and then went back again. I have got to like this place very much: and the people here — five or six of them — and the whole manner of living pleases me. We have 200 men to play with, anyhow we like so long as the excavations go on, and they are

was I? Aha ... I got down to Akabah alone and on foot, since my idiot camels went astray. Alone in Arabia! However it was only a day and a night, but by Jove, I was glad to see a tent (not mine) at the end of it. 48 hrs later, up came my camels, not smiling in the least.

Kaimmakam of Akaba was a bad man. He had (or said he had) no news of us and our little games: and so he forbade Newcombe to map, and me to photograph or archaeologize. I photographed what I could, I archaeologized everywhere. In especial there was an island, said to be full of meat. The bay of Akaba is full of sharks, hungry sharks (shivers) and the island was half a mile off shore. So, of course I engaged a boat ... and it never came, for the boatman went to prison at once. That looked to me a chance of a cheap sail, so I carried off the manless boat ... but a squad of police cut me off and robbed me of my treasure. I was alone alas! Well, I sent word to the Kaimmakam that upon his head was the forbidding me to go, and he said yes ... and while his police were carrying on mutual recriminations I puffed a zinc tank full of air, tied to its tail another for Dahoum, and one for a camera and tape and things ... and splashed off for the island with a couple of planks as paddles. The police returning a little later found my fleet sailing slowly seawards, and they had no boat, and no zinc tanks, and so could only weep while we worked. I had tied Dahoum to my tail, since I felt that any intelligent shark would leave me in the cold, but the whole squadron sailed across safely, saw, judged and condemned the ruins as uninteresting, and splashed homewards, very cold and very tired: there was a most unkind breeze in our teeth, and the return took hours. Kaimmakam was informed of his fate, and cursed my religion: he attached to me in revenge a lieutenant and a half company of soldiers to keep me always in sight. I remembered [*name ommited*] 's dysenteric servant, and took about six photographs so, and then dropped all the police in the ravines around Mount Hor. It's a long story ... they had camels, and couldn't walk and couldn't climb as fast as self and Dahoum ... and we walked them out of water, and they were hungry, and we dodged up valleys and slipped their trails; until the desired happened, and the last one left us, and I spent a splendid morning all in peace on top of Aaron's tomb in Mount Hor. Perfect peace without ... rather a strained situation within, mitigated partly by a sweet rain-pool, partly by the finding of my tents next afternoon after a two-day absence. I shot a partridge on the hill at dawn, and we cooked it over brushwood, and ate half each. A very good partridge but a small one. The night just under the hill-top was bitterly cold, with a huge wind and blinding squalls of rain. We curled up in a knot under a not-sufficiently-overhanging rock and packed our sheepskin cloaks under and over and round us, and still were as cold and cross as bears. Not thirsty though, at all.

We had luck, since we found the two great cross-roads through the hills of the Arabah, that serve modern raiding parties entering Sinai, and which served the Israelites a bit earlier. Nobody would show them us, of the Arabs, which accounts for our rather insane wanderings without a guide ... but we did it all well. ...

Petra [*name omitted*] is the most wonderful place in the world, not for the sake of its ruins, which are quite a secondary affair, but for the colour of its rocks, all red and black and grey with streaks of green and blue, in little wriggly lines ... and for the shape of its cliffs and crags and pinnacles, and for the wonderful gorge it has, always running deep in spring-water, full of oleanders, and ivy and ferns, and only just wide enough for a camel at a time, and a couple of miles long. But I have read hosts of most beautifully written accounts of it, and they give one no idea of it at all ... and I am sure I cannot write nearly as nicely as they have ... so you will never know what Petra is like, unless you come out here ... Only be assured that till you have seen it you have not the glimmering of an idea how beautiful a place can be.

I came up here on the Hedjaz line, after arresting three policemen at Maan, and marching them disarmed through the streets to the Serail, while my camels, which they had arrested, escaped. But that labour requires a letter to itself. Au revoir.

L.

[The local knowledge obtained on this trip was vitally important for the strategy of the whole Arab campaign and it should be borne in mind that, during it, every advance took Lawrence into country better known to him.]

from THE WILDERNESS OF ZIN

FROM this plain one comes quite suddenly to the edge of the plateau, the pilgrim way from Suez falls in on the right, and the united roads turn sharply down a little valley that is the beginning of the Nagb or pass of Akaba.

The way down is very splendid. In the hill-sides all sorts of rocks are mingled in confusion; grey-green limestone cliffs run down sheer for hundreds of feet, in tremendous ravines whose faces are a medley of colours wherever crags of black porphyry and diorite jut out, or where soft sandstone, washed down, has left long pink and red smudges on the lighter colours. The confusion of materials makes the road-laying curiously uneven. The surface is in very few cases made up; wherever possible the road was cut to rock, with little labour, since the stone is always brittle and in thin, flat layers. So the masons had at once ready to their hand masses of squared blocks for parapets or retaining walls. Yet this same facility of the stone has been disastrous to the abandoned road, since the rains of a few seasons chisel the softer parts into an irregular giant staircase; while in the limestone the torrent has taken the road-cutting as a convenient course, and left it deep buried under a sliding mass of water-worn pebbles.

The great descent takes about an hour and a half on foot from the plateau to the bridge in Wady el Masri; and from there to the beach in Wady Araba is another hour and a half of easy road across the buttresses and soft foothills of the cliffs, down wadies and over ridges. The crests of some of these are cut through to ease the gradient, but it is only petty work.

The road finally reaches sea level on the extreme north-west beach of the Gulf of Akaba, and runs over the sand of the shore and through the old site of Aila between the palm-gardens into the modern village. It thus has to traverse the whole width of Wady Araba, a perfectly flat sandy expanse, very salt, with a few dom palms and many date palms and a little scrub to disguise its ugliness. Sweet water, or at least water not very brackish, is to be found by digging a hole a few feet deep anywhere near the beach.

The other point of capital interest at the head of the Gulf, after Akaba itself, is certainly the small island off the western (Egyptian) coast near Taba, called by a variety of names, but at Akaba commonly Geziret Faraun. The Crusaders called it Graye consistently. It is, as seen from the shore, a small double island formed of two sharp points of rock, about 50 feet high each, united by a strip of sandbank raised only a few feet above the level of the sea. Between it and the mainland is a deep channel, perhaps 400 yards across. The island has been strongly fortified at several periods. All round the shore at sea level are to be seen the remains of a built wall of rough masonry about 4 feet thick, entirely destroyed down to the level of the beach. The Akaba water seems to have a curious effect of petrifaction (perhaps due to the coral there), which cements the shores into a single slab of conglomerate; this wall therefore looks as natural a tipped stratum as need be, save for the tool-marks still showing on the inner edges of some stones. The date of this first wall it is impossible to determine. Within it there is a narrow beach of sand round the northern peak, the larger of the two rock masses of which the island is made up; facing shorewards is a square tower of split porphyritic granite, the material of the island, and of all the buildings upon it. This tower has a window or door in its face about 8 feet above the water, which is shallow; the real entrance to the fort was, however, probably from the sand beach on the seaward side. There is here a narrow path running up the cliff face, elsewhere nearly precipitous. The actual door into the fort is very narrow, and the fort itself is small, though no smaller than the top of the rock, every inch of which it covers with its buildings. In the central block or keep there are about a dozen tolerable rooms, and in the extension to the north along the backbone of the ridge there are a few more. Attached to the keep, but half-way down the slope towards the sandy waist of the island, is a little mosque with plain plastered *miḥrab* full of inscriptions cut by officers and men of H.M.S. *Diana* in 1896. The southern peak of the island is nearly as high as the northern, but much smaller, and the buildings on it are more ruined. It has a tower or two still standing, and some well-made rooms and passages with barrel vaults to their roofs. On the sandbank which unites the two peaks lie half buried some rough stone huts and circles, and there is also on it a little pool of salt water, perhaps 50 yards long. It is now filled with sand and debris, but has been deeper, and probably had an entrance from the sea. Set round the pond, as though for ornament, are some drums of columns in soft white limestone. There were two similar drums in a room in the keep of the northern building, and (from their stone-dressing) they seem of different period from the rest of the place. Of course they may well have been shipped across from some ruin at Akaba.

The actual mason-work of the castle is of the worst description. It is built of small split pieces of the red granite of the island and the mainland, and there has been little attempt to square any of the stones. Around the openings of windows, and in doors, and sometimes even at corners of the buildings, are worked blocks of soft yellow limestone, very roughly finished and without mouldings. Door and window heads are usually made of palm-logs, many of which remain in a rotten condition, and in the northern half of the buildings the roofs and the chemin-de-ronds of the curtain walls were also of this wood, with leaf and rib overlay. The walls are nearly mortarless, but inside were plugged with a hard, smooth yellow lime plaster, that the great rooms might appear reasonably habitable. The remains of this pargetting are only to be seen in some inner window openings, which are rectangular and small. These had proved too numerous for later inhabitants of the fort, and two out of three of them have been walled up. The walls are usually about a yard thick (in places, more or less), and their tops are parapeted in very simple style. The outer windows of the fort are nearly all of the loophole type, very narrow outside, and broad within. The southern half of the fort is so much more ruinous than the north that it would suggest an earlier abandonment; also its construction is so much better on the whole, with free use of lime cut stone and vaulting, that one would suspect it of being a twelfth-century construction. The pottery found in it was, however, not very early; practically all of it was metallic-glazed. The pottery of the north end of the fort was nearly modern, and its abandonment may have been as recent as a century or so ago. The only stone which showed any attempt at ornament was built incongruously sideways into the head of a half-destroyed window opening to the east on the northern rock. It was a roll moulding and some angle-ribs, and looked very much like a springer of a twelfth-century French roof; but it was such a tiny fragment that no reliance whatever can be placed on it. It has certainly, however, been re-used in its present position.

It is very hard to give dates to a building so characterless. There are some vaulted store-pits or cisterns that should be twelfth- or thirteenth-century Arab work, and the southern ruins may be of the same period, with later repairs. The whole of the north half of the fort is more like fifteenth- or sixteenth-century work, repaired in the eighteenth century. The loopholes and windows are some of them intended for cannon fire, and some seem more suitable for archery, so that a date in a transitional period is the most probable one. At the same time Akaba is a very out of the way place, and the roughness of the building may be due more to an emergency which forbade choice of materials than to a decadent period.

[As soon as Lawrence and Woolley had finished their respective surveys, and before beginning to write up the results, they started the new season's excavation work at Carchemish. The method of paying workmen bonuses on all antiquities discovered had led to a happy partnership of all engaged in the dig, a state of affairs in marked contrast to that between their near neighbours the German engineers building the Baghdad railway and their workmen, who were largely Kurds. The Germans offered high wages but had a system of fines, and of docking men for food and water, which led to continual friction. They maintained their authority with a guard of armed Circassians. The explosion came in March, the day after Lawrence and Woolley had returned, and the Englishmen were able to save their German neighbours from the consequences of their folly and inflict a moral punishment which must have been particularly galling. The fullest details are contained in the following letter written two or three months later, after Lawrence had returned to England, to amuse his friend the poet James Elroy Flecker who was dying in a sanatorium in Switzerland.]

TO JAMES ELROY FLECKER

Monday [*June* 1914]   [*From England*]

Seeing that you still show an unhealthy interest in the little fuss at Carchemish, despite my letter of explanation & derision from Aleppo, I have bought a large packet of thin paper, & with the help of the parcel post I will declare to you in order, most excellent Theophilus, all things that I have seen & heard.

Now for descriptions

The struggle was about the bridge-head, where the Company had built a little office & pay-house between two embankments. The bridge is only the temporary wooden thing, & at the moment they were making the permanent bank, thirty yards to the North of the temporary one. Each bank was about 8 feet high. North again of the new bank is the town-wall of Carchemish, *our wall*, a heap of earth grass-covered, perhaps forty feet high.

The Company was paying off some workmen on the completion of a subcontract, & as the contractor was bankrupt, they seized his books, & began to pay his workmen themselves. Unfortunately they omitted the very necessary inquiry (above all in Syria) as to whether the books were up to date, so naturally there was a little difficulty, when a certain Ali, a Kurd from Mesopotamia, found he was only to get 5 piastres for a full month's work. He protested, but the paymaster refused to listen to him. This paymaster was a German clerk, an awful rotter who used to treat his men as beasts, & to swindle them in wages right & left; he used to charge for water and for bread, even though the men never ate the Company's bread. Of course they had to drink the water — but that was Euphrates, & the only cost of it was the wage of a water-boy to carry it. However, when Ali found his complaints unheeded, he threw his money back on the table. The German said to his Circassian 'Hit him', & the Circassian knocked the Kurd down. Getting up, he grabbed a stone & slung it at the Circassian who pulled out a revolver & shot at him. Then the other hundred or hundred & fifty Kurds waiting their pay also picked up stones, & flung a volley, which broke the windows of the office in which three or four Germans were. They all grabbed rifles & revolvers, & through the windows blazed out at everyone they saw. These were mostly their own men at work on the Northern embankment thirty yards away, & they wounded five or six of them in the back.

After that of course everyone, Kurd or Arab, took cover behind the upper bank, & those who had revolvers let them off at the office. The Germans telephoned over the bridge & to their camp, & soldiers & Circassians rushed down with other engineers & foremen & mechanics, till they had about 30 wildly excited men with rifles about the bridge-head, shooting up & down stream, & across the bridge & at the embankment & in the air like lunatics.

Our house was only about 200 yards off, & we were down there immediately after the first shots were fired. We stood on the top of our town-wall & saw this happen. Then a Circassian stepped out from behind the office & took aim at Woolley & missed him badly. The bullet hit near his feet. The man was only about 60 yards off, & our men, about 7 or 8 of whom were with us, wanted to shoot the bounder. We said no, but ran down ourselves over the bank (now empty of men). I went to the office & told the chief Engineer that his men mustn't shoot at us. He at once gave orders thusly to his Circassians & subs, & we went back to our wall-top. When we got there we found to our astonishment that there were crowds of men coming up from the back. All the Kurd attackers, plus the men shot at by the

Company from the Office, had slipped into the town ruins between the wall & the river, & were coming up to the hill top to take the bridge-builders in the rear. They had just to run down across the first bank & drive them into the river. When in cover behind the wall, they had all loaded their guns, & those unarmed had picked up iron bars or pick-axes or hatchets from a forge just below the wall. So they were feeling pretty fit, & very wild; about 300 of them.

We told our men — the seven or eight — to help us hold back these fellows. So we talked to them, & pushed them back, & took away their guns: even knocked down one or two, quite good-humouredly, & kept them on the wall-top. The Germans & the Circassians meanwhile were shooting at everything, & in particular at an unfortunate German on an island in the river. He had been working there, & was about 100 yards from the bank: but the bullets were fairly whizzing round him. He was dancing about & shaking his fist at them & talking in German, not softly, until finally some Kurds in a boat landed on the island & took him ashore with them. Our men laughed at this a bit, & things were getting easier, when for lack of other targets the German idiots began shooting again at us. They shot very badly, only hitting one boy next me, but it made the Kurds by us very wild, & we had an awful job to hold them in. However, our men who were with us helped us like anything, & we were able to prevent any rush or any shooting from our side. From beginning to end of the affair not a single shot was fired from the wall.

Finally about an hour later we managed to work the crowd back along the wall, & to get them up to the village. The Germans went to their camp & wired to Aleppo frantically about firing on the bridge. So the Railway Company sent out Aleppo's amateur fire-brigade by a special train about midnight. Next day the Government sent up 250 soldiers, & all the Consuls & Valis & Kaims. & Mutasarrifs & Commandants came out also & made independent inquiries. We got very sick of this, so we enrolled our men (the dispute happened on the day of our arrival only), & got to work. The Company thought it was going to make capital out of the row, so magnified it enormously, & said the whole country was thirsting for Christian blood. They said 200 soldiers were not enough to make safe their work. So the Vali trotted down to us and asked how many soldiers we had for our 250 men. We said of course that we didn't hold with soldiers, & the Germans were jeered at; but turned it off by saying that our side, the Syrian one, was quite safe, that it was in Mesopotamia that the danger lay. So to biff that, Woolley & I walked over next day to Meso-potamia alone & picked a lot of moon-daisies & came back, meeting the Government officials & the Consuls & Engineers by accident at the bridge-head. So that was a further source of grief to them. The whole country was absolutely at peace, you know, all along.

The next day up came the German Consul, one Rössler, to our house at dusk alone. Fontana was holding forth upon Martial, but stopped. Old Rössler said that he had come to ask our help, that the Turkish Government was only fooling as usual & that as the German Consul he felt himself responsible for a peaceful settlement with the Kurds. We of course were inwardly chortling, but were quite polite, I hope. We pointed out how serious the matter was. First of all they had killed one Kurd, and wounded about twenty. We suggested £80 blood-money for the dead man, & about £40 in compensation for the rest. Rössler boggled a bit, but consented in the end. Then we pointed out that all the Circassians must go (each German had one as personal guard, & they were the Membidj bullies, & not true Circassians, but awful bounders): this Rössler at once agreed to. Then we suggested that the paymaster & another engineer must go: this he promised: then we proposed about a dozen Kurds being put on the line to watch pay-days in the Kurdish interest, & in case of dispute to have appeal to him. This also was agreed to, so two days later we brought in the chief of that Kurdish tribe, a man called Busrawi, a very good fellow, whom we knew very well; & he went down with safe-conduct to Fontana, & thence to the German Consulate, & signed a treaty of peace on the above terms, with a very fat present to himself.

It's really very comic now — every engineer walks about with a huge frowning Kurd behind him, armed to the teeth & very ready to shoot him down if he misbehaves. The improvement in German manners is incredible: only they don't seem to love us more than before.

There now, for your amusement I have detailed the wretched thing at full length. The only amusing part is the peace-making, which gave us great joy.

I don't think you can ever have got my Aleppo letter, written just after *Alsander*[1] & your letter came. I wrote to a pension Rheingold — perhaps it was too late, or did the Turkish post covet my letter. They often do, I'm afraid.

[1] *The King of Alsander*, a novel by James Elroy Flecker.

PART II
WAR AND DIPLOMACY

Sunday [Autumn 1914]

This job is not going to be prolific in letters: — because there isn't much to say, and most of that shouldn't be said. No matter.

Today has been an awful scramble, for some unit (report says K's.[1] private sec.) asked for a complete map of Sinai, showing all roads and wells, with capacity of latter, and a rough outline of hills. As Sinai is in manuscript in 68 sheets it meant a little trouble, for the sheets (because the surveyors were not like yourself) were not numbered or labelled, and so nobody could put them together. I came up like St. George in shining armour and delivered them (i.e. Col. Hedley said 'You go down and see what you can do with the damned thing') and by night behold there was a map of Sinai eighteen feet each way in three colours. Some of it was accurate, and the rest I invented. It took the three of us just eleven hours to get the thing traced.

It was proclaimed very good, and the request was made for an extension fifty miles to the E: that is Newcombe's part. However by good hap the draughtsmen were gone to bed. So that remains for tomorrow.

Sinais are in much demand just at present . . . if the P.E.F.[2] publish that thing of ours next month it will be confiscated probably: and I will have to do the confiscating. The position is an involved one, but no matter. I didn't get paid for it . . . Though I'm not appointed to anything, yet they can't sack me now, as I know the most of their secrets. So I wait in a sure hope. The W.O. people are slow, except in the map department!

L.

TO D. G. HOGARTH

18 *March* [1915]   *Grand Continental Hotel, Cairo*

This letter is not going to be censored, so I'm going to let fly.

The Turks aren't coming back, they have only 50,000 disaffected troops in Syria, (200,000 Dardanelles, 200,000 Caucasus, 50,000 Mesopotamia) and the whole country is mad against them. Ibn Rashid

[1] Kitchener.   [2] Palestine Exploration Fund.

has been heavily defeated by Ibn Saoud (Shakespear unfortunately killed in the battle): Idrisi is at open war with the Turks in Assyr: Sherif has almost declared himself, & the Vali & staff of Hedjaz have taken refuge in Damascus. We have sent troops from the Canal to Basra, to reinforce everybody there, (Indian troops there are shaky it seems), the Australians & New Zealanders, & some Indians are going to the Dardanelles, with the French & Ian Hamilton's army. We will be left here in Egypt with 20,000 men or so. The French insist upon Syria — which we are conceding to them: there remains Alexandretta, which is the key of the whole place as you know. It's going to be the head of the Baghdad line, & ∴ the natural outlet for N. Syria & N. Mesopotamia: it's the only easy road from Cilicia & Asia Minor into Asia etc. etc. Also it's a wonderful harbour, & thanks to Ras Khanzir on the S. can be made impregnable. It is cut off from Syria, & is neither Syria nor Asia Minor. In the hands of France it will provide a sure base for naval attacks on Egypt — and remember with her in Syria, & compulsory service there, she will be able any time to fling 100,000 men against the canal in 12 days from declaration of war. The Sinai desert is not really any obstacle in the spring — or at any time when the railway (which is inevitable) is built. The only place from which a fleet can operate against Egypt is Alexandretta, because there is no English port from which one can blockade it. Smyrna & Constantinople are shut in by islands: whereas Alexandretta has only Cyprus in front of it, & the water round that is too deep for a large naval harbour to be built.

If Russia has Alexandretta it's all up with us in the Near East. And in any case in the next war the French will probably be under Russia's finger in Syria. Therefore I think it absolutely necessary that we hold Alexandretta . . . and thanks to the Amanus we needn't hold anything else, either in Syria or in Asia Minor. The High Commissioner is strongly of the same opinion, & General Maxwell also, [6 *words omitted*]. K. has pressed it on us: Winston seems uncertain, & Someone — not Grey — perhaps Parker in the F.O. is blocking it entirely. I think that perhaps you can get a move on.

K. is behind you in any case. Can you get someone to suggest to Winston that there is a petrol spring on the beach (very favourably advised on by many engineers, but concessions always refused by the Turks) huge iron deposits near Deurtyol 10 miles to the N. and coal also. Point out also that it is a splendid natural naval base (which *we* don't want but which no one else can have without detriment to us).

If Winston settles on a thing he gets it, I fancy: especially with K's help.

Then go to the F.O. if possible. Point out that in Baghdad Convention France gave up Alexandretta, to Germans, & agreed that it formed no part of Syria. Swear that it doesn't form part of Syria — and you know it speaks Turkish: & also tell F.O. (not Parker, whom I shall murder some day) that it is vitally important we hold it. One cannot go on betting that France will always be our friend. If F. has all Syria south of Alex, she ought to be content: — she is now trying to fob off Jerusalem on us. Don't touch it with a barge-pole.[1]

By occupying Alexandretta with 10,000 men we are impregnable and we cut

I. Communication between Asia Minor & Syria.

II. Communication between Asia Minor & Baghdad, where the English are likely to be very hard pressed shortly.

III. We also relieve the Caucasus, especially after the centre of Turkey shifts to Konia. We must I think look for a renaissance of the Turk when he has lost Constantinople.[2] They will be much more formidable militarily — and less so politically.   TEL.

[To a letter written on March 31st, 1929, to Liddell Hart on the latter's *Decisive Wars of History*, Lawrence appended the following note:

'I am unrepentant about the Alexandretta scheme which was, from beginning to end, my invention, put forward necessarily through my chiefs (I was a 2nd Lieut. of 3 months seniority!). Actually K. accepted it, and ordered it, for the Australian and N.Z. forces: and then was met by a French ultimatum. A landing at Alexandretta in Feb. 1915 would have handed over Syria and Mespot. to their native (Arab) troops, then all in their home stations, and complete, and automatically established local governments there: and then attracted to Ayas (it was Ayas, not Alexandretta) the whole bulk of the *real* Turkish armies:* and that would have been the moment for the Dardanelles naval effort.'

*to fritter itself against the Arabs, not against us.

The following letter is probably the most remarkable document Lawrence ever wrote. It shows that he had already planned the campaign which he was to carry to a victorious conclusion three years later.]

[1] Far-sighted!   [2] Far-sighted again.

TO D. G. HOGARTH

March 22 [1915]   *Port Said*

Another uncensored letter: at half an hour's notice last week I sent you a flood of stuff about Alex: please try & push it through for I think it is our only chance in face of a French Syria. I hope my letter was clear — because I dashed it off in such a sweat that I had no time to think of it at all.

This week is something else. You know India[1] used to be in control of Arabia — and used to do it pretty badly, for they hadn't a man who knew Syria or Turkey, & they used to consider only the Gulf, & the preservation of peace in the Aden Hinterland. So they got tied into horrid knots with the Imam,[2] who is a poisonous blighter at the best. Egypt (which is one Clayton, a very good man) got hold of the Idrisi family, who are the Senussi and Assyr together, as you know: and for some years we had a little agreement together. Then this war started, & India went on the old game of balancing the little powers there. I want to pull them all together, & to roll up Syria by way of the Hedjaz in the name of the Sherif. You know how big his repute is in Syria. This could be done by Idrisi only, so we drew out a beautiful alliance, giving him all he wanted: & India refused to sign. So we cursed them, & I think that Newcombe & myself are going down to Kunfida as his advisers. If Idrisi is anything like as good as we hope[3] we can rush right up to Damascus, & biff the French out of all hope of Syria. It's a big game, and at last one worth playing. Of course India has no idea what we are playing at: if we can only get to Assyr we can do the rest — or have a try at it. So if I write & tell you that it's all right, & I'm off, you will know where for. Wouldn't you like to be on it? Though I don't give much for my insurance chances again. If only India will let us go. Won't the French be mad if we win through? Don't talk of it yet.   TEL.

[Will Lawrence who had joined the Royal Flying Corps as an observer was shot down in September 1915. Lawrence took his death for granted, though proof of it did not come until the following May. The death of Will, his favourite brother, was a great shock to Lawrence, and in a letter of November 16th, 1915, he expressed a feeling that it was not right for him to go on living safely in Cairo, and a dread of what returning to Oxford would be like. D. G. Hogarth (by that time

---

[1] i.e. the Government of India.   [2] Ruler of Yemen.
[3] These hopes were disappointed.

a Lieutenant-Commander in the R.N.V.R.) had come out and Lawrence was grateful for his companionship.

In the spring of 1916 the Arab Bureau began to publish *The Arab Bulletin* — set up and printed by the Egyptian Government Press at Bulaq. Lawrence was responsible for the early numbers.

Soon afterwards he was sent with Aubrey Herbert, with secret instructions from the War Office, to negotiate with the Turkish Commander, Khalil Pasha, beseiging General Townshend's force in Kut. General Townshend had conceived the plan of buying off the Turkish Commander besieging him for a cash payment. Lord Kitchener had adopted it and General Lake, commanding in Mesopotamia, had accepted it. Most of the British officers in Mesopotamia were against it as they felt it was dishonourable. Sir Percy Cox opposed it as worse for British prestige than the surrender of the garrison. Lawrence believed it was impracticable as Khalil would certainly refuse. However Colonel Beach, Aubrey Herbert and Lawrence were sent to parley with Khalil, offering him first a million pounds, and on his refusal, two million pounds to let the besieged garrison go free. Khalil refused contemptuously, and of course published the facts of the offer which were most damaging to British prestige.

In 1932 Liddell Hart submitted a long interrogatory to Lawrence in which are the following questions and answers.

33. How did you come to receive instructions for Mespot Mission?
I had put the Grand Duke Nicholas in touch with certain disaffected Arab officers in Erzerum. Did it through the War Office and our Military Attaché in Russia. So the War Office thought I could do the same thing over Mespot, and accordingly wired out to Clayton.

34. When did you become a captain?
I was Staff Captain. I lost it on going to Mespot, so Hedley arranged a local captaincy.

35. Were the General Staff going to get rid of you too?
While they were together on Maxwell's staff Holdich was my greatest ally. When appointed to Murray's staff his attitude changed — Holdich decent but a lunacy streak.[1]]

---

[1] Liddell Hart provides the following note: 'Newcombe says that he used to hear from Holdich, now dead, who was very bitter about L. – jealousy and resentment of what was regarded as L.'s cheek. The Murray crowd were trying to down Clayton as well as Lawrence. Further remark about this period: Philip Graves and L. got out Handbook of Turkish Army; may have been a dozen editions; L. supervised the printing of them. L. and Graves spent most of their time among the Turkish prisoners and came to know more about the Turkish Army than the Turks themselves.'

TO HIS MOTHER

May 18 [1916.]

We are at sea, somewhere off Aden, I suppose, so before it gets too late I am going to tell you something of what I saw in Mesopotamia ... Colonel Beach, one of the Mesopotamian staff, Aubrey Herbert (who was with us in Cairo) and myself were sent up to see the Turkish Commander in chief, and arrange the release, if possible, of Townshend's wounded. From our front trenches we waved a white flag vigorously: then we scrambled out, and walked about half-way across the five hundred yards of deep meadow grass between our lines and the Turkish trenches. Turkish officers came out to meet us, and we explained what we wanted. They were tired of shooting so kept us sitting there with our flag as a temporary truce, while they told Halil Pasha that we were coming — and eventually in the early afternoon we were taken blindfolded through their lines and about ten miles Westward (till within four miles of Kut) to his Headquarters. He is a nephew of Enver's and suffered a violent defeat in the Caucasus so they sent him to Mesopotamia as G.O.C. hoping he would make a reputation. He is about 32 or 33, very keen and energetic, but not clever or intelligent I think. He spoke French to us and was very polite, but of course the cards were all in his hands, and we could not get much out of him. However he let about 1000 wounded go without any condition but the release of as many Turks — which was all we could hope for. We spent the night in his camp, and they gave us a most excellent dinner in Turkish style — which was a novelty to Colonel Beach but pleased Aubrey and myself. Next morning we looked at Kut in the distance, and then came back blindfolded as before. We took with us a couple of young Turkish officers, one the brother in law of Enver, and they afterwards went up to Kut from our camp in the hospital ship that removed the wounded. The ill-feeling between Arabs and Turks has grown to such a degree that Halil cannot trust any of his Arabs in the firing line. . . .

I wonder if I ever told you about a magnificent storm we had at Carchemish one night — Mr. Hogarth and the Fontanas were staying with us? It was a very cold week and after dinner we had all moved round the hearth, on which there was a big fire of olive logs burning. Busrawi had sent in his two musicians at our request. One was an old man, who had been a shepherd nearly all his life. He had a long white beard and a quiet weather-beaten face. He played on a pipe about 2 feet long that was of a kind of reed but looked like polished brass. Its tone was hoarse but flute like and had a wonderful range: he goes from high to very low notes which sound just like the wind dragging over rocky hill sides rustling in the dried grass of the valleys. The other man younger also plays a two stringed [*one word illegible*] and sings. He is darker and thin faced with very deep set [*one word illegible*] eyes. I think he is blind: at any rate he has wound a very massive turban and head-cloth over his forehead, so that his face is always in deep shade ... and he generally keeps his eyes shut as he sings. They had been playing and singing Kurd war-songs, and love-songs and dirges for about half an hour when the storm suddenly broke. There was a torrential burst of rain which hissed down in sheets, and rattled over the shingle in our court-yard like the footsteps of a great crowd of men; then there would come a clap of thunder, and immediately after a blue flash of lightning which made our open door and window livid gaps in the pitch-black wall ... through which we caught odd glimpses of the sculptures outside shining in the rain and dazzle of light. I remember particularly the seven foot figure of a helmeted god striding along an inscription towards the doorway: — and the dripping jaws of the two lions of the pedestal which seemed in the alternate glare and shadow of the flashes to be grinning at us through the window. The musicians did not stop, but changed their song for a wild improvisation which kept time with the storm. The pipe shrilled out whenever the thunder pealed and fell down again slow and heavy for the strained silences in between. One did not realize that they were men playing independently: the rhythm seemed so born of the bursts of wind and rain, so made to bind together the elements of the night into one great thunder-song.

[On his return to Egypt Lawrence submitted a report of Mesopotamian affairs in which, in the words of Colonel Stirling, 'he criticized the quality of the stones used for lithographing, the system of berthing barges alongside the quays, the inefficiency of the cranes for handling stores, the lack of system in shunting and entraining on the railways, the want of adequate medical stores, the blindness of the medical authorities and their want of imagination as to their probable requirements. And, horror of horrors, he criticized the Higher Command and the conduct of the campaign in general!'

His report was hurriedly bowdlerized by his staff officers before being shown to Sir Archibald Murray, the Commander-in-Chief in Egypt. The visit to Mesopotamia and Lawrence's sweeping criticism was the beginning of a hostility to him on the part of the Indian Army authorities and the Indian Government which lasted for the rest of his career.

On June 5th, 1916, Sherif Ali, the eldest son of the Sherif of Mecca, and Sherif Feisal, the third son, attacked Medina with several thousand Arabs but failed to take it by storm.

On June 9th the Sherif of Mecca revolted against the Turks and after three days smoked out and captured the small Turkish force in the Holy City. When Hogarth and other members of the Arab Bureau landed at Jidda on June 6th, they found to their surprise that the revolt had broken out. The situation which Lawrence had planned over a year before had come to pass, but it was many months before he could begin to exploit it.]

from SEVEN PILLARS OF WISDOM

HOWEVER it was, things in the Hejaz went from bad to worse. No proper liaison was provided for the Arab forces in the field, no military information was given the Sherifs, no tactical advice or strategy was suggested, no attempt made to find out the local conditions and adapt existing Allied resources in material to suit their needs. The French Military Mission (which Clayton's prudence had suggested be sent to Hejaz to soothe our very suspicious allies by taking them behind the scenes and giving them a purpose there), was permitted to carry on an elaborate intrigue against Sherif Hussein in his towns of Jidda and Mecca, and to propose to him and to the British authorities measures that must have ruined his cause in the eyes of all Moslems. Wingate, now in military control of our co-operation with the Sherif, was induced to land some foreign troops at Rabegh, half-way between Medina and Mecca, for the defence of Mecca and to hold up the further advance of the reinvigorated Turks from Medina. McMahon, in the multitude of counsellors, became confused, and gave a handle to Murray to cry out against his inconsistencies. The Arab Revolt became discredited; and Staff Officers in Egypt gleefully prophesied to us its near failure and the stretching of Sherif Hussein's neck on a Turkish scaffold.

My private position was not easy. As Staff Captain under Clayton in Sir Archibald Murray's Intelligence Section, I was charged with the 'distribution' of the Turkish Army and the preparation of maps. By natural inclination I had added to them the invention of the Arab Bulletin, a secret weekly record of Middle-Eastern politics; and of necessity Clayton came more and more to need me in the military wing of the Arab Bureau, the tiny intelligence and war staff for foreign affairs, which he was now organizing for McMahon. Eventually Clayton was driven out of the General Staff; and Colonel Holdich, Murray's intelligence officer at Ismailia, took his place in command of us. His first intention was to retain my services; and, since he clearly did not need me, I interpreted this, not without some friendly evidence, as a method of keeping me away from the Arab affair. I decided that I must escape at once, if ever. A straight request was refused; so I took to stratagems. I became, on the telephone (G.H.Q. were at Ismailia, and I in Cairo) quite intolerable to the Staff on the Canal. I took every opportunity to rub into them their comparative ignorance and in-efficiency in the department of intelligence (not difficult!) and irritated them yet further by literary airs, correcting Shavian split infinitives and tautologies in their reports.

In a few days they were bubbling over on my account, and at last determined to endure me no longer. I took this strategic opportunity to ask for ten days' leave, saying that Storrs was going down to Jidda on business with the Grand Sherif, and that I would like a holiday and joy-ride in the Red Sea with him. They did not love Storrs, and were glad to get rid of me for the moment. So they agreed at once, and began to prepare against my return some official shelf for me. Needless to say, I had no intention of giving them such a chance; for, while very ready to hire my body out on petty service, I hesitated to throw my mind frivolously away. So I went to Clayton and confessed my affairs; and he arranged for the Residency to make telegraphic application to the Foreign Office for my transfer to the Arab Bureau. The Foreign Office would treat directly with the War Office; and the Egypt command would not hear of it, till all was ended.

Storrs and I then marched off together, happily. In the East they swore that by three sides was the decent way across a square; and my trick to escape was in this sense oriental. But I justified myself by my confidence in the final success of the Arab Revolt if properly advised.

I had been a mover in its beginning; my hopes lay in it. The fatalistic subordination of a professional soldier (intrigue being unknown in the British army) would have made a proper officer sit down and watch his plan of campaign wrecked by men who thought nothing of it, and to whose spirit it made no appeal. *Non nobis, Domine.* . . .

Jeddah had pleased us, on our way to the Consulate: so after lunch, when it was a little cooler, or at least when the sun was not so high, we wandered out to see the sights under the guidance of Young, Wilson's assistant, a man who found good in many old things, but little good in things now being made.

It was indeed a remarkable town. The streets were alleys, wood roofed in the main bazaar, but elsewhere open to the sky in the little gap between the tops of the lofty white-walled houses. These were built four or five stories high, of coral rag tied with square beams and decorated by wide bow-windows running from ground to roof in grey wooden panels. There was no glass in Jidda, but a profusion of good lattices, and some very delicate shallow chiselling on the panels of window casings. The doors were heavy two-leaved slabs of teak-wood, deeply carved, often with wickets in them; and they had rich hinges and ring-knockers of hammered iron. There was much moulded or cut plastering, and on the older houses fine stone heads and jambs to the windows looking on the inner courts.

The style of architecture was like crazy Elizabethan half-timber work, in the elaborate Cheshire fashion, but gone gimcrack to an incredible degree. House-fronts were fretted, pierced and pargetted till they looked as though cut out of cardboard for a romantic stage-setting. Every storey jutted, every window leaned one way or other; often the very walls sloped. It was like a dead city, so clean underfoot, and so quiet. Its winding, even streets were floored with damp sand solidified by time and as silent to the tread as any carpet. The lattices and wall-returns deadened all reverberation of voice. There were no carts, nor any streets wide enough for carts, no shod animals, no bustle anywhere. Everything was hushed, strained, even furtive. The doors of houses shut softly as we passed. There were no loud dogs, no crying children: indeed, except in the bazaar, still half asleep, there were few wayfarers of any kind; and the rare people we did meet, all thin, and as it were wasted by disease, with scarred, hairless faces and screwed-up eyes, slipped past us quickly and cautiously, not looking at us. Their skimp, white robes, shaven polls with little skull-caps, red cotton shoulder-shawls, and bare feet were so same as to be almost a uniform.

The atmosphere was oppressive, deadly. There seemed no life in it. It was not burning hot, but held a moisture and sense of great age and exhaustion such as seemed to belong to no other place: not a passion of smells like Smyrna, Naples or Marseilles, but a feeling of long use, of the exhalations of many people, of continued bath-heat and sweat. One would say that for years Jidda had not been swept through by a firm breeze: that its streets kept their air from year's end to year's end, from the day they were built for so long as the houses should endure. There was nothing in the bazaars to buy.

In the evening the telephone rang; and the Sherif called Storrs to the instrument. He asked if we would not like to listen to his band. Storrs, in astonishment, asked What band? and congratulated his holiness on having advanced so far towards urbanity. The Sherif explained that the headquarters of the Hejaz Command under the Turks had had a brass band, which played each night to the Governor General; and when the Governor General was captured by Abdulla at Taif his band was captured with him. The other prisoners were sent to Egypt for internment; but the band was excepted. It was held in Mecca to give music to the victors. Sherif Hussein laid his receiver on the table of his reception hall, and we, called solemnly one by one to the telephone, heard the band in the Palace at Mecca forty-five miles away. Storrs expressed the general gratification; and the Sherif, increasing his bounty replied that the band should be sent down by forced march to Jidda, to play in our courtyard also, 'And,' said he, 'you may then do me the pleasure of ringing me up from your end, that I may share your satisfaction. . . .'

In the evening Abdulla came to dine with Colonel Wilson. We received him in the courtyard on the house steps. Behind him were his brilliant household servants and slaves; and behind them a pale crew of bearded, emaciated men with woe-begone faces, wearing tatters of military uniform, and carrying tarnished brass instruments of music. Abdulla waved his hand towards them and crowed with delight, 'My Band'. We sat them on benches in the forecourt, and Wilson sent them cigarettes, while we went up to the dining room, where the shuttered balcony was opened right out, hungrily, for a sea breeze. As we sat down, the band, under the guns and swords of Abdulla's retainers, began, each instrument apart, to play heartbroken Turkish airs. Our ears ached with noise: but Abdulla beamed. . . .

We got tired of Turkish music, and asked for German. Aziz stepped out on the balcony and called down to the bandsmen in Turkish to play us something foreign. They struck shakily into 'Deutschland über Alles' just as the Sherif came to his telephone in Mecca to listen to the music of our feast. We asked for more German music; and they played 'Eine feste Burg'. Then in the midst they died away into flabby discords of drums. The parchment had stretched in the damp air of Jidda. They cried for fire; and Wilson's servants and Abdulla's bodyguard brought them piles of straw and packing cases. They warmed the drums, turning them round and round before the blaze, and then broke into what they said was the Hymn of Hate, though no one could recognize a European progression in it all. Sayed Ali turned to Abdulla and said, 'It is a death march'. Abdulla's eyes widened; but Storrs who spoke in quickly to the rescue turned the moment to laughter; and we sent out rewards with the leavings of the feast to the sorrowful musicians, who could take no pleasure in our praises, but begged to be sent home. Next morning I left Jidda by ship for Rabegh. . . .

[At Rabegh Lawrence gave Sidi Ali, Hussein's eldest son, the 'orders' to dispatch him to Feisal's camp, which Storrs and he had extorted from Hussein and Abdulla.]

Ali would not let me start till after sunset, lest any of his followers see me leave the camp. He kept my journey a secret even from his slaves, and gave me an Arab cloak and headcloth to wrap round myself and my uniform, that I might present a proper silhouette in the dark upon my camel . . . My camel was a delight to me, for I had not been on such an animal before. There were no good camels in Egypt; and those of the Sinai Desert, while hardy and strong, were not taught to pace fair and softly and swiftly, like these rich mounts of the Arabian princes.

Yet her accomplishments were to-day largely wasted, since they were reserved for riders who had the knack and asked for them and not for me, who expected to be carried, and had no sense of how to ride. It was easy to sit on a camel's back without falling off, but very difficult to understand and get the best out of her so as to do long journeys without fatiguing either rider or beast. Tafas gave me hints as we went: indeed, it was one of the few subjects on which he would speak. His orders to preserve me from contact with the world seemed to have closed even his mouth. A pity, for his dialect interested me. . . .

Hamra opened on our left. It seemed a village of about one hundred houses, buried in gardens among mounds of earth some twenty feet in height. We forded a little stream, and went up a walled path between trees to the top of one of these mounds, where we made our camels kneel by the yard-gate of a long, low house. Tafas said something to a slave who stood there with silver-hilted sword in hand. He led me to an inner court, on whose further side, framed between the uprights of a black doorway, stood a white figure waiting tensely for me. I felt at first glance that this was the man I had come to Arabia to seek — the leader who would bring the Arab Revolt to full glory. Feisal looked very tall and pillar-like, very slender, in his long white silk robes and his brown head-cloth bound with a brilliant scarlet and gold cord. His eyelids were dropped; and his black beard and colourless face were like a mask against the strange, still watchfulness of his body. His hands were crossed in front of him on his dagger.

I greeted him. He made way for me into the room, and sat down on his carpet near the door. As my eyes grew accustomed to the shade, they saw that the little room held many silent figures, looking at me or at Feisal steadily. He remained staring down at his hands, which were twisting slowly about his dagger. At last he inquired softly how I had found the journey. I spoke of the heat and he asked how long from Rabegh, commenting that I had ridden fast for the season.

'And do you like our place here in Wadi Safra?'

'Well; but it is far from Damascus.'

The word had fallen like a sword in their midst. There was a quiver. Then everybody present stiffened where he sat, and held his breath for a silent minute. Some, perhaps, were dreaming of far off success: others may have thought it a reflection on their late defeat. Feisal at length lifted his eyes, smiling at me, and said, 'Praise be to God, there are Turks nearer us than that.' We all smiled with him; and I rose and excused myself for the moment. . . .

We wrangled while Feisal sat by and grinned delightedly at us.

This talk had been for him a holiday. He was encouraged even by the trifle of my coming; for he was a man of moods, flickering between glory and despair, and just now dead-tired. He looked years older than thirty-one; and his dark, appealing eyes, set a little sloping in his face, were bloodshot, and his hollow cheeks deeply lined and puckered with reflection. His nature grudged thinking, for it crippled his speed in action: the labour of it shrivelled his features into swift lines of pain. In appearance he was tall, graceful and vigorous, with the most beautiful gait, and a royal dignity of head and shoulders. Of course he knew it, and a great part of his public expression was by sign and gesture.

His movements were impetuous. He showed himself hot-tempered and sensitive, even unreasonable, and he ran off soon on tangents. Appetite and physical weakness were mated in him, with the spur of courage. His personal charm, his imprudence, the pathetic hint of frailty as the sole reserve of this proud character made him the idol of his followers. One never asked if he were scrupulous; but later he showed that he could return trust for trust, suspicion for suspicion. He was fuller of wit than of humour.

His training in Abdul Hamid's entourage had made him past-master in diplomacy. His military service with the Turks had given him a working knowledge of tactics. His life in Constantinople and in the Turkish Parliament had made him familiar with European questions and manners. He was a careful judge of men. If he had the strength to realize his dreams he would go very far, for he was wrapped up in his work and lived for nothing else; but the fear was that he would wear himself out by trying to seem to aim always a little higher than the truth or that he would die of too much action. His men told me how, after a long spell of fighting, in which he had to guard himself, and lead the charges, and control and encourage them, he had collapsed physically and was carried away from his victory, unconscious, with the foam flecking his lips.

Meanwhile, here, as it seemed, was offered to our hand, which had only to be big enough to take it, a prophet who, if veiled, would give cogent form to the idea behind the activity of the Arab revolt. It was all and more than we had hoped for, much more than our halting course deserved. The aim of my trip was fulfilled.

My duty was now to take the shortest road to Egypt with the news: and the knowledge gained that evening in the palm wood grew and blossomed in my mind into a thousand branches, laden with fruit and shady leaves, beneath which I sat and half-listened and saw visions, while the twilight deepened, and the night; until a line of slaves with lamps came down the winding paths between the palm trunks, and with Feisal and Maulud we walked back through the gardens to the little house, with its courts still full of waiting people, and to the hot inner room in which the familiars were assembled; and there we sat down together to the smoking bowl of rice and meat set upon the food-carpet for our supper by the slaves. . . .

Later I saw Feisal again, and promised to do my best for him. My chiefs would arrange a base at Yenbo, where the stores and supplies he needed would be put ashore for his exclusive use. We would try to get him officer-volunteers from among the prisoners of war captured in Mesopotamia or on the Canal. We would form gun crews and machine-gun crews from the rank and file in the internment camps, and provide them with such mountain guns and light machine guns as were obtainable in Egypt. Lastly, I would advise that British Army officers, professionals, be sent down to act as advisers and liaison officers with him in the field.

This time our talk was of the pleasantest, and ended in warm thanks from him, and an invitation to return as soon as might be.

from THE ARAB BULLETIN, 26 *November* 1916

PERSONAL NOTES ON THE SHERIFIAL FAMILY

ONE can see that to the nomads the Sherif and his three elder sons are heroes. Sherif Hussein (Sayidna as they call him), is outwardly so gentle and considerate as to seem almost weak, but this appearance hides a deep and crafty policy, wide ambitions and an un-Arabian foresight, strength of character and persistence. There was never any pan-Arab secret society in Mecca, because the Sherif has always been the Arab Government. His influence was so strong in the tribes and country districts, as to be tantamount to administration; and in addition he played Arabs' advocate in the towns against the Turkish Government.

Particularly have his tastes and sympathies been always tribal. The son of a Circassian mother, he is endowed with qualities foreign to both Turk and Arab, but he determined to secure the hearts of the nomads by making his sons Bedouins. The Turks had insisted that they be educated in Constantinople, and Sherif Hussein agreed most willingly. They have all had a first-class Turkish education, and profit by their knowledge of the world. However, when they came back from Constantinople as young Levantines, wearing strange clothes and with Turkish manners, Sherif Hussein at once made them change into Arab things, and rub up their Arabic. He gave them Arab companions, and a little later sent for them, to put them in command of some small bodies of Arab camel corps, patrolling the pilgrim roads against the Auf. The young Sherifs fell in with the plan, as they thought it might be amusing, but were rather dashed when they were forbidden to take with them special food, or bedding, or saddle cushions, and still more when they were not given permission to come to Mecca for the Feast, but had to spend all the season out in the desert with their men, guarding the roads day and night, meeting nomads only, and learning to know their country and their manners.

They are now all thorough Bedouins, and as well have from their education the knowledge and experience of Turkish officials, and from their descent that blend of native intelligence and vigour which so often comes from a cross of Circassian and Arab blood. This makes them a most formidable family group, at once admired and efficient. It has, however, left them curiously isolated in their world. None of them seems to have a confidant or adviser or minister, and it is doubtful whether any one of them is fully intimate with another or with their father, of whom they all stand in awe.

Sidi Ali. — Short and slim, looking a little old already, though only thirty-seven. Slightly bent. Skin rather sallow, large deep brown eyes, nose thin and a little hooked, face somewhat worn and full of lines and hollows, mouth drooping. Beard spare and black. Has very delicate hands. His manners are perfectly simple, and he is obviously a very conscientious, careful, pleasant, gentleman, without force of character, nervous and rather tired. His physical weakness makes him subject to quick fits of shaking passion with more frequent moods of infirm obstinacy. Apparently not ambitious for himself, but swayed somewhat too easily by the wishes of others. Is bookish, and learned in law and religion. Shows his Arab blood more than his brothers.

Sidi Abdullah. — Aged thirty-five, but looks younger. Short and thick built, apparently as strong as a horse, with merry dark brown eyes, a round smooth face, full but short lips, straight nose, brown beard. In manner affectedly open and very charming, not standing at all on ceremony, but jesting with the tribesmen like one of their own sheikhs. On serious occasions he judges his words carefully, and shows himself a keen dialectician. Is probably not so much the brain as the spur of his father. He is obviously working to establish the greatness of the family, and has large ideas, which no doubt include his own particular advancement. The clash between him and Feisal will be interesting. The Arabs consider him a most astute politician, and a far-seeing statesman: but he has possibly more of the former than of the latter in his composition.

Sidi Feisal. — Is tall, graceful, vigorous, almost regal in appearance. Aged thirty-one. Very quick and restless in movement. Far more imposing personally than any of his brothers, knows it and trades on it. Is as clear-skinned as a pure Circassian, with dark hair, vivid black eyes set a little sloping in his face, strong nose, short chin. Looks like a European, and very like the monument of Richard I, at Fontevraud. He is hot tempered, proud and impatient, sometimes unreasonable, and runs off easily at tangents. Possesses far more personal magnetism and life than his brothers, but less prudence. Obviously very clever, perhaps not over scrupulous. Rather narrow-minded, and rash when he acts on impulse, but usually with enough strength to reflect, and then exact in judgment. Had he been brought up the wrong way might have become a barrack-yard officer. A popular idol, and ambitious; full of dreams, and the capacity to realize them, with keen personal insight, and a very efficient man of business.

Sherif Zeid. — Aged about twenty. Is quite overshadowed by the reputation of his half-brothers. His mother was Turkish and he takes after her. Is fond of riding about, and playing tricks. Has not so far been entrusted with any important commission, but is active. In manner a little loutish, but not a bad fellow. Humorous in outlook, and perhaps a little better balanced, because less intense, than his brothers. Shy.

Yenbo, October 27, 1916   T. E. L.

from THE ARAB BULLETIN, 18 *November* 1916

EXTRACTS FROM A REPORT ON FEISAL'S OPERATIONS

... (*Looked at locally the bigness of the Revolt impresses me*). We have here a well-peopled province, extending from Um Lejj to Kunfida, more than a fortnight long in camel journeys, whose whole nomad and semi-nomad population have been suddenly changed from casual pilferers to deadly enemies of the Turks, fighting them, not perhaps in our manner, but effectively enough in their own way, in the name of the religion which so lately preached a Holy War against us. This has now been going on for five months, during which time they have created, out of nothing, a sort of constitution and scheme of government for the areas behind the firing line. (*They believe that in liberating the Hejaz they are vindicating the rights of all Arabs to a national political existence, and without envisaging one state or even a federation, they are definitely looking North towards Syria and Bagdad. They do not question the independence of the Imam or of ibn Saud. They wish to confirm them . . . but they want to add an autonomous Syria to the Arab estate.*

Above and beyond everything we have let loose a wave of anti-Turkish feeling, which embittered as it has been by some generations of subjection may die very hard. There is in the tribes in the firing line a nervous enthusiasm common I suppose to all national risings. A rebellion on such a scale as this does more to weaken a country than unsuccessful foreign wars, and I suspect that Turkey has been harmed here more than it will be harmed elsewhere till Constantinople is captured and the Sultan made the puppet of European advisers.)

The Yeni Turan movement is keenly discussed in the Hejaz, where its anti-Arab and anti-Islamic character is well understood. The peace conference will, I think, see a demand from the Sherif for the transfer of the Holy relics from Constantinople to Mecca, as a sign that the Turks are unworthy longer to be the guardian of such things.

The Arab leaders have quite a number of intelligent level-headed men among them, who, if they do not do things as we would do them, are successful in their generation. Of course they lack experience — except of Turkish officialdom, which is a blind leader — and theory; for the study of practical economies has not been encouraged. However, I no longer question their capacity to form a government in the Hejaz, which is better, so far as the interest of the subjects are concerned, than the Turkish system which they have replaced. (*They are weak in material resources and always will be, for their world is agricultural and pastoral and can never be very rich or strong. If it were otherwise we would have had to weigh more deeply the advisability of creating in the Near East a new power with such exuberant national sentiment. As it is, their military weakness which for the moment incommodes us should henceforward ensure us advantages immeasurably greater than the money, arms and ammunition we are now called upon to spare.*)

Yenbo, October 30   T. E. L.

from SEVEN PILLARS OF WISDOM

KHARTUM felt cool after Arabia, and nerved me to show Sir Reginald Wingate my long reports written in those days of waiting at Yenbo. I urged that the situation seemed full of promise. The main need was skilled assistance; and the campaign should go prosperously if some Regular British officers, professionally competent and speaking Arabic, were attached to the Arab leaders as technical advisers, to keep us in proper touch.

Wingate was glad to hear a hopeful view. The Arab Revolt had been his dream for years. While I was at Khartum chance gave him the power to play the main part in it; for the workings against Sir Henry McMahon came to a head, were successful, and ended in his recall to England. Sir Reginald Wingate was ordered down to Egypt in his stead. So after two or three comfortable days in Khartum, resting and reading the *Morte d'Arthur* in the hospitable palace, I went down towards Cairo, feeling that the responsible person had all my news. The Nile trip became a holiday.

Egypt was, as usual, in the throes of a Rabegh question. Some aeroplanes were being sent there; and it was being argued whether to send a brigade of troops after them or not. The head of the French Military Mission at Jidda, Colonel Bremond (Wilson's counterpart, but with more authority; for he was a practising light in native warfare, a success in French Africa, and an ex-chief of staff of a Corps on the Somme) strongly urged the landing of Allied forces in Hejaz. To tempt us he had brought to Suez some artillery, some machine guns, and some cavalry and infantry, all Algerian Moslem rank and file, with French officers. These added to the British troops would give the force an international flavour.

Bremond's specious appreciation of the danger of the state of affairs in Arabia gained upon Sir Reginald. Wingate was a British General, commander of a nominal expeditionary force, the Hejaz Force, which in reality comprised a few liaison officers and a handful of storemen and instructors. If Bremond got his way he would be G.O.C. of a genuine brigade of mixed British and French troops, with all its pleasant machinery of responsibility and dispatches, and its prospect of increment and official recognition. Consequently he wrote a guarded despatch, half-tending towards direct interference.

As my experience of Arab feeling in the Harb country had given me strong opinions on the Rabegh question (indeed, most of my opinions were strong), I wrote for General Clayton, to whose Arab Bureau I was now formally transferred, a violent memorandum on the whole subject. Clayton was pleased with my view that the tribes might defend Rabegh for months if lent advice and guns, but that they would certainly scatter to their tents again as soon as they heard of the landing of foreigners in force. Further, that the intervention-plans were technically unsound, for a brigade would be quite insufficient to defend the position, to forbid the neighbouring water-supplies to the Turks, and to block their road towards Mecca. I accused Colonel Bremond of having motives of his own, not military, nor taking account of Arab interests and of the importance of the revolt to us; and quoted his words and acts in Hejaz as evidence against him. They gave just plausible colour to my charge.

Clayton took the memorandum to Sir Archibald Murray, who, liking its acidity and force, promptly wired it all home to London as proof that the Arab experts asking this sacrifice of valuable troops from him were divided about its wisdom and honesty, even in their own camp. London asked for explanations; and the atmosphere slowly cleared, though in a less acute form the Rabegh question lingered for two months more.

My popularity with the Staff in Egypt, due to the sudden help I had lent to Sir Archibald's prejudices, was novel and rather amusing. They began to be polite to me, and to say that I was observant, with a pungent style, and character. They pointed out how good of them it was to spare me to the Arab cause in its difficulties. I was sent for by the Commander-in-Chief, but on my way to him was intercepted by a waiting and agitated aide, and led first into the presence of the Chief of Staff, General Lynden Bell. To such an extent had he felt it his duty to support Sir Archibald in his whimsies that people generally confounded the two as one enemy. So I was astonished when, as I came in, he jumped to his feet, leaped forward, and gripped me by the shoulder, hissing, 'Now you're not to frighten him: don't you forget what I say!'

My face probably showed bewilderment, for his one eye turned bland and he made me sit down, and talked nicely about Oxford, . . .

I was hugely amused, inwardly, and promised to be good, but pointed out that my object was to secure the extra stores and arms and officers the Arabs needed, and how for this end I must enlist the interest, and, if necessary (for I would stick at nothing in the way of duty), even the excitement of the Commander-in-Chief; whereupon General Lynden Bell took me up, saying that supplies were his part, and in them he did everything without reference, and he thought he might at once, here and now, admit his new determination to do all he could for us.

I think he kept his word and was fair to us thereafter. I was very soothing to his chief.

Clayton a few days later told me to return to Arabia and Feisal. This being much against my grain I urged my complete unfitness for the job: said I hated responsibility — obviously the position of a conscientious adviser would be responsible — and that in all my life objects had been gladder to me than persons, and ideas than objects. So the duty of succeeding with men, of disposing them to any purpose, would be doubly hard to me. They were not my medium: I was not practised in that technique. . . .

My journey was to Yenbo, now the special base of Feisal's army, where Garland single-handed was teaching the Sherifians how to blow up railways with dynamite, and how to keep army stores in systematic order. The first activity was the better. Garland was an enquirer in physics, and had years of practical knowledge of explosives. He had his own devices for mining trains and felling telegraphs and cutting metals; and his knowledge of Arabic and freedom from the theories of the ordinary sapper-school enabled him to teach the art of demolition to unlettered Beduin in a quick and ready way. His pupils admired a man who was never at a loss.

Incidentally he taught me to be familiar with high explosive. Sappers handled it like a sacrament, but Garland would shovel a handful of detonators into his pocket, with a string of primers, fuse, and fusees, and jump gaily on his camel for a week's ride to the Hejaz Railway. His health was poor and the climate made him regularly ill. A weak heart troubled him after any strenuous effort or crisis; but he treated these troubles as freely as he did detonators, and persisted till he had derailed the first train and broken the first culvert in Arabia. Shortly afterwards he died. . . .

After starting, we cantered for three unbroken hours. That had shaken down our bellies far enough for us to hold more food, and we stopped and ate bread and drank coffee till sunset, while Abd el Kerim rolled about his carpet in a dog-fight with one of the men. When he was exhausted he sat up; and they told stories and japed, till they were breathed enough to get up and dance. Everything was very free, very good-tempered, and not at all dignified. . . .

As we got near we saw through the palm-trees flame, and the flame-lit smoke of many fires, while the hollow ground re-echoed with the roaring of thousands of excited camels, and volleying of shots or shoutings in the darkness of lost men, who sought through the crowd to rejoin their friends. . . .

. . . Feisal with his camel corps had just arrived, and we were to go down and join him. . . .

There were hundreds of fires of thorn-wood, and round them were Arabs making coffee or eating, or sleeping muffled like dead men in their cloaks, packed together closely in the confusion of camels. So many camels in company made a mess indescribable, couched as they were or tied down all over the camping ground, with more ever coming in, and the old ones leaping up on three legs to join them, roaring with hunger and agitation. Patrols were going out, caravans being unloaded, and dozens of Egyptian mules bucking angrily over the middle of the scene.

We ploughed our way through this din, and in an island of calm at the very centre of the valley bed found Sherif Feisal. We halted our camels by his side. On his carpet, spread barely over the stones, he was sitting between Sherif Sharraf, the Kaimmakam both of the Imaret and of Taif, his cousin, and Maulud, the rugged, slashing old Mesopotamian patriot, now acting as his A.D.C. In front of him knelt a secretary taking down an order, and beyond him another reading reports aloud by the light of a silvered lamp which a slave was holding. The night was windless, the air heavy, and the unshielded flame poised there stiff and straight.

Feisal, quiet as ever, welcomed me with a smile until he could finish his dictation. After it he apologized for my disorderly reception, and waved the slaves back to give us privacy . . . Then he explained to me what unexpected things had happened in the last twenty-four hours on the battle front. . . .

This lasted till half-past four in the morning. It grew very cold as the damp of the valley rose through the carpet and soaked our clothes. The camp gradually stilled as the tired men and animals went one by one to sleep; a white mist collected softly over them and in it the fires became slow pillars of smoke. Immediately behind us, rising out of the bed of mist, Jebel Rudhwa, more steep and rugged than ever, was brought so close by the hushed moonlight that it seemed hanging over our heads.

Feisal at last finished the urgent work. We ate half-a-dozen dates, a frigid comfort, and curled up on the wet carpet. As I lay there in a shiver, I saw the Biasha guards creep up and spread their cloaks gently over Feisal, when they were sure that he was sleeping. . . .

Suddenly Feisal asked me if I would wear Arab clothes like his own while in the camp. I should find it better for my own part, since it was a comfortable dress in which to live Arab-fashion as we must do. Besides, the tribesmen would then understand how to take me. The only wearers of khaki in their experience had been Turkish officers, before whom they took up an instinctive defence. If I wore Meccan clothes, they would behave to me as though I were really one of the leaders; and I might slip in and out of Feisal's tent without making a sensation which he had to explain away each time to strangers.

I agreed at once, very gladly; for army uniform was abominable when camel-riding, or when sitting about on the ground; and the Arab things, which I had learned to manage before the war, were cleaner and more decent in the desert. Hejris was pleased, too, and exercised his fancy in fitting me out in splendid white silk and gold-embroidered wedding garments which had been sent to Feisal lately (was it a hint?) by his great-aunt in Mecca. I took a stroll in the new looseness of them round the palm-gardens of Mubarak and Bruka, to accustom myself to their feel. . . .

The march became rather splendid and barbaric. First rode Feisal in white, then Sharraf at his right in red head-cloth and henna-dyed tunic and cloak, myself on his left in white and scarlet, behind us three banners of faded crimson silk with gilt spikes, behind them the drummers playing a march, and behind them again the wild mass of twelve hundred bouncing camels of the bodyguard, packed as closely as they could move, the men in every variety of coloured clothes and the camels nearly as brilliant in their trappings. We filled the valley to its banks with our flashing stream. . . .

Next day we rode easily. A breakfast suggested itself, upon our finding some more little water-pools, in a bare valley flowing down from El Sukhur, a group of three extraordinary hills like granite bubbles blown through the earth. The journey was pleasant, for it was cool; there were a lot of us; and we two Englishmen had a tent in which we could shut ourselves up and be alone. A weariness of the desert was the living always in company, each of the party hearing all that was said and seeing all that was done by the others day and night. Yet the craving for solitude seemed part of the delusion of self-sufficiency, a factitious making-rare of the person to enhance its strangeness in its own estimation. To have privacy, as Newcombe and I had, was ten thousand times more restful than the open life, but the work suffered by the creation of such a bar between the leaders and men. Among the Arabs there were no distinctions, traditional or natural, except the unconscious power given a famous sheikh by virtue of his accomplishment; and they taught me that no man could be their leader except he ate the ranks' food, wore their clothes, lived level with them, and yet appeared better in himself. . . .

At last we camped, and when the camels were unloaded and driven out to pasture, I lay down under the rocks and rested. My body was very sore with headache and high fever, the accompaniments of a sharp attack of dysentery which had troubled me along the march and had laid me out twice that day in short fainting fits, when the more difficult parts of the climb had asked too much of my strength. Dysentery of this Arabian coast sort used to fall like a hammer blow, and crush its victims for a few hours, after which the extreme effects passed off; but it left men curiously tired, and subject for some weeks to sudden breaks of nerve.

My followers had been quarrelling all day; and while I was lying near the rocks a shot was fired. I paid no attention; for there were hares and birds in the valley; but a little later Suleiman roused me and made me follow him across the valley to an opposite bay in the rocks, where one of the Ageyl, a Boreida man, was lying stone dead with a bullet through his temples. The shot must have been fired from close by; because the skin was burnt about one wound. The remaining Ageyl were running frantically about; and when I asked what it was Ali, their head man, said that Hamed the Moor had done the murder. I suspected Suleiman, because of the feud between the Atban and Ageyl which had burned up in Yenbo and Wejh; but Ali assured me that Suleiman had been with him three hundred yards further up the valley gathering sticks when the shot was fired. I sent all out to search for Hamed, and crawled back to the baggage, feeling that it need not have happened this day of all days when I was in pain.

As I lay there I heard a rustle, and opened my eyes slowly upon Hamed's back as he stooped over his saddle-bags, which lay just beyond my rock. I covered him with a pistol and then spoke. He had put down his rifle to lift the gear; and was at my mercy till the others came. We held a court at once; and after a while Hamed confessed that, he and Salem having had words, he had seen red and shot him suddenly. Our inquiry ended. The Ageyl, as relatives of the dead man, demanded blood for blood. The others supported them; and I tried vainly to talk the gentle Ali round. My head was aching with fever and I could not think; but hardly even in health, with all eloquence, could I have begged Hamed off; for Salem had been a friendly fellow and his sudden murder a wanton crime.

Then rose up the horror which would make civilized man shun justice like a plague if he had not the needy to serve him as hangman for wages. There were other Moroccans in our army; and to let the Ageyl kill one in feud meant reprisals by which our unity would have been endangered. It must be a formal execution, and at last, desperately, I told Hamed that he must die for punishment, and laid the burden of his killing on myself. Perhaps they would count me not qualified for feud. At least no revenge could lie against my followers; for I was a stranger and kinless.

I made him enter a narrow gully of the spur, a dank twilight place overgrown with weeds. Its sandy bed had been pitted by trickles of water down the cliffs in the late rain. At the end it shrank to a crack a few inches wide. The walls were vertical. I stood in the entrance and gave him a few moments' delay which he spent crying on the ground. Then I made him rise and shot him through the chest. He fell down on the weeds shrieking, with the blood coming out in spurts over his clothes, and jerked about till he rolled nearly to where I was. I fired again, but was shaking so that I only broke his wrist. He went on calling out, less loudly, now lying on his back with his feet towards me, and I leant forward and shot him for the last time in the thick of his neck under the jaw. His body shivered a little, and I called the Ageyl; who buried him in the gully where he was. Afterwards the wakeful night dragged over me, till, hours before dawn, I had the men up and made them load, in my longing to be set free of Wadi Kitan. They had to lift me into the saddle. . . .

The day, now at its zenith, was very hot; and my weakness had so increased that my head hardly held up against it. The puffs of feverish wind pressed like scorching hands against our faces, burning our eyes. My pain made me breathe in gasps through the mouth; the wind cracked my lips and seared my throat till I was too dry to talk, and drinking became sore; yet I always needed to drink, as my thirst would not let me lie still and get the peace I longed for. The flies were a plague.

The bed of the valley was of fine quartz gravel and white sand. Its glitter thrust itself between our eyelids; and the level of the ground seemed to dance as the wind moved the white tips of stubble grass to and fro. The camels loved this grass, which grew in tufts, about sixteen inches high, on slate-green stalks. They gulped down great quantities of it until the men drove them in and couched them by me. At the moment I hated the beasts, for too much food made their breath stink; and they rumblingly belched up a new mouthful from their stomachs each time they had chewed and swallowed the last, till a green slaver flooded out between their loose lips over the side teeth, and dripped down their sagging chins.

Lying angrily there, I threw a stone at the nearest, which got up and wavered about behind my head: finally it straddled its back legs and staled in wide, bitter jets; and I was so far gone with the heat and weakness and pain that I just lay there and cried about it unhelping....

I rejoiced that we were so nearly in, for fever was heavy on me. I was afraid that perhaps I was going to be really ill, and the prospect of falling into the well-meaning hands of tribesmen in such a state was not pleasant. Their treatment of every sickness was to burn holes in the patient's body at some spot believed to be the complement of the part affected. It was a cure tolerable to such as had faith in it, but torture to the unbelieving: to incur it unwillingly would be silly, and yet certain; for the Arab's good intentions, selfish as their good digestions, would never heed a sick man's protesting.

The morning was easy, over open valleys and gentle rides into Wadi Ais. We arrived at Abu Markha, its nearest watering-place, just a few minutes after Sherif Abdulla had dismounted there ... I gave him the documents from Feisal, explaining the situation in Medina, and the need we had of haste to block the railway. I thought he took it coolly; but, without argument, went on to say that I was a little tired after my journey, and with his permission would lie down and sleep a while. He pitched me a tent next to his great marquee, and I went into it and rested myself at last. It had been a struggle against faintness day-long in the saddle to get here at all: and now the strain was ended with the delivery of my message, I felt that another hour would have brought the breaking point.

About ten days I lay in that tent, suffering a bodily weakness which made my animal self crawl away and hide till the shame was passed. As usual in such circumstances my mind cleared, my senses became more acute, and I began at last to think consecutively of the Arab Revolt, as an accustomed duty to rest upon against the pain ... and as I pondered slowly, it dawned on me that we had won the Hejaz war.

Out of every thousand square miles of Hejaz nine hundred and ninety-nine were now free. . . .

The next day a great complication of boils developed out, to conceal my lessened fever, and to chain me down yet longer in impotence upon my face in this stinking tent. When it grew too hot for dreamless dozing, I picked up my tangle again, and went on ravelling it out, considering now the whole house of war in its structural aspect, which was strategy, in its arrangements, which were tactics, and in the sentiment of its inhabitants, which was psychology; for my personal duty was command, and the commander, like the master architect, was responsible for all.

The first confusion was the false antithesis between strategy, the aim in war, the synoptic regard seeing each part relative to the whole, and tactics, the means towards a strategic end, the particular steps of its staircase. They seemed only points of view from which to ponder the elements of war, the Algebraical element of things, a Biological element of lives, and the Psychological element of ideas.

The algebraical element looked to me a pure science, subject to mathematical law, inhuman. It dealt with known variables, fixed conditions, space and time, inorganic things like hills and climates and railways, with mankind in type-masses too great for individual variety, with all artificial aids and the extensions given our faculties by mechanical invention. It was essentially formulable.

Here was a pompous, professorial beginning. My wits, hostile to the abstract, took refuge in Arabia again. Translated into Arabic, the algebraic factor would first take practical account of the area we wished to deliver, and I began idly to calculate how many square miles: sixty: eighty: one hundred: perhaps one hundred and forty thousand square miles. And how would the Turks defend all that? No doubt by a trench line across the bottom, if we came like an army with banners; but suppose we were (as we might be) an influence, an idea, a thing intangible, invulnerable, without front or back, drifting about like a gas? Armies were like plants, immobile, firm-rooted, nourished through long stems to the head. We might be a vapour, blowing where we listed. Our kingdoms lay in each man's mind; and as we wanted nothing material to live on, so we might offer nothing material to the killing. It seemed a regular soldier might be helpless without a target, owning only what he sat on, and subjugating only what, by order, he could poke his rifle at.

Then I figured out how many men they would need to sit on all this ground, to save it from our attack-in-depth, sedition putting up her head in every unoccupied one of those hundred thousand square miles. I knew the Turkish Army exactly, and even allowing for their recent extension of faculty by aeroplanes and guns and armoured trains (which made the earth a smaller battlefield) still it seemed they would have need of a fortified post every four square miles, and a post could not be less than twenty men. If so, they would need six hundred thousand men to meet the illwills of all the Arab peoples, combined with the active hostility of a few zealots.

How many zealots could we have? At present we had nearly fifty thousand: sufficient for the day. It seemed the assets in this element of war were ours. If we realized our raw materials and were apt with them, then climate, railway, desert, and technical weapons could also be attached to our interests. The Turks were stupid; the Germans behind them dogmatical. They would believe that rebellion was absolute like war, and deal with it on the analogy of war. Analogy in human things was fudge, anyhow; and war upon rebellion was messy and slow, like eating soup with a knife.

This was enough of the concrete; so I sheered off ἐπιστήμη, the mathematical element, and plunged into the nature of the biological factor in command. Its crisis seemed to be the breaking point, life and death, or less finally, wear and tear. The war-philosophers had properly made an art of it, and had elevated one item, 'effusion of blood', to the height of an essential, which became humanity in battle, an act touching every side of our corporal being, and very warm. A line of variability. Man, persisted like leaven through its estimates, making them irregular. The components were sensitive and illogical, and generals guarded themselves by the device of a reserve, the significant medium of their art. Goltz had said that if you knew the enemy's strength, and he was fully deployed, then you could dispense with a reserve: but this was never. The possibility of accident, of some flaw in materials was always in the general's mind, and the reserve unconsciously held to meet it.

The 'felt' element in troops, not expressible in figures, had to be guessed at by the equivalent of Plato's δόξα, and the greatest commander of men was he whose intuitions most nearly happened. Nine-tenths of tactics were certain enough to be teachable in schools; but the irrational tenth was like the kingfisher flashing across the pool, and in it lay the test of generals. It could be ensued only by instinct (sharpened by thought practising the stroke) until at the crisis it came naturally, a reflex. There had been men whose δόξα so nearly approached perfection that by its road they reached the certainty of ἐπιστήμη. The Greeks might have called such genius for command νόησις had they bothered to rationalize revolt.

My mind see-sawed back to apply this to ourselves, and at once knew that it was not bounded by mankind, that it applied also to materials. In Turkey things were scarce and precious, men less esteemed than equipment. Our cue was to destroy, not the Turk's army, but his minerals. The death of a Turkish bridge or rail, machine or gun or charge of high explosive, was more profitable to us than the death of a Turk. In the Arab Army at the moment we were chary both of materials and of men. Governments saw men only in mass; but our men, being irregulars, were not formations, but individuals. An individual death, like a pebble dropped in water, might make but a brief hole; yet rings of sorrow widened out therefrom. We could not afford casualties.

Materials were easier to replace. It was our obvious policy to be superior in some one tangible branch; gun-cotton or machine guns or whatever could be made decisive. Orthodoxy had laid down the maxim, applied to men, of being superior at the critical point and moment of attack. We might be superior in equipment in one dominant moment or respect; and for both things and men we might give the doctrine a twisted negative side, for cheapness' sake, and be weaker than the enemy everywhere except in that one point or matter. The decision of what was critical would always be ours. Most wars were wars of contact, both forces striving into touch to avoid tactical surprise. Ours should be a war of detachment. We were to contain the enemy by the silent threat of a vast unknown desert, not disclosing ourselves till we attacked. The attack might be nominal, directed not against him, but against his stuff; so it would not seek either his strength or his weakness, but his most accessible material. In railway-cutting it would be usually an empty stretch of rail; and the more empty, the greater the tactical success. We might turn our average into a rule (not a law, since war was antinomian) and develop a habit of never engaging the enemy. This would chime with the numerical plea for never affording a target. Many Turks on our front had no chance all the war to fire on us, and we were never on the defensive except by accident and in error.

The corollary of such a rule was perfect 'intelligence', so that we could plan in certainty. The chief agent must be the general's head; and his understanding must be faultless, leaving no room for chance.

Morale, if built on knowledge, was broken by ignorance. When we knew all about the enemy we should be comfortable. We must take more pains in the service of news than any regular staff.

I was getting through my subject. The algebraical factor had been translated into terms of Arabia, and fitted like a glove. It promised victory. The biological factor had dictated to us a development of the tactical line most in accord with the genius of our tribesmen. There remained the psychological element to build up an apt shape. I went to Xenophon and stole, to name it, his word *diathetics*, which had been the art of Cyrus before he struck.

Of this our 'propaganda' was the stained and ignoble offspring. It was the pathic, almost the ethical, in war. Some of it concerned the crowd, an adjustment of its spirit to the point where it became useful to exploit in action, and the pre-direction of this changing spirit to a certain end. Some of it concerned the individual, and then it became a rare art of human kindness, transcending, by purposed emotion, the gradual logical sequence of the mind. It was more subtle than tactics, and better worth doing, because it dealt with uncontrollables, with subjects incapable of direct command. It considered the capacity for mood of our men, their complexities and mutability, and the cultivation of whatever in them promised to profit our intention. We had to arrange their minds in order of battle just as carefully and as formally as other officers would arrange their bodies. And not only our own men's minds, though naturally they came first. We must also arrange the minds of the enemy, so far as we could reach them; then those other minds of the nation supporting us behind the firing line, since more than half the battle passed there in the back; then the minds of the enemy nation waiting the verdict; and of the neutrals looking on; circle beyond circle.

There were many humiliating material limits, but no moral impossibilities; so that the scope of our diathetical activities was unbounded. On it we should mainly depend for the means of victory on the Arab front: and the novelty of it was our advantage. The printing press, and each newly-discovered method of communication favoured the intellectual above the physical, civilization paying the mind always from the body's funds. We kindergarten soldiers were beginning our art of war in the atmosphere of the twentieth century, receiving our weapons without prejudice. To the regular officer, with the tradition of forty generations of service behind him, the antique arms were the most honoured. As we had seldom to concern ourselves with what our men did, but always with what they thought, the diathetic for us would be more than half the command. In Europe it was set a little aside, and entrusted to men outside the General Staff. In Asia the regular elements were so weak that irregulars could not let the metaphysical weapon rust unused.

Battles in Arabia were a mistake, since we profited in them only by the ammunition the enemy fired off. Napoleon had said it was rare to find generals willing to fight battles; but the curse of this war was that so few would do anything else. Saxe had told us that irrational battles were the refuges of fools: rather they seemed to me impositions on the side which believed itself weaker, hazards made unavoidable either by lack of land room or by the need to defend a material property dearer than the lives of soldiers. We had nothing material to lose, so our best line was to defend nothing and to shoot nothing. Our cards were speed and time, not hitting power. The invention of bully beef had profited us more than the invention of gunpowder, but gave us strategical, rather than tactical strength, since in Arabia range was more than force, space greater than the power of armies.

I had now been eight days lying in this remote tent, keeping my ideas general,* till my brain, sick of unsupported thinking, had to be dragged to its work by an effort of will, and went off into a doze whenever that effort was relaxed. The fever passed: my dysentery ceased; and with restored strength the present again became actual to me. Facts concrete and pertinent thrust themselves into my reveries; and my inconstant wit bore aside towards all these roads of escape. So I hurried into line my shadowy principles, to have them once precise before my power to evoke them faded.

It seemed to me proven that our rebellion had an unassailable base, guarded not only from attack, but from the fear of attack. It had a sophisticated alien enemy, disposed as an army of occupation in an area greater than could be dominated effectively from fortified posts. It had a friendly population, of which some two in the hundred were active, and the rest quietly sympathetic to the point of not betraying

---

* Not perhaps as successfully as here. I thought out my problems mainly in terms of Hejaz, illustrated by what I knew of its men and its geography. These would have been too long if written down; and the argument has been compressed into an abstract form in which it smells more of the lamp than of the field. All military writing does, worse luck.

the movements of the minority. The active rebels had the virtues of secrecy and selfcontrol, and the qualities of speed, endurance and independence of arteries of supply. They had technical equipment enough to paralyse the enemy's communications. A province would be won when we had taught the civilians in it to die for our ideal of freedom. The presence of the enemy was secondary. Final victory seemed certain, if the war lasted long enough for us to work it out. . . .

Feisal might be a free gas: Sir Archibald's army, probably the most cumbrous in the world, had to be laboriously pushed forward on its belly. It was ridiculous to suppose it could keep pace with ethical conceptions as nimble as the Arab Movement: doubtful even if it would understand them. However, perhaps by hindering the railway we could frighten the Turks off their plan to evacuate Medina, and give them reason to remain in the town on the defensive: a conclusion highly serviceable to both Arabs and English, though possibly neither would see it, yet.

Accordingly, I wandered into Abdulla's tent, announcing my complete recovery and an ambition to do something to the Hejaz railway.

from THE ARAB BULLETIN, *Wednesday, April 4*

RODE at 5.30 a.m. and at 6.15 a.m. crossed the level bed of Wadi Turaa, and Wadi Hamdh at 6.45 a.m. The Hamdh was as full of *aslam* wood as at Abu Zereibat and had the same hummocky bed, with sandy blisters over it — but it was only about 200 yards wide, and shallow. We halted at 8 a.m. in W. Tubja, which was a sort of wilderness garden, with a profusion of grass and shrubs in which the camels rejoiced. The weather was very hot, with a burning sun that made the sandy ground impossible for me to walk on barefoot. The Arabs had soles like asbestos, and made little complaint, except of the warmth of the air. There had been thunder all yesterday, and half a dozen showers of rain last night and today. J. Serd and J. Kasim were wrapped in shafts and sheets of a dark blue and yellow vapour that seemed motionless and solid. We marched across W. Tubja again at 1.20 p.m. About 1.40 p.m. we noticed that part of the yellow cloud from J. Serd was approaching us, against the wind, raising scores of dust-devils before its feet. It also produced two dust-spouts, tight and symmetrical — stationary columns, like chimneys — one to the right and one to the left of its advance.

When it got nearer, the wind, which had been scorching us from the north-east, changed suddenly, and became bitterly cold and damp, from the south-west. It increased greatly in violence, and at the same time the sunlight disappeared and the air became thick and ochre-yellow. About three minutes later the advancing brown wall (I think it was about 1,500 feet high) struck us, and proved to be a blanket of dust, and large grains of sand, twisting and turning most violently with itself, and at the same time advancing east at about forty miles an hour. The internal whirling winds had the most bizarre effect. They tore our cloaks from us, turned our camels sometimes right round, and sometimes drew them together in a vortex, and large bushes, tufts of grass, and small trees were torn up clean by the roots, in a dense cloud of the soil about them, and were driven against us, or dashed over our heads, with sometimes dangerous force. We were never blinded — it was always possible to see seven or eight feet each side — but it was risky to look out, since one never knew if one would meet a flying tree, or a rush of pebbles, or a column of dust.

This *habub* lasted for eighteen minutes, and then ceased nearly as suddenly as it had come, and while we and our clothes and camels were all smothered in dust and yellow from head to foot, down burst torrents of rain, and muddied us to the skin. The wind swung round to the north, and the rain drove before it through our cloaks, and chilled us through and through. At 3 p.m. we had crossed the plain and entered the bare valley of W. Dhaiji, which cuts through J. Jindal at its southern end, from the railway to the Hamdh. It is fairly broad at first, sandy, with precipitous rock walls. We rode up it till 4 p.m. and left our camels in a side valley, and climbed a hill to see the line. The hill was of naked rock, and with the wet and the numbing cold the Ateibah servant of Sultan el-Abbud lost his nerve, pitched over a cliff, and smashed his skull to pieces. It was our only casualty on the trip.

When we got to the hill-top it was too thick weather to see the railway, so I returned to the camels, and shivered by them for an hour or two. We were stumbled upon by a mounted man, with whom we exchanged ineffectual shots, and were annoyed by this, as surprise was essential, and we could hear the bugles of Madahrij sounding recall and supper in the station, which was also an irritation. However, at 9 p.m. the explosives came up, with the rest of the party, and I started out with Sultan, Dakhilallah and Mohammed el-Gadhi for the line.

We had some delay in finding a machine-gun position, for the railway runs everywhere near the eastern hills of the valley, and the valley is about 3,000 yards broad. However, eventually, we found a place opposite kilometre 1121, and I laid a mine (trigger central, with rail-cutting charges 15 yards north and south of it respectively) with some difficulty owing to the rain, at 12 p.m. It took till 1.45 a.m. to cover up the traces of the digging, and we left the whole bank, and the sandy plain each side, as covered with huge footmarks as though a school of elephants had danced on it, and made tracks that a blind man could have felt. I wiped out most of those on the embankment itself, however, by walking up and down in shoes over it. Such prints are indistinguishable from the daily footmarks of the patrol inspecting the line.

We got back to the new position at 2.30 a.m. (still raining and blowing and very cold) and sat about on stones till dawn, when the camels and machine-gun came up. Dakhilallah, who had been guide and leader all night, now sent out patrols and sentries and outposts in all directions, and went on a hilltop himself with glasses to watch the line. The sun fortunately came out, so we were able to get dry and warm, and by midday were again gasping in the heat. A cotton shirt is a handy garment, but not adaptable to such sudden changes of temperature.

from SEVEN PILLARS OF WISDOM

THE tribal propaganda was marching forward: all was for the best, and I was about to take my leave when Suleiman, the guest-master, hurried in and whispered to Feisal, who turned to me with shining eyes, trying to be calm, and said, 'Auda is here'. I shouted, 'Auda abu Tayi,' and at that moment the tent-flap was drawn back, before a deep voice which boomed salutations to Our Lord, the Commander of the Faithful. There entered a tall, strong figure, with a haggard face, passionate and tragic. This was Auda, and after him followed Mohammed, his son, a child in looks, and only eleven years old in truth.

Feisal had sprung to his feet. Auda caught his hand and kissed it, and they drew aside a pace or two and looked at each other — a splendidly unlike pair, typical of much that was best in Arabia, Feisal the prophet, and Auda the warrior, each filling his part to perfection, and immediately understanding and liking the other. They sat down.

from THE ARAB BULLETIN

T H E head man of the Abu Tayi is, of course, the inimitable Auda. He must be nearly fifty now (he admits forty) and his black beard is tinged with white, but he is still tall and straight, loosely built, spare and powerful, and as active as a much younger man. His lined and haggard face is pure Bedouin: broad low forehead, high sharp hooked nose, brown-green eyes, slanting outward, large mouth (now unfortunately toothless, for his false teeth were Turkish, and his patriotism made him sacrifice them with a hammer, the day he swore allegiance to Feisal in Wejh), pointed beard and moustache, with the lower jaw shaven clean in the Howeitat style. The Howeitat pride themselves on being altogether Bedu, and Auda is the essence of the Abu Tayi. His hospitality is sweeping (inconvenient, except to very hungry souls), his generosity has reduced him to poverty, and devoured the profits of a hundred successful raids. He has married twenty-eight times, has been wounded thirteen times, and in his battles has seen all his tribesmen hurt, and most of his relations killed. He has only reported his 'kill' since 1900, and they now stand at seventy-five Arabs; Turks are not counted by Auda when they are dead. Under his handling the Toweihah have become the finest fighting force in Western Arabia. He raids as often as he can each year ('but a year passes so quickly, Sidi') and has seen Aleppo, Basra, Taif, Wejh and Wadi Dawasir in his armed expeditions.

In his way, Auda is as hard-headed as he is hot-headed. His patience is extreme, and he receives (and ignores) advice, criticism, or abuse with a smile as constant as it is very charming. Nothing on earth would make him change his mind or obey an order or follow a course he disapproved. He sees life as a saga and all events in it are significant and all personages heroic. His mind is packed (and generally over-flows) with stories of old raids and epic poems of fights. When he cannot secure a listener he sings to himself in his tremendous voice, which is also deep and musical. In the echoing valleys of Arnousa, our guide in night marches was this wonderful voice of Auda's, conversing far in the van, and being rolled back to us from the broken faces of the cliffs. He speaks of himself in the third person, and he is so sure of his fame that he delights to roar out stories against himself. At times he seems seized with a demon of mischief and in large gatherings shouts appalling stories of the private matters of his host or guests: with all this he is modest, simple as a child, direct, honest, kind-hearted, affectionate, and warmly loved even by those to whom he is most trying — his friends.

He is rather like Caesar's tribe, in his faculty for keeping round him a free territory, and then a great ring of enemies. Nuri Shaalan pretends only to love Auda — but in reality he and the Sukhur, and all friendly chiefs also, go about in terror lest they should offend in some way against Auda's pleasure. He loses no opportunity of adding to his enemies and relishes the new situation most because it is an ideal excuse to take on the Turkish Government. 'To the Mutessarif of Kerak from Auda abu Tayi . . . greeting. Take notice to quit Arab territory before the end of Ramadan. We want it for ourselves. Should you not go, I declare you outlawed and God will decide between us.' Such was Auda's cartel to the Government the day we struck.

After Auda, Mohammed el Dheilan is the chief figure in the tribe. He is taller than Auda, and massively built, a square-headed intelligent, thoughtful man of perhaps thirty-five, with a sour humour and a kind heart carefully concealed beneath it. In his youth he was notoriously wild, but reformed himself the night he was condemned to be hanged by Nevris Bey, Sami Pasha's Staff Officer, and has repaid many of the injuries he once wrought. He acted as business manager of the Abu Tayi and their spokesman with the Government. His tastes are rather luscious, and his ploughed land at Tafileh and his little house at Maan introduced him to luxuries which took root among the tribe: hence the mineral waters and parasols of a Howeitat *Ghazzu*. Mohammed is greedy, richer than Auda, more calculating, deeper — but a fine fighting man, too, and one who knows how to appeal to everything in his hearers' natures, and to bend them to his will by words.

Zaal ibn Motlog is Auda's nephew. He is about twenty-five, with *petite* features, carefully curled moustache, polished teeth, trimmed and pointed beard, like a French professional man. He, too, is greedy (of all Arabs I have met the Howeitat were the most open, most constant, most shameless beggars, wearying one day and night with their mean importunities and preposterous demands), sharp as a needle, of no great mental strength, but trained for years by Auda as chief scout to the tribe, and therefore a most capable and dashing commander of a raid.

Auda ibn Zaal is the fourth great man of Abu Tayi. He is silent and more usual in type than Auda, Mohammed, or Zaal, but the Howeitat flock to his side when there is a raid, and say that in action for concentrated force he is second only to Auda, with something of the skill of Mohammed super-added. Personally I have seen all four chiefs under fire, and saw in them all a headlong unreasoning dash and courage that accounted easily for the scarred and mutilated figures of their tribesmen.

The fighting strength of the Abu Tayi is 535 camelmen and twenty-five horsemen.   T.E.L.

from SEVEN PILLARS OF WISDOM

I WAS working out with Auda abu Tayi a march to the Howeitat in their spring pastures of the Syrian Desert. From them we might raise a mobile camel force, and rush Akaba from the eastward without guns or machine-guns.

The eastern was the unguarded side, the line of least resistance, the easiest for us. Our march would be an extreme example of a turning movement, since it involved a desert journey of six hundred miles to capture a trench within gunfire of our ships: but there was no practicable alternative, and it was so entirely in the spirit of my sick-bed ruminations that its issue might well be fortunate, and would surely be instructive. Auda thought all things possible with dynamite and money, and that the smaller clans about Akaba would join us. Feisal, who was already in touch with them, also believed that they would help if we won a preliminary success up by Maan and then moved in force against the port. The Navy raided it while we were thinking, and their captured Turks gave us such useful information that I became eager to go off at once.

The desert route to Akaba was so long and so difficult that we could take neither guns nor machine-guns, nor stores nor regular soldiers. Accordingly the element I would withdraw from the railway scheme was only my single self; and, in the circumstances, this amount was negligible, since I felt so strongly against it that my help there would have been half-hearted. So I decided to go my own way, with or without orders. I wrote a letter full of apologies to Clayton, telling him that my intentions were of the best: and went. . . .

Our business was to reach Arfaja alive.

So we wisely marched on, over monotonous, glittering sand; and over those worse stretches, 'Giaan', of polished mud, nearly as white and smooth as laid paper, and often whole miles square. They blazed back the sun into our faces with glassy vigour, so we rode with its light raining direct arrows upon our heads, and its reflection glancing up from the ground through our inadequate eyelids. It was not a steady pressure, but a pain ebbing and flowing; at one time piling itself up and up till we nearly swooned; and then falling away coolly, in a moment of false shadow like a black web crossing the retina: these gave us a moment's breathing space to store new capacity for suffering, like the struggles to the surface of a drowning man. . . .

Only Gasim was not there: they thought him among the Howeitat, for his surliness offended the laughing soldiery and kept him commonly with the Beduin, who were more of his kidney.

There was no one behind, so I rode forward wishing to see how his camel was: and at last found it, riderless, being led by one of the Howeitat. His saddle-bags were on it, and his rifle and his food, but he himself nowhere; gradually it dawned on us that the miserable man was lost. This was a dreadful business, for in the haze and mirage the caravan could not be seen two miles, and on the iron ground it made no tracks: afoot he would never overtake us.

Everyone had marched on, thinking him elsewhere in our loose line; but much time had passed and it was nearly midday, so he must be miles back. His loaded camel was proof that he had not been forgotten asleep at our night halt. The Ageyl ventured that perhaps he had dozed in the saddle and fallen, stunning or killing himself: or perhaps someone of the party had borne him a grudge. Anyway they did not know. He was an ill-natured stranger, no charge on any of them, and they did not greatly care.

True: but it was true also that Mohammed, his countryman and fellow, who was technically his road-companion, knew nothing of the desert, had a foundered camel, and could not turn back for him.

If I sent him, it would be murder. That shifted the difficulty to my shoulders. The Howeitat, who would have helped, were away in the mirage out of sight, hunting or scouting. Ibn Dgheithir's Ageyl were so clannish that they would not put themselves about except for one another. Besides Gasim was my man: and upon me lay the responsibility of him.

I looked weakly at my trudging men, and wondered for a moment if I could change with one, sending him back on my camel to the rescue. My shirking the duty would be understood, because I was a foreigner: but that was precisely the plea I did not dare set up, while I yet presumed to help these Arabs in their own revolt. It was hard, anyway, for a stranger to influence another people's national movement, and doubly hard for a Christian and a sedentary person to sway Moslem nomads. I should make it impossible for myself if I claimed, simultaneously, the privileges of both societies.

So, without saying anything, I turned my unwilling camel round, and forced her, grunting and moaning for her camel friends, back past the long line of men, and past the baggage into the emptiness behind. My temper was very unheroic, for I was furious with my other servants, with my own play-acting as a Beduin, and most of all with Gasim, a gap-toothed, grumbling fellow, skrimshank in all our marches, bad-tempered, suspicious, brutal, a man whose engagement I regretted, and of whom I had promised to rid myself as soon as we reached a discharging-place. It seemed absurd that I should peril my weight in the Arab adventure for a single worthless man. . . .

I had ridden about an hour and a half, easily, for the following breeze had let me wipe the crust from my red eyes and look forward almost without pain: when I saw a figure, or large bush, or at least something black ahead of me. The shifting mirage disguised height or distance; but this thing seemed moving, a little east of our course. On chance I turned my camel's head that way, and in a few minutes saw that it was Gasim. When I called he stood confusedly; I rode up and saw that he was nearly blinded and silly, standing there with his arms held out to me, and his black mouth gaping open. The Ageyl had put our last water in my skin, and this he spilled madly over his face and breast, in haste to drink. He stopped babbling, and began to wail out his sorrows. I sat him, pillion, on the camel's rump; then stirred her up and mounted.

At our turn the beast seemed relieved, and moved forward freely. I set an exact compass course, so exact that often I found our old tracks, as little spurts of paler sand scattered over the brown-black flint. In spite of our double weight the camel began to stride out, and at times she even put her head down and for a few paces developed that fast and most comfortable shuffle to which the best animals, while young, were broken by skilled riders. This proof of reserve spirit in her rejoiced me, as did the little time lost in search.

Gasim was moaning impressively about the pain and terror of his thirst: I told him to stop; but he went on, and began to sit loosely; until at each step of the camel he bumped down on her hinder quarters with a crash, which, like his crying, spurred her to greater pace. There was danger in this, for we might easily founder her so. Again I told him to stop, and when he only screamed louder, hit him and swore that for another sound I would throw him off. The threat, to which my general rage gave colour, worked. After it he clung on grimly without sound.

Not four miles had passed when again I saw a black bubble, lunging and swaying in the mirage ahead. It split into three, and swelled. I wondered if they were enemy. A minute later the haze unrolled with the disconcerting suddenness of illusion; and it was Auda with two of Nasir's men come back to look for me. I yelled jests and scoffs at them for abandoning a friend in the desert. Auda pulled his beard and grumbled that had he been present I would never have gone back. Gasim was transferred with insults to a better rider's saddle-pad, and we ambled forward together.

Auda pointed to the wretched hunched-up figure and denounced me, 'For that thing, not worth a camel's price . . .' I interrupted him with 'Not worth a half-crown, Auda,' and he, delighted in his simple mind, rode near Gasim, and struck him sharply, trying to make him repeat, like a parrot, his price. Gasim bared his broken teeth in a grin of rage and afterwards sulked on. In another hour we were on the heels of the baggage camels, and as we passed up the inquisitive line of our caravan, Auda repeated my joke to each pair, perhaps forty times in all, till I had seen to the full its feebleness.

Gasim explained that he had dismounted to ease nature, and had missed the party afterwards in the dark: but, obviously, he had gone to sleep, where he dismounted, with the fatigue of our slow, hot journeying. We rejoined Nasir and Nesib in the van. Nesib was vexed with me, for perilling the lives of Auda and myself on a whim. It was clear to him that I reckoned they would come back for me. Nasir was shocked at his ungenerous outlook, and Auda was glad to rub into a townsman the paradox of tribe and city; the collective responsibility and group-brotherhood of the desert, contrasted with the isolation and competitive living of the crowded districts. . . .

So we agreed to camp for the night where we were, and to make beacon fires for the slave of Nuri Shaalan, who like Gasim, had disappeared from our caravan to-day.

We were not greatly perturbed about him. He knew the country and his camel was under him. It might be that he had intentionally taken the direct way to Jauf, Nuri's capital, to earn the reward of first news that we came with gifts. However it was, he did not come that night, nor next day; and when, months after, I asked Nuri of him, he replied that his dried body had lately been found, lying beside his unplundered camel far out in the wilderness. He must have lost himself in the sand-haze and wandered till his camel broke down; and there died of thirst and heat. Not a long death — even for the very strongest a second day in summer was all — but very painful; for thirst was an active malady; a fear and panic which tore at the brain and reduced the bravest man to a stumbling babbling maniac in an hour or two: and then the sun killed him. . . .

Each morning, between eight and ten, a little group of blood mares under an assortment of imperfect saddlery would come to our camping place, and on them Nasir, Nesib, Zeki and I would mount, and with perhaps a dozen of our men on foot would move solemnly across the valley by the sandy paths between the bushes. Our horses were led by our servants, since it would be immodest to ride free or fast. So eventually we would reach the tent which was to be our feast-hall for that time; each family claiming us in turn, and bitterly offended if Zaal, the adjudicator, preferred one out of just order.

As we arrived, the dogs would rush out at us, and be driven off by onlookers — always a crowd had collected round the chosen tent — and we stepped in under the ropes to its guest half, made very large for the occasion and carefully dressed with its wall-curtain on the sunny side to give us the shade. The bashful host would murmur and vanish again out of sight. The tribal rugs, lurid red things from Beyrout, were ready for us, arranged down the partition curtain, along the back wall and across the dropped end, so that we sat down on three sides of an open dusty space. We might be fifty men in all. . . .

Then would follow an awkward pause, which our friends would try to cover, by showing us on its perch the household hawk (when possible a sea-bird taken young on the Red Sea coast) or their watch-cockerel, or their greyhound. Once a tame ibex was dragged in for our admiration: another time an oryx. When these interests were exhausted they would try and find a small talk to distract us from the household noises, and from noticing the urgent whispered cookery-directions wafted through the dividing curtain with a powerful smell of boiled fat and drifts of tasty meat-smoke.

After a silence the host or a deputy would come forward and whisper 'Black or white?' an invitation for us to choose coffee or tea. Nasir would always answer 'Black', and the slave would be beckoned forward with the beaked coffee-pot in one hand, and three or four clinking cups of white ware in the other. He would dash a few drops of coffee into the uppermost cup, and proffer it to Nasir; then pour the second for me, and the third for Nesib; and pause while we turned the cups about in our hands, and sucked them carefully, to get apprecia-tively from them the last richest drop.

As soon as they were empty his hand was stretched to clap them noisily one above the other, and toss them out with a lesser flourish for the next guest in order, and so on round the assembly till all had drunk. Then back to Nasir again. This second cup would be tastier than the first, partly because the pot was yielding deeper from the brew, partly because of the heel-taps of so many previous drinkers present in the cups; whilst the third and fourth rounds, if the serving of the meat delayed so long, would be of surprising flavour.

However, at last, two men came staggering through the thrilled crowd, carrying the rice and meat on a tinned copper tray or shallow bath, five feet across, set like a great brazier on a foot. In the tribe there was only this one food-bowl of the size, and an incised inscription ran round it in florid Arabic characters: 'To the glory of God, and in trust of mercy at the last, the property of His poor suppliant, Auda abu Tayi'. It was borrowed by the host who was to entertain us for the time; and, since my urgent brain and body made me wakeful, from my blankets in the first light I would see the dish going across country, and by marking down its goal would know where we were to feed that day.

The bowl was now brim-full, ringed round its edge by white rice in an embankment a foot wide and six inches deep, filled with legs and ribs of mutton till they toppled over. It needed two or three victims to make in the centre a dressed pyramid of meat such as honour pre-scribed. The centre-pieces were the boiled, upturned heads, propped on their severed stumps of necks, so that the ears, brown like old leaves, flapped out on the rice surface. The jaws gaped emptily upward, pulled open to show the hollow throat with the tongue, still pink, clinging to the lower teeth; and the long incisors whitely crowned the pile, very prominent above the nostrils' pricking hair and the lips which sneered away blackly from them.

This load was set down on the soil of the cleared space between us, where it steamed hotly, while a procession of minor helpers bore small cauldrons and copper vats in which the cooking had been done. From them, with much-bruised bowls of enamelled iron, they ladled out over the main dish all the inside and outside of the sheep; little bits of yellow intestine, the white tail-cushion of fat, brown muscles and meat and bristly skin, all swimming in the liquid butter and grease of the seething. The bystanders watched anxiously, muttering satisfactions when a very juicy scrap plopped out.

The fat was scalding. Every now and then a man would drop his baler with an exclamation, and plunge his burnt fingers, not reluctantly, in his mouth to cool them: but they persevered till at last their scooping rang loudly on the bottoms of the pots; and, with a gesture of triumph, they fished out the intact livers from their hiding place in the gravy and topped the yawning jaws with them.

Two raised each smaller cauldron and tilted it, letting the liquid splash down upon the meat till the rice-crater was full, and the loose grains at the edge swam in the abundance: and yet they poured, till, amid cries of astonishment from us, it was running over, and a little pool congealing in the dust. That was the final touch of splendour, and the host called us to come and eat.

We feigned a deafness, as manners demanded: at last we heard him, and looked surprised at one another, each urging his fellow to move first; till Nasir rose coyly, and after him we all came forward to sink on one knee round the tray, wedging in and cuddling up till the twenty-two for whom there was barely space were grouped around the food. We turned back our right sleeves to the elbow, and, taking lead from Nasir with a low 'In the name of God the merciful, the loving-kind', we dipped together.

The first dip, for me, at least, was always cautious, since the liquid fat was so hot that my unaccustomed fingers could seldom bear it: and so I would toy with an exposed and cooling lump of meat till others' excavations had drained my rice-segment. We would knead between the fingers (not soiling the palm), neat balls of rice and fat and liver and meat cemented by gentle pressure, and project them by leverage of the thumb from the crooked fore-finger into the mouth. With the right trick and the right construction the little lump held together and came clean off the hand; but when surplus butter and odd fragments clung, cooling, to the fingers, they had to be licked carefully to make the next effort slip easier away.

As the meat pile wore down (nobody really cared about rice: flesh was the luxury) one of the chief Howeitat eating with us would draw his dagger, silver hilted, set with turquoise, a signed masterpiece of Mohammed ibn Zari, of Jauf, and would cut criss-cross from the larger bones long diamonds of meat easily torn up between the fingers; for it was necessarily boiled very tender, since all had to be disposed of with the right hand which alone was honourable.

Our host stood by the circle, encouraging the appetite with pious ejaculations. At top speed we twisted, tore, cut and stuffed: never speaking, since conversation would insult a meal's quality, though it was proper to smile thanks when an intimate guest passed a select fragment, or when Mohammed el Dheilan gravely handed over a huge barren bone with a blessing. On such occasions I would return the compliment with some hideous impossible lump of guts, a flippancy which rejoiced the Howeitat, but which the gracious, aristocratic Nasir saw with disapproval.

At length some of us were nearly filled, and began to play and pick; glancing sideways at the rest till they too grew slow, and at last ceased eating, elbow on knee, the hand hanging down from the wrist over the tray edge to drip, while the fat, butter and scattered grains of rice cooled into a stiff white grease which gummed the fingers together. When all had stopped, Nasir meaningly cleared his throat, and we rose up together in haste with an explosive 'God requite it you, O host,' to group ourselves outside among the tent-ropes while the next twenty guests inherited our leaving.

Those of us who were nice would go to the end of the tent where the flap of the roof-cloth, beyond the last poles, drooped down as an end curtain; and on this clan handkerchief (whose coarse goat-hair mesh was pliant and glossy with much use) would scrape the thickest of the fat from the hands. Then we would make back to our seats, and re-take them sighingly; while the slaves, leaving aside their portion, the skulls of the sheep, would come round our rank with a wooden bowl of water, and a coffee-cup as dipper, to splash over our fingers, while we rubbed them with the tribal soap-cake.

Meantime the second and third sittings by the dish were having their turn, and then there would be one more cup of coffee, or a glass of syrup-like tea; and at last the horses would be brought and we would slip out to them, and mount, with a quiet blessing to the hosts as we passed by. When our backs were turned the children would run in disorder upon the ravaged dish, tear our gnawed bones from one another, and escape into the open with valuable fragments to be devoured in security behind some distant bush: while the watchdogs of all the camp prowled round snapping, and the master of the tent fed the choicest offal to his greyhound.

. . . I still saw the liberation of Syria happening in steps, of which Akaba was the indispensable first. I now saw these steps coming close together; and as soon as Nesib was out of the way planned to go off myself, rather in his fashion, on a long tour of the north country. I felt that one more sight of Syria would put straight the strategic ideas given me by the Crusaders and the first Arab conquest, and adjust them to the two new factors — the railways, and Murray in Sinai.

Also a rash adventure suited my abandoned mood. It should have been happiness, this lying out free as air, with the visible life striving its utmost along my own path; but the knowledge of the axe I was secretly grinding destroyed all my assurance.

The Arab Revolt had begun on false pretences. To gain the Sherif's help our Cabinet had offered, through Sir Henry McMahon, to support the establishment of native governments in parts of Syria and Mesopotamia, 'saving the interests of our ally, France'. The last modest clause concealed a treaty (kept secret, till too late, from McMahon, and therefore from the Sherif) by which France, England and Russia agreed to annex some of these promised areas, and to establish their respective spheres of influence over all the rest.

Rumours of the fraud reached Arab ears, from Turkey. In the East persons were more trusted than institutions. So the Arabs, having tested my friendliness and sincerity under fire, asked me, as a free agent, to endorse the promises of the British Government. I had had no previous or inner knowledge of the McMahon pledges and the Sykes-Picot treaty, which were both framed by war-time branches of the Foreign Office. But, not being a perfect fool, I could see that if we won the war the promises to the Arabs were dead paper. Had I been an honourable adviser I would have sent my men home, and not let them risk their lives for such stuff. Yet the Arab inspiration was our main tool in winning the Eastern war. So I assured them that England kept her word in letter and spirit. In this comfort they performed their fine things: but, of course, instead of being proud of what we did together, I was continually and bitterly ashamed.

Clear sight of my position came to me one night, when old Nuri Shaalan in his aisled tent brought out a file of documents and asked which British pledge was to be believed. In his mood, upon my answer, lay the success or failure of Feisal. My advice, uttered with some agony of mind, was to trust the latest in date of the contradictions. This disingenuous answer promoted me, in six months, to be chief confidence-man. In Hejaz the Sherifs were everything, and I had allayed my conscience by telling Feisal how hollow his basis was. In Syria England was mighty and the Sherif very low. So I became the principal.

In revenge I vowed to make the Arab Revolt the engine of its own success, as well as handmaid to our Egyptian campaign: and vowed to lead it so madly in the final victory that expediency should counsel to the Powers a fair settlement of the Arabs' moral claims. This presumed my surviving the war, to win the later battle of the Council Chamber — immodest presumptions, which still balance in fulfilment.[*] Yet the issue of the fraud was beside the point.

Clearly I had no shadow of leave to engage the Arabs, unknowing, in a gamble of life and death. Inevitably and justly we should reap bitterness, a sorry fruit of heroic endeavour. So in resentment at my false place (did ever second lieutenant so lie abroad for his betters?) I undertook this long, dangerous ride, in which to see the more important of Feisal's secret friends, and to study key-positions of our future campaigns: but the results were incommensurate with the risks, and the act artistically unjustifiable, like the motive. I had whispered to myself 'Let me chance it, now, before we begin', seeing truly that this was the last chance, and that after a successful capture of Akaba I

[*]1919: but two years later Mr. Winston Churchill was entrusted by our harassed Cabinet with the settlement of the Middle East; and in a few weeks, at his conference in Cairo, he made straight all the tangle, finding solutions fulfilling (I think) our promises in letter and spirit (where humanly possible) without sacrificing any interest of our Empire or any interest of the peoples concerned. So we were quit of the war-time Eastern adventure, with clean hands, but three years too late to earn the gratitude which peoples, if not states, can pay.

would never again possess myself freely, without association, in the security lurking for the obscure in their protective shadow.

Before me lay a vista of responsibility and command, which disgusted my thought-riddled nature. I felt mean, to fill the place of a man of action; for my standards of value were a wilful reaction against theirs, and I despised their happiness. Always my soul hungered for less than it had, since my senses, sluggish beyond the senses of most men, needed the immediacy of contact to achieve perception; they distinguished kinds only, not degrees.

from THE ARAB BULLETIN

TO GENERAL CLAYTON[1]

10th *July*, 1917   SECRET   *Cairo*

GENERAL CLAYTON, I left Wejh on May 9th, 1917 with Sherif★ Nasir Ibn Ali Ibn Radhi Beni Hussein of Medina as O.C. Expedition, and Nessib Bey El Bekri as Political Officer to deal with villagers and townspeople. Sherif Feisal's instructions were to open Akaba for use as a base of supply for the Arab forces, and to sound the possibilities of Sherifian action in East and South Syria.

We marched to Abu Raga where we increased our force to 36 men, and thence to the Railway at km. 810.5 which we dynamited on May 19th. Our route then lay by Fejr to Maigua in Wadi Soilan, for Jarf to see Nuri and Nawwaf. We heard however that they were to the North of us, so marched to Nebk (near Kaf) on June 2nd, where we met

★ Nasir proved most capable, hard working and straightforward during the expedition. I took a personal liking to him, and think him (after Faisal and Shakir) the best of the Ashraf I have had to work with.

[1] Chief of Intelligence in Egypt and head of the Arab Bureau. See *Seven Pillars of Wisdom*, chaps. VI and VII.

Auda Abu Tayi, and the Huweitat. Sherif Nasir stayed in Kaf to enrol Rualla, Shererat and Huweitat for the Akaba expedition.

I rode on June 4th with 2 men into Wald Ali* country, via Burga and Seba Biar to Ain El Barida near Tudmor on June 8th. Here I met Sheikh Dhami of the Kawakiba Aneza and heard that Hachim was away N.E. and Ibn Murshid confined in Damascus. I therefore went West with Dhami and his 35 men (whom I enrolled) to Ras Baalbek on June 10th and dynamited a small plate girder bridge there.† From Ras Baalbek we rode South to El Gabban, in the Ghuta 3 miles from Damascus where on June 13th I met Ali Riza Pasha Rehabi,‡ G.O.C. Damascus. Thence I rode to El Rudeine where I met Sheikh Saad Ed Din Ibn Ali of the Leja,§ and passed on to Salkhad to see Hussein Bey El Atrash.‡ From Salkhad we went to Azrak and saw Nuri and Nawwaf**, and returned to Nebk on June 18th.

I found the enrolment finished. Nessib Bey El Bekri went to Salk-

---

* My object was to meet the Bishr and compose their feud with the Howeitat with a view to working between Homs and Aleppo. The plan failed, but Dhami is in a position to act as go-between, or to provide men to destroy the Orontes bridges when required. He is now in Akaba — a good man.

† The effect on the traffic was of course very slight, but the Metowila of Baalbek were most excited, and it was to arouse them that I did it. The noise of dynamite explosions we find everywhere the most effective propagandist measure possible.

‡ Ali Riza is the well known Turkish Engineer General, President of the Syrian branch of the Arab Secret Society. He informed me that he had only 500 Turkish gendarmes and three unarmed Labour battalions in Damascus, and was not in a position to demonstrate his real feelings unaided.

§ With Saad Ed Din I discussed a provisional plan of action from the Leja when the need arises.

‖ Hussein told me the terms on which the Druses are prepared to rise. They seem to me to offer a basis for negotiation.

** Their action depends on that of the Druses. I am sure that by himself Nuri would do nothing, but he recognizes the certainty of his being involved in the struggle, and is profoundly pro-Arab and pro-Sherif. He is now collecting his annual corn supply in the Nugra, and is playing double till we require him.

had with Hussein El Atrash with the instructions attached,* and with Nasir I marched on June 19th to Bair where we re-opened the dynamited wells. From Bair I rode to Ziza and saw Fawaz Ibn Faiz,† and thence West of Amman to Um Keis on June 23rd where I looked at railway bridge Z in the Yarmuk valley and saw Shererat and Beni Hassan Sheikhs. From Um Keis I went to Ifdein (Mafrak on the map) the first station below Deraa, and destroyed a stretch of curved rails at km. 173.‡ From Ifdein we rode to Zerga, and thence to Atwi, where we failed to take the station, but killed 3 out of the 5 of the garrison, captured a large flock of sheep and destroyed a telegraph party of 4 men repairing the wire. We also dynamited a stretch of line. From Atwi I rode back to Bair, and rejoined Sherif Nasir who had meantime prepared the Western Huweitat. On June 30th we moved to El Jefer, clearing one well, and thence to km. 479 which we destroyed on a large scale, while a column was attacking N. of Maan near Aneyza. We then marched towards Fuweileh, where the gendarmes post had been destroyed by an advance column. They met us with the news of the re-occupation of Fuweileh by the belated relief expedition of 4/174/59 from Maan. We wiped out the battalion on July 2nd (taking the O.C., a mountain gun and 160 prisoners) at Abu El Lissan, and sent a flying column North which defeated the Turkish post at Hisha (railhead 5 miles East of Shobek), occupied Wadi Musa, Shobek, Tafileh, and is now near Kerak to take action there.

From Fuweileh we captured the post of Mreigha and then moved to Guweira where we met Ibn Jad of the Akaba Huweitat, and took 100 men and 5 officers. From Guweira we marched on to El Kethira (wiping out a post of 3 officers and 140 men) and thence to El Khadra in the North of Wadi Ithm, where the Akaba garrison surrendered at discretion. We entered Akaba on July 6th, with 600 prisoners, about

* Nessib El Bekri is volatile and short-sighted, as are most town-Syrians, and will not carry them out exactly — but no other agent was available.

† Who was fair spoken, but I am convinced pro-Turk at heart. The Beni Saklhad will mostly follow Trad and Ibn Zebbu, who are our men.

‡ The curved rails took 3 days to replace: the repair train then proceeded South, and at km. 174 exploded a very large compound Garland mine, and fell off a 15 foot high culvert into a valley. This caused a further delay of two days while the line was being searched.

20 officers, and a German unter-offizier well-borer. I rode the same day for Suez with 8 men and arrived at El Shatt on July 9th.

As a result of the journeys and interviews noted above, between June 5th and July 6th, I am of opinion that given the necessary material assistance Arab Forces can be arranged about the end of August as in the sketch map attached. These levies will not (any more than the Hedjaz Beduin) be capable of fighting a pitched battle, but forces 1, 2, 4 & 5 may be able to ensure a cessation of traffic on the railways in their areas, and forces 6 & 7 should suffice for the expulsion of all Turkish posts in their districts, and the occupation of all ways of communication. Force 3 is our striking force (of perhaps 6,000 not bad men) and may be able to rush Deraat, or at least should cut off the garrison there and hold up the line in the neighbourhood. I would propose to cut the bridge at Hemmah[1] from Um Keis by force 2, if possible, as a preliminary of action, and if Damascus could be taken over by a part of force 3 it would mean a great accession of strength to the Arab cause.

These various operations fortunately need not be accurately concerted. If they took place in numerical order (as in the map) it would be easiest — but there is little hope of things working out just as planned. If they come off the L. of C.[2] of the Turkish force in the Jerusalem area would appear threatened — but I do not think the Arabs can be advised to take action unless the E.E.[3] Force can retain the Turks in front of them by a holding attack, to prevent large drafts being sent up to the Hauran. Force 3 is capable of only one effort (lasting perhaps 2 months) and if it is crushed Arab hopes in Syria will depend on the yet untried possibility of action between Homs and Aleppo — on which it is too soon to speak.

Sherif Nasir asked me to discuss with E.E. Force the situation, his needs, and the possibility of joint action by E.E. Force and himself against the Turkish forces in Palestine, as outlined above.

T. E. L.

[1] Thus cutting the only Turkish Railway into Palestine.
[2] Lines of Communication.
[3] Egyptian Expeditionary.

ABSTRACT OF INSTRUCTIONS GIVEN TO NESSIB BEY EL BEKRI AT KAF
ON JUNE 18TH, 1917

1. Arrange an Intelligence Service with resident agents in Damascus, Deraat and Amman, to collect Military information.
2. Reconcile the Druse leaders to one another.
3. Get into touch with the Druses of Hasbeya and the Lebanon: also with the Metowala of the Jebel Amr and the Belad Bishara (using Sid Nasir's name), and re-assure the Maronites of the area on the nature of the Sherif's administration in the future.
4. Get in touch with the Ghawarineh of Lake Huleh and Merj Ayum.
5. Send Zeki Effendi to Leja, to examine the roads and water supply.
6. Send me an estimate of the needs of the Druses in warlike stores.
7. Discuss with Nuri the elimination of the Circassian colonies of the Nugra and Kuneitra.
8. Approach some of the chief Baalbek Metowila and find out what they are prepared to do.
9. Prepare the villagers of J. El Sheikh, J. El Shergi, and J. Kalamun.
10. Get on speedy terms with the Bishr.

from SEVEN PILLARS OF WISDOM

WHEN I returned it was June 16th, and Nasir was still labouring in his tent. . . .

Sunset came down, delightfully red, and after the feast the whole party lay round the outside coffee-hearth lingering under the stars, while Auda and others told us stories. In a pause I remarked casually that I had looked for Mohammed el Dheilan in his tent that afternoon, to thank him for the milch camel he had given me, but had not found him. Auda shouted for joy, till everybody looked at him; and then, in the silence which fell that they might learn the joke, he pointed to Mohammed sitting dismally beside the coffee mortar, and said in his huge voice:

'Ho! Shall I tell why Mohammed for fifteen days has not slept in his tent?' Everybody chuckled with delight, and conversation stopped; all the crowd stretched out on the ground, chins in hands, prepared to take the good points of the story which they had heard perhaps twenty times. The women, Auda's three wives, Zaal's wife, and some of Mohammed's, who had been cooking, came across, straddling their bellies in the billowy walk which came of carrying burdens on their heads, till they were near the partition-curtain; and there they listened like the rest while Auda told at length how Mohammed had bought publicly in the bazaar at Wejh a costly string of pearls, and had not given it to any of his wives, and so they were all at odds, except in their common rejection of him.

The story was, of course, a pure invention — Auda's elvish humour heightened by the stimulus of Revolt — and the luckless Mohammed, who had dragged through the fortnight guesting casually with one or other of the tribesmen, called upon God for mercy, and upon me for witness that Auda lied. I cleared my throat solemnly. Auda asked for silence, and begged me to confirm his words.

I began with the introducing phrase of a formal tale: 'In the name of God the merciful, the loving-kind. We were six in Wejh. There were Auda, and Mohammed, and Zaal, Gasim el Shimt, Mufaddhi and the poor man (myself); and one night just before dawn, Auda said, "Let us make a raid against the market". And we said, "in the name of God". And we went; Auda in a white robe and a red head-cloth, and Kasim sandals of pieced leather; Mohammed in a silken tunic of "seven kings" and barefoot; Zaal . . . I forget Zaal. Gasim wore cotton, and Mufaddhi was in silk of blue stripes with an embroidered head-cloth. Your servant was as your servant.'

My pause was still with astonishment. This was a close parody of Auda's epic style; and I mimicked also his wave of the hand, his round voice, and the rising and dropping tone which emphasized the points, or what he thought were points, of his pointless stories. The Howeitat sat silent as death, twisting their full bodies inside their sweat-stiffened shirts for joy, and staring hungrily at Auda; for they all recognized the original, and parody was a new art to them and to him. The coffee man, Mufaddhi, a Shammar refugee from the guilt of blood, himself a character, forgot to pile fresh thorns on his fire for fixity of listening to the tale.

I told how we left the tents, with a list of the tents, and how we walked down towards the village, describing every camel and horse we saw, and all the passers-by, and the ridges, 'all bare of grazing for by God that country was barren. And we marched: and after we had marched the time of a smoked cigarette, we heard something, and Auda stopped and said, "Lads, I hear something". And Mohammed stopped and said, "Lads, I hear something". And Zaal, "By God, you are right". And we stopped to listen, and there was nothing, and the poor man said, "By God, I hear nothing". And Zaal said, "By God, I hear nothing". And Mohammed said, "By God, I hear nothing". And Auda said, "By God, you are right."

'And we marched and we marched, and the land was barren, and we heard nothing. And on our right hand came a man, a negro, on a donkey. The donkey was grey, with black ears, and one black foot, and on its shoulder was a brand like this' (a scrabble in the air), 'and its tail moved and its legs: Auda saw it, and said, "By God, a donkey". And Mohammed said, "By the very God, a donkey and a slave". And we marched. And there was a ridge, not a great ridge, but a ridge as great as from the here to the what-do-you-call-it (*lil biliyeh el hok*) that is yonder: and we marched to the ridge and it was barren. That land is barren: barren: barren.

'And we marched: and beyond the what-do-you-call-it there was a what-there-is as far as hereby from hence, and thereafter a ridge: and we came to that ridge, and went up that ridge: it was barren, all that land was barren: and as we came up that ridge, and were by the head of that ridge, and came to the end of the head of that ridge, by God, by my God, by very God, the sun rose upon us.'

It ended the session. Everyone had heard that sunrise twenty times, in its immense bathos; an agony piled up of linked phrases, repeated and repeated with breathless excitement by Auda to carry over for hours the thrill of a raiding story in which nothing happened; and the trivial rest of it was exaggerated the degree which made it like one of Auda's tales; and yet, also, the history of the walk to market at Wejh which many of us had taken. The tribe was in waves of laughter on the ground.

Auda laughed the loudest and longest, for he loved a jest upon himself; and the fatuousness of my epic had shown him his own sure mastery of descriptive action. He embraced Mohammed, and confessed the invention of the necklace. In gratitude Mohammed invited the camp to breakfast with him in his regained tent on the morrow, an hour before we started for the swoop on Akaba. We should have a sucking camel-calf boiled in sour milk by his wives: famous cooks, and a legendary dish! . . .

We made hurried plans, and scattered.to the work, knowing we could not go forward to Akaba with this battalion in possession of the pass. Unless we dislodged it, our two months' hazard and effort would fail before yielding even first-fruits.

Fortunately the poor handling of the enemy gave us an unearned advantage. They slept on, in the valley, while we crowned the hills in wide circle about them unobserved. We began to snipe them steadily in their positions under the slopes and rock-faces by the water, hoping to provoke them out and up the hill in a charge against us. Meanwhile, Zaal rode away with our horsemen and cut the Maan telegraph and telephone in the plain.

This went on all day. It was terribly hot — hotter than ever before I had felt it in Arabia — and the anxiety and constant moving made it hard for us. Some even of the tough tribesmen broke down under the cruelty of the sun, and crawled or had to be thrown under rocks to recover in their shade. We ran up and down to supply our lack of numbers by mobility, ever looking over the long ranges of hill for a new spot from which to counter this or that Turkish effort. The hill-sides were steep, and exhausted our breath, and the grasses twined like little hands about our ankles as we ran, and plucked us back. The sharp reefs of limestone which cropped out over the ridges tore our feet, and long before evening the more energetic men were leaving a rusty print upon the ground with every stride.

Our rifles grew so hot with sun and shooting, that they seared our hands; and we had to be grudging of our rounds, considering every shot and spending great pains to make it sure. The rocks on which we flung ourselves for aim were burning, so that they scorched our breasts and arms, from which later the skin drew off in ragged sheets. The present smart made us thirst. Yet even water was rare with us; we could not afford men to fetch enough from Batra, and if all could not drink, it was better that none should. . . .

Just after noon I had a heat-stroke, or so pretended, for I was dead weary of it all, and cared no longer how it went. So I crept into a hollow where there was a trickle of thick water in a muddy cup of the hills, to suck some moisture off its dirt through the filter of my sleeve. Nasir joined me, panting like a winded animal, with his cracked and bleeding lips shrunk apart in his distress: and old Auda appeared, striding powerfully, his eyes bloodshot and staring, his knotty face working with excitement.

He grinned with malice when he saw us lying there, spread out to find coolness under the bank, and croaked at me harshly, 'Well, how

is it with the Howeitat? All talk and no work?' 'By God, indeed,'
spat I back again, for I was angry with everyone and with myself, 'they
shoot a lot and hit a little.' Auda almost pale with rage, and trembling,
tore his head-cloth off and threw it on the ground beside me. Then he
ran back up the hill like a madman, shouting to the men in his dreadful
strained and rustling voice.

They came together to him, and after a moment scattered away
downhill. I feared things were going wrong, and struggled to where
he stood alone on the hill-top, glaring at the enemy; but all he would
say to me was, 'Get your camel if you want to see the old man's work'.
Nasir called for his camel and we mounted.

The Arabs passed before us into a little sunken place, which rose to
a low crest; and we knew that the hill beyond went down in a facile
slope to the main valley of Aba el Lissan, somewhat below the spring.
All our four hundred camel men were here tightly collected, just out
of sight of the enemy. We rode to their head, and asked the Shimt
what it was and where the horsemen had gone.

He pointed over the ridge to the next valley above us, and said,
'With Auda there': and as he spoke yells and shots poured up in a
sudden torrent from beyond the crest. We kicked our camels furiously
to the edge, to see our fifty horsemen coming down the last slope into
the main valley, like a run-away, at full gallop, shooting from the
saddle. As we watched, two or three went down, but the rest thundered
forward at marvellous speed, and the Turkish infantry, huddled together under the cliff ready to cut their desperate way out towards
Maan, in the first dusk began to sway in and out, and finally broke
before the rush, adding their flight to Auda's charge.

Nasir screamed at me, 'Come on', with his bloody mouth; and we
plunged our camels madly over the hill, and down towards the head
of the fleeing enemy. The slope was not too steep for a camel-gallop,
but steep enough to make their pace terrific, and their course uncon-
trollable: yet the Arabs were able to extend to right and left and to
shoot into the Turkish brown. The Turks had been too bound up in
the terror of Auda's furious charge against their rear to notice us as we
came over the eastward slope: so we also took them by surprise and in
the flank; and a charge of ridden camels going nearly thirty miles an
hour was irresistible.

My camel, the Sherari racer, Naama, stretched herself out, and
hurled downhill with such might that we soon out-distanced the others.
The Turks fired a few shots, but mostly only shrieked and turned to

run: the bullets they did send at us were not very harmful, for it took much to bring a charging camel down in a dead heap.

I had got among the first of them, and was shooting, with a pistol of course, for only an expert could use a rifle from such plunging beasts; when suddenly my camel tripped and went down emptily upon her face, as though pole-axed. I was torn completely from the saddle, sailed grandly through the air for a great distance, and landed with a crash which seemed to drive all the power and feeling out of me. I lay there, passively waiting for the Turks to kill me, continuing to hum over the verses of a half-forgotten poem, whose rhythm something, perhaps the prolonged stride of the camel, had brought back to my memory as we leaped down the hill-side:

For Lord I was free of all Thy flowers, but I chose the world's sad roses.
And that is why my feet are torn and mine eyes are blind with sweat.

While another part of my mind thought what a squashed thing I should look when all that cataract of men and camels had poured over.

After a long time I finished my poem, and no Turks came, and no camel trod on me: a curtain seemed taken from my ears: there was a great noise in front. I sat up and saw the battle over, and our men driving together and cutting down the last remnants of the enemy. My camel's body had lain behind me like a rock and divided the charge into two streams; and in the back of its skull was the heavy bullet of the fifth shot I fired. . . .

Auda came swinging up on foot, his eyes glazed over with the rapture of battle, and the words bubbling with incoherent speed from his mouth. 'Work, work, where are words, work, bullets, Abu Tayi' . . . and he held up his shattered field-glasses, his pierced pistol-holster, and his leather sword-scabbard cut to ribbons. He had been the target of a volley which had killed his mare under him, but the six bullets through his clothes had left him scathless. . . .

He was wildly pleased with the fight, most of all because he had confounded me and shown what his tribe could do. Mohammed was wroth with us for a pair of fools, calling me worse than Auda, since I had insulted him by words like flung stones to provoke the folly which had nearly killed us all: though it had killed only two of us, one Rueili and one Sherari.

It was, of course, a pity to lose any one of our men, but time was of importance to us, and so imperative was the need of dominating Maan, to shock the little Turkish garrisons between us and the sea into surrender, that I would have willingly lost much more than two. On occasions like this Death justified himself and was cheap.

I questioned the prisoners about themselves, and the troops in Maan; but the nerve crisis had been too severe for them. Some gaped at me and some gabbled, while others with helpless weepings, embraced my knees, protesting at every word from us that they were fellow Moslems and my brothers in the faith.

Finally I got angry and took one of them aside and was rough to him, shocking him by new pain into a half-understanding, when he answered well enough, and reassuringly, that their battalion was the only reinforcement, and it merely a reserve battalion; the two companies in Maan would not suffice to defend its perimeter.

This meant we could take it easily, and the Howeitat clamoured to be led there, lured by the dream of unmeasured loot, though what we had taken here was a rich prize. However, Nasir, and afterwards Auda, helped me to stay them. We had no supports, no regulars, no guns, no base nearer than Wejh, no communications, no money even, for our gold was exhausted, and we were issuing our own notes, promises to pay 'when Akaba is taken', for daily expenses. Besides, a strategic scheme was not changed to follow up a tactical success. We must push to the coast, and re-open sea-contact with Suez. . . .

To an Arab an essential part of the triumph of victory was to wear the clothes of an enemy: and next day we saw our force transformed (as to the upper half) into a Turkish force, each man in a soldier's tunic: for this was a battalion straight from home, very well found and dressed in new uniforms.

The dead men looked wonderfully beautiful. The night was shining gently down, softening them into new ivory. Turks were white-skinned on their clothed parts, much whiter than the Arabs; and these soldiers had been very young. Close round them lapped the dark wormwood, now heavy with dew, in which the ends of the moon-beams sparkled like sea-spray. The corpses seemed flung so pitifully on the ground, huddled anyhow in low heaps. Surely if straightened they would be comfortable at last. So I put them all in order, one by one, very wearied myself, and longing to be of these quiet ones, not of the restless, noisy, aching mob up the valley, quarrelling over the plunder, boasting of their speed and strength to endure God knew how many toils and pains of this sort; with death, whether we won or lost, waiting to end the history. . . .

To-day was the fourth of July. Time pressed us, for we were hungry, and Akaba was still far ahead behind two defences. The nearer post, Kethira, stubbornly refused parley with our flags. Their cliff commanded the valley — a strong place which it might be costly to take. We assigned the honour, in irony, to ibn Jad and his unwearied men, advising him to try it after dark. He shrank, made difficulties, pleaded the full moon: but we cut hardly into this excuse, promising that tonight for a while there should be no moon. By my diary there was an eclipse. Duly it came, and the Arabs forced the post without loss, while the superstitious soldiers were firing rifles and clanging copper pots to rescue the threatened satellite. . . .

The narrows of Wadi Itm increased in intricate ruggedness as we penetrated deeper. Below Kethira we found Turkish post after Turkish post, empty. Their men had been drawn in to Khadra, the entrenched position (at the mouth of Itm), which covered Akaba so well against a landing from the sea. Unfortunately for them the enemy had never imagined attack from the interior, and of all their great works not one trench or post faced inland. Our advance from so new a direction threw them into panic.

In the afternoon we were in contact with this main position, and heard from the local Arabs that the subsidiary posts about Akaba had been called in or reduced, so that only a last three hundred men barred us from the sea. We dismounted for a council, to hear that the enemy were resisting firmly in bomb-proof trenches with a new artesian well. Only it was rumoured that they had little food. . . .

We had a third try to communicate with the Turks, by means of a little conscript, who said that he understood how to do it. He undressed and went down the valley in little more than boots. An hour later he proudly brought us a reply, very polite, saying that in two days, if help did not come from Maan, they would surrender.

Such folly (for we could not hold our men indefinitely) might mean the massacre of every Turk. I held no great brief for them, but it was better they be not killed, if only to spare us the pain of seeing it. Besides we might have suffered loss. Night operations in the staring moon would be nearly as exposed as day. Nor was this, like Aba el Lissan, an imperative battle.

We gave our little man a sovereign as earnest of reward, walked down close to the trenches with him, and sent in for an officer to speak with us. After some hesitation this was achieved, and we explained the situation on the road behind us; our growing forces; and our short control over their tempers. The upshot was that they promised to surrender at daylight. So we had another sleep (an event rare enough to chronicle) in spite of our thirst.

Next day at dawn fighting broke out on all sides, for hundreds more hill-men, again doubling our number, had come in the night; and, not knowing the arrangement, began shooting at the Turks, who defended themselves. Nasir went out, with ibn Dgheithir and his Ageyl marching in fours, down the open bed of the valley. Our men ceased fire. The Turks then stopped, for their rank and file had no more fight in them and no more food, and thought we were well supplied. So the surrender went off quietly after all.

As the Arabs rushed in to plunder I noticed an engineer in grey uniform, with red beard and puzzled blue eyes; and spoke to him in German. He was the well-borer, and knew no Turkish. Recent doings had amazed him, and he begged me to explain what we meant. I said that we were a rebellion of the Arabs against the Turks. This, it took him time to appreciate. He wanted to know who was our leader. I said the Sherif of Mecca. He supposed he would be sent to Mecca. I said rather to Egypt. He inquired the price of sugar, and when I replied, 'cheap and plentiful', he was glad.

The loss of his belongings he took philosophically, but was sorry for the well, which a little work would have finished as his monument. He showed me where it was, with the pump only half-built. By pulling on the sludge bucket we drew enough delicious clear water to quench our thirsts. Then we raced through a driving sand-storm down to Akaba, four miles further, and splashed into the sea on July the sixth, just two months after our setting out from Wejh. . . .

Supper taught us the urgent need to send news over the one hundred and fifty miles to the British at Suez for a relief-ship. I decided to go across myself with a party of eight, mostly Howeitat, on the best camels in the force — one even was the famous Jedhah, the seven-year-old for whom the Nowasera had fought the beni Sakhr. As we rode round the bay we discussed the manner of our journey. If we went gently, sparing the animals, they might fail with hunger. If we rode hard they might break down with exhaustion or sore feet in mid-desert.

Finally we agreed to keep at a walk, however tempting the surface, for so many hours of the twenty-four as our endurance would allow. On such time-tests the man, especially if he were a foreigner, usually collapsed before the beast: in particular, I had ridden fifty miles a day for the last month, and was near my limit of strength. If I held out, we should reach Suez in fifty hours of a march; and, to preclude cooking-halts upon the road, we carried lumps of boiled camel and broiled dates in a rag behind our saddles. . . .

Our aim was the Shatt, a post opposite Suez on the Asiatic bank of the Canal, and we gained it at last near three in the afternoon, forty-nine hours out of Akaba. For a tribal raid this would have been fair time, and we were tired men before ever we started.

Shatt was in unusual disorder, without even a sentry to stop us, plague having appeared there two or three days before. So the old camps had been hurriedly cleared, left standing, while the troops bivouacked out in the clean desert. Of course we knew nothing of this, but hunted in the empty offices till we found a telephone. I rang up Suez headquarters and said I wanted to come across.

They regretted that it was not their business. The Inland Water Transport managed transit across the Canal, after their own methods. There was a sniff of implication that these methods were not those of the General Staff. Undaunted, for I was never a partisan of my nominal branch of the service, I rang up the office of the Water Board, and explained that I had just arrived in Shatt from the desert with urgent news for Headquarters. They were sorry, but had no free boats just then. They would be sure to send first thing in the morning, to carry me to the Quarantine Department: and rang off.

Now I had been four months in Arabia continually on the move. In the last four weeks I had ridden fourteen hundred miles by camel, not sparing myself anything to advance the war; but I refused to spend a single superfluous night with my familiar vermin. I wanted a bath, and something with ice in it to drink: to change these clothes, all sticking to my saddle sores in filthiness: to eat something more tractable than green date and camel sinew. I got through again to the Inland Water Transport and talked like Chrysostom. It had no effect, so I became vivid. Then, once more, they cut me off. I was growing very vivid, when friendly northern accents from the military exchange floated down the line: 'It's no bluidy good, sir, talking to them fookin water boogers.'

This expressed the apparent truth; and the broad-spoken operator worked me through to the Embarkation Office. Here, Lyttleton, a major of the busiest, had added to his innumerable labours that of catching Red Sea warships one by one as they entered Suez roads and persuading them (how some loved it!) to pile high their decks with stores for Wejh or Yenbo. In this way he ran our thousands of bales and men, free, as a by-play in his routine; and found time as well to smile at the curious games of us curious folk.

He never failed us. As soon as he heard who and where I was, and what was not happening in the Inland Water Transport, the difficulty was over. His launch was ready: would be at the Shatt in half an hour. I was to come straight to his office: and not explain (till perhaps now after the war) that a common harbour launch had entered the sacred canal without permission of the Water Directorate. All fell out as he said. I sent my men and camels north to Kubri, where, by telephone from Suez, I would prepare them rations and shelter in the animal camp on the Asiatic shore. Later, of course, came their reward of hectic and astonishing days in Cairo.

Lyttleton saw my weariness and let me go at once to the hotel. Long ago it had seemed poor, but now was become splendid; and, after conquering its first hostile impression of me and my dress, it produced the hot baths and the cold drinks (six of them) and the dinner and bed of my dreams. A most willing intelligence officer, warned by spies of a disguised European in the Sinai Hotel, charged himself with the care of my men at Kubri and provided tickets and passes for me to Cairo next day.

The strenuous 'control' of civilian movement in the canal zone entertained a dull journey. A mixed body of Egyptian and British military police came round the train, interrogating us and scrutinizing our passes. It was proper to make war on permit-men, so I replied crisply in fluent English, 'Sherif of Mecca — Staff', to their Arabic inquiries. They were astonished. The sergeant begged my pardon: he had not expected to hear. I repeated that I was in the Staff uniform of the Sherif of Mecca. They looked at my bare feet, white silk robes and gold head-rope and dagger. Impossible! 'What army, sir?' 'Meccan.' 'Never heard of it: don't know the uniform.' 'Would you recognize a Montenegrin dragoon?'

This was a home-thrust. Any Allied troops in uniform might travel without pass. The police did not know all the allies, much less their uniforms. Mine might really be some rare army. They fell back into the corridor and watched me while they wired up the line. Just before Ismailia, a perspiring intelligence officer in wet khaki boarded the train to check my statements. As we had almost arrived I showed him the special pass with which the forethought of Suez had twice-armed my innocence. He was not pleased.

At Ismailia passengers for Cairo changed, to wait until the express from Port Said was due. In the other train shone an opulent saloon, from which descended Admiral Wemyss and Burmester and Neville, with a very large and superior general. A terrible tension grew along the platform as the party marched up and down it in weighty talk. Officers saluted once: twice: still they marched up and down. Three times was too much. Some withdrew to the fence and stood permanently to attention. These were the mean souls. Some fled: these were the contemptibles. Some turned to the bookstall and studied book-backs avidly: these were shy. Only one was blatant.

Burmester's eye caught my staring. He wondered who it was, for I was burned crimson and very haggard with travel. (Later I found my weight to be less than seven stone.) However, he answered; and I explained the history of our unannounced raid on Akaba. It excited him. I asked that the admiral send a storeship there at once. Burmester said the *Dufferin*, which came in that day, should load all the food in Suez, go straight to Akaba, and bring back the prisoners. (Splendid!) He would order it himself, not to interrupt the Admiral and Allenby.

'Allenby! what's he doing here?' cried I. 'Oh, he's in command now.' 'And Murray?' 'Gone home.' This was news of the biggest, importantly concerning me: and I climbed back and fell to wondering if this heavy, rubicund man was like ordinary generals, and if we should have trouble for six months teaching him. Murray and Belinda had begun so tiresomely that our thought those first days had been, not to defeat the enemy, but to make our own chiefs let us live. Only by time and performance had we converted Sir Archibald and his Chief of Staff who in their last months, wrote to the War Office commending the Arab venture, and especially Feisal in it. This was generous of them and our secret triumph, for they were an odd pair in one chariot — Murray all brains and claws, nervous, elastic, changeable; Lynden Bell so solidly built up of layers of professional opinion, glued together after Government testing and approval, and later trimmed and polished to standard pitch.

At Cairo my sandalled feet slip-slapped up the quiet Savoy corridors to Clayton, who habitually cut the lunch hour to cope with his thronging work. As I entered he glanced up from his desk with a muttered 'Mush fadi' (Anglo-Egyptian for 'engaged') but I spoke and got a surprised welcome. In Suez the night before I had scribbled a short report; so we had to talk only of what needed doing. Before the hour ended, the Admiral rang up to say that the *Dufferin* was loading flour for her emergency trip.

Clayton drew sixteen thousand pounds in gold and got an escort to take it to Suez by the three o'clock train. This was urgent, that Nasir might be able to meet his debts. The notes we had issued at Bair, Jefer and Guweira were pencilled promises, on army telegraph forms, to pay so much to bearer in Akaba. It was a great system, but no one had dared issue notes before in Arabia, because the Beduins had neither pockets in their shirts nor strong-rooms in their tents, and notes could not be buried for safety. So there was an unconquerable prejudice against them, and for our good name it was essential that they be early redeemed.

Afterwards, in the hotel, I tried to find clothes less publicly exciting than my Arab get-up; but the moths had corrupted all my former store, and it was three days before I became normally ill-dressed.

Meanwhile I heard of Allenby's excellence, and of the last tragedy of Murray, that second attack on Gaza, which London forced on one too weak or too politic to resist; and how we went into it, everybody, generals and staff-officers, even soldiers, convinced that we should lose. . . .

Five thousand eight hundred was the casualty bill. They said Allenby was getting armies of fresh men, and hundreds of guns, and all would be different.

Before I was clothed the Commander-in-Chief sent for me, curiously. In my report, thinking of Saladin and Abu Obeida, I had stressed the strategic importance of the eastern tribes of Syria, and their proper use as a threat to the communications of Jerusalem. This jumped with his ambitions, and he wanted to weigh me.

It was a comic interview, for Allenby was physically large and confident, and morally so great that the comprehension of our littleness came slow to him. He sat in his chair looking at me — not straight, as his custom was, but sideways, puzzled. He was newly from France where for years he had been a tooth of the great machine grinding the enemy. He was full of Western ideas of gun power and weight — the worst training for our war — but, as a cavalryman, was already half persuaded to throw up the new school, in this different world of Asia, and accompany Dawnay and Chetwode along the worn road of manœuvre and movement; yet he was hardly prepared for anything so odd as myself — a little bare-footed silk-skirted man offering to hobble the enemy by his preaching if given stores and arms and a fund of two hundred thousand sovereigns to convince and control his converts.

Allenby could not make out how much was genuine performer and how much charlatan. The problem was working behind his eyes, and I left him unhelped to solve it. He did not ask many questions, nor talk much, but studied the map and listened to my unfolding of Eastern Syria and its inhabitants. At the end he put up his chin and said quite directly, 'Well, I will do for you what I can', and that ended it. I was not sure how far I had caught him; but we learned gradually that he meant exactly what he said; and that what General Allenby could do was enough for his very greediest servant.

from THE ARAB BULLETIN, 20 *August* 1917

TWENTY-SEVEN ARTICLES

T H E following notes have been expressed in commandment form for greater clarity and to save words. They are, however, only my personal conclusions, arrived at gradually while I worked in the Hejaz and now put on paper as stalking horses for beginners in the Arab armies. They are meant to apply only to Bedu; townspeople or Syrians require totally different treatment. They are of course not suitable to any other person's need, or applicable unchanged in any particular situation. Handling Hejaz Arabs is an art, not a science, with exceptions and no obvious rules. At the same time we have a great chance there; the Sherif trusts us, and has given us the position (towards his Government) which the Germans wanted to win in Turkey. If we are tactful, we can at once retain his goodwill and carry out our job, but to succeed we have got to put into it all the interest and skill we possess.

1. Go easy for the first few weeks. A bad start is difficult to atone for, and the Arabs form their judgments on externals that we ignore. When you have reached the inner circle in a tribe, you can do as you please with yourself and them.

2. Learn all you can about your Ashraf and Bedu. Get to know their families, clans and tribes, friends and enemies, wells, hills and roads. Do all this by listening and by indirect inquiry. Do not ask questions. Get to speak their dialect of Arabic, not yours. Until you

can understand their allusions, avoid getting deep into conversation, or you will drop bricks. Be a little stiff at first.

3. In matters of business deal only with the commander of the army, column, or party in which you serve. Never give orders to anyone at all, and reserve your directions or advice for the C.O., however great the temptation (for efficiency's sake) of dealing direct with his under-lings. Your place is advisory, and your advice is due to the commander alone. Let him see that this is your conception of your duty, and that his is to be the sole executive of your joint plans.

4. Win and keep the confidence of your leader. Strengthen his prestige at your expense before others when you can. Never refuse or quash schemes he may put forward; but ensure that they are put forward in the first instance privately to you. Always approve them, and after praise modify them insensibly, causing the suggestions to come from him, until they are in accord with your own opinion. When you attain this point, hold him to it, keep a tight grip of his ideas, and push him forward as firmly as possibly, but secretly, so that no one but himself (and he not too clearly) is aware of your pressure.

5. Remain in touch with your leader as constantly and unobtrusively as you can. Live with him, that at meal times and at audiences you may be naturally with him in his tent. Formal visits to give advice are not so good as the constant dropping of ideas in casual talk. When stranger sheikhs come in for the first time to swear allegiance and offer service, clear out of the tent. If their first impression is of foreigners in the confidence of the Sherif, it will do the Arab cause much harm.

6. Be shy of too close relations with the subordinates of the expedi-tion. Continual intercourse with them will make it impossible for you to avoid going behind or beyond the instructions that the Arab C.O. has given them on your advice, and in so disclosing the weakness of his position you altogether destroy your own.

7. Treat the sub-chiefs of your force quite easily and lightly. In this way you hold yourself above their level. Treat the leader, if a Sherif, with respect. He will return your manner and you and he will then be alike, and above the rest. Precedence is a serious matter among the Arabs, and you must attain it.

8. Your ideal position is when you are present and not noticed. Do not be too intimate, too prominent, or too earnest. Avoid being identified too long or too often with any tribal sheikh, even if C.O. of the expedition. To do your work you must be above jealousies, and you lose prestige if you are associated with a tribe or clan, and its

inevitable feuds. Sherifs are above all blood-feuds and local rivalries, and form the only principle of unity among the Arabs. Let your name therefore be coupled always with a Sherif's, and share his attitude towards the tribes. When the moment comes for action put yourself publicly under his orders. The Bedu will then follow suit.

9. Magnify and develop the growing conception of the Sherifs as the natural aristocracy of the Arabs. Intertribal jealousies make it impossible for any sheikh to attain a commanding position, and the only hope of union in nomad Arabs is that the Ashraf be universally acknowledged as the ruling class. Sherifs are half-townsmen, half-nomad, in manner and life, and have the instinct of command. Mere merit and money would be insufficient to obtain such recognition; but the Arab reverence for pedigree and the Prophet gives hope for the ultimate success of the Ashraf.

10. Call your Sherif 'Sidi' in public and in private. Call other people by their ordinary names, without title. In intimate conversation call a Sheikh 'Abu Annad', 'Akhu Alia' or some similar by-name.

11. The foreigner and Christian is not a popular person in Arabia. However friendly and informal the treatment of yourself may be, remember always that your foundations are very sandy ones. Wave a Sherif in front of you like a banner and hide your own mind and person. If you succeed, you will have hundreds of miles of country and thousands of men under your orders, and for this it is worth bartering the outward show.

12. Cling tight to your sense of humour. You will need it every day. A dry irony is the most useful type, and repartee of a personal and not too broad character will double your influence with the chiefs. Reproof, if wrapped up in some smiling form, will carry further and last longer than the most violent speech. The power of mimicry or parody is valuable, but use it sparingly, for wit is more dignified than humour. Do not cause a laugh at a Sherif except among Sherifs.

13. Never lay hands on an Arab; you degrade yourself. You may think the resultant obvious increase of outward respect a gain to you; but what you have really done is to build a wall between you and their inner selves. It is difficult to keep quiet when everything is being done wrong, but the less you lose your temper the greater your advantage. Also then you will not go mad yourself.

14. While very difficult to drive, the Bedu are easy to lead, if you have the patience to bear with them. The less apparent your interferences the more your influence. They are willing to follow your

advice and do what you wish, but they do not mean you or anyone else to be aware of that. It is only after the end of all annoyances that you find at bottom their real fund of goodwill.

15. Do not try to do too much with your own hands. Better the Arabs do it tolerably than that you do it perfectly. It is their war, and you are to help them, not to win it for them. Actually, also, under the very odd conditions of Arabia, your practical work will not be as good as, perhaps, you think it is.

16. If you can, without being too lavish, forestall presents to yourself. A well-placed gift is often most effective in winning over a suspicious sheikh. Never receive a present without giving a liberal return, but you may delay this return (while letting its ultimate certainty be known) if you require a particular service from the giver. Do not let them ask you for things, since their greed will then make them look upon you only as a cow to milk.

17. Wear an Arab headcloth when with a tribe. Bedu have a malignant prejudice against the hat, and believe that our persistence in wearing it (due probably to British obstinacy of dictation) is founded on some immoral or irreligious principle. A thick headcloth forms a good protection against the sun, and if you wear a hat your best Arab friends will be ashamed of you in public.

18. Disguise is not advisable. Except in special areas, let it be clearly known that you are a British officer and a Christian. At the same time, if you can wear Arab kit when with the tribes, you will acquire their trust and intimacy to a degree impossible in uniform. It is, however, dangerous and difficult. They make no special allowances for you when you dress like them. Breaches of etiquette not charged against a foreigner are not condoned to you in Arab clothes. You will be like an actor in a foreign theatre, playing a part day and night for months, without rest, and for an anxious stake. Complete success, which is when the Arabs forget your strangeness and speak naturally before you, counting you as one of themselves, is perhaps only attainable in character: while half-success (all that most of us will strive for; the other costs too much) is easier to win in British things, and you yourself will last longer, physically and mentally, in the comfort that they mean. Also then the Turks will not hang you, when you are caught.

19. If you wear Arab things, wear the best. Clothes are significant among the tribes, and you must wear the appropriate, and appear at ease in them. Dress like a Sherif, if they agree to it.

20. If you wear Arab things at all, go the whole way. Leave your

English friends and customs on the coast, and fall back on Arab habits entirely. It is possible, starting thus level with them, for the European to beat the Arabs at their own game, for we have stronger motives for our action, and put more heart into it than they. If you can surpass them, you have taken an immense stride toward complete success, but the strain of living and thinking in a foreign and half-understood language, the savage food, strange clothes, and stranger ways, with the complete loss of privacy and quiet, and the impossibility of ever relaxing your watchful imitation of the others for months on end, provide such an added stress to the ordinary difficulties of dealing with the Bedu, the climate, and the Turks, that this road should not be chosen without serious thought.

21. Religious discussions will be frequent. Say what you like about your own side, and avoid criticism of theirs, unless you know that the point is external, when you may score heavily by proving it so. With the Bedu, Islam is so all-pervading an element that there is little religiosity, little fervour, and no regard for externals. Do not think from their conduct that they are careless. Their conviction of the truth of their faith, and its share in every act and thought and principle of their daily life is so intimate and intense as to be unconscious, unless roused by opposition. Their religion is as much a part of nature to them as is sleep or food.

22. Do not try to trade on what you know of fighting. The Hejaz confounds ordinary tactics. Learn the Bedu principles of war as thoroughly and as quickly as you can, for till you know them your advice will be no good to the Sherif. Unnumbered generations of tribal raids have taught them more about some parts of the business than we will ever know. In familiar conditions they fight well, but strange events cause panic. Keep your unit small. Their raiding parties are usually from one hundred to two hundred men, and if you take a crowd they only get confused. Also their sheikhs, while admirable company commanders, are too 'set' to learn to handle the equivalents of battalions or regiments. Don't attempt unusual things, unless they appeal to the sporting instinct Bedu have so strongly, or unless success is obvious. If the objective is a good one (booty) they will attack like fiends, they are splendid scouts, their mobility gives you the advantage that will win this local war, they make proper use of their knowledge of the country (don't take tribesmen to places they do not know), and the gazelle-hunters, who form a proportion of the better men, are great shots at visible targets. A sheikh from one tribe

cannot give orders to men from another; a Sherif is necessary to command a mixed tribal force. If there is plunder in prospect, and the odds are at all equal, you will win. Do not waste Bedu attacking trenches (they will not stand casualties) or in trying to defend a position, for they cannot sit still without slacking. The more unorthodox and Arab your proceedings, the more likely you are to have the Turks cold, for they lack initiative and expect you to. Don't play for safety.

23. The open reason that Bedu give you for action or inaction may be true, but always there will be better reasons left for you to divine. You must find these inner reasons (they will be denied, but are none the less in operation) before shaping your arguments for one course or other. Allusion is more effective than logical exposition: they dislike concise expression. Their minds work just as ours do, but on different premises. There is nothing unreasonable, incomprehensible, or inscrutable in the Arab. Experience of them, and knowledge of their prejudices will enable you to foresee their attitude and possible course of action in nearly every case.

24. Do not mix Bedu and Syrians, or trained men and tribesmen. You will get work out of neither, for they hate each other. I have never seen a successful combined operation, but many failures. In particular, ex-officers of the Turkish army, however Arab in feelings and blood and language, are hopeless with Bedu. They are narrow-minded in tactics, unable to adjust themselves to irregular warfare, clumsy in Arab etiquette, swollen-headed to the extent of being incapable of politeness to a tribesman for more than a few minutes, impatient, and, usually, helpless without their troops on the road and in action. Your orders (if you were unwise enough to give any) would be more readily obeyed by Beduins than those of any Mohammedan Syrian officer. Arab townsmen and Arab tribesmen regard each other mutually as poor relations, and poor relations are much more objectionable than poor strangers.

25. In spite of ordinary Arab example, avoid too free talk about women. It is as difficult a subject as religion, and their standards are so unlike our own that a remark, harmless in English, may appear as unrestrained to them, as some of their statements would look to us, if translated literally.

26. Be as careful of your servants as of yourself. If you want a sophisticated one you will probably have to take an Egyptian, or a Sudani, and unless you are very lucky he will undo on trek much of the good you so laboriously effect. Arabs will cook rice and make

coffee for you, and leave you if required to do unmanly work like cleaning boots or washing. They are only really possible if you are in Arab kit. A slave brought up in the Hejaz is the best servant, but there are rules against British subjects owning them, so they have to be lent to you. In any case, take with you an Ageyli or two when you go up country. They are the most efficient couriers in Arabia, and understand camels.

27. The beginning and ending of the secret of handling Arabs is unremitting study of them. Keep always on your guard; never say an unnecessary thing: watch yourself and your companions all the time: hear all that passes, search out what is going on beneath the surface, read their characters, discover their tastes and their weaknesses, and keep everything you find out to yourself. Bury yourself in Arab circles, have no interests and no ideas except the work in hand, so that your brain is saturated with one thing only, and you realize your part deeply enough to avoid the little slips that would counteract the painful work of weeks. Your success will be proportioned to the amount of mental effort you devote to it.

from SEVEN PILLARS OF WISDOM

ABDULLA and I went off before dawn, and in the afternoon, after a friendly ride, reached Rumm to find all safe: . . .

In the idleness forced on him by our absence, Lewis had explored the cliff, and reported the springs very good for washing in; . . .

Its rushing noise came from my left, by a jutting bastion of cliff over whose crimson face trailed long falling runners of green leaves. The path skirted it in an undercut ledge. On the rock-bulge above were clear-cut Nabathæan inscriptions, and a sunk panel incised with a monogram or symbol. Around and about were Arab scratches, including tribe-marks, some of which were witnesses of forgotten migrations: but my attention was only for the splashing of water in a crevice under the shadow of the overhanging rock.

From this rock a silver runlet issued into the sunlight. I looked in to see the spout, a little thinner than my wrist, jetting out firmly from a fissure in the roof, and falling with that clean sound into a shallow, frothing pool, behind the step which served as entrance. The walls and roof of the crevice dripped with moisture. Thick ferns and grasses of the finest green made it a paradise just five feet square.

Upon the water-cleansed and fragrant ledge I undressed my soiled body, and stepped into the little basin, to taste at last a freshness of moving air and water against my tired skin. It was deliciously cool. I lay there quietly, letting the clear, dark red water run over me in a ribbly stream, and rub the travel-dirt away. While I was so happy, a grey-bearded, ragged man, with a hewn face of great power and weariness, came slowly along the path till opposite the spring; and there he let himself down with a sigh upon my clothes spread out over a rock beside the path, for the sun-heat to chase out their thronging vermin.

He heard me and leaned forward, peering with rheumy eyes at this white thing splashing in the hollow beyond the veil of sun-mist. After a long stare he seemed content, and closed his eyes, groaning, 'The love is from God; and of God; and towards God.'

His low-spoken words were caught by some trick distinctly in my water pool. They stopped me suddenly. I had believed Semites unable to use love as a link between themselves and God, indeed, unable to conceive such a relation except with the intellectuality of Spinoza, who loved so rationally and sexlessly, and transcendently that he did not seek, or rather had not permitted, a return. Christianity had seemed to me the first creed to proclaim love in this upper world, from which the desert and the Semite (from Moses to Zeno) had shut it out: and Christianity was a hybrid, except in its first root not essentially Semitic. . . .

Islam, too, had inevitably changed from continent to continent . . . In Arabia, however, it had kept a Semitic character, or rather the Semitic character had endured through the phase of Islam (as through all the phases of the creeds with which the town-dwellers continually vested the simplicity of faith), expressing the monotheism of open spaces, the pass-through-infinity of pantheism and its everyday usefulness of an all-pervading, household God.

By contrast with this fixity, or with my reading of it, the old man of Rumm loomed portentous in his brief, single sentence, and seemed to overturn my theories of the Arab nature. In fear of a revelation, I put an end to my bath, and advanced to recover my clothes. He shut his eyes with his hands and groaned heavily. Tenderly I persuaded him to rise up and let me dress, and then to come with me along the crazy path which the camels had made in their climbing to and from the other water-springs. He sat down by our coffee-place, where Mohammed blew up the fire while I sought to make him utter doctrine.

When the evening meal was ready we fed him, so checking for some minutes his undercurrent of groans and broken words. Late at night, he rose painfully to his feet and tottered deafly into the night, taking his beliefs, if any, with him. The Howeitat told me that life-long he had wandered among them moaning strange things, not knowing day or night, not troubling himself for food or work or shelter. He was given bounty of them all, as an afflicted man: but never replied a word, or talked aloud, except when abroad by himself or alone among the sheep and goats. . . .

The sergeants set up their toys on a terrace, while we went down to the bridge to dig a bed between the ends of two steel sleepers, wherein to hide my fifty pounds of gelatine. We had stripped off the paper wrapping of the individual explosive plugs and kneaded them together by help of the sun-heat into a shaking jelly in a sand-bag.

The burying of it was not easy. The embankment was steep, and in the sheltered pocket between it and the hill-side was a wind-laid bank of sand. No one crossed this but myself, stepping carefully; yet I left unavoidable great prints over its smoothness. The ballast dug out from the track I had to gather in my cloak for carriage in repeated journeys to the culvert, whence it could be tipped naturally over the shingle bed of the watercourse.

It took me nearly two hours to dig in and cover the charge: then came the difficult job of unrolling the heavy wires from the detonator to the hills whence we would fire the mine. The top sand was crusted and had to be broken through in burying the wires. They were stiff wires, which scarred the wind-rippled surface with long lines like the belly marks of preposterously narrow and heavy snakes. When pressed down in one place they rose into the air in another. At last they had to be weighted down with rocks which, in turn, had to be buried at the cost of great disturbance of the ground.

Afterwards it was necessary, with a sand-bag, to stipple the marks into a wavy surface; and, finally, with a bellows and long fanning sweeps of my cloak, to simulate the smooth laying of the wind. The whole job took five hours to finish; but then it was well finished: neither myself nor any of us could see where the charge lay, or that double wires led out underground from it to the firing point two hundred yards off, behind the ridge marked for our riflemen. . . .

The men with rifles posted themselves in a long line behind the spur running from the guns past the exploder to the mouth of the valley. From it they would fire directly into the derailed carriages at less than one hundred and fifty yards, whereas the ranges for the Stokes and Lewis guns were about three hundred yards. An Arab stood up on high behind the guns and shouted to us what the train was doing — a necessary precaution, for if it carried troops and detrained them behind our ridge we should have to face about like a flash and retire fighting up the valley for our lives. Fortunately it held on at all the speed the two locomotives could make on wood fuel.

It drew near where we had been reported, and opened random fire into the desert. I could hear the racket coming, as I sat on my hillock by the bridge to give the signal to Salem, who danced round the exploder on his knees, crying with excitement, and calling urgently on God to make him fruitful. The Turkish fire sounded heavy, and I wondered with how many men we were going to have affair, and if the mine would be advantage enough for our eighty fellows to equal them. It would have been better if the first electrical experiment had been simpler.

However, at that moment the engines, looking very big, rocked with screaming whistles into view around the bend. Behind them followed ten box-wagons, crowded with rifle-muzzles at the windows and doors; and in little sand-bag nests on the roofs Turks precariously held on, to shoot at us. I had not thought of two engines, and on the moment decided to fire the charge under the second, so that however little the mine's effect, the uninjured engine should not be able to uncouple and drag the carriages away.

Accordingly, when the front 'driver' of the second engine was on the bridge, I raised my hand to Salem. There followed a terrific roar, and the line vanished from sight behind a spouting column of black dust and smoke a hundred feet high and wide. Out of the darkness came shattering crashes and long, loud metallic clangings of ripped steel, with many lumps of iron and plate; while one entire wheel of a locomotive whirled up suddenly black out of the cloud against the sky, and sailed musically over our heads to fall slowly and heavily into the desert behind. Except for the flight of these, there succeeded a deathly silence, with no cry of men or rifle-shot, as the now grey mist of the explosion drifted from the line towards us, and over our ridge until it was lost in the hills.

In the lull, I ran southward to join the sergeants. Salem picked up his rifle and charged out into the murk. Before I had climbed to the guns the hollow was alive with shots, and with the brown figures of the Beduin leaping forward to grips with the enemy. I looked round to see what was happening so quickly, and saw the train stationary and dismembered along the track, with its waggon sides jumping under the bullets which riddled them, while Turks were falling out from the far doors to gain the shelter of the railway embankment.

As I watched, our machine-guns chattered out over my head, and the long rows of Turks on the carriage roofs rolled over, and were swept off the top like bales of cotton before the furious shower of bullets which stormed along the roofs and splashed clouds of yellow chips from the planking. The dominant position of the guns had been an advantage to us so far.

When I reached Stokes and Lewis the engagement had taken another turn. The remaining Turks had got behind the bank, here about eleven feet high, and from cover of the wheels were firing point-blank at the Beduin twenty yards away across the sand-filled dip. The enemy in the crescent of the curving line were secure from the machine-guns; but Stokes slipped in his first shell, and after a few seconds there came a crash as it burst beyond the train in the desert.

He touched the elevating screw, and his second shot fell just by the trucks in the deep hollow below the bridge where the Turks were taking refuge. It made a shambles of the place. The survivors of the group broke out in a panic across the desert, throwing away their rifles and equipment as they ran. This was the opportunity of the Lewis gunners. The sergeant grimly traversed with drum after drum, till the open sand was littered with bodies. Mushagraf, the Sherari boy behind the second gun, saw the battle over, threw aside his weapon with a yell, and dashed down at speed with his rifle to join the others who were beginning, like wild beasts, to tear open the carriages and fall to plunder. It had taken nearly ten minutes.

I looked up-line through my glasses and saw the Mudowwara patrol breaking back uncertainly towards the railway to meet the train-fugitives running their fastest northward. I looked south, to see our thirty men cantering their camels neck and neck in our direction to share the spoils. The Turks there, seeing them go, began to move after them with infinite precaution, firing volleys. Evidently we had a half-hour respite, and then a double threat against us.

I ran down to the ruins to see what the mine had done. The bridge was gone; and into its gap was fallen the front waggon, which had been filled with sick. The smash had killed all but three or four and had rolled dead and dying into a bleeding heap against the splintered end. One of those yet alive deliriously cried out the word typhus. So I wedged shut the door, and left them there, alone.

Succeeding waggons were derailed and smashed: some had frames irreparably buckled. The second engine was a blanched pile of smoking iron. Its driving wheels had been blown upward, taking away the side of the fire-box. Cab and tender were twisted into strips, among the piled stones of the bridge abutment. It would never run again. The front engine had got off better: though heavily derailed and lying half-over, with the cab burst, yet its steam was at pressure, and driving-gear intact.

Our greatest object was to destroy locomotives, and I had kept in my arms a box of gun-cotton with fuse and detonator ready fixed, to make sure such a case. I now put them in position on the outside cylinder. On the boiler would have been better, but the sizzling steam made me fear a general explosion which would sweep across my men (swarming like ants over the booty) with a blast of jagged fragments. Yet they would not finish their looting before the Turks came. So I lit the fuse, and in the half-minute of its burning drove the plunderers a little back, with difficulty. Then the charge burst, blowing the cylinder to smithers, and the axle too. At the moment I was distressed with uncertainty whether the damage were enough; but the Turks later, found the engine beyond use and broke it up.

The valley was a weird sight. The Arabs, gone raving mad, were rushing about at top speed bareheaded and half-naked, screaming, shooting into the air, clawing one another nail and fist, while they burst open trucks and staggered back and forward with immense bales, which they ripped by the rail-side, and tossed through, smashing what they did not want. The train had been packed with refugees and sick men, volunteers for boat-service on the Euphrates, and families of Turkish officers returning to Damascus.

There were scores of carpets spread about; dozens of mattresses and flowered quilts, blankets in heaps, clothes for men and women in full variety; clocks, cooking-pots, food, ornaments and weapons. To one side stood thirty or forty hysterical women, unveiled, tearing their clothes and hair; shrieking themselves distracted. The Arabs without regard to them went on wrecking the household goods; looting their absolute fill. Camels had become common property. Each man frantically loaded the nearest with what it could carry and shooed it westward into the void, while he turned to his next fancy.

Seeing me tolerably unemployed, the women rushed, and caught at me with howls for mercy. I assured them that all was going well: but they would not get away till some husbands delivered me. These knocked their wives off and seized my feet in a very agony of terror of instant death. A Turk so broken down was a nasty spectacle: I kicked them off as well as I could with bare feet, and finally broke free.

Next a group of Austrians, officers and non-commissioned officers, appealed to me quietly in Turkish for quarter. I replied with my halting German; whereupon one, in English, begged a doctor for his wounds. We had none: not that it mattered, for he was mortally hurt and dying. I told them the Turks would return in an hour and care for them. But he was dead before that, as were most of the others (instructors in the new Skoda mountain howitzers supplied to Turkey for the Hejaz war), because some dispute broke out between them and my own bodyguard, and one of them fired a pistol shot at young Rahail. My infuriated men cut them down, all but two or three, before I could return to interfere.

So far as could be seen in the excitement, our side had suffered no loss. Among the ninety military prisoners were five Egyptian soldiers, in their underclothes. They knew me, and explained that in a night raid of Davenport's, near Wadi Ais, they had been cut off by the Turks and captured. They told me something of Davenport's work: of his continual pegging away in Abdulla's sector, which was kept alive by him for month after month, without any of the encouragement lent to us by success and local enthusiasm. His best helpers were such stolid infantrymen as these, whom I made lead the prisoners away to our appointed rallying place at the salt rocks.

Lewis and Stokes had come down to help me. I was a little anxious about them; for the Arabs, having lost their wits, were as ready to assault friend as foe. Three times I had had to defend myself when they pretended not to know me and snatched at my things. However, the sergeants' war-stained khaki presented few attractions. Lewis went out east of the railway to count the thirty men he had slain; and incidentally, to find Turkish gold and trophies in their haversacks. Stokes strolled through the wrecked bridge, saw there the bodies of twenty Turks torn to pieces by his second shell, and retired hurriedly.

Ahmed came up to me with his arms full of booty and shouted (no Arab could speak normally in the thrill of victory) that an old woman in the last waggon but one wished to see me. I sent him at once, empty-handed, for my camel and some baggage camels to remove the guns; for the enemy's fire was now plainly audible, and the Arabs, sated with spoils, were escaping one by one towards the hills, driving tottering camels before them into safety. It was bad tactics to leave the guns until the end: but the confusion of a first, overwhelmingly successful, experiment had dulled our judgement.

In the end of the waggon sat an ancient and very tremulous Arab dame, who asked me what it was all about. I explained. She said that though an old friend and hostess of Feisal, she was too infirm to travel and must wait her death there. I replied that she would not be harmed. The Turks were almost arrived and would recover what remained of the train. She accepted this, and begged me to find her old negress, to bring her water. The slave woman filled a cup from the spouting tender of the first engine (delicious water, from which Lewis was slaking his thirst), and then I led her to her grateful mistress. Months after there came to me secretly from Damascus a letter and a pleasant little Baluchi carpet from the lady Ayesha, daughter of Jellal el Lel, of Medina, in memory of an odd meeting. . . .

In the best circumstances, waiting for action was hard. To-day it was beastly. Even enemy patrols stumbled along without care, perfunctorily against the rain. At last, near noon, in a snatch of fine weather, the watchmen on the south peak flagged their cloaks wildly in signal of a train. We reached our positions in an instant, for we had squatted the late hours on our heels in a streaming ditch near the line, so as not to miss another chance. The Arabs took cover properly. I looked back at their ambush from my firing point, and saw nothing but the grey hill-sides.

I could not hear the train coming, but trusted, and knelt ready for perhaps half an hour, when the suspense became intolerable, and I signalled to know what was up. They sent down to say it was coming very slowly, and was an enormously long train. Our appetites stiffened. The longer it was the more would be the loot. Then came word that it had stopped. It moved again.

Finally, near one o'clock, I heard it panting. The locomotive was evidently defective (all these wood-fired trains were bad), and the heavy load on the up-gradient was proving too much for its capacity. I crouched behind my bush, while it crawled slowly into view past the south cutting, and along the bank above my head towards the culvert.

The first ten trucks were open trucks, crowded with troops. However, once again it was too late to choose, so when the engine was squarely over the mine I pushed down the handle of the exploder. Nothing happened. I sawed it up and down four times.

Still nothing happened; and I realized that it had gone out of order, and that I was kneeling on a naked bank, with a Turkish troop train crawling past fifty yards away. The bush, which had seemed a foot high, shrank smaller than a fig-leaf; and I felt myself the most distinct object in the country-side. Behind me was an open valley for two hundred yards to the cover where my Arabs were waiting and wondering what I was at. It was impossible to make a bolt for it, or the Turks would step off the train and finish us. If I sat still, there might be just a hope of my being ignored as a casual Bedouin.

So there I sat, counting for sheer life, while eighteen open trucks, three box-waggons, and three officers' coaches dragged by. The engine panted slower and slower, and I thought every moment that it would break down. The troops took no great notice of me, but the officers were interested, and came out to the little platforms at the ends of their carriages, pointing and staring. I waved back at them, grinning nervously, and feeling an improbable shepherd in my Meccan dress, with its twisted golden circlet about my head. Perhaps the mud-stains, the wet and their ignorance made me accepted. The end of the brake van slowly disappeared into the cutting on the north.

As it went, I jumped up, buried my wires, snatched hold of the wretched exploder, and went like a rabbit uphill into safety. There I took breath and looked back to see that the train had finally stuck. It waited, about five hundred yards beyond the mine, for nearly an hour to get up a head of steam, while an officers' patrol came back and searched very carefully, the ground where I had been sitting. However the wires were properly hidden: they found nothing: the engine plucked up heart again, and away they went. . . .

Just at that moment the watchman on the north cried a train. We left the fire and made a breathless race of the six hundred yards down hill to our old position. Round the bend, whistling its loudest, came the train, a splendid two-engined thing of twelve passenger coaches, travelling at top speed on the favouring grade. I touched off under the first driving wheel of the first locomotive, and the explosion was terrific. The ground spouted blackly into my face, and I was sent spinning, to sit up with the shirt torn to my shoulder and the blood dripping from long ragged scratches on my left arm. Between my knees lay the exploder, crushed under a twisted sheet of sooty iron. In front of me was the scalded and smoking upper half of a man. When I peered through the dust and steam of the explosion the whole boiler of the first engine seemed to be missing.

I dully felt that it was time to get away to support; but when I moved, learnt that there was a great pain in my right foot, because of which I could only limp along, with my head swinging from the shock. Movement began to clear away this confusion, as I hobbled towards the upper valley, whence the Arabs were now shooting fast into the crowded coaches. Dizzily I cheered myself by repeating aloud in English 'Oh, I wish this hadn't happened'.

When the enemy began to return our fire, I found myself much between the two. Ali saw me fall, and thinking that I was hard hit, ran out, with Turki and about twenty men of his servants and the Beni Sakhr, to help me. The Turks found their range and got seven of them in a few seconds. The others, in a rush, were about me — fit models, after their activity, for a sculptor. Their full white cotton drawers drawn in, bell-like, round their slender waists and ankles, their hairless brown bodies; and the love-locks plaited tightly over each temple in long horns, made them look like Russian dancers.

We scrambled back into cover together, and there, secretly, I felt myself over, to find I had not once been really hurt; though besides the bruises and cuts of the boiler-plate and a broken toe, I had five different bullet-grazes on me (some of them uncomfortably deep) and my clothes ripped to pieces.

From the watercourse we could look about. The explosion had destroyed the arched head of the culvert, and the frame of the first engine was lying beyond it, at the near foot of the embankment down which it had rolled. The second locomotive had toppled into the gap, and was lying across the ruined tender of the first. Its bed was twisted. I judged them both beyond repair. The second tender had disappeared over the further side; and the first three waggons had telescoped and were smashed in pieces.

The rest of the train was badly derailed, with the listing coaches butted end to end at all angles, zigzagged along the track. One of them was a saloon, decorated with flags. In it had been Mehmed Jemal Pasha, commanding the Eighth Army Corps, hurrying down to defend Jerusalem against Allenby. His chargers had been in the first waggon; his motor-car was on the end of the train, and we shot it up. Of his staff we noticed a fat ecclesiastic, whom we thought to be Assad

Shukair, Imam to Ahmed Jemal Pasha, and a notorious pro-Turk pimp. So we blazed at him till he dropped.

It was all long bowls. We could see that our chances of carrying the wreck were slight. There had been some four hundred men on board, and the survivors, now recovered from the shock, were under shelter and shooting hard at us. At the first moment our party on the north spur had closed, and nearly won the game. Mifleh on his mare chased the officers from the saloon into the lower ditch. He was too excited to stop and shoot, and so they got away scathless. The Arabs following him had turned to pick up some of the rifles and medals littering the ground, and then to drag bags and boxes from the train. If we had had a machine gun posted to cover the far side, according to my mining practice, not a Turk would have escaped.

Mifleh and Adhub rejoined us on the hill, and asked after Fahad. One of the Serahin told how he had led the first rush, while I lay knocked out beside the exploder, and had been killed near it. They showed his belt and rifle as proof that he was dead and that they had tried to save him. Adhub said not a word, but leaped out of the gully, and raced downhill. We caught our breaths till our lungs hurt us, watching him; but the Turks seemed not to see. A minute later he was dragging a body behind the left-hand bank.

Mifleh went back to his mare, mounted, and took her down behind a spur. Together they lifted the inert figure on to the pommel, and returned. A bullet had passed through Fahad's face, knocking out four teeth, and gashing the tongue. He had fallen unconscious, but had revived just before Adhub reached him, and was trying on hands and knees, blinded with blood to crawl away. He now recovered poise enough to cling to a saddle. So they changed him to the first camel they found and led him off at once. . . .

We were now only about forty left, and obviously could do no good against them. So we ran in batches up the little stream-bed, turning at each sheltered angle to delay them by pot-shots . . . Ali was angry with me for retiring slowly. In reality my raw hurts crippled me, but to hide from him this real reason I pretended to be easy, interested in and studying the Turks. Such successive rests while I gained courage for a new run kept him and Turki far behind the rest.

At last we reached the hill-top. Each man there jumped on the nearest camel, and made away at full speed eastward into the desert, for an hour. Then in safety we sorted our animals. The excellent Rahail, despite the ruling excitement, had brought off with him, tied to his saddle-girth, a huge haunch of the camel slaughtered just as the train arrived. He gave us the motive for a proper halt, five miles farther on as a little party of four camels appeared marching in the same direction. It was our companion, Matar, coming back from his home village to Azrak with loads of raisins and peasant delicacies.

So we stopped at once, under a large rock in Wadi Dhuleil, where was a barren fig-tree, and cooked our first meal for three days. There, also we bandaged up Fahad, who was sleepy with the lassitude of his severe hurt . . . Next day we moved into Azrak, having a great welcome, and boasting — God forgive us — that we were victors.

TO A FRIEND

Sept 24, '17   *Akaba*

Dear [*name omitted*], I'm sorry, but I felt the usual abrupt beginning would be too much for your nerves, and that you would fall exhausted on to the floor, without even a Turkish carpet to break the shock of my writing at last. What can have happened? I was pondering last night how for a year I had written no private letter (except to my people, and those don't count, for my mails are sunk or censored!) and today I go and break the habit. Perhaps it's because it was a habit, and I'm getting old and stiff (not to say tired, for every year out in Arabia counts ten) and habits must be nipped in their shells.

I'm in Akaba for two days — that for me spells civilization, though it doesn't mean other than Arab togs and food, but it means you lunch where you dined, and not further on — and therefore happy. The last stunt has been a few days on the Hejaz Railway, in which I potted a train with two engines (oh, the Gods were kind) and we killed superior numbers, and I got a good Baluch prayer-rug and lost all my kit, and nearly my little self.

I'm not going to last out this game much longer: nerves going and temper wearing thin, and one wants an unlimited account of both. However while it lasts it's a show between Gilbert and Carroll, and one can retire on it, with that feeling of repletion that comes after a hearty meal. By the way hearty meals are like the chopped snow that one scatters over one's bowl of grapes in Damascus at midsummer. Ripping, to write about —

This letter isn't going to do you much good, for the amount of information it contains would go on a pin's head and roll about. However it's not a correspondence, but a discourse held with the only person to whom I have ever written regularly, and one whom I have shamefully ill-used by not writing to more frequently. On a show so narrow and voracious as this one loses one's past and one's balance, and becomes hopelessly self-centred. I don't think I ever think except about shop, and I'm quite certain I never do anything else. That must be my excuse for dropping everyone, and I hope when the nightmare ends that I will wake up and become alive again. This killing and killing of Turks is horrible. When you charge in at the finish and find them all over the place in bits, and still alive many of them, and know that you have done hundreds in the same way before and must do hundreds more if you can. . . .

from SEVEN PILLARS OF WISDOM

RAIN had set in steadily, and the country was sodden wet . . . Azrak lay favourably for us, and the old fort would be convenient headquarters if we made it habitable, no matter how severe the winter.

So I established myself in its southern gate-tower, and set my six Haurani boys (for whom manual labour was not disgraceful) to cover with brushwood, palm-branches, and clay the ancient split stone rafters, which stood open to the sky. Ali took up his quarters in the south-east corner tower, and made that roof tight. The Indians weather-proofed their own north-west rooms. We arranged the stores on the ground floor of the western tower, by the little gate, for it was the soundest, driest place. The Biasha chose to live under me in the south gate. So we blocked that entry and made a hall of it. Then we opened a great arch from the court to the palm-garden, and made a ramp, that our camels might come inside each evening.

Hassan Shah we appointed Seneschal. As a good Moslem his first care was for the little mosque in the square. It had been half unroofed and the Arabs had penned sheep within the walls. He set his twenty men to dig out the filth, and wash the pavement clean. The mosque then became a most attractive house of prayer. What had been a place shut off, dedicated to God alone, Time had broken open to the Evanescent with its ministering winds and rain and sunlight; these entering into the worship taught worshippers how the two were one.

Our prudent Jemadar's next labour was to make positions for machine-guns in the upper towers, from whose tops the approaches lay at mercy. Then he placed a formal sentry (a portent and cause of wonder in Arabia) whose main duty was the shutting of the postern gate at sundown. The door was a poised slab of dressed basalt, a foot thick, turning on pivots of itself, socketed into threshold and lintel. It took a great effort to start swinging, and at the end went shut with a clang and crash which made tremble the west wall of the old castle. . . .

Then began our flood of visitors. All day and every day they came, now in the running column of shots, raucous shouting and rush of camel-feet which meant a Bedouin parade, it might be of Rualla, or Sherarat, or Serahin, Serdiyeh, or Beni Sakhr, chiefs of great name like ibn Zuhair, ibn Kaebir, Rafa el Khoreisha, or some little father of a family demonstrating his greedy goodwill before the fair eyes of Ali ibn el Hussein. Then it would be a wild gallop of horse: Druses, or the ruffling warlike peasants of the Arab plain. Sometimes it was a cautious, slow-led caravan of ridden camels, from which stiffly dismounted Syrian politicians or traders not accustomed to the road. One day arrived a hundred miserable Armenians, fleeing starvation and the suspended terror of the Turks. Again would come a spick and span group of mounted officers, Arab deserters from the Turkish armies, followed, often as not, by a compact company of Arab rank and file. Always they came, day after day, till the desert, which had been trackless when we came, was starred out with grey roads. . . .

In these slow nights we were secure against the world. For one thing, it was winter, and in the rain and the dark few men would venture either over the labyrinth of lava or through the marsh — the two approaches to our fortress; and, further, we had ghostly guardians. The first evening we were sitting with the Serahin, Hassan Shah had made the rounds, and the coffee was being pounded by the hearth, when there rose a strange, long wailing round the towers outside. Ibn Bani seized me by the arm and held to me, shuddering. I whispered to him, 'What is it?' and he gasped that the dogs of the Beni Hillal, the mythical builders of the fort, quested the six towers each night for their dead masters.

We strained to listen. Through Ali's black basalt window-frame crept a rustling, which was the stirring of the night-wind in the withered palms, an intermittent rustling, like English rain on yet-crisp fallen leaves. Then the cries came again and again and again, rising slowly in power, till they sobbed round the walls in deep waves to die away choked and miserable. At such times our men pounded the coffee harder while the Arabs broke into sudden song to occupy their ears against the misfortune. No Bedouin would lie outside in wait for the mystery, and from our windows we saw nothing but the motes of water in the dank air which drove through the radiance of our firelight. So it remained a legend: but wolves or jackals, hyænas, or hunting dogs, their ghost-watch kept our ward more closely than arms could have done.

In the evening, when we had shut-to the gate, all guests would assemble, either in my room or in Ali's, and coffee and stories would go round until the last meal, and after it, till sleep came. On stormy nights we brought in brushwood and dung and lit a great fire in the middle of the floor. About it would be drawn the carpets and the saddle-sheepskins, and in its light we would tell over our own battles, or hear the visitors' traditions. The leaping flames chased our smoke-ruffled shadows strangely about the rough stone wall behind us, distorting them over the hollows and projections of its broken face. When these stories came to a period, our tight circle would shift over, uneasily, to the other knee, or elbow; while coffee-cups went clinking round, and a servant fanned the blue reek of the fire towards the loophole with his cloak, making the glowing ash swirl and sparkle with his draught. Till the voice of the story-teller took up again, we would hear the rain-spots hissing briefly as they dripped from the stone-beamed roof into the fire's heart.

At last the sky turned solidly to rain, and no man could approach us. In loneliness we learned the full disadvantages of imprisonment within such gloomy ancient unmortared palaces. The rains guttered down within the walls' thickness and spouted into the rooms from their chinks. We set rafts of palm-branches to bear us clear of the streaming floor, covered them with felt mats, and huddled down on them under sheepskins, with another mat over us like a shield to throw off the water. It was icy cold, as we hid there, motionless, from the murky daylight until dark, our minds seeming suspended within these massive walls, through whose every shot-window the piercing mist streamed like a white pennant. Past and future flowed over us like an uneddying river. We dreamed ourselves into the spirit of the place; sieges and feasting, raids, murders, love-singing in the night. . . .

As I was thinking how I would ride, there came to us, unheralded, one morning in the rain, Talal el Hareidhin, sheikh of Tafas. He was a famous outlaw with a price upon his head; but so great that he rode about as he pleased. In two wild years he had killed, according to report, some twenty-three of the Turks. His six followers were splendidly mounted, and himself the most dashing figure of a man in the height of Hauran fashion. His sheepskin coat was finest Angora covered in green broadcloth, with silk patches and designs in braid. His other clothes were silk; and his high boots, his silver saddle, his sword, dagger, and rifle matched his reputation.

He swaggered to our coffee-hearth, as a man sure of his welcome, greeting Ali boisterously (after our long sojourn with the tribes all peasants sounded boisterous), laughing broad-mouthed at the weather and our old fort and the enemy. He looked about thirty-five, was short and strong, with a full face, trimmed beard and long, pointed moustaches. His round eyes were made rounder, larger and darker by the antimony loaded on in villager style. He was ardently ours, and we rejoiced, since his name was one to conjure with in Hauran. When a day had made me sure of him, I took him secretly to the palm-garden, and told him my ambition to see his neighbourhood. The idea delighted him, and he companioned me for the march as thoroughly and cheerfully as only a Syrian on a good horse could. Halim and Faris, men specially engaged, rode with me as guards. . . .

Properly to round off this spying of the hollow land of Hauran, it was necessary to visit Deraa, its chief town. Talal, however, could not venture in with me since he was too well known in the place. So we parted from him with many thanks on both sides, and rode southward along the line until near Deraa. There we dismounted. The boy, Halim, took the ponies, and set off for Nisib, south of Deraa. My plan was to walk round the railway station and town with Faris, and reach Nisib after sunset. Faris was my best companion for the trip, because he was an insignificant peasant, old enough to be my father, and respectable . . . I was in Halim's wet things, with a torn Hurani jacket, and was yet limping from the broken foot acquired when we blew up Jemal's train. The slippery track made walking difficult, unless we spread out our toes widely and took hold of the ground with them: and doing this for mile after mile was exquisitely painful to me. Because pain hurt me so, I would not lay weight always on my pains in our revolt: yet hardly one day in Arabia passed without a physical ache to increase the corroding sense of my accessory deceitfulness towards the Arabs, and the legitimate fatigue of responsible command. . . .

At the corner of the aerodrome by the south end of the station we struck over towards the town. There were old Albatros machines in the sheds, and men lounging about. One of these, a Syrian soldier, began to question us about our villages, and if there was much 'government' where we lived. He was probably an intending deserter, fishing for a refuge. We shook him off at last and turned away. Someone called out in Turkish. We walked on deafly; but a sergeant came after, and took me roughly by the arm, saying 'The Bey wants you'. There were too many witnesses for fight or flight, so I went readily. He took no notice of Faris.

I was marched through the tall fence into a compound set about with many huts and a few buildings. We passed to a mud room, outside which was an earth platform, whereon sat a fleshy Turkish officer, one leg tucked under him. He hardly glanced at me when the sergeant brought me up and made a long report in Turkish. He asked my name: I told him Ahmed ibn Bagr, a Circassian from Juneitra. 'A deserter?' 'But we Circassians have no military service'. He turned, stared at me, and said very slowly 'You are a liar. Enrol him in your section, Hassan Chowish, and do what is necessary till the Bey sends for him'.

They led me into a guard-room, mostly taken up by large wooden cribs, on which lay or sat a dozen men in untidy uniforms. They took away my belt, and my knife, made me wash myself carefully, and fed me. I passed the long day there. They would not let me go on any terms, but tried to reassure me. A soldier's life was not all bad. To-morrow, perhaps, leave would be permitted, if I fulfilled the Bey's pleasure this evening. The Bey seemed to be Nahi, the Governor. If he was angry, they said, I would be drafted for infantry training to the depot in Baalbek. I tried to look as though, to my mind, there was nothing worse in the world than that.

Soon after dark three men came for me. It had seemed a chance to get away, but one held me all the time. I cursed my littleness. Our march crossed the railway, where were six tracks, besides the sidings of the engine-shop. We went through a side gate, down a street, past a square, to a detached, two-storied house. There was a sentry outside, and a glimpse of others lolling in the dark entry. They took me upstairs to the Bey's room; or to his bedroom, rather. He was another bulky man, a Circassian himself, perhaps, and sat on the bed in a night-gown, trembling and sweating as though with fever. When I was pushed in he kept his head down, and waved the guard out. In a breathless voice he told me to sit on the floor in front of him, and after that was dumb; while I gazed at the top of his great head, on which the bristling hair stood up, no longer than the dark stubble on his cheeks and chin. At last he looked me over, and told me to stand up: then to turn round. I obeyed; he flung himself back on the bed, and dragged me down with him in his arms. When I saw what he wanted I twisted round and up again, glad to find myself equal to him, at any rate in wrestling.

He began to fawn on me, saying how white and fresh I was, how fine my hands and feet, and how he would let me off drills and duties, make me his orderly, even pay me wages, if I would love him.

I was obdurate, so he changed his tone, and sharply ordered me to take off my drawers. When I hesitated, he snatched at me; and I pushed him back. He clapped his hands for the sentry, who hurried in and pinioned me. The Bey cursed me with horrible threats: and made the man holding me tear my clothes away, bit by bit. His eyes rounded at the half-healed places where the bullets had flicked through my skin a little while ago. Finally he lumbered to his feet, with a glitter in his look, and began to paw me over. I bore it for a little, till he got too beastly; and then jerked my knee into him.

He staggered to his bed, squeezing himself together and groaning with pain, while the soldier shouted for the corporal and the other three men to grip me hand and foot. As soon as I was helpless the Governor regained courage, and spat at me, swearing he would make me ask pardon. He took off his slipper, and hit me repeatedly with it in the face, while the corporal braced my head back by the hair to receive the blows. He leaned forward, fixed his teeth in my neck and bit till the blood came. Then he kissed me. Afterwards he drew one of the men's bayonets. I thought he was going to kill me, and was sorry: but he only pulled up a fold of the flesh over my ribs, worked the point through, after considerable trouble, and gave the blade a half-turn. This hurt, and I winced, while the blood wavered down my side and dripped to the front of my thigh. He looked pleased and dabbled it over my stomach with his finger-tips.

In my despair I spoke. His face changed and he stood still, then controlled his voice with an effort, to say significantly, 'You must understand that I know: and it will be easier if you do as I wish'. I was dumbfounded, and we stared silently at one another, while the men who felt an inner meaning beyond their experience, shifted uncomfortably. But it was evidently a chance shot, by which he himself did not, or would not, mean what I feared. I could not again trust my twitching mouth, which faltered always in emergencies, so at last threw up my chin, which was the sign for 'No' in the East; then he sat down, and half-whispered to the corporal to take me out and teach me everything.

They kicked me to the head of the stairs, and stretched me over a guard-bench, pommelling me. Two knelt on my ankles, bearing down on the back of my knees, while two more twisted my wrists till they cracked, and then crushed them and my neck against the wood. The corporal had run downstairs; and now came back with a whip of the Circassian sort, a thong of supple black hide, rounded, and tapering from the thickness of a thumb at the grip (which was wrapped in silver) down to a hard point finer than a pencil.

He saw me shivering, partly I think, with cold, and made it whistle over my ear, taunting me that before his tenth cut I would howl for mercy, and at the twentieth beg for the caresses of the Bey; and then he began to lash me madly across and across with all his might, while I locked my teeth to endure this thing which lapped itself like flaming wire about my body.

To keep my mind in control I numbered the blows, but after twenty lost count, and could feel only the shapeless weight of pain, not tearing claws, for which I had prepared, but a gradual cracking apart of my whole being by some too-great force whose waves rolled up my spine till they were pent within my brain, to clash terribly together. Somewhere in the place a cheap clock ticked loudly, and it distressed me that their beating was not in its time. I writhed and twisted, but was held so tightly that my struggles were useless. After the corporal ceased, the men took up, very deliberately, giving me so many, and then an interval during which they would squabble for the next turn, ease themselves, and play unspeakably with me. This was repeated often, for what may have been no more than ten minutes. Always for the first of every new series, my head would be pulled round, to see how a hard white ridge, like a railway, darkening slowly into crimson, leaped over my skin at the instant of each stroke, with a bead of blood where two ridges crossed. As the punishment proceeded the whip fell more and more upon existing weals, biting blacker or more wet, till my flesh quivered with accumulated pain, and with terror of the next blow coming. They soon conquered my determination not to cry, but while my will ruled my lips I used only Arabic, and before the end a merciful sickness choked my utterance.

At last when I was completely broken they seemed satisfied. Somehow I found myself off the bench, lying on my back on the dirty floor, where I snuggled down, dazed, panting for breath, but vaguely comfortable. I had strung myself to learn all pain until I died, and no longer actor, but spectator, thought not to care how my body jerked and squealed. Yet I knew or imagined what passed about me.

I remembered the corporal kicking with his nailed boot to get me up; and this was true, for the next day my right side was dark and lacerated, and a damaged rib made each breath stab me sharply. I remembered smiling idly at him, for a delicious warmth, probably sexual, was swelling through me: and then that he flung up his arm and hacked with the full length of his whip into my groin. This doubled me half-over, screaming, or, rather, trying impotently to scream, only shuddering through my open mouth. One giggled with amusement. A voice cried, 'Shame, you've killed him'. Another slash followed. A roaring, and my eyes went black: while within me the core of life seemed to heave slowly up through the rending nerves, expelled from its body by this last indescribable pang.

By the bruises perhaps they beat me further: but I next knew that I was being dragged about by two men, each disputing over a leg as though to split me apart: while a third man rode me astride. It was momently better than more flogging. Then Nahi called. They splashed water in my face, wiped off some of the filth, and lifted me between them retching and sobbing for mercy, to where he lay: but he now rejected me in haste, as a thing too torn and bloody for his bed, blaming their excess of zeal which had spoilt me: whereas no doubt they had laid into me much as usual, and the fault rested mainly upon my indoor skin, which gave way more than an Arab's.

So the crestfallen corporal, as the youngest and best-looking of the guard, had to stay behind, while the others carried me down the narrow stair into the street. The coolness of the night on my burning flesh, and the unmoved shining of the stars after the horror of the past hour, made me cry again. The soldiers, now free to speak, warned me that men must suffer their officer's wishes or pay for it, as I had just done, with greater suffering.

They took me over an open space, deserted and dark, and behind the Government house to a lean-to wooden room, in which were many dusty quilts. An Armenian dresser appeared, to wash and bandage me in sleepy haste. Then all went away, the last soldier delaying by my side a moment to whisper in his Druse accent that the door into the next room was not locked.

I lay there in a sick stupor, with my head aching very much, and growing slowly numb with cold, till the dawn light came shining through the cracks of the shed, and a locomotive whistled in the station. These and a draining thirst brought me to life, and I found I was in no pain. Pain of the slightest had been my obsession and secret terror, from a boy. Had I now been drugged with it, to bewilderment? Yet the first movement was anguish: in which I struggled nakedly to my feet, and rocked moaning in wonder that it was not a dream, and myself back five years ago, a timid recruit at Khalfati, where something, less staining, of the sort had happened.

The next room was a dispensary. On its door hung a suit of shoddy clothes. I put them on slowly and unhandily, because of my swollen wrists: and from the drugs chose corrosive sublimate, as safeguard against recapture. The window looked on a long blank wall. Stiffly I climbed out, and went shaking down the road towards the village, past the few people already astir. They took no notice: indeed there was nothing peculiar in my dark broadcloth, red fez and slippers: but it was only by the full urge of my tongue silently to myself that I refrained from being foolish out of sheer fright. Deraa felt inhuman with vice and cruelty, and it shocked me like cold water when a soldier laughed behind me in the street.

By the bridge were the wells, with men and women about them. A side trough was free. From its end I scooped up a little water in my hands, and rubbed it over my face; then drank, which was precious to me; and afterwards wandered along the bottom of the valley, towards the south, unobtrusively retreating out of sight. This valley provided the hidden road by which our projected raid could attain Deraa town secretly, and surprise the Turks. So, in escaping I solved, too late, the problem which had brought me to Deraa.

Further on, a Serdi, on his camel, overtook me hobbling up the road towards Nisib. I explained that I had business there, and was already footsore. He had pity and mounted me behind him on his bony animal to which I clung the rest of the way, learning the feelings of my adopted name-saint on his gridiron. The tribe's tents were just in front of the village, where I found Faris and Halim anxious about me, and curious to learn how I had fared. Halim had been up to Deraa in the night, and knew by the lack of rumour that the truth had not been discovered. I told them a merry tale of bribery and trickery, which they promised to keep to themselves, laughing aloud at the simplicity of the Turks.

During the night I managed to see the great stone bridge by Nisib. Not that my maimed will now cared a hoot about the Arab Revolt (or about anything but mending itself); yet, since the war had been a hobby of mine, for custom's sake I would force myself to push it through. Afterwards we took horse, and rode gently and carefully towards Azrak, without incident, except that a raiding party of Wuld Ali let us and our horses go unplundered when they heard who we were. This was an unexpected generosity, the Wuld Ali being not yet of our fellowship. Their consideration (rendered at once, as if we had deserved men's homage) momently stayed me to carry the burden, whose certainty the passing days confirmed: how in Deraa that night the citadel of my integrity had been irrevocably lost. . . .

I had never been a lofty person; on the contrary I had tried to be accessible to everyone, even if it continually felt as though most of them came and saw me every day. I had striven as eloquently as I could by my own example to keep plain the standard of existence. I had had no tents, no cooks, no body-servants: just my guards, who were fighting men, not servile: and behold these Byzantine shop-keepers endeavouring to corrupt our simplicity! So I flung away from them in a rage, determined to go south and see if anything active could be done, in the cold weather, about the Dead Sea, which the enemy held as a trench dividing us from Palestine.

My remaining money was handed over to Sherif Ali, for his main-tenance till the spring; and the Indians were commended to his care. Particularly we bought them fresh riding-camels, in case the need to move came suddenly upon them in the winter; though the daily news of a threat by the Turks against Azrak was scornfully discounted by young Ali. He and I took affectionate leave of one another. Ali gave me half his wardrobe: shirts, head-cloths, belts, tunics. I gave him an equivalent half of mine, and we kissed like David and Jonathan, each wearing the other's clothes. Afterwards, with Rahail only, on my two best camels, I struck away southward.

We left Azrak one evening, riding into a glowing west, while over our heads schools of cranes flew into the sunset like the out-drawn barbs of arrows. It was toilsome from the start. Night was deep by

Wadi Butum, where the conditions became even worse. All the plain was wet, and our poor camels slithered and fell time and again. We fell as often as they did, but at least our part of sitting still, between falls, was easier than their part of movement. By midnight we had crossed the Ghadaf and the quag felt too awful for further progress. Also the mishandling at Deraa had left me curiously faint; my muscles seemed at once pappy and inflamed, and all effort frightened me in anticipation. So we halted.

We slept where we were, in the mud; rose up plated with it at dawn; and smiled crackily at one another. The wind blew, and the ground began to dry. It was important, for I wanted to reach Akaba before Wood's men had left it with the return caravan, and their eight days' start called for speed. My body's reluctance to ride hard was another (and perverse) reason for forcing the march. Until noon we made poor travelling, for the camels still broke through the loose crust of flints, and foundered in the red under-clay. After noon, on the higher ground, we did better, and began rapidly to close the white sky-tents which were the Thlaithakhwat peaks.

Suddenly shots rang out at close range, and four mouthing men dashed down the slope towards us. I stopped my camel peaceably. Seeing this they jumped off, and ran to us brandishing their arms. They asked who I was: volunteering that they were Jazi Howeitat. This was an open lie, because their camel-brands were Faiz. They covered us with rifles at four yards, and told us to dismount. I laughed at them, which was good tactics with Beduin at a crisis. They were puzzled. I asked the loudest if he knew his name. He stared at me, thinking I was mad. He came nearer, with his finger on the trigger, and I bent down to him and whispered that it must be 'Teras' since no other tradesman could be so rude. As I spoke, I covered him with a pistol hidden under my cloak.

It was a shooting insult, but he was so astonished that anyone should provoke an armed man, as to give up for the moment his thought of murdering us. He took a step back, and looked around, fearful that there was a reserve somewhere, to give us confidence. At once I rode off slowly, with a creepy feeling in my back, calling Rahail to follow. They let him go too, unhurt. When we were a hundred yards away, they repented themselves, and began to shoot, but we dashed over the watershed into the next depression, and across it cantered more confidently into safe ground.

From the ridge at sunset we looked back for an instant upon the northern plain, as it sank away from us greyly, save that here and there glowed specks or great splashes of crimson fire, the reflection of the dying sun in shallow pools of rain-water on the flats. These eyes of a dripping bloody redness were so much more visible than the plain that they carried our sight miles into the haze, and seemed to hang detached in the distant sky, tilted up, like mirage.

We passed Bair long after dark, when only its latest tent-fires still shone. As we went we saw the stars mirrored in a valley bottom, and were able to water our breathless camels in a pool of yesterday's rain. After their drink, we eased them for half an hour. This night-journeying was hard on both men and animals. By day the camels saw the irregularities of their path, and undulated over them; and the rider could swing his body to miss the jerk of a long or short stride: but by night everything was blinded, and the march racked with shocks. I had a heavy bout of fever on me, which made me angry, so that I paid no attention to Rahail's appeals for rest. That young man had maddened all of us for months by his abundant vigour, and by laughing at our weaknesses; so this time I was determined to ride him out, showing no mercy. Before dawn he was blubbering with self-pity; but softly, lest I hear him.

Dawn in Jefer came imperceptibly through the mist like a ghost of sunlight, which left the earth untouched, and demonstrated itself as a glittering blink against the eyes alone. Things at their heads stood matt against the pearl-grey horizon, and at their feet melted softly into the ground. Our shadows had no edge: we doubted if that faint stain upon the soil below was cast by us or not. In the forenoon we reached Auda's camp; and stopped for a greeting, and a few Jauf dates. Auda could not provide us a relay of camels. We mounted again to get over the railway in the early night. Rahail was past protest now. He rode beside me white-faced, bleak and silent, wrought up only to outstay me, beginning to take a half pride in his pains.

Even had we started fair, he had the advantage anyhow over me in strength, and now I was nearly finished. Step by step I was yielding myself to a slow ache which conspired with my abating fever and the numb monotony of riding to close up the gate of my senses. I seemed at last approaching the insensibility which had always been beyond my reach: but a delectable land: for one born so slug-tissued that nothing this side fainting would let his spirit free. Now I found myself dividing into parts. There was one which went on riding wisely, sparing or helping every pace of the wearied camel. Another hovering above and to the right bent down curiously, and asked what the flesh was doing. The flesh gave no answer, for, indeed, it was conscious only of a ruling impulse to keep on and on; but a third garrulous one talked and wondered, critical of the body's self-inflicted labour, and contemptuous of the reason for effort.

The night passed in these mutual conversations. My unseeing eyes saw the dawn-goal in front; the head of the pass, below which that other world of Rumm lay out like a sunlit map, and my parts debated that the struggle might be worthy, but the end foolishness and a re-birth of trouble. The spent body toiled on doggedly and took no heed, quite rightly, for the divided selves said nothing which I was not capable of thinking in cold blood; they were all my natives. Telesius, taught by some such experience, split up the soul. Had he gone on, to the furthest limit of exhaustion, he would have seen his conceived regiment of thoughts and acts and feelings ranked around him as separate creatures; eyeing, like vultures, the passing in their midst of the common thing which gave them life.

Rahail collected me out of my death-sleep by jerking my head-stall and striking me, while he shouted that we had lost our direction, and were wandering toward the Turkish lines at Aba el Lissan. He was right, and we had to make a long cut back to reach Batra safely. We walked down the steeper portions of the pass, and then stumbled along Wadi Hafira. In its midst a gallant little Howeiti, aged perhaps four-teen, darted out against us, finger on trigger, and told us to stand and explain; which we did, laughing. The lad blushed, and pleaded that his father's camels kept him always in the field so that he had not known us either by sight or by description. He begged that we would not do him shame by betraying his error. The incident broke the tension between Rahail and myself; and, chatting, we rode out upon the Gaa. There under the tamarisk we passed the middle hour of the day in sleep, since by our slowness in the march over Batra we had lost the possibility of reaching Akaba within the three days from Azrak. The breaking of our intention we took quietly. Rumm's glory would not let a man waste himself in feverish regrets.

We rode up its valley in the early afternoon; easier now and ex-changing jests with one another, as the long winter evening crept down. When we got past the Khazail in the ascent we found the sun veiled behind level banks of low clouds in the west, and enjoyed a rich twi-light of the English sort. In Itm the mist steamed up gently from the soil, and collected into wool-white masses in each hollow. We reached

Akaba at midnight, and slept outside the camp till breakfast, when I called on Joyce, and found the caravan not yet ready to start: indeed Wood was only a few days returned.

Later came urgent orders for me to go up at once to Palestine by air. Croil flew me to Suez. Thence I went up to Allenby's headquarters beyond Gaza. He was so full of victories that my short statement that we had failed to carry a Yarmuk bridge was sufficient, and the miserable details of failure could remain concealed.

While I was still with him, word came from Chetwode that Jerusalem had fallen; and Allenby made ready to enter in the official manner which the catholic imagination of Mark Sykes had devised. He was good enough, although I had done nothing for the success, to let Clayton take me along as his staff officer for the day. The personal Staff tricked me out in their spare clothes till I looked like a major in the British Army. Dalmeny lent me red tabs, Evans his brass hat; so that I had the gauds of my appointment in the ceremony of the Jaffa gate, which for me was the supreme moment of the war. . . .

On our return to Akaba domestic affairs engaged the remaining free days. My part mostly concerned the bodyguard which I formed for private protection, as rumour gradually magnified my importance. On our first going up country from Rabegh and Yenbo, the Turks had been curious: afterwards they were annoyed; to the point of ascribing to the English the direction and motive force of the Arab Revolt, much as we used to flatter ourselves by attributing the Turkish efficiency to German influence.

However, the Turks said it often enough to make it an article of faith, and began to offer a reward of one hundred pounds for a British officer alive or dead. As time went on they not only increased the general figure, but made a special bid for me. After the capture of Akaba the price became respectable; while after we blew up Jemal Pasha they put Ali and me at the head of their list; worth twenty thousand pounds alive or ten thousand dead.

Of course, the offer was rhetorical; with no certainty whether in gold or paper, or that the money would be paid at all. Still, perhaps, it might justify some care. I began to increase my people to a troop, adding such lawless men as I found, fellows whose dash had got them into trouble elsewhere. I needed hard riders and hard livers; men proud of themselves, and without family. By good fortune three or four of this sort joined me at the first, setting a tone and standard. . . .
He examined the applicants for my service, and, thanks to him and

to the Zaagi, my other commander (a stiff man of normal officer cut), a wonderful gang of experts grew about me. The British at Akaba called them cut-throats; but they cut throats only to my order. Perhaps in others' eyes it was a fault that they would recognize no authority but mine. Yet when I was away they were kind to Major Marshall, and would hold him in incomprehensible talk about points of camels, their breeds and ailments, from dawn till night time. Marshall was very patient; and two or three of them would sit attentive by his bed-side, from the first daylight, waiting to continue his education as soon as he became conscious.

A good half (nearly fifty of the ninety) were Ageyl, the nervous limber Nejdi villagers who made the colour and the parade in Feisal's army, and whose care for their riding camels was such a feature of their service. They would call them by name, from a hundred yards away, and leave them in charge of the kit when they dismounted. The Ageyl, being mercenaries, would not do well unless well paid, and for lack of that condition had fallen into disrepute: yet the bravest single effort of the Arab war belonged to that one of them who twice swam down the subterranean water-conduit into Medina, and returned with a full report of the invested town.

I paid my men six pounds a month, the standard army wage for a man and camel, but mounted them on my own animals, so that the money was clear income: this made the service enviable, and put the eager spirits of the camp at my disposal. For my time-table's sake, since I was more busy than most, my rides were long, hard and sudden. The ordinary Arab, whose camel represented half his wealth, could not afford to founder it by travelling my speed: also such riding was painful for the man.

Consequently, I had to have with me picked riders, on my own beasts. We bought at long prices the fastest and strongest camels to be obtained. We chose them for speed and power, no matter how hard and exhausting they might be under the saddle: indeed, often we chose the hard-paced as the more enduring. They were changed or rested in our own camel-hospital when they became thin; and their riders were treated likewise. The Zaagi held each man bodily responsible for his mount's condition, and for the fitness of his saddlery.

Fellows were very proud of being in my bodyguard, which developed a professionalism almost flamboyant. They dressed like a bed of tulips, in every colour but white; for that was my constant wear, and they did not wish to seem to presume. In half an hour they would make ready for a ride of six weeks, that being the limit for which food could be carried at the saddle-bow. Baggage camels they shrank from as a disgrace. They would travel day and night at my whim, and made it a point of honour never to mention fatigue. If a new man grumbled the others would silence him, or change the current of his complaint, brutally.

They fought like devils, when I wanted, and sometimes when I did not, especially with Turks or with outsiders. For one guardsman to strike another was the last offence. They expected extravagant reward and extravagant punishment. They made boast throughout the army of their pains and gains. By this unreason in each degree they were kept apt for any effort, any risk.

Abdulla and the Zaagi ruled them, under my authority, with a savagery palliated only by the power of each man to quit the service if he wished. Yet we had but one resignation. The others, though adolescents full of carnal passion, tempted by this irregular life, well-fed, exercised, rich, seemed to sanctify their risk, to be fascinated by their suffering. Servitude, like other conduct, was profoundly modified to Eastern minds by their obsession with the antithesis between flesh and spirit. These lads took pleasure in subordination; in degrading the body: so as to throw into greater relief their freedom in equality of mind: almost they preferred servitude as richer in experience than authority, and less binding in daily care.

Consequently the relation of master and man in Arabia was at once more free and more subject than I had experienced elsewhere. Servants were afraid of the sword of justice and of the steward's whip, not because the one might put an arbitrary term to their existence, and the other print red rivers of pain about their sides, but because these were the symbols and the means to which their obedience was vowed. They had a gladness of abasement, a freedom of consent to yield to their master the last service and degree of their flesh and blood, because their spirits were equal with his and the contract voluntary. Such boundless engagement precluded humiliation, repining and regret.

In this pledging of their endurance, it disgraced men, if from weakness of nerve or insufficiency of courage, they fell short of the call. Pain was to them a solvent, a cathartic, almost a decoration, to be fairly worn while they survived it. Fear, the strongest motive in slothful man, broke down with us, since love for a cause — or for a person — was aroused. For such an object, penalties were discounted, and loyalty became open-eyed, not obedient. To it men dedicated their being, and in its possession they had no room for virtue or vice. Cheerfully they nourished it upon what they were; gave it their lives; and, greater than that, the lives of their fellowship: it being many times harder to offer than to endure sacrifice. . . .

However, for the time the Arabs were possessed, and cruelty of governance answered their need. Besides, they were blood enemies of thirty tribes, and only for my hand over them would have murdered in the ranks each day. Their feuds prevented them combining against me; while their unlikeness gave me sponsors and spies wherever I went or sent, between Akaba and Damascus, between Beersheba and Bagdad. In my service nearly sixty of them died.

With quaint justice, events forced me to live up to my bodyguard, to become as hard, as sudden, as heedless. The odds against me were heavy, and the climate cogged the die. In the short winter I outdid them, with my allies of the frost and snow: in the heat they outdid me. In endurance there was less disparity. For years before the war I had made myself trim by constant carelessness. I had learned to eat much one time: then to go two, three, or four days without food; and after to overeat. I made it a rule to avoid rules in food; and by a course of exceptions accustomed myself to no custom at all.

So, organically, I was efficient in the desert, felt neither hunger nor surfeit, and was not distracted by thought of food. On the march I could go dry between wells, and, like the Arabs, could drink greatly to-day for the thirst of yesterday and of to-morrow.

In the same way, though sleep remained for me the richest pleasure in the world, I supplied its place by the uneasy swaying in the saddle of a night-march, or failed of it for night after laborious night without undue fatigue. Such liberties came from years of control (contempt of use might well be the lesson of our manhood), and they fitted me peculiarly for our work: but, of course, in me they came half by training, half by trying, out of mixed choice and poverty, not effortlessly, as with the Arabs. Yet in compensation stood my energy of motive. Their less taut wills flagged before mine flagged, and by comparison made me seem tough and active.

Into the sources of my energy of will I dared not probe. The conception of antithetical mind and matter, which was basic in the Arab self-surrender, helped me not at all. I achieved surrender (so far as I did achieve it) by the very opposite road, through my notion that mental and physical were inseparably one: that our bodies, the universe, our thoughts and tactilities were conceived in and of the molecular sludge of matter, the universal element through which form drifted as clots and patterns of varying density. It seemed to me unthinkable that assemblages of atoms should cogitate except in atomic terms. My perverse sense of values constrained me to assume that abstract and concrete, as badges, did not denote oppositions more serious than Liberal and Conservative.

The practice of our revolt fortified the nihilist attitude in me. During it, we often saw men push themselves or be driven to a cruel extreme of endurance: yet never was there an intimation of physical break. Collapse rose always from a moral weakness eating into the body, which of itself, without traitors from within, had no power over the will. While we rode we were disbodied, unconscious of flesh or feeling: and when at an interval this excitement faded and we did see our bodies, it was with some hostility, with a contemptuous sense that they reached their highest purpose, not as vehicles of the spirit, but when, dissolved, their elements served to manure a field. . . .

'Us' proved to be about sixty men, clustered behind the ridge in two bunches, one near the bottom, one by the top. The lower was made up of peasants, on foot, blown, miserable, and yet the only warm things I had seen that day. They said their ammunition was finished, and it was all over. I assured them it was just beginning and pointed to my populous reserve ridge, saying that all arms were there in support. I told them to hurry back, refill their belts and hold on to it for good. Meanwhile we would cover their retreat by sticking here for the few minutes yet possible.

They ran off, cheered, and I walked about among the upper group quoting how one should not quit firing from one position till ready to fire from the next. In command was young Metaab, stripped to his skimp riding-drawers for hard work, with his black love-curls awry, his face stained and haggard. He was beating his hands together and crying hoarsely with baffled vexation, for he had meant to do so well in this, his first fight for us.

My presence at the last moment, when the Turks were breaking through, was bitter; and he got angrier when I said that I only wanted to study the landscape. He thought it flippancy, and screamed something about a Christian going into battle unarmed. I retorted with a quip from Clausewitz, about a rearguard effecting its purpose more by being than by doing: but he was past laughter, and perhaps with justice, for the little flinty bank behind which we sheltered was crackling with fire. The Turks, knowing we were there, had turned twenty machine-guns upon it. It was four feet high and fifty feet long, of bare flinty ribs, off which the bullets slapped deafeningly: while the air above so hummed or whistled with ricochets and chips that it felt like death to look over. Clearly we must leave very soon, and as I had no horse I went off first, with Metaab's promise that he would wait where he was if he dared, for another ten minutes.

The run warmed me. I counted my paces, to help in ranging the Turks when they ousted us; since there was only that one position for them, and it was poorly protected against the south. In losing this Motalga ridge we would probably win the battle. The horsemen held on for almost their ten minutes, and then galloped off without hurt. Metaab lent me his stirrup to hurry me along, till we found ourselves breathless among the Ageyl. It was just noon, and we had leisure and quiet in which to think.

Our new ridge was about forty feet up, and a nice shape for defence. We had eighty men on it, and more were constantly arriving. My guards were in place with their gun; Lutfi, an engine-destroyer, rushed up hotly with his two, and after him came another hundred Ageyl. The thing was becoming a picnic, and by saying 'excellent' and looking overjoyed, we puzzled the men, and made them consider the position dispassionately. The automatics were put on the skyline, with orders to fire occasional shots, short, to disturb the Turks a little, but not too much, after the expedient of Massena in delaying enemy deployment. Otherwise a lull fell; I lay down in a sheltered place which caught a little sun, and no wind, and slept a blessed hour, while the Turks occupied the old ridge, extending over it like a school of geese, and about as wisely. Our men left them alone, being contented with a free exhibition of themselves.

In the middle of the afternoon Zeid arrived, with Mastur, Rasim and Abdulla. They brought our main body comprising twenty mounted infantry on mules, thirty Motalga horsemen, two hundred villagers, five automatic rifles, four machine-guns and the Egyptian Army mountain gun which had fought about Medina, Petra and Jurf. This was magnificent, and I woke up to welcome them.

The Turks saw us crowding, and opened with shrapnel and machine-gun fire: but they had not the range and fumbled it. We reminded one another that movement was the law of strategy, and started moving. Rasim became a cavalry officer, and mounted with all our eighty riders of animals to make a circuit about the eastern ridge and envelop the enemy's left wing, since the books advised attack not upon a line, but upon a point, and by going far enough along any finite wing it would be found eventually reduced to a point of one single man: Rasim liked this, my conception of his target.

He promised, grinningly, to bring us that last man: but Hamd el Arar took the occasion more fittingly. Before riding off he devoted himself to the death for the Arab cause, drew his sword ceremoniously, and made to it, by name, a heroic speech. Rasim took five automatic guns with him; which was good.

We in the centre paraded about, so that their departure might be unseen of the enemy, who were bringing up an apparently endless procession of machine-guns and dressing them by the left at intervals along the ridge as though in a museum. It was lunatic tactics. The ridge was flint, without cover for a lizard. We had seen how, when a bullet struck the ground, it and the ground spattered up in a shower of deadly chips. Also we knew the range and elevated our Vickers guns carefully, blessing their long, old-fashioned sights; our mountain gun was propped into place ready to let go a sudden burst of shrapnel over the enemy when Rasim was at grips.

As we waited, a reinforcement was announced of one hundred men from Aima. They had fallen out with Zeid over war-wages the day previous, but had grandly decided to sink old scores in the crisis. Their arrival convinced us to abandon Marshal Foch and to attack from, at any rate, three sides at once. So we sent the Aima men, with three automatic guns, to outflank the right, or western wing. Then we opened against the Turks from our central position, and bothered their exposed lines with hits and ricochets.

The enemy felt the day no longer favourable. It was passing, and sunset often gave victory to defenders yet in place. Old General Hamid Fakhri collected his Staff and Headquarters, and told each man to take a rifle. 'I have been forty years a soldier, but never saw I rebels fight like these. Enter the ranks' . . . but he was too late. Rasim pushed forward an attack of his five automatic guns, each with its two-man crew. They went in rapidly, unseen till they were in position, and crumpled the Turkish left.

The Aima men, who knew every blade of grass on these, their own village pastures, crept, unharmed, within three hundred yards of the Turkish machine-guns. The enemy, held by our frontal threat, first knew of the Aima men when they, by a sudden burst of fire, wiped out the gun-teams and flung the right wing into disorder. We saw it, and cried advance to the camel men and levies about us.

Mohamed el Ghasib, comptroller of Zeyd's household, led them on his camel, in shining wind-billowed robes, with the crimson banner of the Ageyl over his head. All who had remained in the centre with us, our servants, gunners and machine-gunners, rushed after him in a wide vivid line.

The day had been too long for me, and I was now only shaking with desire to see the end: but Zeid beside me clapped his hands with joy at the beautiful order of our plan unrolling in the frosty redness of the setting sun. On the one hand Rasim's cavalry were sweeping a broken left wing into the pit beyond the ridge: on the other the men of Aima were bloodily cutting down fugitives. The enemy centre was pouring back in disorder through the gap, with our men after them on foot, on horse, on camel. The Armenians, crouching behind us all day anxiously, now drew their knives and howled to one another in Turkish as they leaped forward.

I thought of the depths between here and Kerak, the ravine of Hesa, with its broken, precipitous paths, the undergrowth, the narrows and defiles of the way. It was going to be a massacre and I should have been crying-sorry for the enemy; but after the angers and exertions of the battle my mind was too tired to care to go down into that awful place and spend the night saving them. By my decision to fight, I had killed twenty or thirty of our six hundred men, and the wounded would be perhaps three times as many. It was one-sixth of our force gone on a verbal triumph, for the destruction of this thousand poor Turks would not affect the issue of the war.

In the end we had taken their two mountain howitzers (Skoda guns, very useful to us), twenty-seven machine-guns, two hundred horses and mules, two hundred and fifty prisoners. Men said only fifty got back, exhausted fugitives, to the railway. The Arabs on their track rose against them and shot them ignobly as they ran. Our own men gave up the pursuit quickly, for they were tired and sore and hungry, and it was pitifully cold. A battle might be thrilling at the moment for generals, but usually their imagination played too vividly beforehand, and made the reality seem sham; so quiet and unimportant that they ranged about looking for its fancied core. This evening there was no glory left, but the terror of the broken flesh, which had been our own men, carried past us to their homes.

As we turned back it began to snow; and only very late, and by a last effort did we get our hurt men in. The Turkish wounded lay out, and were dead next day. It was indefensible, as was the whole theory of war: but no special reproach lay on us for it. We risked our lives in the blizzard (the chill of victory bowing us down) to save our own fellows; and if our rule was not to lose Arabs to kill even many Turks, still less might we lose them to save Turks.

Next day and the next it snowed yet harder. We were weather-bound, and as the days passed in monotony we lost the hope of doing. We should have pushed past Kerak on the heels of victory, frighting the Turks to Amman with our rumour: as it was, nothing came of all the loss and effort, except a report which I sent over to the British headquarters in Palestine for the Staff's consumption. It was meanly written for effect, full of quaint similes and mock simplicities; and made them think me a modest amateur, doing his best after the great models; not a clown, leering after them where they with Foch, band-master, at their head went drumming down the old road of effusion of blood into the house of Clausewitz. Like the battle, it was nearly-proof parody of regulation use. Headquarters loved it, and innocently, to crown the jest, offered me a decoration on the strength of it. We should have more bright breasts in the Army if each man was able without witnesses, to write out his own despatch. . . .

For myself I felt quite fresh and happy, averse from the delay of needless tribal hospitality. Zeid's penniless state was excellent pretext for a trial of strength with the Edomite winter. Shobek was only ten miles further, and daylight had yet five hours to run. So I decided to go on alone. It would be quite safe, for in such weather neither Turk nor Arab was abroad, and the roads were mine. I took their four thousand pounds from Serj and Rameid, and cursed them into the valley for cowards: which really they were not. Rameid was catching his breath in great sobs, and Serj's nervous pain marked each lurch of his camel with a running moan. They raved with miserable rage when I dismissed them and turned away.

The truth was that I had the best camel. The excellent Wodheiha struggled gamely forward under the weight of the extra gold. In flat places I rode her: at ascents and descents we used to slide together side by side with comic accidents, which she seemed rather to enjoy.

By sunset the snow-fall ceased; we were coming down to the river of Shobek, and could see a brown track straggling over the opposite hill towards the village. I tried a short cut, but the frozen crust of the mud-banks deceived me, and I crashed through the cat-ice (which was sharp, like knives) and bogged myself so deeply that I feared I was going to pass the night there, half in and half out of the sludge: or wholly in which would be a tidier death.

Wodheiha, sensible beast, had refused to enter the morass: but she stood at a loss on the hard margin, and looked soberly at my mud-larking. However, I managed, with the still-held head-stall, to per-suade her a little nearer. Then I flung my body suddenly backward against the squelching quag, and, grabbing wildly behind my head, laid hold of her fetlock. She was frightened, and started back: and her purchase dragged me clear. We crawled farther down the bed to a safe place, and there crossed: after I had hesitatingly sat in the stream and washed off the weight of stinking clay.

Shiveringly I mounted again. We went over the ridge and down to the base of the shapely cone, whose mural crown was the ring-wall of the old castle of Monreale, very noble against the night sky. The chalk was hard, and it was freezing; snow-drifts lay a foot deep each side of the spiral path which wound up the hill. The white ice crackled desolately under my naked feet as we neared the gate, where, to make a stage entry, I climbed up by Wodheiha's patient shoulder into the saddle. Then I repented, since only by throwing myself sideways along her neck did I avoid the voussoirs of the arch as she crashed underneath in half-terror of this strange place.

I knew that Sherif Abd el Main should be still at Shobek, so rode boldly up the silent street in the reeded starlight, which played with the white icicles and their underlying shadow among the walls and snowy roofs and ground. The camel stumbled doubtfully over steps hidden beneath a thick covering of snow: but I had no care of that, having reached my night's goal, and having so powdery a blanket to fall on. At the crossways I called out the salutation of a fair night: and after a minute, a husky voice protested to God through the thick sacking which stuffed a loophole of the mean house on my right. I asked for Abd el Mayein, and was told 'in the Government house' which lay at the further end of the old castle's enceinte.

Arrived there I called again. A door was flung open, and a cloud of smoky light streamed recklessly across, whirling with motes, through which black faces peered to know who I was. I hailed them friendly, by name, saying that I was come to eat a sheep with the master: upon which these slaves ran out, noisy with astonishment, and relieved me of Wodheiha, whom they led into the reeking stable where themselves lived. One lit me with a flaming spar up the stone outside stairs to the house door, and between more servants, down a winding passage dripping with water from the broken roof, into a tiny room. There lay Abd el Muein upon a carpet, face down, breathing the least smoky level of air.

My legs were shaky, so I dropped beside him, and gladly copied his position to avoid the choking fumes of a brass brazier of flaming wood which crackled in a recessed shot-window of the mighty outer wall. He searched out for me a waist-cloth, while I stripped off my things and hung them to steam before the fire, which became less smarting to the eyes and throat as it burned down into red coals. Meanwhile Abd el Mayin clapped his hands for supper to be hastened and served 'Fauzan' (tea in Harith slang, so named from his cousin, governor of their village) hot and spiced and often, till the mutton, boiled with raisins in butter, was carried in.

He explained, with his blessings on the dish, that next day they would starve or rob, since he had here two hundred men, and no food or money, and his messengers to Feisal were held up in the snow. Whereat I, too, clapped hands, commanding my saddle-bags, and presented him with five hundred pounds on account, till his subsidy came. This was good payment for the food, and we were very merry over my oddness of riding alone, in winter, with a hundredweight and more of gold for baggage. I repeated that Zeid, like himself, was straitened; and told of Serj and Rameid with the Arabs. The Sherif's eyes darkened and he made passes in the air with his riding-stick. I explained, in extenuation of their failure, that the cold did not trouble me, since the English climate was of this sort most of the year. 'God forbid it,' said Abd el Muyein. . . .

In the morning I rose with a splitting headache, and said I must go on. Two men were found to ride with me, though all said we should not reach Tafileh that night. However, I thought it could not be worse than yesterday; so we skated timorously down the rapid path to the plain across which still stretched the Roman road with its groups of fallen milestones, inscribed by famous emperors.

From this plain the two faint-hearts with me slipped back to their fellows on the castle-hill. I proceeded, alternately on and off my camel, like the day before, though now the way was all too slippery, except on the ancient paving, the last footprint of Imperial Rome which had once so much more preciously, played the Turk to the desert dwellers. On it I could ride: but I had to walk and wade the dips where the floods of fourteen centuries had washed the road's foundations out. Rain came on, and soaked me, and then it blew fine and freezing till I crackled in armour of white silk, like a theatre knight: or like a bridal cake, hard iced.

The camel and I were over the plain in three hours; wonderful going: but our troubles were not ended. The snow was indeed as my guides had said, and completely hid the path, which wound uphill between walls and ditches, and confused piles of stone. It cost me an infinity of pain to turn the first two corners. Wodheiha, tired of wading to her bony knees in useless white stuff, began perceptibly to flag. However, she got up one more steep bit, only to miss the edge of the path in a banked place. We fell together some eighteen feet down the hill-side into a yard-deep drift of frozen snow. After the fall she rose to her feet whimpering and stood still, in a tremble.

When he-camels so baulked, they would die on their spot, after days; and I feared that now I had found the limit of effort in she-camels. I plunged to my neck in front of her, and tried to tow her out, vainly. Then I spent a long time hitting her behind. I mounted, and she sat down, I jumped off, heaved her up, and wondered if, perhaps, it was that the drift was too thick. So I carved her a beautiful little road, a foot wide, three deep, and eighteen paces long, using my bare feet and hands as tools. The snow was so frozen on the surface that it took all my weight, first to break it down, and then to scoop it out. The crust was sharp, and cut my wrists and ankles till they bled freely, and the roadside became lined with pink crystals, looking like pale, very pale, water-melon flesh.

Afterwards I went back to Wodheiha, patiently standing there, and climbed into the saddle. She started easily. We went running at it, and such was her speed that the rush carried her right over the shallow stuff, back to the proper road. Up this we went cautiously, with me afoot, sounding the path in front with my stick, or digging new passes when the drifts were deep. In three hours we were on the summit, and found it wind-swept on the western side. So we left the track, and scrambled unsteadily along the very broken crest, looking down across the chess-board houses of Dana village, into sunny Arabah, fresh and green thousands of feet below.

When the ridge served no more we did further heavy work, and at last Wodheiha baulked again. It was getting serious, for the evening was near; suddenly I realized the loneliness, and that if the night found us yet beyond help on this hill-top, Wodheiha would die, and she was a very noble beast. There was also the solid weight of gold, and I felt not sure how far, even in Arabia, I could safely put six thousand sovereigns by the roadside with a signet as mark of ownership, and leave them for a night. So I took her back a hundred yards along our beaten track, mounted, and charged her at the bank. She responded. We burst through and over the northern lip which looked down on the Senussi village of Rasheidiya.

This face of the hill, sheltered from the wind and open to the sun all afternoon, had thawed. Underneath the superficial snow lay wet and muddy ground; and when Wodheiha ran upon this at speed her feet went from under her and she sprawled, with her four feet locked. So on her tail, with me yet in the saddle, we went sliding round and down a hundred feet. Perhaps it hurt the tail (there were stones under the snow) for on the level she sprang up unsteadily, grunting, and lashed it about like a scorpion's. Then she began to run at ten miles an hour down the greasy path towards Rasheidiya, sliding and plunging wildly: with me, in terror of a fall and broken bones, clinging to the horns of the saddle.

A crowd of Arabs, Zeid's men, weather-bound here on their way to Feysal, ran out when they heard her trumpeting approach, and shouted with joy at so distinguished an entry to the village. I asked them the news; they told me all was well. Then I remounted, for the last eight miles into Tafileh, where I gave Zeid his letters and some money, and went gladly to bed . . . flea-proof for another night.

They told us Jericho was just taken. I went through to Allenby's headquarters. Hogarth was there on the platform. To him I confessed that I had made a mess of things: and had come to beg Allenby to find me some smaller part elsewhere. I had put all myself into the Arab business, and had come to wreck because of my sick judgement; the occasion being Zeid, own brother to Feisal, and a little man I really liked. I now had no tricks left worth a meal in the Arab market-place, and wanted the security of custom: to be conveyed; to pillow myself on duty and obedience: irresponsibly.

I complained that since landing in Arabia I had had options and requests, never an order: that I was tired to death of free-will, and of many things beside free-will. For a year and a half I had been in motion, riding a thousand miles each month upon camels: with added nervous hours in crazy aeroplanes, or rushing across country in power-ful cars. In my last five actions I had been hit, and my body so dreaded further pain that now I had to force myself under fire. Generally I had been hungry: lately always cold: and frost and dirt had poisoned my hurts into a festering mass of sores.

However, these worries would have taken their due petty place, in my despite of the body, and of my soiled body in particular, but for the rankling fraudulence which had to be my mind's habit: that pretence to lead the national uprising of another race, the daily posturing in alien dress, preaching in alien speech: with behind it a sense that the 'promises' on which the Arabs worked were worth what their armed strength would be when the moment of fulfilment came. . . .

There was no escape for me. I must take up again my mantle of fraud in the East. With my certain contempt for half-measures I took it up quickly and wrapped myself in it completely. . . .

As I road up the bank my camel's feet scrambled in the loose ballast, and out of the long shadow of a culvert to my left, where, no doubt, he had slept all day, rose a Turkish soldier. He glanced wildly at me and at the pistol in my hand, and then with sadness at his rifle against the abutment, yards beyond. He was a young man; stout, but sulky-looking. I stared at him, and said softly, 'God is merciful'. He knew the sound and sense of the Arabic phrase, and raised his eyes like a flash to mine, while his heavy sleep-ridden face began slowly to change into incredulous joy.

However, he said not a word. I pressed my camel's hairy shoulder with my foot, she picked her delicate stride across the metals and down the further slope, and the little Turk was man enough not to shoot me in the back, as I rode away, feeling warm towards him, as ever towards a life one has saved. At a safe distance I glanced back. He put thumb to nose, and twinkled his fingers at me. . . .

We reached it together, and found there one dead Turk, and Farraj terribly wounded through the body, lying by the arch just as he had fallen from his camel. He looked unconscious; but, when we dismounted, greeted us, and then fell silent, sunken in that loneliness which came to hurt men who believed death near. We tore his clothes away and looked uselessly at the wound. The bullet had smashed right through him, and his spine seemed injured. The Arabs said at once that he had only a few hours to live.

We tried to move him, for he was helpless, though he showed no pain. We tried to stop the wide, slow bleeding, which made poppy-splashes in the grass; but it seemed impossible, and after a while he told us to let him alone, as he was dying, and happy to die, since he had no care of life. Indeed, for long he had been so, and men very tired and sorry often fell in love with death, with that triumphal weakness coming home after strength has been vanquished in a last battle.

While we fussed about him Abd el Latif shouted an alarm. He could see about fifty Turks working up the line towards us, and soon after a motor trolley was heard coming from the north. We were only sixteen men, and had an impossible position. I said we must retire at once, carrying Farraj with us. They tried to lift him, first in his cloak, afterwards in a blanket; but consciousness was coming back, and he screamed so pitifully that we had not the heart to hurt him more.

We could not leave him where he was, to the Turks, because we had seen them burn alive our hapless wounded. For this reason we were all agreed, before action, to finish off one another, if badly hurt: but I had never realized that it might fall to me to kill Farraj.

I knelt down beside him, holding my pistol near the ground by his head, so that he should not see my purpose; but he must have guessed it, for he opened his eyes, and clutched me with his harsh, scaly hand, the tiny hand of these unripe Nejd fellows. I waited a moment, and he said, 'Daud will be angry with you', the old smile coming back so strangely to this grey shrinking face. I replied, 'Salute him from me'. He returned the formal answer, 'God will give you peace', and at last wearily closed his eyes.

The Turkish trolley was now very close, swaying down the line towards us like a dung-beetle: and its machine-gun bullets stung the air about our heads as we fled back into the ridges. Mohsin led Farraj's camel, on which were his sheepskin and trappings, still with the shape of his body in them just as he had fallen by the bridge. Near dark we halted; and the Zaagi came whispering to me that all were wrangling as to who should ride the splendid animal next day. He wanted her for himself; but I was bitter that these perfected dead had again robbed my poverty: and to cheapen the great loss with a little one I shot the poor beast with my second bullet. . . .

Our acquaintance of before the war had been renewed secretly a year before, when three of us crept in after sunset to their rich family tents near Ziza. Fawaz, the senior Faiz, was a notable Arab, a committee-man of the Damascus group, prominent in the party of independence. He received me with fair words and hospitality, fed us richly, and brought out, after we had talked, his richest bed-quilts.

I had slept an hour or two when a charged voice whispered through a smoke-smelling beard into my ear. It was Nawaf, the brother, to say that, behind the friendly seeming, Fawaz had sent horsemen to Ziza and soon the troops would be here to take me. We were certainly caught. My Arabs crouched in their place, meaning to fight like cornered animals, and kill at least some of the enemy before they themselves died. Such tactics displeased me. When combats came to the physical, bare hand against hand, I was finished. The disgust of being touched revolted me more than the thought of death and defeat: perhaps because one such terrible struggle in my youth had given me an enduring fear of contact: or because I so reverenced my wits and despised my body that I would not be beholden to the second for the life of the first.

I whispered to Nawaf for counsel. He crawled back through the tent-curtain; we followed dragging my few things in their light saddle-pouch. Behind the next tent, his own, sat the camels, knee-haltered and saddled. We mounted circumspectly. Nawaf led out his mare, and guided us, loaded rifle across his thigh, to the railway and beyond it into the desert. There he gave us the star-direction of our supposed goal in Bair. A few days later Sheikh Fawaz was dead.

TO V. W. RICHARDS

15.7.18

Well, it was wonderful to see your writing again, and very difficult to read it: also pleasant to have a letter which doesn't begin 'Reference your GS 102487b of the 45th'. Army prose is bad, and one has so much of it that one fears contamination in one's own. I cannot write to anyone just now. Your letter came to me in Aba Lissan, a little hill-fort on the plateau of Arabia S.E. of the Dead Sea, and I carried it with me down to Akaba, to Jidda, and then here to answer. Yet with all that I have had it only a month, and you wrote it three months ago. This letter will be submarined, and then it is all over for another three years.

It always seemed to me that your eyes would prevent all service for you, and that in consequence you might preserve your continuity. For myself, I have been so violently uprooted and plunged so deeply into a job too big for me, that everything feels unreal. I have dropped everything I ever did, and live only as a thief of opportunity, snatching chances of the moment when and where I see them. My people have probably told you that the job is to foment an Arab rebellion against Turkey, and for that I have to try and hide my frankish exterior, and be as little out of the Arab picture as I can. So it's a kind of foreign stage, on which one plays day and night, in fancy dress, in a strange language, with the price of failure on one's head if the part is not well filled.

You guessed rightly that the Arab appealed to my imagination. It is the old, old civilization, which has refined itself clear of household gods, and half the trappings which ours hastens to assume. The gospel of bareness in materials is a good one, and it involves apparently a sort of moral bareness too. They think for the moment, and endeavour to slip through life without turning corners or climbing hills. In part it is a mental and moral fatigue, a race trained out, and to avoid difficulties they have to jettison so much that we think honourable and grave: and yet without in any way sharing their point of view, I think I can understand it enough to look at myself and other foreigners from their direction, and without condemning it. I know I'm a stranger to them, and always will be: but I cannot believe them worse, any more than I could change to their ways.

This is a very long porch to explain why I'm always trying to blow up railway trains and bridges instead of looking for the Well at the World's End. Anyway these years of detachment have cured me of any desire ever to do anything for myself. When they untie my bonds I will not find in me any spur to action. However actually one never thinks of afterwards: the time from the beginning is like one of those dreams which seems to last for aeons, and then you wake up with a start, and find that it has left nothing in your mind. Only the different thing about this dream is that so many people do not wake up in this life again.

I cannot imagine what my people can have told you. Until now we have only been preparing the groundwork and basis of our revolt, and do not yet stand on the brink of action. Whether we are going to win or lose, when we do strike, I cannot ever persuade myself. The whole thing is such a play, and one cannot put conviction into one's day dreams. If we succeed I will have done well with the materials given me, and that disposes of your 'lime light'. If we fail, and they have patience, then I suppose we will go on digging foundations. Achievement, if it comes, will be a great disillusionment, but not great enough to wake one up.

Your mind has evidently moved far since 1914. That is a privilege you have won by being kept out of the mist for so long. You'll find the rest of us aged undergraduates, possibly still unconscious of our unfitting grey hair. For that reason I cannot follow or return your steps. A house with no action entailed upon one, quiet, and liberty to think and abstain as one wills — yes, I think abstention, the leaving everything alone and watching the others still going past, is what I would choose today, if they ceased driving one. This may be only the reaction from four years opportunism, and is not worth trying to resolve into terms of geography and employment.

Of course the ideal is that of the lords who are still certainly expected, but the certainty is not for us, I'm afraid. Also for very few would the joy be so perfect as to be silent. Those words, peace, silence, rest, and the others take on a vividness in the midst of noise and worry and weariness like a lighted window in the dark. Yet what on earth is the good of a lighted window? and perhaps it is only because one is over-borne and tired. You know when one marches across an interminable plain a hill (which is still the worst hill on earth) is a banquet, and after searing heat cold water takes on a quality (what would they have said about this word before?) impossible in the eyes of a fen-farmer. Probably I'm only a sensitized film, turned black or white by the objects projected on me: and if so what hope is there that next week or year, or tomorrow, can be prepared for today?

This is an idiot letter, and amounts to nothing except cry for a further change which is idiocy, for I change my abode every day, and my job every two days, and my language every three days, and still remain always unsatisfied. I hate being in front, and I hate being back and I don't like responsibility, and I don't obey orders. Altogether no good just now. A long quiet like a purge and then a contemplation and decision of future roads, that is what [there] is to look forward to.

You want apparently some vivid colouring of an Arab costume, or of a flying Turk, and we have it all, for that is part of the mise en scène of the successful raider, and hitherto I am that. My bodyguard of fifty Arab tribesmen, picked riders from the young men of the deserts, are more splendid than a tulip garden, and we ride like lunatics and with our Beduins pounce on unsuspecting Turks and destroy them in heaps: and it is all very gory and nasty after we close grips. I love the preparation, and the journey, and loathe the physical fighting. Disguises, and prices on one's head, and fancy exploits are all part of the pose: how to reconcile it with the Oxford pose I know not. Were we flamboyant there?

If you reply — you will perceive I have matting of the brain — and your thoughts are in control, please tell me of Berry,[1] and if possible, Winkworth.[1] The latter was the man for all these things, because he would take a baresark beery pleasure in physical outputs. Very many thanks for writing. It has opened a very precious casement.

L.

from SEVEN PILLARS OF WISDOM

AT Guweira, Siddons had an aeroplane waiting. Nuri Shaalan and Feisal wanted me at once in Jefer. The air was thin and bumpy, so that we hardly scraped over the crest of Shtar. I sat wondering if we would crash, almost hoping it. I felt sure Nuri was about to claim fulfilment of our dishonourable half-bargain, whose execution seemed more impure than its thought. Death in the air would be a clean escape; yet I scarcely hoped it, not from fear, for I was too tired to be much afraid: nor from scruple, for our lives seemed to me absolutely our own, to keep or give away: but from habit, for lately I had risked myself only when it seemed profitable to our cause.

I was busy compartmenting-up my mind, finding instinct and reason as ever at strong war. Instinct said 'Die', but reason said that was only to cut the mind's tether, and loose it into freedom: better to seek some mental death, some slow wasting of the brain to sink it below these puzzlements. An accident was meaner than deliberate fault. If I did not hesitate to risk my life, why fuss to dirty it? Yet life and honour seemed in different categories, not able to be sold one for another: and for honour, had I not lost that a year ago when I assured the Arabs that England kept her plighted word?

Or was honour like the Sybil's leaves, the more that was lost the more precious the little left? Its part equal to the whole? My self-secrecy had left me no arbiter of responsibility. The debauch of physical work yet ended in a craving for more, while the everlasting doubt, the questioning, bound up my mind in a giddy spiral and left me never space for thought.

[1] Friends of their undergraduate days.

So we came at last, alive, to Jefer, where met us Feisal and Nuri in the smoothest spirits, with no mention of my price. It seemed incredible that this old man had freely joined our youth. For he was very old; livid, and worn, with a grey sorrow and remorse about him and a bitter smile the only mobility of his face. Upon his coarse eyelashes the eyelids sagged down in tired folds, through which, from the overhead sun, a red light glittered into his eye-sockets and made them look like fiery pits in which the man was slowly burning. Only the dead black of his dyed hair, only the dead skin of the face, with its net of lines, betrayed his seventy years. . . .

The irony was in my loving objects before life or ideas; the incongruity in my answering the infectious call of action, which laid weight on the diversity of things. It was a hard task for me to straddle feeling and action. I had had one craving all my life — for the power of self-expression in some imaginative form — but had been too diffuse ever to acquire a technique. At last accident, with perverted humour, in casting me as a man of action had given me place in the Arab Revolt, a theme ready and epic to a direct eye and hand, thus offering me an outlet in literature, the technique-less art. Whereupon I became excited only over mechanism. The epic mode was alien to me, as to my generation. Memory gave me no clue to the heroic, so that I could not feel such men as Auda in myself. He seemed fantastic as the hills of Rumm, old as Mallory.

Among the Arabs I was the disillusioned, the sceptic, who, envied their cheap belief. The unperceived sham looked so well-fitting and becoming a dress for shoddy man. The ignorant, the superficial, the deceived were the happy among us. By our swindle they were glorified. We paid for them our self-respect, and they gained the deepest feeling of their lives. The more we condemned and despised ourselves, the more we could cynically take pride in them, our creatures. It was so easy to overcredit others: so impossible to write down their motives to the level of our own uncharitable truth. They were our dupes, wholeheartedly fighting the enemy. They blew before our intentions like chaff, being not chaff, but the bravest, simplest and merriest of men. *Credo quia sum?* But did not the being believed by many make for a distorted righteousness? The mounting together of the devoted hopes of years from near-sighted multitudes, might endow even an unwilling idol with Godhead, and strengthen It whenever men prayed silently to Him. . . .

King Hussein behaved truly to type, protesting fluently, with endless circumlocution, showing no understanding of the grave effect of his incursion into Northern Army affairs. To clear his mind we sent him plain statements which drew abusive but involved returns. His telegrams came through Egypt and by wireless to our operators in Akaba, and were sent up to me by car, for delivery to Feisal. The Arabic ciphers were simple, and I had undesirable passages mutilated by rearranging their figures into nonsense, before handing them in code to Feisal. By this easy expedient the temper of his entourage was not needlessly complicated.

The play went on for several days, Mecca never repeating a message notified corrupt, but telegraphing in its place a fresh version toned down at each re-editing from the previous harshness. Finally, there came a long message, the first half a lame apology and withdrawal of the mischievous proclamation, the second half a repetition of the offence in a new form. I suppressed the tail, and took the head marked 'very urgent' to Feisal's tent, where he sat in the full circle of his staff officers.

His secretary worked out the despatch, and handed the decipher to Feisal. My hints had roused expectation, and all eyes were on him as he read it. He was astonished, and gazed wonderingly at me, for the meek words were unlike his father's querulous obstinacy. Then he pulled himself together, read the apology aloud, and at the end said thrillingly, 'The telegraph has saved all our honour'.

A chorus of delight burst out, during which he bent aside to whisper in my ear, 'I mean the honour of nearly all of us'. It was done so delightfully that I laughed, and said demurely, 'I cannot understand what you mean'. He replied, 'I offered to serve for this last march under your orders: why was that not enough?' 'Because it would not go with your honour'. He murmured, 'You prefer mine always before your own', and then sprang energetically to his feet, saying, 'Now, Sirs, praise God and work'.

In three hours we had settled time-tables, and arranged for our successors here in Aba el Lissan, with their spheres and duties. I took my leave. Joyce had just returned to us from Egypt, and Feisal promised that he would come, with him and Marshall, to Azrak to join me on the twelfth at latest. All the camp was happy as I got into a Rolls tender and set off northward, hoping yet to rally the Rualla under Nuri Shaalan in time for our attack on Deraa. . . .

My bodyguard waited in two long lines on the hill-side. Joyce was staying at Tell Arar as covering force, with a hundred of Nuri Said's

THE ESSENTIAL T. E. LAWRENCE

men, the Rualla, the Ghurkas and the cars; while we slipped across to break the Palestine Railway. My party would look like Beduins, so I determined to move openly to Mezerib by the quickest course, for we were very late.

Unfortunately we drew enemy attention. An aeroplane crawled over us, dropping bombs: one, two, three, misses: the fourth into our midst. Two of my men went down. Their camels, in bleeding masses, struggled on the ground. The men had not a scratch, and leaped up behind two of their friends. Another machine floated past us, its engine cut off. Two more bombs, and a shock which spun my camel round, and knocked me half out of the saddle with a burning numbness in my right elbow. I felt I was hard hit, and began to cry for the pity of it: to be put out just when another day's control would have meant a vast success. The blood was running down my arm: perhaps if I did not look at it I might carry on as if I were unhurt.

My camel swung to a spatter of machine-gun bullets. I clutched at the pommel, and found my damaged arm there and efficient. I had judged it blown off. My left hand threw the cloak aside and explored for the wound — to feel only a very hot little splinter of metal, too light to do real harm after driving through the massed folds of my cloak. The trifle showed how much my nerve was on edge. Curiously enough it was the first time I had been hit from the air. . . .

Meanwhile it was breakfast time with a smell of sausage in the air. We sat round, very ready: but the watcher on the broken tower yelled 'Aeroplane up', seeing one coming over from Deraa. Our Australians, scrambling wildly to their yet-hot machines, started them in a moment. Ross Smith, with his observer, leaped into one, and climbed like a cat up the sky. After him went Peters, while the third pilot stood beside the D.H.9 and looked hard at me.

I seemed not to understand him. Lewis guns, scarfe mountings, sights, rings which turned, vanes, knobs which rose and fell on swinging parallel bars; to shoot, one aimed with this side of the ring or with that, according to the varied speed and direction of oneself and the enemy. I had been told the theory, could repeat some of it: but it was in my head, and rules of action were only snares of action till they had run out of the empty head into the hands, by use. No: I was not going up to air-fight, no matter what caste I lost with the pilot. He was an Australian, of a race delighting in additional risks, not an Arab to whose gallery I must play.

He was too respectful to speak: only he looked reproach at me while
we watched the battle in the air. There were one enemy two-seater
and three scouts. Ross Smith fastened on the big one, and, after five
minutes of sharp machine-gun rattle, the German dived suddenly
towards the railway line. As it flashed behind the low ridge, there
broke out a pennon of smoke, and from its falling place a soft, dark
cloud. An 'Ah!' came from the Arabs about us. Five minutes later
Ross Smith was back, and jumped gaily out of his machine, swearing
that the Arab front was the place. Our sausages were still hot. . . .

The nearer two thousand seemed more our size. We would meet
them with half our regulars, and two of Pisani's guns. Tallal was
anxious, for their indicated route would bring them through Tafas,
his own village. He determined us to make speed there and seize the
ridge south of it. Unfortunately speed was only a relative term with
men so tired. I rode with my troop to Tafas, hoping to occupy a
shadow position beyond it and fight a retiring action till the rest came
up. Half-way on the road, there met us mounted Arabs, herding a
drove of stripped prisoners towards Sheikh Saad. They were driving
them mercilessly, the bruises of their urging blue across the ivory backs;
but I left them to it, for these were Turks of the police battalion of
Deraa, beneath whose iniquities the peasant-faces of the neighbourhood
had run with tears and blood, innumerable times.

The Arabs told us that the Turkish column — Jemal Pasha's lancer
regiment — was already entering Tafas. When we got within sight,
we found they had taken the village (from which sounded an occasional
shot) and were halted about it. Small pyres of smoke were going up
from between the houses. On the rising ground to this side, knee-deep
in the thistles, stood a remnant of old men, women and children, telling
terrible stories of what had happened when the Turks rushed in an hour
before. . . .

Nuri came with Pisani. Before their ranks rode Auda abu Tayi,
expectant, and Tallal, nearly frantic with the tales his people poured out
of the sufferings of the village. The last Turks were now quitting it.
We slipped down behind them to end Tallal's suspense, while our
infantry took position and fired strongly with the Hotchkiss; Pisani
advanced his half battery among them; so that the French high
explosive threw the rearguard into confusion.

The village lay stilly under its slow wreaths of white smoke, as we
rode near, on our guard. Some grey heaps seemed to hide in the long

grass, embracing the ground in the close way of corpses. We looked away from these, knowing they were dead; but from one a little figure tottered off, as if to escape us. It was a child, three or four years old, whose dirty smock was stained red over one shoulder and side, with blood from a large half-fibrous wound, perhaps a lance thrust, just where neck and body joined.

The child ran a few steps, then stood and cried to us in a tone of astonishing strength (all else being very silent), 'Don't hit me, Baba'.[1] Abd el Aziz, choking out something — this was his village, and she might be of his family — flung himself off his camel, and stumbled, kneeling, in the grass beside the child. His suddenness frightened her, for she threw up her arms and tried to scream; but, instead, dropped in a little heap, while the blood rushed out again over her clothes; then, I think, she died.

We rode past the other bodies of men and women and four more dead babies, looking very soiled in the daylight, towards the village; whose loneliness we now knew meant death and horror. By the outskirts were low mud walls, sheepfolds, and on one something red and white. I looked close and saw the body of a woman folded across it, bottom upwards, nailed there by a saw bayonet whose haft stuck hideously into the air from between her naked legs. She had been pregnant, and about her lay others, perhaps twenty in all, variously killed, but set out in accord with an obscene taste.

The Zaagi burst into wild peals of laughter, the more desolate for the warm sunshine and clear air of this upland afternoon. I said, 'The best of you brings me the most Turkish dead', and we turned after the fading enemy, on our way shooting down those who had fallen out by the roadside, and came imploring our pity. One wounded Turk, half naked, not able to stand, sat and wept to us. Abdulla turned away his camel's head, but the Zaagi, with curses, crossed his track and whipped three bullets from his automatic through the man's bare chest. The blood came out with his heart beats, throb, throb, throb, slower and slower.

Tallal had seen what we had seen. He gave one moan like a hurt animal; then rode to the upper ground and sat there awhile on his mare, shivering and looking fixedly after the Turks. I moved near to speak to him, but Auda caught my rein and stayed me. Very slowly Tallal drew his head-cloth about his face; and then he seemed suddenly to take hold of himself, for he dashed his stirrups into the mare's flanks

[1] Dad.

and galloped headlong, bending low and swaying in the saddle, right at the main body of the enemy.

It was a long ride down a gentle slope and across a hollow. We sat there like stone while he rushed forward, the drumming of his hoofs unnaturally loud in our ears, for we had stopped shooting, and the Turks had stopped. Both armies waited for him; and he rocked on in the hushed evening till only a few lengths from the enemy. Then he sat up in the saddle and cried his war-cry, 'Tallal, Tallal', twice in a tremendous shout. Instantly their rifles and machine-guns crashed out, and he and his mare, riddled through and through with bullets, fell dead among the lance points.

Auda looked very cold and grim. 'God give him mercy; we will take his price.' He shook his rein and moved slowly after the enemy. We called up the peasants, now drunk with fear and blood, and sent them from this side and that against the retreating column. The old lion of battle waked in Auda's heart, and made him again our natural, inevitable leader. By a skilful turn he drove the Turks into bad ground and split their formation into three parts.

The third part, the smallest, was mostly made up of German and Austrian machine-gunners grouped round three motor-cars, and a handful of mounted officers or troopers. They fought magnificently and repulsed us time and again despite our hardiness. The Arabs were fighting like devils, the sweat blurring their eyes, dust parching their throats; while the flame of cruelty and revenge which was burning in their bodies so twisted them, that their hands could hardly shoot. By my order we took no prisoners, for the only time in our war.

At last we left this stern section behind, and pursued the faster two. They were in panic; and by sunset we had destroyed all but the smallest pieces of them, gaining as and by what they lost. Parties of peasants flowed in on our advance. At first there were five or six to a weapon: then one would win a bayonet, another a sword, a third a pistol. An hour later those who had been on foot would be on donkeys. Afterwards every man had a rifle, and a captured horse. By nightfall the horses were laden, and the rich plain was scattered over with dead men and animals. In a madness born of the horror of Tafas we killed and killed, even blowing in the heads of the fallen and of the animals; as though their death and running blood could slake our agony.

Just one group of Arabs, who had not heard our news, took prisoner the last two hundred men of the central section. Their respite was short. I had gone up to learn why it was, not unwilling that this remnant be let live as witnesses of Tallal's price; but a man on the ground behind them screamed something to the Arabs, who with pale faces led me across to see. It was one of us — his thigh shattered. The blood had rushed out over the red soil, and left him dying; but even so he had not been spared. In the fashion of to-day's battle he had been further tormented by bayonets hammered through his shoulder and other leg into the ground, pinning him out like a collected insect.

He was fully conscious. When we said, 'Hassan, who did it?' he drooped his eyes towards the prisoners, huddling together so hopelessly broken. They said nothing in the moments before we opened fire. At last their heap ceased moving; and Hassan was dead; and we mounted again and rode home slowly (home was my carpet three or four hours from us at Sheikh Saad) in the gloom, which felt so chill now that the sun had gone down.

However, what with wounds and aches and weariness I could not rest from thinking of Tallal, the splendid leader, the fine horseman, the courteous and strong companion of the road; and after a while I had my other camel brought, and with one of my bodyguard rode out into the night to join our men hunting the greater Deraa column.

It was very dark, with a wind beating in great gusts from the south and east; and only by the noise of shots it tossed across to us and by occasional gun flashes, did we at length come to the fighting. Every field and valley had its Turks stumbling blindly northward. Our men were clinging on. The fall of night had made them bolder, and they were now closing with the enemy. Each village, as the fight rolled to it, took up the work; and the black, icy wind was wild with rifle-fire, shoutings, volleys from the Turks, and the rush of gallops, as small parties of either side crashed frantically together.

The enemy had tried to halt and camp at sunset, but Khalid had shaken them again into movement. Some marched, some stayed. Many dropped asleep in their tracks with fatigue. They had lost order and coherence, and were drifting through the blast in lorn packets, ready to shoot and run at every contact with us or with each other; and the Arabs were as scattered, and nearly as uncertain.

Exceptions were the German detachments; and here, for the first time, I grew proud of the enemy who had killed my brothers. They were two thousand miles from home, without hope and without guides, in conditions mad enough to break the bravest nerves. Yet their sections held together, in firm rank, sheering through the wrack of Turk and Arab like armoured ships, high-faced and silent. When attacked they halted, took position, fired to order. There was no haste, no crying, no hesitation. They were glorious.

At last I found Khalid, and asked him to call off the Rualla and leave this rout to time and the peasantry. Heavier work, perhaps, lay to the southward. At dusk a rumour had passed across our plain that Deraa was empty, and Trad, Khalid's brother, with a good half of the Anazeh, had ridden off to see. I feared a reverse for him, since there must still be Turks in the place, and more struggling towards it up the railway and through the Irbid Hills. Indeed, unless Barrow, last reported to us as delayed in Remthe, had lost contact with his enemy, there must be a fighting rearguard yet to follow.

I wanted Khalid to support his brother. After an hour or two of shouting his message down the wind, hundreds of horsemen and camel men had rallied to him. On his way to Deraa he charged through and over several detachments of Turks in the star-blink, and arrived to find Trad in secure possession. He had won through in the later twilight, taking the station at a gallop, jumping trenches and blotting out the scanty Turkish elements which still tried to resist.

With local help the Rualla plundered the camp, especially finding booty in the fiercely burning storehouses whose flaming roofs imperilled their lives; but this was one of the nights in which mankind went crazy, when death seemed impossible, however many died to the right and left, and when others' lives became toys to break and throw away. . . .

I inquired about General Barrow. A man just ridden in from the west told us he had been fired on by the English, as they deployed to attack the town. To prevent such an accident the Zaagi and I rode up the Buweib, on whose crest was visible a strong post of Indian machine-gunners. They trained their weapons on us, proud of such splendidly dressed prizes. However, an officer showed himself, with some British troopers, and to them I explained myself. They were indeed in the midst of an enveloping movement against Deraa, and, while we watched, their aeroplanes bombed the luckless Nuri Said as he rode into the railway station. This was his penalty for losing the race from Sheikh Saad: but, to stop it, I hurried down to where General Barrow was inspecting outposts in a car. . . .

He had had no orders as to the status of the Arabs. Clayton did us this service, thinking we should deserve what we could assert: so Barrow, who had come in thinking of them as a conquered people, though dazed at my calm assumption that he was my guest, had no option but to follow the lead of such assurance. My head was working full speed in these minutes, on our joint behalf, to prevent the fatal first steps by which the unimaginative British, with the best will in the world, usually deprived the acquiescent native of the discipline of responsibility, and created a situation which called for years of agitation and successive reforms and riotings to mend.

I had studied Barrow and was ready for him. Years before, he had published his confession of faith in Fear as the common people's main incentive to action in war and peace. Now I found fear a mean, over-rated motive; no deterrent, and, though a stimulant, a poisonous stimulant, whose every injection served to consume more of the system to which it was applied. I could have no alliance with his pedant belief of scaring men into heaven: better that Barrow and I part at once. My instinct with the inevitable was to provoke it. Therefore, I was very spiny and high.

Barrow surrendered himself by asking me to find him forage and food-stuffs. Indeed, soon we got on well. In the square I showed him Nasir's little silk pennon, propped on the balcony of the charred Government office, with a yawning sentry underneath. Barrow drew himself up and saluted sharply, while a thrill of pleasure at the General's compliment ran round Arab officers and men. . . .

Sleep would not come, so before the light, I woke Stirling and my drivers, and we four climbed into the Blue Mist, our Rolls tender, and set out for Damascus, along the dirt road which was first rutted, and then blocked by the transport columns and rearguard of Barrow's division. We cut across country to the French railway, whose old ballast gave us a clear, if rugged road; then we put on speed. At noon we saw Barrow's pennon at a stream, where he was watering his horses. My bodyguard were near by, so I took my camel and rode over to him. Like other confirmed horsemen, he had been a little contemptuous of the camel; and had suggested, in Deraa, that we might hardly keep up with his cavalry, which was going to Damascus in about three forced marches.

So when he saw me freshly riding up he was astonished, and asked when we left Deraa. 'This morning.' His face fell. 'Where will you stop to-night?' 'In Damascus,' said I gaily; and rode on, having made another enemy. It a little smote me to play tricks, for he was generous towards my wishes: but the stakes were high, beyond his sight, and I cared nothing what he thought of me so that we won. . . .

. . . as the night fell, we saw the break-up of the enemy, who abandoned their guns, their transport and all their stuff and went streaming up the col towards the two peaks of Mania, escaping into what they thought was empty land beyond.

However, in the empty land was Auda; and in that night of his last battle the old man killed and killed, plundered and captured, till dawn showed him the end. There passed the Fourth Army, our stumbling-block for two years. . . .

We sought a retired spot; but already there were men by the thousand everywhere. . . .

The strange power of war which made us all as a duty so demean ourselves! These Australians, shouldering me in unceremonious horse-play, had put off half civilization with their civil clothes. They were dominant to-night, too sure of themselves to be careful: and yet: — as they lazily swaggered those quick bodies, all curves with never a straight line, but with old and disillusioned eyes: and yet: — I felt them thin-tempered, hollow, instinctive; always going to do great things; with the disquieting suppleness of blades half-drawn from the scabbard. Disquieting: not dreadful.

The English fellows were not instinctive, nor negligent like the Australians, but held themselves, with a slow-eyed, almost sheepish care. They were prim in dress, and quiet; going shyly in pairs. The Australians stood in groups and walked singly: the British clung two and two, in a celibate friendliness which expressed the level of the ranks: the commonness of their Army clothes. 'Holding together' they called it: a war-time yearning to keep within four ears such thoughts as were deep enough to hurt.

About the soldiers hung the Arabs: gravely-gazing men from another sphere. My crooked duty had banished me among them for two years. To-night I was nearer to them than to the troops, and I resented it, as shameful. The intruding contrast mixed with longing for home, to sharpen my faculties and make fertile my distaste, till not merely did I see the unlikeness of race, and hear the unlikeness of language, but I learned to pick between their smells: the heavy, standing, curdled sourness of dried sweat in cotton, over the Arab crowds; and the feral smell of English soldiers: that hot pissy aura of thronged men in woollen clothes: a tart pungency, breath-catching, ammoniacal; a fervent fermenting naphtha-smell. . . .

When we came in there had been some miles of people greeting us: now there were thousands for every hundred then. Every man, woman and child in this city of a quarter-million souls seemed in the streets, waiting only the spark of our appearance to ignite their spirits. Damascus went mad with joy. The men tossed up their tarbushes to cheer, the women tore off their veils. Householders threw flowers, hangings, carpets, into the road before us: their wives leaned, screaming with laughter, through the lattices and splashed us with bath-dippers of scent.

Poor dervishes made themselves our running footmen in front and behind, howling and cutting themselves with frenzy; and over the local cries and the shrilling of women came the measured roar of men's voices, chanting, 'Feisal, Nasir, Shukri, Urens', in waves which began here, rolled along the squares, through the market down long streets to East gate, round the wall, back up the Meidan; and grew to a wall of shouts around us by the citadel.

They told me Chauvel was coming; our cars met in the southern outskirts. I described the excitement in the city, and how our new government could not guarantee administrative services before the following day, when I would wait on him, to discuss his needs and mine. Meanwhile I made myself responsible for public order: only begging him to keep his men outside, because to-night would see such carnival as the town had not held for six hundred years, and its hospitality might pervert their discipline.

Chauvel unwillingly followed my lead, his hesitations ruled by my certainty. Like Barrow, he had no instructions what to do with the captured city; and as we had taken possession, knowing our road, with clear purpose, prepared processes, and assets in hand, he had no choice but to let us carry on. His chief of staff who did his technical work, Godwin, a soldier, was delighted to shelve the responsibility of civil government. His advocacy confirmed my assumption.

Indeed, it was confirmed in Chauvel's next words, which asked liberty for himself to drive round the town. I gave it so gladly that he asked if it would be convenient for him to make formal entry with his troops on the morrow. I said certainly, and we thought a little of the route. There flashed into my head the pleasure of our men at Deraa when Barrow saluted their flag — and I quoted it as an example good to follow before the Town Hall when he marched past. It was a casual thought of mine, but he saw significance in it: and a grave difficulty if he saluted any flag except the British. I wanted to make faces at his folly: but instead, in kindness I kept him company, seeing equal difficulty in his passing the Arab flag deliberately not noticed. We stumbled round this problem, while the joyful, unknowing crowd cheered us. As a compromise I suggested we leave out the Town Hall, and invent another route, passing, let us say, by the Post Office. I meant this for farce, since my patience had broken down; but he took it seriously, as a helpful idea; and in return would concede a point for my sake and the Arabs. In place of an 'entry' he would make a 'march through': it meant that instead of going in the middle he would go at the head, or instead of the head, the middle. I forgot, or did not well hear, which: for I should not have cared if he had crawled under or flown over his troops, or split himself to march both sides. . . .

At lunch an Australian doctor implored me, for the sake of humanity, to take notice of the Turkish hospital. I ran over in my mind our three hospitals, the military, the civil, the missionary, and told him they were cared for as well as our means allowed. The Arabs could not invent drugs, nor could Chauvel give them to us. He enlarged further; describing an enormous range of filthy buildings without a single medical officer or orderly, packed with dead and dying; mainly dysentery cases, but at least some typhoid; and it was only to be hoped, no typhus or cholera.

In his descriptions I recognized the Turkish barracks, occupied by two Australian companies of town reserve. Were there sentries at the gates? Yes, he said, that was the place, but it was full of Turkish sick. I walked across and parleyed with the guard, who distrusted my single appearance on foot. They had orders to keep out all natives lest they massacre the patients — a misapprehension of the Arab fashion of making war. At last my English speech got me past the little lodge whose garden was filled with two hundred wretched prisoners in exhaustion and despair.

Through the great door of the barrack I called, up the dusty echoing corridors. No one answered. The huge, deserted, sun-trapping court was squalid with rubbish. The guard told me that thousands of prisoners from here had yesterday gone to a camp beyond the town. Since then no one had come in or out. I walked over to the far thoroughfare, on whose left was a shuttered lobby, black after the blazing sunlight of the plastered court.

I stepped in, to meet a sickening stench: and, as my eyes grew open, a sickening sight. The stone floor was covered with dead bodies, side by side, some in full uniform, some in underclothing, some stark naked. There might be thirty there, and they crept with rats, who had gnawed wet red galleries into them. A few were corpses nearly fresh, perhaps only a day or two old: others must have been there for long. Of some the flesh, going putrid, was yellow and blue and black. Many were already swollen twice or thrice life-width, their fat heads laughing with black mouth across jaws harsh with stubble. Of others the softer parts were fallen in. A few had burst open, and were liquescent with decay.

Beyond was the vista of a great room, from which I thought there came a groan. I trod over to it, across the soft mat of bodies, whose clothing, yellow with dung, crackled dryly under me. Inside the ward the air was raw and still, and the dressed battalion of filled beds so quiet that I thought these too were dead, each man rigid on his stinking pallet, from which liquid muck had dripped down to stiffen on the cemented floor.

I picked forward a little between their lines, holding my white skirts about me, not to dip my bare feet in their puddled running: when suddenly I heard a sigh and turned abruptly to meet the open beady eyes of an outstretched man, while 'Aman, Aman' (pity, pity, pardon) rustled from the twisted lips. There was a brown waver as several tried to lift their hands, and a thin fluttering like withered leaves, as they vainly fell back again upon their beds.

No one of them had strength to speak, but there was something which made me laugh at their whispering in unison, as if by command. No doubt occasion had been given them to rehearse their appeal all the last two days, each time a curious trooper had peered into their halls and gone away.

I ran through the arch into the garden, across which Australians were picketed in lines, and asked them for a working-party. They refused. Tools? They had none. Doctors? Busy. Kirkbride came; the Turkish doctors, we heard, were upstairs. We broke open a door to find seven men in night-gowns sitting on unmade beds in a great room, boiling coffee. We convinced them quickly that it would be wise to sort out living and dead, and prepare me, in half an hour, a tally of their numbers. Kirkbride's heavy frame and boots fitted him to oversee this work: while I saw Ali Riza Pasha, and asked him to detail us one of the four Arab army doctors.

When we came we pressed the fifty fittest prisoners in the lodge as labour party. We bought biscuits and fed them: then armed them with Turkish tools and set them in the backyard to dig a common grave. The Australian officers protested it was an unfit place, the smell arising from which might drive them from their garden. My jerky reply was that I hoped to God it would.

It was cruelty to work men so tired and ill as our miserable Turks, but haste gave us no choice. By the kicks and blows of their victor-serving non-commissioned officers they were at last got obedient. We began operations on a six-foot hole to one side of the garden. This hole we tried to deepen, but beneath was a cement floor; so I said it would do if they enlarged the edges. Near by was much quicklime, which would cover the bodies effectually.

The doctors told us of fifty-six dead, two hundred dying, seven hundred not dangerously ill. We formed a stretcher party to carry down the corpses, of which some were lifted easily, others had to be scraped up piecemeal with shovels. The bearers were hardly strong enough to stand at their work: indeed, before the end, we had added the bodies of two to the heap of dead men in the pit.

The trench was small for them, but so fluid was the mass that each newcomer, when tipped in, fell softly, just jellying out the edges of the pile a little with his weight. Before the work finished it was midnight, and I dismissed myself to bed, exhausted, since I had not slept three hours since we left Deraa four days ago. Kirkbride (a boy in years, doing two men's work these days) stayed to finish the burying, and scatter earth and lime over the grave.

At the hotel waited a bunch of urgent matters: some death sentences, a new justiciary, a famine in barley for the morrow if the train did not work. Also a complaint from Chauvel that some of the Arab troops had been slack about saluting *Australian* officers!

By morning, after the sudden fashion of troubles, they were ended and our ship sailing under a clear sky. The armoured cars came in, and the pleasure of our men's sedate faces heartened me. Pisani arrived, and made me laugh, so bewildered was the good soldier by the political hubbub. He gripped his military duty as a rudder to steer him through. Damascus was normal, the shops open, street merchants trading, the electric tramcars restored, grain and vegetables and fruits coming in well.

The streets were being watered to lay the terrible dust of three war-years' lorry traffic. The crowds were slow and happy, and numbers of British troops were wandering in the town, unarmed. The tele-graph was restored with Palestine, and with Beyrout, which the Arabs had occupied in the night. As long ago as Wejh I had warned them, when they took Damascus to leave Lebanon for sop to the French and take Tripoli instead; since as a port it outweighed Beyrout, and England would have played the honest broker for it on their behalf in the Peace Settlement. So I was grieved by their mistake, yet glad they felt grown-up enough to reject me.

Even the hospital was better. I had urged Chauvel to take it over, but he would not. At the time I thought he meant to overstrain us, to justify his taking away our government of the town. However, since, I have come to feel that the trouble between us was a delusion of the ragged nerves which were jangling me to distraction these days. Certainly Chauvel won the last round, and made me feel mean, for when he heard that I was leaving he drove round with Godwin and thanked me outright for my help in his difficulties. Still, the hospital was improving of itself. Fifty prisoners had cleaned the courtyard, burning the lousy rubbish. A second gang had dug another great grave-pit in the garden, and were zealously filling it as opportunity offered. Others had gone through the wards, washing every patient, putting them into cleaner shirts, and reversing their mattresses to have a tolerably decent side up. We had found food suitable for all but critical cases, and each ward had some Turkish-spoken orderly within hearing if a sick man called. One room we had cleared, brushed out and disinfected, meaning to transfer into it the less ill cases, and do their room in turn.

At this rate three days would have seen things very fit, and I was proudly contemplating other benefits when a medical major strode up and asked me shortly if I spoke English. With a brow of disgust for my skirts and sandals he said, 'You're in charge?' Modestly I smirked that in a way I was, and then he burst out, 'Scandalous, disgraceful, outrageous, ought to be shot . . .' At this onslaught I cackled out like a chicken, with the wild laughter of strain; it did feel extraordinarily funny to be so cursed just as I had been pluming myself on having bettered the apparently hopeless.

The major had not entered the charnel house of yesterday, nor smelt it, nor seen us burying those bodies of ultimate degradation, whose memory had started me up in bed, sweating and trembling, a few hours since. He glared at me, muttering 'Bloody brute'. I hooted out again, and he smacked me over the face and stalked off, leaving me more ashamed than angry, for in my heart I felt he was right, and that anyone who pushed through to success a rebellion of the weak against their masters must come out of it so stained in estimation that afterward nothing in the world would make him feel clean. However, it was nearly over.

When I got back to the hotel crowds were besetting it, and at the door stood a grey Rolls-Royce, which I knew for Allenby's. I ran in and found him there with Clayton and Cornwallis and other noble people. In ten words he gave his approval to my having impertinently imposed Arab Governments, here and at Deraa, upon the chaos of victory. He confirmed the appointment of Ali Riza Rikabi as his Military Governor, under the orders of Feisal, his Army Commander, and regulated the Arab sphere and Chauvel's.

He agreed to take over my hospital and the working of the railway. In ten minutes all the maddening difficulties had slipped away. Mistily I realized that the harsh days of my solitary battling had passed. The lone hand had won against the world's odds, and I might let my limbs relax in this dreamlike confidence and decision and kindness which were Allenby.

Then we were told that Feisal's special train had just arrived from Deraa. A message was hurriedly sent him by Young's mouth, and we waited till he came, upon a tide of cheering which beat up against our windows. It was fitting the two chiefs should meet for the first time in the heart of their victory; with myself still acting as the interpreter between them.

Allenby gave me a telegram from the Foreign Office, recognizing to the Arabs the status of belligerents; and told me to translate it to the Emir: but none of us knew what it meant in English, let alone in Arabic: and Feisal, smiling through the tears which the welcome of his people had forced from him, put it aside to thank the Commander-in-Chief for the trust which had made him and his movement. They were a strange contrast: Feisal, large-eyed, colourless and worn, like a fine dagger; Allenby, gigantic and red and merry, fit representative of the Power which had thrown a girdle of humour and strong dealing round the world.

When Feisal had gone, I made to Allenby the last (and also I think the first) request I ever made him for myself — leave to go away. For a while he would not have it; but I reasoned, reminding him of his year-old promise, and pointing out how much easier the New Law would be if my spur were absent from the people. In the end he agreed; and then at once I knew how much I was sorry.

DAMASCUS *had not seemed a sheath for my sword when I landed in Arabia: but its capture disclosed the exhaustion of my main springs of action. The strongest motive throughout had been a personal one, not mentioned here, but present to me, I think, every hour of these two years. Active pains and joys might fling up, like towers, among my days, but, refluent as air, this hidden urge re-formed, to be the persisting element of life, till near the end. It was dead, before we reached Damascus.*

Next in force had been a pugnacious wish to win the war: yoked to the conviction that without Arab help England could not pay the price of winning its Turkish sector. When Damascus fell, the Eastern war — probably the whole war — drew to an end.

Then I was moved by curiosity. 'Super flumina Babylonis', read as a boy, had left me longing to feel myself the node of a national movement. We took Damascus, and I feared. More than three arbitrary days would have quickened in me a root of authority.

There remained historical ambition, insubstantial as a motive by itself. I had dreamed, at the City School in Oxford, of hustling into form, while I lived: the new Asia which time was inexorably bringing upon us. Mecca was to lead to Damascus; Damascus to Anatolia, and afterwards to Bagdad; and then there was Yemen. Fantasies, these will seem, to such as are able to call my beginning an ordinary effort.

[Passages from the Introductory Chapter and Chapter I of *Seven Pillars of Wisdom* have been printed here after the main excerpts from that book as they contain Lawrence's criticism of the Arab war and the part he played in it. Chapter I was omitted from the Subscribers' Edition of *Seven Pillars of Wisdom*.]

T H E story which follows was first written out in Paris during the Peace Conference, from notes jotted daily on the march, strengthened by some reports sent to my chiefs in Cairo. Afterwards, in the autumn of 1919, this first draft and some of the notes were lost. It seemed to me historically needful to reproduce the tale, as perhaps no one but myself in Feisal's army had thought of writing down at the time what we felt, what we hoped, what we tried. So it was built again with heavy repugnance in London in the winter of 1919-20 from memory and my surviving notes. The record of events was not dulled in me and perhaps few actual mistakes crept in — except in details of dates or numbers — but the outlines and significance of things had lost edge in the haze of new interests.

Dates and places are correct, so far as my notes preserved them: but the personal names are not. Since the adventure some of those who worked with me have buried themselves in the shallow grave of public duty. Free use has been made of their names. Others still possess themselves, and here keep their secrecy. Sometimes one man carried various names. This may hide individuality and make the book a scatter of featureless puppets, rather than a group of living people: but once good is told of a man, and again evil, and some would not thank me for either blame or praise.

This isolated picture throwing the main light upon myself is unfair to my British colleagues. Especially I am most sorry that I have not told what the non-commissioned of us did. They were inarticulate, but wonderful, especially when it is taken into account that they had not the motive, the imaginative vision of the end, which sustained the officers. Unfortunately my concern was limited to this end, and the book is just a designed procession of Arab freedom from Mecca to Damascus. It is intended to rationalize the campaign, that everyone may see how natural the success was and how inevitable, how little dependent on direction or brain, how much less on the outside assistance of the few British. It was an Arab war waged and led by Arabs for an Arab aim in Arabia.

My proper share was a minor one, but because of a fluent pen, a free speech, and a certain adroitness of brain, I took upon myself, as I describe it, a mock primacy. In reality I never had any office among the Arabs: was never in charge of the British mission with them. Wilson, Joyce, Newcombe, Dawnay, and Davenport were all over my head. I flattered myself that I was too young, not that they had more heart or mind in the work. I did my best. Wilson, Newcombe, Joyce, Dawnay, Davenport, Buxton, Marshall, Stirling, Young, Maynard, Ross, Scott, Winterton, Lloyd, Wordie, Siddons, Goslett, Stent, Henderson, Spence, Gilman, Garland, Brodie, Makins, Nunan, Leeson, Hornby, Peake, Scott-Higgins, Ramsay, Wood, Hinde, Bright, MacIndoe, Greenhill, Grisenthwaite, Dowsett, Bennett, Wade, Gray, Pascoe and the others also did their best.

It would be impertinent in me to praise them. When I wish to say ill of one outside our number, I do it: though there is less of this than was in my diary, since the passage of time seems to have bleached out men's stains. When I wish to praise outsiders, I do it: but our family affairs are our own. We did what we set out to do, and have the satisfaction of that knowledge. The others have liberty some day to put on record their story, one parallel to mine but not mentioning more of me than I of them, for each of us did his job by himself and as he pleased, hardly seeing his friends.

In these pages the history is not of the Arab movement, but of me in it. It is a narrative of daily life, mean happenings, little people. Here are no lessons for the world, no disclosures to shock peoples. It is filled with trivial things, partly that no one mistake for history the bones from which some day a man may make history, and partly for the pleasure it gave me to recall the fellowship of the revolt. We were fond together, because of the sweep of the open places, the taste of wide winds, the sunlight, and the hopes in which we worked. The morning freshness of the world-to-be intoxicated us. We were wrought up with ideas inexpressible and vaporous, but to be fought for. We lived many lives in those whirling campaigns, never sparing ourselves: yet when we achieved and the new world dawned, the old men came out again and took our victory to re-make in the likeness of the former world they knew. Youth could win, but had not learned to keep: and was pitiably weak against age. We stammered that we had worked for a new heaven and a new earth, and they thanked us kindly and made their peace.

All men dream: but not equally. Those who dream by night in the dusty recesses of their minds wake in the day to find that it was vanity: but the dreamers of the day are dangerous men, for they may act their dream with open eyes, to make it possible. This I did. I meant to make a new nation, to restore a lost influence, to give twenty millions of Semites the foundation on which to build an inspired dream-palace of their national thoughts. So high an aim called out the inherent nobility of their minds, and made them play a generous part in events: but when we won, it was charged against me that the British petrol royalties in Mesopotamia were become dubious, and French Colonial policy ruined in the Levant.

I am afraid that I hope so. We pay for these things too much in honour and in innocent lives. I went up the Tigris with one hundred Devon Territorials, young, clean, delightful fellows, full of the power of happiness and of making women and children glad. By them one saw vividly how great it was to be their kin, and English. And we were casting them by thousands into the fire to the worst of deaths, not to win the war but that the corn and rice and oil of Mesopotamia might be ours. The only need was to defeat our enemies (Turkey among them), and this was at last done in the wisdom of Allenby with less than four hundred killed, by turning to our uses the hands of the oppressed in Turkey. I am proudest of my thirty fights in that I did not have any of our own blood shed. All our subject provinces to me were not worth one dead Englishman.

We were three years over this effort and I have had to hold back many things which may not yet be said. Even so, parts of this book will be new to nearly all who see it, and many will look for familiar things and not find them. Once I reported fully to my chiefs, but learnt that they were rewarding me on my own evidence. This was not as it should be. Honours may be necessary in a professional army, as so many emphatic mentions in despatches, and by enlisting we had put ourselves, willingly or not, in the position of regular soldiers.

For my work on the Arab front I had determined to accept nothing. The Cabinet raised the Arabs to fight for us by definite promises of self-government afterwards. Arabs believe in persons, not in institutions. They saw in me a free agent of the British Government, and demanded from me an endorsement of its written promises. So I had to join the conspiracy, and, for what my word was worth, assured the men of their reward. In our two years' partnership under fire they grew accustomed to believing me and to think my Government, like myself, sincere. In this hope they performed some fine things, but, of course, instead of being proud of what we did together, I was continually and bitterly ashamed.

It was evident from the beginning that if we won the war these promises would be dead paper, and had I been an honest adviser of the Arabs I would have advised them to go home and not risk their lives fighting for such stuff: but I salved myself with the hope that, by leading these Arabs madly in the final victory I would establish them, with arms in their hands, in a position so assured (if not dominant) that expediency would counsel to the Great Powers a fair settlement of their claims. In other words, I presumed (seeing no other leader with the will and power) that I would survive the campaigns, and be able to defeat not merely the Turks on the battlefield, but my own country and its allies in the council-chamber. It was an immodest presumption: it is not yet clear if I succeeded: but it is clear that I had no shadow of leave to engage the Arabs, unknowing, in such hazard. I risked the fraud, on my conviction that Arab help was necessary to our cheap and speedy victory in the East, and that better we win and break our word than lose.

The dismissal of Sir Henry McMahon confirmed my belief in our essential insincerity: but I could not so explain myself to General Wingate while the war lasted, since I was nominally under his orders, and he did not seem sensible of how false his own standing was. The only thing remaining was to refuse rewards for being a successful trickster and, to prevent this unpleasantness arising, I began in my reports to conceal the true stories of things, and to persuade the few Arabs who knew to an equal reticence. In this book also, for the last time, I mean to be my own judge of what to say.

Some of the evil of my tale may have been inherent in our circumstances. For years we lived anyhow with one another in the naked desert, under the indifferent heaven. By day the hot sun fermented us; and we were dizzied by the beating wind. At night we were stained by dew, and shamed into pettiness by the innumerable silences of stars. We were a self-centred army without parade or gesture, devoted to freedom, the second of man's creeds, a purpose so ravenous that it devoured all our strength, a hope so transcendent that our earlier ambitions faded in its glare.

As time went by our need to fight for the ideal increased to an unquestioning possession, riding with spur and rein over our doubts. Willy-nilly it became a faith. We had sold ourselves into its slavery, manacled ourselves together in its chain-gang, bowed ourselves to serve its holiness with all our good and ill content. The mentality of ordinary human slaves is terrible — they have lost the world — and we had surrendered, not body alone, but soul to the overmastering greed of victory. By our own act we were drained of morality, of volition, of responsibility, like dead leaves in the wind.

The everlasting battle stripped from us care of our own lives or of others'. We had ropes about our necks, and on our heads prices which showed that the enemy intended hideous tortures for us if we were caught. Each day some of us passed; and the living knew themselves just sentient puppets on God's stage: indeed, our taskmaster was merciless, merciless, so long as our bruised feet could stagger forward on the road. The weak envied those tired enough to die; for success looked so remote, and failure a near and certain, if sharp, release from toil. We lived always in the stretch or sag of nerves, either on the crest or in the trough of waves of feeling. This impotency was bitter to us, and made us live only for the seen horizon, reckless what spite we inflicted or endured, since physical sensation showed itself meanly transient. Gusts of cruelty, perversions, lusts ran lightly over the surface without troubling us; for the moral laws which had seemed to hedge about these silly accidents must be yet fainter words. We had learned that there were pangs too sharp, griefs too deep, ecstasies too high for our finite selves to register. When emotion reached this pitch the mind choked; and memory went white till the circumstances were humdrum once more.

Such exaltation of thought, while it let adrift the spirit, and gave it licence in strange airs, lost it the old patient rule over the body. The body was too coarse to feel the utmost of our sorrows and of our joys. Therefore, we abandoned it as rubbish: we left it below us to march forward, a breathing simulacrum, on its own unaided level, subject to influences from which in normal times our instincts would have shrunk. The men were young and sturdy; and hot flesh and blood unconsciously claimed a right in them and tormented their bellies with strange longings. Our privations and dangers fanned this virile heat, in a climate as racking as can be conceived. We had no shut places to be alone in, no thick clothes to hide our nature. Man in all things lived candidly with man.

The Arab was by nature continent; and the use of universal marriage had nearly abolished irregular courses in his tribes. The public women of the rare settlements we encountered in our months of wandering would have been nothing to our numbers, even had their raddled meat been palatable to a man of healthy parts. In horror of such sordid commerce our youths began indifferently to slake one another's few needs in their own clean bodies — a cold convenience that, by comparison, seemed sexless and even pure. Later, some began to justify this sterile process, and swore that friends quivering together in the yielding sand with intimate hot limbs in supreme embrace, found there hidden in the darkness a sensual co-efficient of the mental passion which was welding our souls and spirits in one flaming effort. Several, thirsting to punish appetites they could not wholly prevent, took a savage pride in degrading the body, and offered themselves fiercely in any habit which promised physical pain or filth.

I was sent to these Arabs as a stranger, unable to think their thoughts or subscribe their beliefs, but charged by duty to lead them forward and to develop to the highest any movement of theirs profitable to England in her war. If I could not assume their character, I could at least conceal my own, and pass among them without evident friction, neither a discord nor a critic but an unnoticed influence. Since I was their fellow, I will not be their apologist or advocate. To-day in my old garments, I could play the bystander, obedient to the sensibilities of our theatre . . . but it is more honest to record that these ideas and actions then passed naturally. What now looks wanton or sadic seemed in the field inevitable, or just unimportant routine.

Blood was always on our hands: we were licensed to it. Wounding and killing seemed ephemeral pains, so very brief and sore was life with us. With the sorrow of living so great, the sorrow of punishment had to be pitiless. We lived for the day and died for it. When there was reason and desire to punish we wrote our lesson with gun or whip immediately in the sullen flesh of the sufferer, and the case was beyond appeal. The desert did not afford the refined slow penalties of courts and gaols.

Of course our rewards and pleasures were as suddenly sweeping as our troubles; but, to me in particular, they bulked less large. Bedouin ways were hard even for those brought up to them, and for strangers terrible: a death in life. When the march or labour ended I had no energy to record sensation, nor while it lasted any leisure to see the spiritual loveliness which sometimes came upon us by the way. In my notes, the cruel rather than the beautiful found place. We no doubt enjoyed more the rare moments of peace and forgetfulness; but I remember more the agony, the terrors, and the mistakes. Our life is not summed up in what I have written (there are things not to be repeated in cold blood for very shame); but what I have written was in and of our life. Pray God that men reading the story will not, for love of the glamour of strangeness, go out to prostitute themselves and their talents in serving another race.

A man who gives himself to be a possession of aliens leads a Yahoo life, having bartered his soul to a brute-master. He is not of them. He may stand against them, persuade himself of a mission, batter and twist them into something which they, of their own accord, would not have been. Then he is exploiting his old environment to press them out of theirs. Or, after my model, he may imitate them so well that they spuriously imitate him back again. Then he is giving away his own environment: pretending to theirs; and pretences are hollow, worthless things. In neither case does he do a thing of himself, nor a thing so clean as to be his own (without thought of conversion), letting them take what action or reaction they please from the silent example.

In my case, the effort for these years to live in the dress of Arabs, and to imitate their mental foundation, quitted me of my English self, and let me look at the West and its conventions with new eyes: they destroyed it all for me. At the same time I could not sincerely take on the Arab skin: it was an affectation only. Easily was a man made an infidel, but hardly might he be converted to another faith. I had dropped one form and not taken on the other, and was become like Mohammed's coffin in our legend, with a resultant feeling of intense loneliness in life, and a contempt, not for other men, but for all they do. Such detachment came at times to a man exhausted by prolonged physical effort and isolation. His body plodded on mechanically, while his reasonable mind left him, and from without looked down critically on him, wondering what that futile lumber did and why. Sometimes these selves would converse in the void; and then madness was very near, as I believe it would be near the man who could see things through the veils at once of two customs, two educations, two environments.

DEMOLITIONS UNDER FIRE[1]

by T.E.L.

WE were interested in the Hejaz Railway, and spent nearly two years on it. The Turkish counter-measures were passive. They garrisoned each station (an average of 14 miles apart) with half a company, entrenched, sometimes with guns, and put in between the stations a chain of small entrenched posts, usually about 2000 yards apart, and sited on small knolls or spurs within 200 yards of the railway, so that each post could see its neighbours and command all the inter-mediate line. Extra posts were put on one or other bank of any large bridge. The 15 or 20 men in the post had to patrol their section of line after dawn each day, and in the afternoon. There was no night activity on their part.

The Turks arrived at their system of defence after considerable experience of our demolition parties, but we were able, till the end of the war, to descend upon the railway when and where we pleased, and effect the damage we wished, without great difficulty. At the same time our ways and means had constantly to be improved. We began with small parties of ten or fifteen Beduins, and we ended with

[1] This article was first published in *The Royal Engineers' Journal*, Vol. XXIX, No. 1, January 1919, and has not hitherto been reprinted.

mobile columns of all arms, including armoured cars; nevertheless I believe that it is impossible for a purely passive defence, such as the Turkish, to prevent a daily interruption of the railway traffic by a decently equipped enemy. Railway defence, to be inviolable, would require a passive force, entrenched with continuous barbed wire fence, and day and night patrol, at a considerable distance from the line, on each side of it; mobile forces, in concentrations not more than 20 miles apart; and liberal air reconnaissance.

The actual methods of demolition we used are perhaps more interesting than our manners of attack. Our explosives were mainly blasting gelatine and guncotton. Of the two we infinitely preferred the former when we could get it. It is rather more powerful in open charges in direct contact, far better for indirect work, has a value of 5 to 1 in super-tamped charges, is quicker to use, and more compact. We used to strip its paper covering, and handle it in sandbags of 50 lbs. weight. These sweated vigorously in the summer heats of Arabia, but did us no harm, beyond the usual headache, from which we never acquired immunity. The impact of a bullet may detonate a sack of it but we found in practice that when running you clasp it to your side, and if it is held on that furthest from the enemy, then the chances are that it will not be hit, except by the bullet that has already inflicted a mortal wound on the bearer. Guncotton is a good explosive, but inferior in the above respects to gelatine, and in addition, we used to receive it packed 16 slabs (of 15 oz. each) in a wooden box of such massive construction that it was nearly impossible to open peacefully. You can break these boxes with an entrenching tool, in about four minutes slashing, but the best thing is to dash the box, by one of its rope or wire beckets against a rock until it splits. The lid of the box is fastened by six screws, but even if there is time to undo all of these, the slabs will not come out, since they are unshakably wedged against the four sides. I have opened boxes by detonating a primer on one corner, but regard this way as unnecessarily noisy wasteful and dangerous for daily use.

Rail Demolition. — Guncotton in 15-ounce slabs is convenient for rail cutting. The usual method of putting a fused and detonated and primed slab against the web is quick and easy, but ineffective. The slab cuts a six-in. section out of the lie, leaving two clean fractured surfaces (Hejaz rails are of a mild Maryland or Cockerill steel). The steel chairs and sleepers are strong, and the enemy used to tap the broken rails again into contact with a sledge, and lay in a new piece whenever the combined fractures were important enough. New rails were ten metres long, but the line worked well on unbolted pieces two or three metres long. Two bolts are enough for a fish plate, and on straights the line will serve slow trains for a mile or two without fish plates, owing to the excellence of the chairs. For curves the Turks, after we had exhausted their curved rails, used short straights. These proved efficient even on 120-metre curves. The rate of repair of a gang 100 strong, in simple demolition is about 250 cuts an hour. A demolition gang of 20 would do about 600 cuts an hour.

A better demolition is to lay two successive slabs on the ballast beneath the bottom flange under the joint and fish plate, in contact with the line. This spoils the fish plate and bolts, and shortens each of two rails by a few inches, for the expenditure of two slabs and one fuse. It takes longer to lay than the simple demolition, but also takes longer to repair, since one or other rail is often not cut, but bent, and in that case the repair party has either to cut it, or to press it straight.

The best demolition we discovered was to dig down in the ballast beside a mid-rail sleeper between the tracks, until the inside of the sleeper (iron of course) could be cleared of ballast, and to lay two slabs in the bottom of the hole, under the sleeper, but not in contact with it. The excavated ballast should then be returned and the end of the fuse left visible over the sleeper for the lighting party. The expansion of air raises the middle of the sleeper 18 in. from the ground, humps the two rails 3 in. from the horizontal, draws them 6 in. nearer together, and warps them from the vertical inwards by the twisting pull of the chairs on the bottom outer flange. A trough is also driven a foot or more deep across the formation. This gives two rails destroyed, one sleeper or two, and the grading, for two slabs and one fuse. The repair party has either to throw away the entire track, or cut a metre out of each rail and re-grade. A gang of 100 will mend about 20 pairs an hour, and a gang of 40 will lay 80 an hour. The appearance of a piece of rail treated by this method is most beautiful, for the sleepers rise up in all manner of varied forms, like the early buds of tulips.

Simple demolitions can be lit with a 12-in. fuse. The fish-plate-flange type should be lit with 30-in. fuses, since the fragments of steel spray the whole earth. The 'tulips' may be lit with a 10-in. fuse, for they only scatter ballast. If, however, the slabs have been allowed to get into contact with the metal of the sleeper they will throw large lumps of it about. With a 10-in. fuse most of these will pass over the head of the lighting man who will be only 15 yards or so away when it goes off. To be further is dangerous. We were provided with Bickford fuse by Ordnance. The shiny black variety causes many accidents, owing to its habits of accelerating or smouldering. The dull black is better, and the white very good. Our instantaneous fuse has an amusing effect if lit at night among friendly tents, since it jumps about and bangs; but it is not good for service conditions. The French instantaneous fuse is reliable. Detonators should always be crimped on to ready-cut fuses, and may be safely carried in the pocket or sandbag, since great violence is required to set them off. We generally used fusees for lighting.

Speaking as a rule rail demolitions are wasteful and ineffective unless the enemy is short of metal or unless they are only made adjuncts to bridge-breaking.

A pleasant demolition, of a hybrid type, is to cut both rails, and turn them over, so as to throw them on their face down the bank. It takes 30 men to start this, but a small gang can then pass up the line, bearing on the overturned part, and the spring of the rails will carry on the reversing process, until you have done miles of it. This is an effective demolition with steel sleepers, since you wreck the ballasting. We tried it once on about 8 miles of a branch line, with a preponderance of spiked wooden sleepers, and it made such a mess of rails and sleepers that the Turks washed their hands of it.

The Hejaz line carried a minimum of traffic, so that there was no special virtue in destroying the points of crossing places.

Bridge Demolitions. — The lightness of traffic affected the tactics of bridge demolition also, since a single break was met either by transport or deviation. As with the rails however, the methods we used are perhaps more important than why we did it. Most of the bridges are of dressed limestone masonry, in 80 to 100-pound blocks, set in lime mortar. The average spans were from four to seven metres, and the piers were usually 15 ft. wide and 4 ft. 6 in. thick. It is of course better to shatter a bridge than to blow it sky-high, since you increase your enemy's labours. We found that a charge of 48 pounds of guncotton, laid against the foot of the pier on the ground, untamped, was hardly enough, and that 64 pounds was often a little too much. Our formula was therefore about $\frac{1}{3}BT^2$ for guncotton charges below 100 pounds, untamped. In a pier 15 ft. broad, had the feet been marked off on it, we would have had no explosive between feet 1 and 3 and 12 and 15. The bulk would have been against 4, 5, and 10, 11, with a continuous but weaker band uniting 5 and 10. Dry guncotton is better than wet for such work; gelatine is about 10 per cent. stronger for these open charges. With charges above 100 lbs. $\frac{1}{8}BT^2$ or $\frac{1}{7}BT^2$ is enough. The larger your object the smaller your formula. Under fire, the inside of the bridge is fairly safe, since enemy posts enfilade the line and not the bridge arches. It is however seldom leisurely enough to allow of tamping a pier charge by digging. When it is, a trench a foot deep is all that is possible, and this does not decrease a guncotton charge by more than 10 per cent. Gelatine profits rather more in proportion by simple tamping.

A quick and cheap method of bringing down the ordinary pier or abutment is by inserting small charges in the drainage holes that are usually present. In the Hejaz line these were in the splay of the arch, and a charge of 5 lbs. of gelatine, or 25 of guncotton, in these would wreck the whole line. The depth and small size of the drainage holes tamp the explosive to an extreme degree. Where the bridge was of many spans we used to charge alternate drainage holes on either side. In the ordinary English abutment where the drainage holes are small and frequent, it would be wise to explode several simultaneously by electricity, since the effect is much greater than by independent firing. Necklacing and digging down from the crown or roadbed are methods too clumsy and slow for active service conditions.

In North Syria, where we came to bridges of great blocks of basalt, with cement joints, we had to increase our charges for untamped work to $\frac{1}{4}$ or even $\frac{1}{3}$ BT.^{2}.

We found guncotton most convenient to handle when we knotted it up into 30-slab blocks by passing cords through the round holes in the middle of the slabs. These large bricks are quick to lay and easy to carry. An armoured car is very useful in bridge demolition, to hold the explosive and the artist. We found in practice that from 30 to 40 seconds was time enough to lay a pier demolition charge, and that only one man was necessary. We usually used 2-ft. fuses.

Girder bridges are more difficult. In lattice bridges where the tension girder is below the roadway, it is best to cut both compression beams. If the tension girder is overhead, it is better to cut both tensions and one compression. It is impossible to do a bridge of this sort very quickly. We had not many cases, but they took ten minutes or more each. When possible we used to wedge the gelatine in the angles of meeting girders. The only quick way is to lay an enormous single charge on the top of the abutment and root it all away with the holdfasts.

This may require 1000 lbs. of gelignite, or more, and a multiplicity of porters complicates things. I never blew up a plate girder.

Mining trains pertains perhaps more to operations than to engineering, and is, any way, a special study in itself. Automatic mines, to work on rail deflection always sounded better than they proved. They require very careful laying and to be efficient have to be four-charge compound. This involves electrical connection. The best mine action we had was made for us by Colonel R. E. M. Russell, R.E., and we were about to give it extended use when the enemy caved in.

The ordinary mine was fired electrically by an observer. It is an infallible but very difficult way of destroying hostile rolling stock, and we made great profit from it. Our standard charge was 50 lbs. of gelatine. Guncotton is very little use.

However mining is too large a subject to treat of. The army electrical gear is good, but the exploder seems needlessly heavy. By using a single strand insulated wire (commercial) we fired four detonators in parallel at 500 metres; army multiple-stranded insulated cables will fire two at 500 metres. In series I have never had occasion to fire more than 25 detonators (at 250 yards), but I see no reason why this number should not be greatly increased. The army electric detonators never failed us. A meter test might show that some of them were defective, but even the defective ones will fire on an exploder. It is usually unnecessary to insulate your joints. The exploder goes out of action quickly if knocked about in a baggage column, or slung on a trotting camel, so I usually carried two as reserve.

from THE EVOLUTION OF A REVOLT

FIRST PUBLISHED IN THE FIRST NUMBER OF *The Army Quarterly*,
OCT 1920.

[Much of the first part of the article appears in Chapter XXXIII of *Seven Pillars of Wisdom* and is therefore omitted here.]

MY chiefs did not follow all these arguments, but gave me leave to try my hand after my own fashion. We went off first to Akaba, and took it easily. Then we took Tafileh and the Dead Sea: then Azrak and Deraa, and finally Damascus, all in successive stages worked out consciously on these sick-bed theories. The process was to set up ladders of tribes, giving us a safe and comfortable route from our sea-bases (Yenbo, Wejh or Akaba) to our advanced bases of operation. These were sometimes three hundred miles away, a long distance in lands without railways or roads, but made short for us by an assiduous cultivation of desert-power, control by camel parties of the desolate and unmapped wilderness which fills up all the centre of Arabia, from Mecca to Aleppo and Bagdad.

In character these operations were more like naval warfare than ordinary land operations, in their mobility, their ubiquity, their independence of bases and communications, their lack of ground features, of strategic areas, of fixed directions, of fixed points. 'He who commands the sea is at great liberty, and may take as much or as little of the war as he will'; he who commands the desert is equally fortunate. Camel raiding-parties, as self-contained as ships, could cruise without danger along any part of the enemy's land frontier, just out of sight of his posts along the edge of cultivation, and tap or raid into his lines where it seemed fittest or easiest or most profitable, with a sure retreat always behind them into an element which the Turks could not enter. We were fortified in our freedom of movement by an intimate knowledge of the desert-front of Syria, a country peculiarly and historically indefensible against attack from the east. I had traversed most of it on foot before the war many times, working out the movements of Saladin or Ibrahim Pasha, and, as our war-experience deepened, we became adepts at that form of geographical intuition, described by Bourcet as wedding unknown land to known in a mental map.

Our tactics were always tip and run, not pushes, but strokes. We never tried to maintain or improve an advantage, but to move off and strike again somewhere else. We used the smallest force, in the quickest time, at the farthest place. If the action had continued till the enemy had changed his dispositions to resist it, we would have been breaking the spirit of our fundamental rule of denying him targets.

The necessary speed and range were attained by the extreme frugality of the desert men, and their high efficiency when mounted on their she-riding-camels. The camel is an intricate animal, and calls for skilled labour in the handling: but she yields a remarkable return. We had no system of supply: each man was self-contained and carried on the saddle, from the sea base at which the raid started, six weeks' food for himself. The six-weeks' ration for ordinary men was a half-bag of flour, forty-five pounds in weight. Luxurious feeders carried some rice also for variety. Each man baked for himself, kneading his own flour into unleavened cakes, and warming it in the ashes of a fire. We carried about a pint of drinking water each, since the camels required to come to water on average every three days, and there was no advantage in our being richer than our mounts. Some of us never drank between wells, but those were hardy men: most of us drank a lot at each well, and had a drink during the intermediate dry day. In the heat of summer Arabian camels will do about two hundred and fifty miles comfortably between drinks: and this represented three days' vigorous marching. The country is not so dry as it is painted, and this radius was always more than we needed. Wells are seldom more than one hundred miles apart. An easy day's march was fifty miles: an emergency march might be up to one hundred and ten miles in the day.

The six weeks' food gave us a range of over a thousand miles out and home, and that (like the pint of water) was more than ever we needed, even in so large a country as Arabia. It was possible (for me, the camel-novice in the Army, 'painful' was a better word) to ride fifteen hundred miles in the month without re-victualling, and there was never a fear of starvation, for each of us was riding on two hundred pounds of potential meat, and when food lacked we would stop and eat the weakest of our camels. Exhausted camel is poor food, but cheaper killing than a fat one, and we had to remember that our future efficiency depended on the number of good camels at our disposal. They lived on grazing as we marched (we never gave them grain or fodder), and after their six weeks on the road they would be worn thin, and have to be sent to pasture for some months' rest, while we called out another tribe in replacement, or found fresh riding-beasts.

We did not hamper ourselves with led-camels. The men carried with them a hundred rounds of ammunition and a rifle, or else two men would be an 'automatic' team, dividing the gun and its drums between them. They slept as they were, in their riding cloaks, and fared well enough till the winter of 1917-18, which caught us on the five-thousand foothills of Edom behind the Dead Sea. Then we lost many men and camels frozen to death, or trapped in the snow, which lay over all the high lands in deep drifts for weeks, while we vainly appealed to Egypt for tents and boots and blankets. In reply we were advised that Arabia was a tropical country!

The equipment of the raiding parties aimed at simplicity, with nevertheless a technical superiority over the Turks in the most critical department. We had great quantities of light machine guns, used not as machine guns, but as automatic rifles, snipers' tools, by men kept deliberately in ignorance of their mechanism, so that the speed of action would not be hampered by attempts at repair. If a gun jammed, the gunner had to throw it away and go on with his rifle. We made another special feature of high explosives, and nearly every one in the revolt was qualified by rule of thumb experience in demolition work. We invented special methods of our own, for rapid work under fire, in the course of our months of practice, and before the end were dealing with any quantity of track and bridges economically and safely.

On some occasions we strengthened tribal raids by armoured cars, manned by Englishmen. Armoured cars, once they have found a possible track, can keep up with a camel party. They are, however, cumbrous and shorter-ranged, because of the difficulty of carrying petrol. Therefore we seldom used them more than a hundred miles from home. On the march to Damascus, when we were nearly four hundred miles off our base, we first maintained them by a baggage train of petrol-laden camels, and afterwards by the help of the Air Force were able to give them further supplies by Handley-Page. Cars are magnificent fighting machines, and decisive whenever they can come into action on their own conditions. But though each has for main principle that of 'fire in movement', yet the tactical employments of cars and camel-corps are so different that I do not recommend their being used in joint operations, except in very special circumstances. We found it demoralizing to both to use armoured and unarmoured cavalry together.

The distribution of the raiding parties was unorthodox. It was impossible to mix or combine tribes, since they disliked or distrusted one another. Likewise we could not use the men of one tribe in the territory of another. In consequence, we aimed at the widest distribution of forces, in order to have the greatest number of raids on hand at once, and we added fluidity to their ordinary speed by using one district on Monday, another on Tuesday, a third on Wednesday. This much reinforced their natural mobility. It gave us priceless advantages in pursuit, for the force renewed itself with fresh men in every new tribal area, and gave us always our pristine energy. Maximum disorder was in a real sense our equilibrium.

The internal economy of the raiding parties was equally curious. We aimed at maximum articulation. We were serving a common ideal, without tribal emulation, and so we could not hope for any *esprit de corps* to reinforce our motives. Soldiers are made a caste either by being given great pay and rewards in money, uniform, or political privileges; or, as in England, by being made outcasts, cut off from their fellows by contempt. We could not knit man to man, for our tribesmen were in arms willingly, by conviction. There have been many armies enlisted voluntarily: there have been few armies serving voluntarily under such trying conditions, for so long a war as ours. Any of the Arabs could go home whenever the conviction failed him. Our only contract was honour.

Consequently we had no discipline, in the sense in which it is restrictive, submergent of individuality, the lowest common denominator of men. In regular armies in peace it means the limit of energy attainable by everybody present: it is the hunt not of an average, but of an absolute, a 100-per-cent. standard, in which the ninety-nine stronger men are played down to the level of the worst. The aim is to render the unit a unit, and the man a type, in order that their effort shall be calculable, their collective output even in grain and in bulk. The deeper the discipline, the lower the individual efficiency, and the more sure the performance. It is a deliberate sacrifice of capacity in order to reduce the uncertain element, the bionomic factor, in enlisted humanity, and its accompaniment is *compound* or social war, that form in which the man in the fighting line has to be the product of the multiplied exertions of the long hierarchy, from workshop to supply unit, which maintains him in the field.

The Arab war was *simple* and individual. Every enrolled man served in the line of battle, and was self-contained. We had no lines of communication or labour troops. The efficiency of each man was his personal efficiency. We thought that in our condition of warfare the sum yielded by single men would be at least equal to the product of a compound system, and it was certainly easier to adjust to tribal life and manners, given elasticity and understanding on the part of the commanding officers. Fortunately for our chances nearly every young Englishman has the roots of eccentricity in him, and so we got on well enough. Of course we used very few Englishmen in the field, not more than one per thousand of the Arab troops. A larger proportion would have created friction, just because they were foreign bodies (pearls if you please) in the oyster: and those who were present controlled by influence and advice, by their superior knowledge, not by an extraneous authority.

In practice we did not employ in the firing line the greater numbers which the adoption of a 'simple' system put theoretically at our disposal. We preferred to use them in relay: otherwise our attack would have become too extended. Each man had to have liberal work-room. In irregular war if two men are together one is being wasted. The moral strain of isolated action makes this simple form of war very exacting on the individual soldier, and demands from him special initiative, endurance and enthusiasm. Our ideal was to make action a series of single combats. Napoleon, in his pregnant valuation of the Mamelukes in terms of French soldiers, first gave me the idea: Ardant du Picq widened its application: the prejudices of historians are generally the richest part of their histories. Our value depended entirely on our quality, not on our quantity. We had to keep always cool, for the excitement of a blood-lust would impair the science of our combatants, and our victory depended on our just use of speed, concealment, accuracy of fire. Irregular war is far more intellectual than a bayonet charge.

The illiteracy of our forces was not harmful, since we worked intentionally in these small numbers and explained our plan verbally to everyone. Their very illiteracy has trained them to a longer memory and a closer hearing of the news. Nor were our tactics too subtle, for they had to be translated into independent action through the heads of our followers, and success was impossible unless most of them used their intelligence to forward our conception against the moral and material accidents of the path. This dilution of tactical ability to the level of the lowest interpreter was regrettable, but not all loss. The only alternative would be independent enterprise, and a mediocre design, persisted in, is grander than a series of brilliant expedients and will overcome them in the end.

By careful persistence, kept strictly within our strength and following the spirit of our theories, we were able eventually to reduce the Turks to helplessness, and complete victory seemed to be almost within our sight when General Allenby by his immense stroke in Palestine threw the enemy's main forces into hopeless confusion and put an immediate end to the Turkish war. We were very happy to have done with all our pains, but sometimes since I have felt a private regret that his too-greatness deprived me of the opportunity of following to the end the dictum of Saxe that a war might be won without fighting battles. It was an irony of fate to entrust this side-show of a side-show, with its opportunity of proving or disproving the theory, to an outsider like myself, not qualified technically to make the best of it. I would have given so much to show that Saxe was the greatest master of this kind of war, but now all I can say is that we worked by his light for two years, and the work stood. This is a pragmatic argument that cannot be wholly derided.

Unfortunately our campaigns lacked a historian as much as an executant. Now that I try to write down what we did, and why, some of our principles look truisms (mankind would so rather believe a sophism) and some look contradictory. The fault must be either in my exposition or in my observation. Savage warfare seems never to have been thought out in English from the savage point of view, and the Arab revolt would have been a great opportunity for a thinker to test its possibilities on a grand scale. Our war was so odd and so far away that coy Authority left us to ourselves. We had no base machinery, no formal staff, no clerks, no government, no telegraphs, no public opinion, no troops of British nationality, no honour, no conventions. The experiment was a thrilling one, which took all our wits. We believed we would prove irregular war or rebellion to be an exact science, and an inevitable success, granted certain factors and if pursued along certain lines. We did not prove it, because the war stopped: but here the thesis is:—

It seemed that rebellion must have an unassailable base, something guarded not merely from attack, but from the fear of it: such a base as we had in the Red Sea Ports, the desert, or in the minds of the men we converted to our creed. It must have a sophisticated alien enemy, in the form of a disciplined army of occupation too small to fulfil the doctrine of acreage: too few to adjust number to space, in order to dominate the whole area effectively from fortified posts. It must have a friendly population, not actively friendly, but sympathetic to the point of not betraying rebel movements to the enemy. Rebellions can be made by 2 per cent. active in a striking force, and 98 per cent. passively sympathetic. The few active rebels must have the qualities of speed and endurance, ubiquity and independence of arteries of supply. They must have the technical equipment to destroy or paralyse the enemy's organized communications, for irregular war is fairly Willisen's definition of strategy, 'the study of communication' in its extreme degree, of attack where the enemy is not. In fifty words: Granted mobility, security (in the form of denying targets to the enemy), time, and doctrine (the idea to convert every subject to friendliness), victory will rest with the insurgents, for the algebraical factors are in the end decisive, and against them perfections of means and spirit struggle quite in vain.

TO C. M. DOUGHTY

25.12.18   *[Carlton Hotel, Pall Mall, London, crossed out]*

Dear Mr. Doughty, It is exceedingly good of you to have written to me: and it happened just when I had made up my mind that I must write to you, and tell you that I had been over much of your country, (more securely and comfortably, but in somewhat the same fashion) meeting many of the people, and sons of the people who knew you out there. It has been a wonderful experience, and I have got quite a lot to tell.

I'm afraid it is not likely to be written for publication, since some of it would give offence to people alive, (including myself!) but I hope to get it put on paper soon.

When I can, I want to come down to Eastbourne and see you. That will not be till after the Peace Conference, I expect. Meanwhile I must tell you that I got a copy of *Arabia Deserta* the other day: the genuine edition!

I'm too late for Christmas: but my very best New Year wishes. Yours sincerely,   T. E. LAWRENCE

P.S. I haven't any initials after my name — except B.A., which it is unusual to put!

TO COLONEL S. F. NEWCOMBE

16. 2. 20.

Dear S.F., I owe you five letters! At first it wasn't worth while for you were reported to me in one week as at Aleppo, Azrak, Bagdad & Cairo: and then it became a habit.

However the arrival of a smaller (I hope not cheaper) edition[1] is an occasion for a bookworm like myself. The editio princeps always has a special value: but in some cases (Shakespeare folios e.g.) new matter is embodied in the reprints, which give them a market reputation little, if any, less than original. At the same time collectors, and especially collectors of sentiment, always prefer the genuine article.

---

[1] Colonel Newcombe's son, Stuart Lawrence Newcombe, had just been born.

However Mrs. Newcombe will regard the graft as the first. These things, as Solomon quoted from Adam's table-talk, depend on the point of view. Please give her my heartiest congratulations.

Then about business. Of course Lawrence may have been the name of your absolutely favourite cousin or aunt, (observe my adroitness in *sex*), and if so I will be dropping an immodest brick by blushing — but if it isn't, aren't you handicapping 'it'? In the history of the world (cheap edition) I'm a sublimated Aladdin, the thousand and second Knight, a Strand-Magazine strummer. In the eyes of 'those who know'[1] I failed badly in attempting a piece of work which a little more resolution would have pushed through, or left un-touched. So either case it is bad for the sprig, unless, as I said, there is a really decent aunt.

As for god-fathering him, I asked two or three people what it meant, & their words were ribald. Perhaps it is because people near me lose that sense of mystery which distance gives. Or else it was because they didn't know it was you — or at least yours. Anyhow I can't find out what it means, and so I shall be delighted to take it on. Everybody agrees it means a silver mug — but tell me first if his complexion is red or white: I wouldn't commit a colour-discord. . . .

I have abandoned Oxford, & wander about town from a bedroom in Pimlico, (temporary, for Bethnal Green is nicer to the nose) looking at the stars. It is nicer than looking at Lord Curzon.

Please give Mrs. Newcombe my very best regards. How odd it must be having married you. Tell her my letter wasn't fit for her to see.   L.

TO V. W. RICHARDS

27.2.20

. . . About the book-to-build-the-house. It is on paper in the first draft to the middle of Book vi: and there are seven books in all. But the first draft is a long way off the last one and I feel hopeless about ever finishing it. I work best utterly by myself: when I speak to no one

---

[1] Translation of Dante's *Color chi sanno*.

for days. So that's a consoling prospect for you in the hut (or Hall: q.e.v.) days of garrulity divided by days of silence. Hoots again. Gardiner to return to business says 'Hut, Hawkes Head'. Stokes & Stokes say 'King's Head': you say 'Pole Hill'. Which? Pole Hill Press sounds nicest. I'm sorry to raise this again. Hawkes are poor eating, and Kings, if eaten, would taste like them. Also heads are the worst part of everything except asparagus.

I haven't read *Boon*; and I don't like Wells. He has written eighty books. . . .

[The administration of Mesopotamia on the Indian model, and with administrators from India, was proving an expensive and unpopular business: unpopular that is to say with the inhabitants and with the British taxpayer. Lawrence had an alternative plan of holding Meso-potamia by air control only, which proved a great economy and success after the establishment of the kingdom of Iraq.]

TO LORD WINTERTON

22. 4. 20   *All Souls College Oxford.*

Dear Winterton, I've hopped off here — more or less broke — for a month. They give one credit. . . .

Yes I saw Trenchard last night. He has, as you say, 'grown' beyond measure. Pre-1914 he'd have been downed for a little-Englander: now I think he is right in all points, and after quite a lot of talk I feel inclined to back his scheme. It means Salmond as H.C.[1] in Bagdad (a happy deliverance from the I.C.S.[2] tradition) with probably the Colonial Secretary nominally responsible, and with an Arab army under an Arab-British administration to defend the country.

Trenchard sounded to me clean & honest (for the Lord's sake don't repeat this!) and means to play fair by the local people. He thinks as little of the worth of bombing as we did!

I told him Joyce would make the Arab army for him[3]: it would be pleasant to see Nuri and Jaafar & the rest doing their job over again.

[1] High Commissioner.   [2] Indian Civil Service.   [3] He did, with Jaafar.

However more of this when we meet: but unless something provokes you beyond measure don't knock him on the head in the House, because I think he means rightly. So odd to find a man without entanglements in the city!

That talk will be great sport, and I'll look forward to it: but I doubt whether Aubrey[1] will come so soon. Albania seems to be revolting in several ways at once, and he will probably assume its crown for a few weeks. Yours ever,   TEL

This letter goes to the H. of C.[2]: a bad address, I think, but I always forget the other.   L.

TO C. M. DOUGHTY

7. 5. 20   *All Souls, Oxford.*

Dear Mr. Doughty, After a great deal of writing Egypt[3] have at last been able to make up their minds — of course wrongly. They say that the arrears due to the interference of the local troubles will take them two years to work off. After that they will be able to take on outside work again.

I do not believe it, for I am sure that their local troubles are not nearly over. It is most unsatisfactory.

There remain possibilities of America, and subscription. The younger poets are very anxious for the latter, since they all want *Arabia Deserta*, and cannot afford her (she now stands at £32. 10. 0) but it would mean getting a very long list (at least a thousand copies, I think) and I do not know if this is possible. As for America, the book is unfortunately not copyright there. However, if I may, I'll have another talk with Duckworth. There is so large and worthy a demand for the book that it seems shameful not to get it out again somehow.

---

[1] Aubrey Herbert.   [2] House of Commons.
[3] Lawrence had hoped to have *Arabia Deserta* reprinted by the Government Press in Cairo.

WAR AND DIPLOMACY

MESOPOTAMIA[1]

BY EX.-LIEUT.-COL. T. E. LAWRENCE
(Fellow of All Souls College, Oxford)

[*Mr. Lawrence, whose organization and direction of the Hedjaz against the Turks was one of the outstanding romances of the war, has written this article at our request in order that the public may be fully informed of our Mesopotamian commitments.*]

The people of England have been led in Mesopotamia into a trap from which it will be hard to escape with dignity and honour. They have been tricked into it by a steady withholding of information. The Bagdad communiqués are belated, insincere, incomplete. Things have been far worse than we have been told, our administration more bloody and inefficient than the public knows. It is a disgrace to our imperial record, and may soon be too inflamed for any ordinary cure. We are to-day not far from a disaster.

The sins of commission are those of the British civil authorities in Mesopotamia (especially of three 'colonels') who were given a free hand by London. They are controlled from no Department of State, but from the empty space which divides the Foreign Office from the India Office. They availed themselves of the necessary discretion of war-time to carry over their dangerous independence into times of peace. They contest every suggestion of real self-government sent them from home. A recent proclamation about autonomy circulated with unction from Bagdad was drafted and published out there in a hurry, to forestall a more liberal statement in preparation in London. 'Self-determination papers' favourable to England were extorted in Mesopotamia in 1919 by official pressure, by aeroplane demonstrations, by deportations to India.

The Cabinet cannot disclaim all responsibility. They receive little more news than the public: tney should have insisted on more, and better. They have sent draft after draft of reinforcements, without enquiry. When conditions became too bad to endure longer, they decided to send out as High Commissioner the original author of the present system, with a conciliatory message to the Arabs that his heart and policy have completely changed.[2]

---

[1] Printed in the *Sunday Times*, August 22nd, 1920.

[2] It had been decided that Sir Percy Cox was to return as High Commissioner the following October to form a provisional Government of Arab notables.

Yet our published policy has not changed, and does not need changing. It is that there has been a deplorable contrast between our profession and our practice. We said we went to Mesopotamia to defeat Turkey. We said we stayed to deliver the Arabs from the oppression of the Turkish Government, and to make available for the world its resources of corn and oil. We spent nearly a million men and nearly a thousand million of money to these ends. This year we are spending ninety-two thousand men and fifty millions of money on the same objects.

Our government is worse than the old Turkish system. They kept fourteen thousand local conscripts embodied, and killed a yearly average of two hundred Arabs in maintaining peace. We keep ninety thousand men, with aeroplanes, armoured cars, gunboats, and armoured trains. We have killed about ten thousand Arabs in this rising this summer. We cannot hope to maintain such an average: it is a poor country, sparsely peopled; but Abd el Hamid would applaud his masters, if he saw us working. We are told the object of the rising was political, we are not told what the local people want. It may be what the Cabinet has promised them. A Minister in the House of Lords said that we must have so many troops because the local people will not enlist. On Friday the Government announce the death of some local levies defending their British officers, and say that the services of these men have not yet been sufficiently recognized because they are too few (adding the characteristic Bagdad touch that they are men of bad character). There are seven thousand of them, just half the old Turkish force of occupation. Properly officered and distributed, they would relieve half our army there. Cromer controlled Egypt's six million people with five thousand British troops; Colonel Wilson[1] fails to control Mesopotamia's three million people with ninety thousand troops.

We have not reached the limit of our military commitments. Four weeks ago the staff in Mesopotamia drew up a memorandum asking for four more divisions. I believe it was forwarded to the War Office, which has now sent three brigades from India. If the North-West Frontier cannot be further denuded, where is the balance to come from? Meanwhile, our unfortunate troops, Indian and British, under hard conditions of climate and supply, are policing an immense area, paying dearly every day in lives for the wilfully wrong policy of the civil administration in Bagdad. General Dyer was relieved of his com-

[1] Not to be confused with Colonel C. E. Wilson.

mand in India for a much smaller error, but the responsibility in this case is not on the Army, which has acted only at the request of the civil authorities. The War Office has made every effort to reduce our forces, but the decisions of the Cabinet have been against them.

The Government in Bagdad have been hanging Arabs in that town for political offences, which they call rebellion. The Arabs are not rebels against us. They are still nominally Turkish subjects, nominally at war with us. Are these illegal executions to provoke the Arabs to reprisals on the three hundred British prisoners they hold? And, if so, is it that their punishment may be more severe, or is it to persuade our other troops to fight to the last?

We say we are in Mesopotamia to develop it for the benefit of the world. All experts say that the labour supply is the ruling factor in its development. How far will the killing of ten thousand villagers and townspeople this summer hinder the production of wheat, cotton and oil? How long will we permit millions of pounds, thousands of Imperial troops, and tens of thousands of Arabs to be sacrificed on behalf of a form of colonial administration which can benefit nobody but its administrators?

TO ROBERT GRAVES

Saturday [*Dec.* 1920]

My Lord, I'd just got as keen as mustard on going out with Kennington[1] when Winston Churchill in his third effort to get me to join his new Middle Eastern Department used arguments which I could not resist.

So I'm a Government servant from yesterday: and Palestine goes fut (or phut?).

Kennington is going all the same: (that man is a great man) and as an official I'll be able to help him even more than ever: but what a beastly mess.

[1] Lawrence had got to know Robert Graves while he was at All Souls, and Graves had introduced him to Eric Kennington who became eager to go out to paint several of the Arab leaders, and members of Lawrence's bodyguard, to illustrate *Seven Pillars of Wisdom*.

They let me fix my own terms: so I said a temporary billet, and £1000: out of evil comes good for——

I had meant to publish the enclosed muck[1] in U.S.A., to raise £1000: and now I've written to say that I've made other arrangements. Will you read them now they are born to blush unseen? They are literal extracts from a book I wrote: but all the personal (subjective) part is left out for dignity's sake. It's bloody cheek asking you to read such muck: but the intrinsic interest may atone for the lack of technique: and as an artist you should be glad to peep behind the scenes of another's affair.

ON ERIC KENNINGTON'S ARAB PORTRAITS

[Sent from Aden on August 25th, 1921. The Catalogue reference numbers have been omitted]

I saw him doing one of these and can testify that he did not know why he was working, nor how he was working. When he felt that he knew things went very badly. When he began to whistle softly, things were moving well; and as some Arabs think that whistling is a speech with devils, many of his subjects must have felt themselves in bad company before their sittings ended. He was drawing odd people, who are very impatient of those they think fools, men without ties, or duties, or claims, rank individualists who cling to their barren country that they may owe nothing to any man, and be owed nothing in return. Very difficult sitters they are.

It was a strange chance which put him in contact with this society, but he rose to his occasion and brought a full selection of his opportunities back with him in his portfolio.

He has drawn camel-men, and princes of the desert, donkey-boys, officers, descendants of the Prophet, a vice-president of the Turkish Chamber, slaves, sheikhs and swordsmen. They represent a fair choice of the real Arab, not the Algerian or Egyptian or Syrian so commonly palmed off on us, not the noisy, luxury-loving, sensual, passionate, greedy person, but a man whose ruling characteristic is hardness, of body, mind, heart and head.

This is no doubt where my being asked to write a note comes in,

[1] Four articles in *The World's Work*.

for I know these odd people who sat to him, and some of them have been my friends. The causes of his going out to Arabia were, a poet, something a man said, and an unpublished book of mine. His Arabs were amongst those who fought gallantly for their freedom in the War. Freedom is a profane, not a saintly body, for which they cared too exclusively to have spare mind to see themselves in action. It never occurred to them that their children might want to know what they did, and so they wrote down nothing of their story. I felt that this was a mistake, and set about making loose notes in the leisure and detachment I had, for our race has been free so long that by now we have forgotten that first wonderful taste; indeed age has made it cloying, and sometimes we wish for chains as a variety.

This book was something for the future, but it was an outside view, from an odd angle, and words, especially an amateur's words, are unsatisfactory to describe persons. It seemed to us that it would be balanced somewhat by an expert view, from another angle: and so Kennington went out to correct my men. He was to have had me as his guide, but circumstances prevented this, and plunged him alone into a great Arab camp, which was in a state of semi-warfare. There he had nothing better than a bell-tent for working in, and an atmosphere of unrest and uncertainty which made work difficult.

I had meant to help him in his selection of subjects to draw: as events turned out he was thrown on his own judgment. It is interesting to see that instinctively he drew the men of the desert. Where he was there were ten settled men to every nomad: yet his drawings show nearly ten desert men to every peasant. This has strengthened in me the unflattering suspicion that the nomad is the richer creature.

The Arab townsman or villager is like us and our villagers, with our notion of property, our sense of gain and our appetite for material success. He has our premises as well as our processes. The Beduin, on the other hand, while his sense is as human and his mind as logical as ours, begins with principles quite other than our own, and gets further from us as his character strengthens. He has a creed and practice of not-possessing which is a tough armour against our modern wiles. It defends him against all sentiment.

Somehow or other Kennington persuaded them to sit; and when he came home, and turned over his sheets of paper in front of me, the experience was very wonderful. I saw first one and then another of the men whom I had known, and at once learned to know them better. This may point indirectly to the power of the drawings as works of art: it pointed without contest to their literary completeness as illustrations of my memory of the men in action: and I think it is praise of psychology. There is quite admirable character.

Some are curiously typical. Of course they are individual enough, speaking portraits of the men in many of their moods and attitudes: but often Kennington has reached behind the particular, and made them also types. Perhaps it was because of the language bar, which forced him to rely entirely on his visual powers. However it is, in this study and in that you see not only So and So, son of So and So, but a representation of all the Ageyl who ever rode out from Bagdad, or of all the freedom of the palm-oases of Nejd. In his Sherifs and in his Sheikhs you see the spirit of the race of sherifs, or of the class of sheikhs sitting within these men's clothes, inhabiting their features, giving a broader significance to their shapes. These drawings are deep and sharp renderings of all that Western Arabians are.

They are quite literal, not prettied or idealized in any way. Yet it would not be fair to call them average. Kennington chose some of the finest men within his reach for his sitters. Auda abu Tayi is the best man in Arabia to have beside you in a fight: you are good enough if you can keep near him for long. He is a mosaic of quixotic splendours: and when he dies the 'Middle Ages' of the desert will have ended. Said el Sikeini is a dour puritan, who saw his men dragging chests of gold and rich merchandise from the train which he had blown up by a mine. He left them plundering while he carefully rolled up and carried away the wire and electrical gear with which he had fired this mine, and with which he meant to fire the next. There is Sherif Shakir, the finest horseman in Arabia, and one of its bravest and richest and most beloved men. There is the boy Mahmas whom our standards would make a murderer. He is short-tempered and proud, and cannot endure to be worsted in argument. When it happens he leans forward with his little knife and kills the other party. Three times he did it before people learnt to respect his convictions, however ill-expressed. His elder brother, a responsible parent, each time saved him from odium by discharging on the nail the blood-money which heals the dispute and compensates the bereaved. There is Emir Abdulla who will read this note, and would not thank me for either praise or blame of him. His complexity comes out in the portrait.

At the other end of the scale is the spy who was our most excellent informant in the War, but is looked down upon by his fellows because he took money for his work. He lost the money in a bad trading venture after the armistice, and now without either friends or substance must serve as a donkey-boy where he once walked free. His face shows his sense of the broken world about him: but when he was sent for to be drawn he ran home and put on his best clothing. It was not very good, but evidently he still has hope and self-respect.

Ali ibn Hussein, Fahad, Matar, Mohammad Sheri, Sindah: the desert is full of songs and legends of their fighting, books could be written round them by the Arabs, and personally I am very content to have had a share in causing to be made these records of their faces while the knowledge of what they did is fresh in men's minds. Whoever writes those books will have to write well if he is to do honour to his illustrations.

[The following letter appeared in the *Morning Post* of July 20th, 1922, under the heading, 'Arabian Politics: Resignation of Colonel Lawrence as Adviser'.]

TO SIR JOHN SHUCKBURGH

4th July, 1922

My dear Shuckburgh, It seems to me that the time has come when I can fairly offer my resignation from the Middle East Department. You will remember that I was an emergency appointment, made because Mr. Churchill meant to introduce changes in our policy, and because he thought that my help would be useful during the expected stormy period.

Well, that was eighteen months ago; but since we 'changed direction', we have not had, I think, a British casualty in Palestine or Arabia or the Arab provinces of Irak. Political questions there are still, of course, and wide open; there always will be, but their expression and conduct has been growing steadily more constitutional. For long there has not been an outbreak of any kind; and while it would be foolish to seem too hopeful, yet at the same time I think there is no present prospect of trouble.

As I said, I think of myself as an emergency appointment. There are many other things I want to do and I came in unwillingly in the first place. While things run along the present settled and routine lines I can see no justification for the Department's continuing my employment — and little for me to do if it is continued. So if Mr. Churchill permits, I shall be very glad to leave so prosperous a ship. I need hardly say that I'm always at his disposal if ever there is a crisis, or any job, small or big, for which he can convince me that I am necessary.

I have to thank you personally for the very pleasant conditions under which I have worked in the Department itself.

yours sincerely,

T. E. LAWRENCE

[It is perhaps appropriate to insert here Lawrence's own view of the work done while he was Churchill's adviser on Arab affairs. The following extract is from the manuscript Preface, dated November 18th, 1922, to an abridgement of the Oxford Text of *Seven Pillars of Wisdom*, made by Edward Garnett but never published. It shows that Lawrence regarded his work as ended.]

18. 11. 22

The book dates itself to 1919, when powerful elements in the British Government were seeking to evade their war-time obligations to the Arabs. That stage ended in March 1921, when Mr. Winston Churchill took charge of the Middle East. He set honesty before expediency in order to fulfil our promises in the letter and in the spirit. He executed the whole McMahon undertaking (called a treaty by some who have not seen it) for Palestine, for Trans-Jordania, and for Arabia. In Mesopotamia he went far beyond its provisions, giving to the Arabs more, and reserving for us much less, than Sir Henry McMahon had thought fit.

In the affairs of French Syria he was not able to interfere, and the Sherif of Mecca can fairly complain that the settlement there is not yet in accordance with the Anglo-French agreement of 1916, or with our word to him. I say 'not yet' advisedly, since the McMahon proposals (being based on racial and economic reasons) were likely to have imposed themselves eventually, even if Mr. Churchill's progressive

British military withdrawal from Mesopotamia had not come to pre-judge the future of all the Arab areas.

I do not wish to publish secret documents, nor to make long explanations: but must put on record my conviction that England is out of the Arab affair with clean hands. Some Arab advocates (the most vociferous joined our ranks after the Armistice) have rejected my judgment on this point. Like a tedious Pensioner I showed them my wounds (over sixty I have, each scar evidence of a pain incurred in Arab service) as proof I had worked sincerely on their side. They found me out-of-date: and I was happy to withdraw from a political milieu which had never been congenial.

PART III

THE ROYAL AIR FORCE

[Lawrence was enlisted at Henrietta Street on August 30th, 1922, under the name of John Hume Ross, A/C 2 No. 352087.]

I.IX.22 [*Uxbridge*]

Dear Swann, I can't ask the corporal how an aircraft hand addresses an air-vice-marshall: — so please take this letter as a work of my late existence! I hadn't meant to write, except when I changed station, but the mess I made of Henrietta St. demands an apology. I thought I was fitter: but when it came to the point, walked up and down the street in a blue funk, and finally went in with my nerves dithering, and my heart dancing. My teeth never were any good, so the doctors threw me straight downstairs again. There Dexter caught me, and lent me what was no doubt his right hand to steer me past the medical, and through other rocks of square roots and essays and decimals. However I was obviously incapable of getting through on my own, so he got another chit from you, and that did the trick satisfactorily. If I'd known I was such a wreck I'd have gone off and recovered before [join]ing up: now the cure and the experiment must proceed together. I'm not very certain of myself, for the crudities, which aren't as bad as I expected, worry me far more than I expected: and physically I can only just scrape through the days. However they are a cheerful crowd; and the N.C.O.s behave with extraordinary gentleness to us (there's no other word fits their tone— except on the square, from which good Lord deliver us!) and I enjoy usually one hour of the sixteen, and often laugh in bed after lights out. If I can get able to sleep, and to eat the food, and to go through the P.T.[1] I'll be all right. The present worry is 90% nerves.

Would you tell the C.A.S.[2] that he's given me the completest change any mortal has had since Nebuchadnezzar: and that so far as I'm concerned it's to go on? Fortunately I told him I wasn't sure how long I could stick it, so that there is always a bridge — but it isn't required yet, and I hope won't be: only it's a comforting thought for the fifteen bad hours.

As for the special reason for which I came in — there's masses of gorgeous stuff lying about: but the scale of it is heart-rending. I found the Arab Revolt too big to write about, and chose this as a smaller subject to write about: but you'd have to be a man and a half to tackle it at all decently.

[1] Physical Training.　　　　　[2] Chief of the Air Staff.

I must say you have an amazing good crowd in the ranks: as a new force it ought to be pretty alive: but its keenness and life is better than I dreamed of.

In case I'm wanted by the Colonial Office I'll send you a note as often as I change station: but not more unless I want something, which will be a sad event. Less than two years won't do what I planned, in my present opinion: and they all say things are easier outside Uxbridge. Also I'll have got used to being a dog's body.

Please tell the C.A.S. that I'm delighted, and most grateful to him and to you for what you have done. Don't bother to keep an eye on what happens to me. Yours sincerely   T E LAWRENCE

from THE MINT

I: RECRUITING OFFICE

G OD, this is awful. Hesitating for two hours up and down a filthy street, lips and hands and knees tremulously out of control, my heart pounding in fear of that little door through which I must go to join up. Try sitting a moment in the churchyard? That's caused it. The nearest lavatory, now. Oh yes, of course, under the church. What was Baker's story about the cornice?

A penny; which leaves me fifteen. Buck up, old seat-wiper: I can't tip you and I'm urgent. Won by a short head. My right shoe is burst along the welt and my trousers are growing fringes. One reason that taught me I wasn't a man of action was this routine melting of the bowels before a crisis. However, now we end it. I'm going straight up and in.

All smooth so far. They are gentle-spoken to us, almost sorry. Won't you walk into my parlour? Wait upstairs for medical exam? 'Righto!' This sodden pyramid of clothes upon the floor is sign of a dirtier man than me in front. My go next? Everything off? (Naked we come into the R.A.F.) Ross? 'Yes, that's me.'

Officers, two of them. . . .

'D'you smoke?'

Not much, Sir.

238

'Well, cut it out. See?'

Six months back, it was, my last cigarette. However, no use giving myself away.

'Nerves like a rabbit.' The scotch-voiced doctor's hard fingers go hammer, hammer, hammer over the loud box of my ribs. I must be pretty hollow.

'Turn over: get up: stand under here: make yourself as tall as you can: he'll just do five foot six, Mac: chest — say 34. Expansion — by Jove, 38. That'll do. Now jump: higher: lift your right leg: hold it there: cough: all right: on your toes: arms straight in front of you: open your fingers wide: hold them so: turn round: bend over. Hullo, what the hell's those marks? Punishment?' 'No Sir, more like persuasion Sir, I think.' Face, neck, chest, getting hot.

'H . . . m . . . m . . ., that would account for the nerves.' His voice sounds softer. 'Don't put them down, Mac. Say *Two parallel scars on ribs.* What were they, boy?'

Superficial wounds, Sir.

'Answer my question.'

A barbed-wire tear, over a fence.

'H . . . m . . . m . . . and how long have you been short of food?'

(O Lord, I never thought he'd spot that. Since April I've been taking off my friends what meals I dared, all that my shame would let me take. I'd haunt the Duke of York steps at lunch-time, so as to turn back with someone to his club for the food whose necessity nearly choked me.[1] Put a good face on it; better.)

Gone a bit short the last three months, Sir. How my throat burns!

'More like six' . . . came back in a growl. The worst of telling lies naked is that the red shows all the way down. A long pause, me shivering in disgrace. He stares so gravely, and my eyes are watering. (Oh, it hurts: I wish I hadn't taken this job on.)

At last, 'All right: get back into your clothes. You aren't as good as we want but after a few weeks at the Depot you'll pull up all right.' Thank you very much, Sir. 'Best of luck, boy,' from Mac. Grunt from the kinder-spoken one. Here's the vegetable market again, not changed. I'm still shaking everyway, but anyhow I've done it. Isn't there a Fuller's down that street? I've half a mind to blow my shilling on a coffee. Seven years now before I need think of winning a meal.

[1] This must be regarded as an indication of Lawrence's state of mind. Colonel Newcombe recalls that at the time in question Lawrence constantly refused or neglected invitations to meals at the houses of friends and the money he received was sufficient for his needs.

2: THE GATE

Our sergeant, trimly erect in creaseless blue uniform, hesitated as we left the station yard. Your fighting-man is shy of giving orders to people possibly disobedient, for an ignored command disgraces would-be authority; and Englishmen (being what they are) resent being bossed except as law or imperious circumstance directs. Then in un-convincing offhand, 'I'm going over to that shop a moment. You fellows keep along this foot-path till I give you a shout' and he crossed the sunny street to pop slickly in and out of a tobacconist's. I suppose he has done such conducting duty daily for months: but he needn't care for the feelings of us six shambling ones. We are moving in a dream.

This main street of an old-fashioned country town clanks with hulking trams labelled Shepherd's Bush. Invaders. We walk till on our left rise the bill-boards of eligible plots and heavy elms bulge through the wall of a broken park. The tyre-polished tarmac glistens before and after these umbrellas of shade. Here is a gateway, high and brick-pillared with bombs atop: and by it a blue sentry with a rifle. A momentary drawing-together of our group. But head in air on the opposite pavement the sergeant strides forward, looking hard to his front. The stone flags ring under the ferrule of his planted stick.

Our sun-softened asphalt declines into a dusty gravel. Shuffle shuffle goes the loose crowd of us, past another gate. The wall gives place to park-paling and wire: there are khaki men in the park, distant. A third gate. The sergeant crosses towards it, heading us off. With a wave of his stick he shepherds our little mob past the sentry who stands firm before a box. For a moment we glance back over the bayonet at the gleaming road with its traffic and its people strolling, freely, in a world that we have quitted.

3: IN THE PARK

They licensed us to wander where we pleased (within gates) through the still autumn afternoon. The clouded breadth of the fallen park, into which this war-time camp had been intruded, made an appeal to me. Across it lay the gentle curve of Park Road, the only formal road in camp and quiet, being out of bounds. With a blue smoothness it stretched between cut lawns, under a rank of trees.

The park dipped in the middle to the ragged edges of a little stream, and huts climbed down each slope from the tops, reaching out over the valley as if they had meant to join roofs across its leafy stream — but something, perhaps the dank, deep grass of the lowland meadows, stayed them.

I paused on the bridge above the stagnant water, which wound into the hollow between banks of thicketed rush and foxglove. By each side were choice-planted great trees. On the western slope swelled the strident activity of red-and-chocolate footballers. Should I be concerned in football again? There had been a rumour of that sinful misery, forced games. The ball at intervals plonked musically against men's boots or on the resistant ground: and each game was edged by its vocal border of khaki and blue. The blue clothes, which pinked their wearers' faces, seemed of a startling richness against the valley-slopes of verdant or yellow grass. Curtains of darkness were drawn around the playing fields by other bulky trees, from whose boughs green shadows dripped.

The particular wilderness of the Pinne's banks seemed also forbidden to troops: in its sallows sang a choir of birds. From the tall spire (where it pricked black against the sky on the ridge behind the pent-roofed camp) fell, quarter by quarter, the Westminster chimes on tubular bells. The gentleness of the river's air added these notes, not as an echo, but as an extra gravity and sweetness to its natural sounds and prolonged them into the distances, which were less distant than silvered with the deepening afternoon and the mists it conjured off the water. The dragging rattle of electric trains and trams, outside the pale, emphasized the aloof purposefulness in which so many men were cloistered here.

By tea-time the football grew languid, and at last ceased. Slowly the mist invaded the lowest ground and slowly it climbed all the grass slope until the lights of the camp were glowing direct into its sea.

4: THE FEAR

After dusk the camp paths became thronged with men, all seeming friends, who met with a freemasonry of unintelligible greeting. I shrank from them and equally from their canteen with its glare and its hospitable smells. The thought of our hut returned to me as a refuge. Thankfully I made for it.

When I opened the door the long interior with its pendent lights offered indeed a refuge against the night. Its colouring was gay:— primary white walls sectioned by pilasters of hot brick, or by slender roof-posts painted green aligning themselves over the concrete floor between the close rows of brown-blanketed identical beds. But there was no one there, and the roof seemed full of staring eyes. I stumbled dizzily, under their view, down the alley of polished linoleum which lay like a black gangway across the concrete. Did the floor pitch slightly, with a rise and fall, like a deck? Or was my head swimming in the brilliant silence which thronged the empty place?

I lay, sickly, on my allotted bed. For a moment my bedfellow was perfect fear. The globes stared unwinking; my external imaginings flocked to the pillow and whispered to each ear that I was attempting the hardest effort of my life. Could a man, who for years had been closely shut up, sifting his inmost self with painful iteration to compress its smallest particles into a book — could he suddenly end his civil war and live the open life, patent for everyone to read?

Accident, achievement, and rumour (cemented equally by my partial friends) had built me such a caddis-shell as almost prompted me to forget the true shape of the worm inside. So I had sloughed them and it right off — every comfort and possession — to plunge crudely amongst crude men and find myself for these remaining years of prime life. Fear now told me that nothing of my present would survive this voyage into the unknown.

Voyage? Yes, the long hold-like hall had the sheer and paint-smell and sense of between decks. The pillars and tie-beams of its louring roof barred it into stalls like the stalls of a cattle boat waiting its load. Awaiting us.

Slowly we drifted in, those who had come with me today, till on the made-up beds five or six of us were lying subdued to the strangeness and the silence: a silence again pointed by that faint external creeping roar of the tramcars which swung along the road behind. Subtly our presences comforted one another.

At ten o'clock the door was flung open and a torrent of others entered, those stagers who had been here for some days and had gained outward assurance. They fought off nervousness by noise, by talk, by Swanee River on the mouth-organ, by loose scrummaging and japes and horseplay. Between the jangles of a sudden song fell bars of quiet, in which man whispered confidentially to man. Then again the chatter, a jay-laugh, that pretence of vast pleasure from a poor jest.

As they swiftly stripped for sleep a reek of body fought with beer and tobacco for the mastery of the room. The horseplay turned to a rough-house: snatching of trousers, and smacks with the flat of hard hands, followed by clumsy steeple-chases over the obstacles of beds which tipped or tilted. We, the last joined, were trembling to think how we should bear the freedom of this fellowship, if they played with us. Our hut-refuge was become libertine, brutal, loud-voiced, unwashed.

At ten-fifteen lights out; and upon their dying flash every sound ceased. Silence and the fear came back to me. Through the white windows streaked white diagonals from the conflicting arc-lamps without. Without there ruled the stupor of first sleep, as of embryos in the natal caul. My observing spirit slowly and deliberately hoisted itself from place to prowl across this striped upper air, leisurely examining the forms stretched out so mummy-still in the strait beds. Our first lesson in the Depot had been of our apartness from life. This second vision was of our sameness, body by body. How many souls gibbered that night in the roof-beams, seeing it? Once more mine panicked, suddenly, and fled back to its coffin-body. Any cover was better than the bareness.

Night dragged. The sleepers, their prime exhaustion sated, began to stir uneasily. Some muttered thickly in the false life of dreams. They moaned or rolled slowly over in their beds, to the metallic twangling of their mattresses of hooked wire. In sleep on a hard bed the body does not rest without sighing. Perhaps all physical existence is a weary pain to man: only by day his alert stubborn spirit will not acknowledge it.

The surge of the trams in the night outside lifted sometimes to a scream as the flying wheels gridded on a curve. Each other hour was marked by the cobbling tic-tac of the relief guard, when they started on their round in file past our walls. Their rhythmic feet momently covered the rustling of the great chestnuts' yellowed leaves, the drone of the midnight rain, and the protestant drip drip of roof-drainings in a gutter.

For two or three such periods of the night I endured, stiff-stretched on the bed, widely awake and open-eyed, realizing myself again one of many after the years of loneliness. And the morrow loomed big with our new (yet certainly not smooth) fate in store. 'They can't kill us, anyhow,' Clarke had said at tea-time. That might, in a way, be the worst of it. Many men would take the death-sentence without a whimper to escape the life-sentence which fate carries in her other hand. When a plane shoots downward out of control, its crew cramp themselves fearfully into their seats for minutes like years, expecting the crash: but the smoothness of that long dive continues to their graves. Only for survivors is there an after-pain.

TO EDWARD GARNETT

Monday 9.x.22   [*Postmarked Uxbridge*]

Your Tuesday letter came, not to the pig-stye but to the barrack square. The Government's scare over Turkey (wind and vanity) has pushed forward our training and we wheel and turn and form fours and mark time and forward and wheel again from dawn till dark. I'm completely dead to decency: but your letter has been a sort of life-line, and I've read it about six times to cheer myself.

It's good of you to (or rather that you should) like my effort more on the re-reading. My test for a book is that one should finish it each time with a mind to read it again — some day. It's particularly interesting that the last fifty pages seem to you alive: I've never been able to see them at all: always by the time I have got so far my eyes have carried forward to the end, and I've gone through the last fighting like a dream. Those pages have been worked at very hard, but I've never got them in perspective: and I've always had a lurking fear that they were flatter than the VIth and VIIth parts (the failure of the bridge and the winter war) and formed an anticlimax — a weak ending. It was impossible for me to last out so long a writing with my wits about me: and I've feared that there would be found no reader long-winded enough to get there either. Your judgment that the book is in excess, as regards lengths, is also, I judge, true as regards intensity and breadth. I've had no pity on myself writing it — nor on my readers reading it. There's a clamour of force in it which deafens. A better artist would have given the effect of a fortissimo with less instrumentality. It's unskilled craftsmen who are profuse.

What you say about the oddity of my brain doesn't surprise me — but it helps to explain the apartness of myself here in this noisy barrack room. I might be one dragon-fly in a world of wasps — or one wasp among the dragon-flies! It's not a comfortable place: but if the oddity of my standing produces a fresh-feeling book, I suppose I shouldn't grouse about my luck.

The personal chapter clearly bothers you. A man (a metaphysician by nature, who was at Oxford with me and knows me very well)[1] read it, and told me that it stood out as the finest chapter in the book. I tend more to your opinion: it's not meant for the ordinary intelligences, and *must* mislead them: but to set it out in plain English would be very painful. However six months away from it, and then a fresh approach may work a change in my feeling towards it: may even give me energy to re-write it. At present nothing sounds less probable. I don't even feel capable (though I'd love to) of writing a fresh book on this place. I've made some rather poor notes, which show me how hard it would be to bring off a picture of the R.A.F. Depot.

I wonder how the reduction seems to you now. If you get it to 150,000 and satisfy yourself, and then I take out 20,000 or so, that should do the trick. What an odd book it will be! It's over-good of you to attempt such a business. I decided yesterday in church (church-parade!) that I ought to publish nothing. Today I feel inclined to publish. Am I neurasthenic or just feeble-willed?

I'm afraid I can't come away, even for a day.   E.L.

(Glad you like Auda, I did!)

TO BERNARD SHAW

7.xii.22

Dear Mr. Shaw, The camel-shooting, first time, was a fluke: and I have not inclination to repeat it. Suddenly it came to my mind that you still had the book: and I remembered that it was the longest book written: and that your time was rubies: and that if you spent hours over it I might be preventing, and would surely be delaying, another *Caesar* or *Heartbreak*: and in remorse I wrote to you. Please don't, out of kindness, bore yourself. It's more like the heaps of stone-chips left in the quarry after the builders had finished, than like the great pyramid itself: though I'll confess that I found the pyramid a sad sight: vulgar in size, untidy in surface, singularly sedative in shape. (As many s's in that as ever Swinburne used.')

[1] V. W Richards.

It's amusing, though probably you meant it without significance, that you mention Caesar. Your picture of him is one of the few of great men with any life in them: and to it and *Heartbreak* are due my sending you the *Seven Pillars*. Also the *Commentaries* are one of my pet books. I carry them, and read them regularly: in fact I'm reading them now. They are the antithesis of mine: indeed I suspect that no successful general ever spilled so much of himself on to paper as I did.

Why Gordon? There is only a superficial likeness I think: though my mother was a Gordon. My father was Anglo Irish, with Dutch strain. The death of Childers struck me as a very definite tragedy: Greek type.

I wonder what you will do with my 'dangerous potentialities' when you have finished the book: if you do finish it, and your letter sounds determined. It won't be so odd as what I've done with myself. I'm now an airman in the Air Force: one of those funny little objects in blue clothes who look forlorn when they walk about the Strand. It keeps me alive (just) and keeps me out of mischief. One of its consequences is that I'm afraid I can't come and see you: they give us very little leave, and rather too much work. At present I'm stationed by Aldershot. As the Press would talk rot about my eccentricity, please don't talk very much of it. It's not a secret, and not common knowledge: you see, people generally took for granted that I had enough money — or the determination to make some: whereas I have none at all, and have never worked for it: and won't.

The book is being abridged. Edward Garnett, a critic, has cut it to 150,000 words, and I'm going to see if a publisher will pay for these miserable orts. If so I'll become a civilian again. You have no idea how repulsive a barrack is as permanent home. It reconciles me to the meanness of the abridgement. Yours sincerely   T E LAWRENCE

TO EDWARD GARNETT

30.1.23

I'm overdue in writing, but have been inordinately worried. The R.A.F. have sacked me, for the crime of possessing too wide a publicity for a ranker: and as I'm as broke as usual the sacking is immediately and physically inconvenient. Also it's annoying to have worked myself up to the point of seeing much good and some thrills in barrack life, and then to be kicked out of it suddenly.

One result is that I'm unlikely to write an epoch-making book about man — or Englishman — in the ranks. . . .

TO BERNARD SHAW

30.1.23

I've now been sacked from the R.A.F., as a person with altogether too large a publicity factor for the ranks: — and feel miserable about it. As a last resort I've written to Trenchard asking for another chance in some remote station, where there are no papers, and no one will have heard of me. The reply to this is still not come. I've only a few days' money, so will do something decisive soon.

Those letters have come back.[1] Decent of the finder to notify you. I dropped them with my cheque book when the bank told me that I hadn't any more need of cheques. It wasn't rage or astonishment, but an agitation of mind which made me stuff them into a slit in my motoring overalls. The slit is a way to a pocket, not a pocket in itself. Also I haven't a motor, but a motor-bike. It goes 80 miles an hour, and is a perfect thing. I hope to eat it shortly . . . or rather, when regretfully I have to eat it, I hope it will last me for a very long while.

I've been wanting to tell you about the misfortunes of my proposed book: (if I remember rightly, your first book also isn't yet published: my only score over you is that I haven't written a second): however: —

When the first foul shout about me came in the *Daily Express* I cancelled (or rather I refused to complete and sign) the contract with Cape for publishing an abridgement. Cape was furious.

My mind is like a lump of putty, so that a while later I was sorry to have cancelled it, and I began to think of publishing, not an abridgement, but the whole story, as you have advised. So I sketched to Cape the possibility of a limited, privately-printed, subscription edition of 2000 copies, illustrated with all the drawings made for me by some twenty of the younger artists. Cape was staggered for the first moment, but then rose to it — suggesting half-profits, and a serial-issue of a

---

[1] A packet of Bernard Shaw's letters to Lawrence had been picked up in Lombard Street by Mr. Cope Hand, a clerk in a City merchant's, who returned them.

quarter of it in the *Observer*, and American copyrights, and all the necessary decorations. It took the form of a beautiful contract, sent me to sign: and that very day I got my dismissal from the Air Ministry, and so I've cancelled it too.

The present position is that nothing is going to appear: and this is the most comfortable state of affairs, so far as my mind is concerned. Whether my body will cry out for more food after it's eaten my quite perfect motor bike, I don't know. Sufficient for the month, anyway: and it's been a bad month, for the R.A.F. was the most interesting thing I ever did (after the squalid difficulty of getting used to it) and I'll regret its loss for good.

Please give Mrs. Shaw my regards. I tried to call last week end.

T.E.L.

TO LADY SCOTT (*afterwards* Lady Kennet)

16. 2. 23   14 *Barton St. S.W.*1

If Your Serenity doesn't think it hitting below the belt (when I fight its with everything anyhow & everywhere) will She carry out Her idea of doing something summary of H. W. Young.[1] (Major, Indian Army)? It would greatly gratify my unworthy self.

This self lacked courage to tell you that it has changed its name, (without proceeding to the dreadful extremity of marriage) and now answers to Mr. J. H. Ross, at Barton Street and where else men do collect.

No luck with the work-hunt, except in the Free State, which is willing, but from which I shrink a little. In fact I've postponed it a week, in the hope that the British Army (to which I've made advances) may offer me a shilling. Light-houses seem to be all booked.   JR.

My mother sends her kind regards. She is called Mrs. Lawrence.

[With the help of some friends in the War Office Lawrence joined the Royal Tank Corps early in March 1923 under the name of T. E. Shaw and was stationed at Bovington Camp, near Wool, Dorset.]

---

[1] Major, now Sir Hubert, Young, had fought with Lawrence in the Arabian campaign. See his book, *The Independent Arab*. Lawrence wanted a portrait of him for *Seven Pillars of Wisdom*, and eventually secured a drawing by Lady Young.

TO LIONEL CURTIS

19.3.23   [*Bovington Camp*]

Lorde, My mind moves me this morning to write you a whole series of letters, to be more splendid than the *Lettres de Mon Moulin*. Nothing will come of it, but meanwhile this page grows blacker with the preliminaries.

What should the preliminaries be? A telling why I joined? As you know I don't know! Explaining it to Dawnay[1] I said 'Mind-suicide': but that's only because I'm an incorrigible phraser. Do you, in reading my complete works, notice that tendency to do up small packets of words foppishly?

At the same time there's the reason why I have twice enlisted, in those same complete works: on my last night in Barton Street I read chapters 113 to 118,[2] and saw implicit in them my late course. The months of politics with Winston were abnormal, and the R.A.F. and Army are natural. The Army (which I despise with all my mind) is more natural than the R.A.F.: for at Farnborough I grew suddenly on fire with the glory which the air should be, and set to work full steam to make the others vibrate to it like myself. I was winning too, when they chucked me out: indeed I rather suspect I was chucked out for that. It hurt the upper story that the ground-floor was grown too keen.

The Army seems safe against enthusiasm. It's a horrible life, and the other fellows fit it. I said to one 'They're the sort who instinctively fling stones at cats' . . . and he said 'Why what do you throw?' You perceive that I'm not yet in the picture: but I will be in time. Seven years of this will make me impossible for anyone to suggest for a responsible position, and that self-degradation is my aim. I haven't the impulse and the conviction to fit what I know to be my power of moulding men and things: and so I always regret what I've created, when the leisure after creation lets me look back and see that the idea was secondhand.

This is a pompous start, and it should be a portentous series of letters: but there is excuse for it, since time moves slower here than elsewhere: and a man has only himself to think about. At reveille I feel like Adam,

---

[1] Colonel Alan Dawnay had helped Lawrence to join the Tank Corps.
[2] Of the Oxford Text of *Seven Pillars of Wisdom*, chapters XCIX to CIII in the published book.

after a night's pondering: and my mind has malice enough rather to enjoy putting Adam through it.

Don't take seriously what I wrote about the other men, above. It's only at first that certain sides of them strike a little crudely. In time I'll join, concerning them, in Blake's astonishing cry 'Everything that is, is holy!' It seems to me one of the best words ever said. Philip Kerr would agree with it (one of the engaging things about Philip is his agreement with my absence), but not many other reflective men come to the same conclusion without a web of mysticism to help them.

I'm not sure either that what I've said about my creations is quite true. I feel confident that Arabia and Trans-Jordan and Mesopotamia, *with what they will breed*, are nearly monumental enough for the seven years' labour of one head: because I knew what I was at, and the others only worked on instinct: and my other creation, that odd and interminable book . . . do you know I'm absolutely hungry to know what people think of it — not when they are telling me, but what they tell to one another. Should I be in this secret case if I really thought it pernicious?

There again, perhaps there's a solution to be found in multiple personality. It's my reason which condemns the book and the revolt, and the new nationalities: because the only rational conclusion to human argument is pessimism such as Hardy's, a pessimism which is very much like the wintry heath, of bog and withered plants and stripped trees, about us. Our camp on its swelling in this desolation feels pustular, and we (all brown-bodied, with yellow spots down our front belly-line), must seem like the swarming germs of its fermentation. That's feeling, exterior-bred feeling, with reason harmonizing it into a picture: but there's a deeper sense which remembers other landscapes, and the changes which summer will bring to this one: and to that sense nothing can be changeless: whereas the rational preference or advantage of pessimism is its finality, the eternity in which it ends: and if there isn't an eternity there cannot be a pessimism pure.

Lorde what a fog of words! What I would say is that reason proves there is no hope, and we therefore hope on, so to speak, on one leg of our minds: a dot and go one progress, which takes me Tuesday Thursday and Saturday and leaves me authentic on the other days. Quelle vie.   R.

TO LIONEL CURTIS

27.3.23   [*Bovington Camp*]

It seems to continue itself today, because I've been wondering about the other fellows in the hut. A main feeling they give me is of difference from the R.A.F. men. There we were excited about our coming service. We talked and wondered of the future, almost exclusively. There was a constant recourse to imagination, and a constant rewarding of ourselves therefore. The fellows were decent, but so wrought up by hope that they were carried out of themselves, and I could not see them mattly. There was a sparkle round the squad.

Here every man has joined because he was down and out: and no one talks of the Army or of promotion, or of trades and accomplishments. We are all here unavoidably, in a last resort, and we assume this world's failure in one-another, so that pretence would be not merely laughed at, but as near an impossibility as anything human. We are social bed-rock, those unfit for life-by-competition: and each of us values the rest as cheap as he knows himself to be.

I suspect that this low estimation is very much the truth. There cannot be classes in England much more raw, more free of all that the upbringing of a lifetime has plastered over you and me. Can there be profit, or truth, in all these modes and sciences and arts of ours? The leisured world for hundreds, or perhaps thousands of years has been jealously working and recording the advance of each generation for the starting-point of the next — and here these masses are as animal, as carnal as were their ancestors before Plato and Christ and Shelley and Dostoevsky taught and thought. In this crowd it's made startlingly clear how short is the range of knowledge, and what poor conductors of it ordinary humans are. You and I know: you have tried (Round Tabling[1] and by mouth) to tell all whom you can reach: and the end is here, a cimmerian darkness with bog-lights flitting wrongly through its gas.

The pity of it is, that you've got to take this black core of things in camp, this animality, on trust. It's a feeling, a spirit which colours every word and action, and I believe every thought, passing in Hut 12. Your mind is like a many-storied building, and you, its sole tenant, flit from floor to floor, from room to room, at the whim of your

[1] Lionel Curtis was Editor of *The Round Table*, a quarterly Review of the Politics of the British Commonwealth.

spirit's moment. (Not that the spirit has moments, but let it pass for the metaphor's sake.) At will you can be gross, and enjoy coffee or a sardine, or rarefy yourself till the diaphancité [sic] of pure mathematics, or of a fluent design in line, is enough to feed you. Here —

I can't write it, because in literature such things haven't ever been, and can't be. To record the acts of Hut 12 would produce a moral-medical case-book, not a work of art but a document. It isn't the filth of it which hurts me, because you can't call filthy the pursuit of a bitch by a dog, or the mating of birds in springtime; and it's man's misfortune that he hasn't a mating season, but spreads his emotions and excitements through the year . . . but I lie in bed night after night with this cat-calling carnality seething up and down the hut, fed by streams of fresh matter from twenty lecherous mouths . . . and my mind aches with the rawness of it, knowing that it will cease only when the slow bugle calls for 'lights out' an hour or so hence . . . and the waiting is so slow. . . .

However the call comes always in the end, and suddenly at last, like God's providence, a dewfall of peace upon the camp . . . but surely the world would be more clean if we were dead or mindless? We are all guilty alike, you know. You wouldn't exist, I wouldn't exist, without this carnality. Everything with flesh in its mixture is the achievement of a moment when the lusty thought of Hut 12 has passed to action and conceived: and isn't it true that the fault of birth rests somewhat on the child? I believe it's we who led our parents on to bear us, and it's our unborn children who make our flesh itch.

A filthy business all of it, and yet Hut 12 shows me the truth behind Freud. Sex is an integer in all of us, and the nearer nature we are, the more constantly, the more completely a product of that integer. These fellows are the reality, and you and I, the selves who used to meet in London and talk of fleshless things, are only the outward wrappings of a core like these fellows. They let light and air play always upon their selves, and consequently have grown very lustily, but have at the same time achieved health and strength in their growing. Whereas our wrappings and bandages have stunted and deformed ourselves, and hardened them to an apparent insensitiveness . . . but it's a callousness, a crippling, only to be yea-said by aesthetes who prefer clothes to bodies, surfaces to intentions.

These fellows have roots, which in us are rudimentary, or long cut off. Before I came I never visualized England except as an organism, an entity . . . but these fellows are local, territorial. They all use dialects, and could be placed by their dialects, if necessary. However it isn't necessary, because each talks of his district, praises it, boasts of it, lives in the memory of it. We call each other 'Brum' or 'Coventry' or 'Cambridge', and the man who hasn't a 'place' is an outsider. They wrangle and fight over the virtues of their homes. Of solidarity, of a nation, of something ideal comprehending their familiar streets in itself — they haven't a notion.

Well, the conclusion of the first letter was that man, being a civil war, could not be harmonized or made logically whole . . . and the end of this is that man, or mankind, being organic, a natural growth, is unteachable: cannot depart from his first grain and colour nor exceed flesh, nor put forth anything not mortal and fleshly.

I fear not even my absence would reconcile Ph.K.[1] to this.

E.L.

TO LIONEL CURTIS

14.V.23.   *Tanktown*

I should have written before, but a split thumb, and the sudden discovery of the authorities that I belonged to a criminal class, have put me out of the mood for subjective writing: — and since politics passed out of me the only theme between us is myself.

There was one injustice in your letter. My crying-out here was not at the foul talk. To me it's meaningless, unobjectionable, on a par with heedless fair-talk. The R.A.F. was foul-mouthed, and the cleanest little mob of fellows. These are foul-mouthed, and behind their mouths is a pervading animality of spirit, whose unmixed bestiality frightens me and hurts me. There is no criticism, indeed it's taken for granted as natural, that you should job a woman's body, or hire out yourself, or abuse yourself in any way. I cried out against it, partly in self-pity because I've condemned myself to grow like them, and partly in premonition of failure, for my masochism remains and will remain, only moral. Physically I can't do it: indeed I get in denial the gratification they get in indulgence. I react against their example into an abstention even more rigorous than of old. Everything bodily is now hateful to me (and in my case hateful is the same as impossible). In

[1] Philip Kerr, afterwards Lord Lothian.

the sports lately (they vex us with set exercises) I was put down to jump, and refused because it was an activity of the flesh. Afterwards to myself I wondered if that was the reason, or was I afraid of failing ridiculously: so I went down alone and privily cleared over twenty feet, and was sick of mind at having tried because I was glad to find I still could jump. It's on a par with the music for which I'm hungry. Henry Lamb is in Poole, and will play wonderfully to me if I go over: and I won't go, though I'm so starved for rhythm that even a soldier's stumbling through a song on the piano makes my blood run smooth (I refuse to hear it with my head).

This sort of thing must be madness, and sometimes I wonder how far mad I am, and if a mad-house would not be my next (and merciful) stage. Merciful compared with this place, which hurts me, body and soul. It's terrible to hold myself voluntarily here: and yet I want to stay here till it no longer hurts me: till the burnt child no longer feels the fire. Do you think there have been many lay monks of my persuasion? One use to think that such frames of mind would have perished with the age of religion: and yet here they rise up, purely secular. It's a lurid flash into the Nitrian desert: seems almost to strip the sainthood from Anthony. How about Teresa?

I consume the day (and myself) brooding, and making phrases and reading and thinking again, galloping mentally down twenty divergent roads at once, as apart and alone as in Barton Street in my attic. I sleep less than ever for the quietness of night imposes thinking on me: I eat breakfast only, and refuse every possible distraction and employment and exercise. When my mood gets too hot and I find myself wandering beyond control I pull out my motor-bike and hurl it top-speed through these unfit roads for hour after hour. My nerves are jaded and gone near dead, so that nothing less than hours of voluntary danger will prick them into life: and the 'life' they reach then is a melancholy joy at risking something worth exactly 2/9 a day.

It's odd, again, that craving for real risk: because in the gymnasium I funk jumping the horse, more than poison. That is physical, which is why it is: I'm ashamed of doing it and of not doing it, unwilling to do it: and most of all ashamed (afraid) of doing it well.

A nice, neurotic letter! What you've done to deserve its receipt God knows . . . perhaps you have listened to me too friendly-like at earlier times. Sorry, and all that. You are a kind of safety-valve perhaps. I wish you were an alienist, and could tell me where or how this ferment will end. It makes me miserable on top of all the curiosity and determination: and sets me so much aside that I hardly blame the powers for jumping on me with their dull punishments.   **L.**

TO LIONEL CURTIS

30.v.23.

My Lord, Your letter was black and white: — white because of that Albright story. There seems a pitiful irony in my helping a mind diseased. A hair of the biter? or was it the picture of a sickness graver than his own? You know with neuroses the causeless ones are worst. If my success had not been so great, and so easy, I would despise it less: and when to my success in action there was added (according to those whose judgement I asked) success in book-writing, also at first venture — why then I broke down, and ran here to hide myself.

Isn't it just faintly possible that part of the virtue apparent in the book lies in its secrecy, its novelty, and its contestability? My hard verdict upon it commands your sympathy? The hope that it isn't as good as Shaw says sustains me . . . And the blackness of your letter? Because it tempts me to run away from here, and so doing it marches with all my wishes against my will. Conscience in healthy men is a balanced sadism, the bitter sauce which makes more tasteful the ordinary sweets of life: and in sick stomachs the desire of condiment becomes a craving, till what is hateful feels therefore wholesome, and what is repugnant to the moral sense becomes (to the mind) therefore pure and righteous and to be pursued. So because my senses hate it, my will forces me to it . . . and a comfortable life would seem now to me sinful.

When I embarked on it, a year ago (it was June '22 that Trenchard accepted me for the R.A.F.) I thought it a mood, and curable: while today I feel that there is no change before me, and no hope of change. That's why your suggestions of one hurt me.

Your arguments, while they make me very grateful to yourself, are not heavy. I called you rich, once, in ideas and in furniture of mind: and you are rich, relative to these poor fellows here. You say my friends feel the absence of me — but personality (which it is my gift to you to exhibit) is of a short range, and in my experience has not touched more than ten or twelve friends at a time: and here I live with twenty very barren men, who feel my being with them. The hut is changed from what it used to be, and unlike what it would be (will be?) if I left. This isn't conceit, but a plain statement; for there would be a change if any one of us twenty was taken away: and I am richer and wider and more experienced than any of the others here. More of the world has passed over me in my 35 years than over all their twenties put together: and your gain, if you did gain by my return, would be their loss. It seems to me that the environment does not matter. Your circle does not draw from me (except superficially) more than theirs: indeed perhaps caenobite man influences as much as man social, for example is eternal, and the rings of its extending influence infinite.

For myself there are consolations. The perfect beauty of this place becomes tremendous, by its contrast with the life we lead, and the squalid huts we live in, and the noisy bullying authority of all our daily unloveliness. The nearly intolerable meanness of man is set in a circle of quiet heath, and budding trees, with the firm level bar of the Purbeck hills behind. The two worlds shout their difference in my ears. Then there is the irresponsibility: I have to answer here only for my cleanness of skin, cleanness of clothes, and a certain mechanical neatness of physical evolution upon the barrack-square. There has not been presented to me, since I have been here, a single choice: everything is ordained — except that harrowing choice of going away from here the moment my will to stay breaks down. With this exception it would be determinism complete — and perhaps in determinism complete there lies the perfect peace I have so longed for. Free-will I've tried, and rejected: authority I've rejected (not obedience, for that is my present effort, to find equality only in subordination. It is dominion whose taste I have been cloyed with): action I've rejected: and the intellectual life: and the receptive senses: and the battle of wits. They were all failures, and my reason tells me therefore that obedience, nescience, will also fail, since the roots of common failure must lie in myself — and yet in spite of reason I am trying it.

Albright should have told his physician to heal himself . . . but yet my best thanks for handing on the story. It cheered me a little bit, as Brutus must have been cheered when the Roman gossip praised his executed son.

This must be the end of egoistic writing: a safety valve may be good for a boiler, in saving it from bursting — but it's an abuse of it, to make it a pretext for habitually overloading the poor engine. Wherefore apologies, and it shall not happen any more.   L.

TO LIONEL CURTIS

27.VI.22 [really 23]

Old thing, This correspondence nearly died: might have died if you had not asked whether I did not join for the sake of the others here. Of course I didn't: things are done in answer to a private urge — not one of altruism.

You've been talking to Hogarth about my discomfort in the Tank Corps: but you know I joined partly to make myself unemployable, or rather impossible, in my old trade: and the burning out of freewill and self-respect and delicacy from a nature as violent as mine is bound to hurt a bit. If I was firmer I wouldn't cry about it.

It isn't all misery here either. There is the famous motor-bike as a temporary escape. Last Sunday was fine, and another day-slave and myself went off with it after church-parade. Wells we got to, and very beautiful it was: — a grey sober town, stiffly built of prim houses, but with nothing of the artificial in it. Everything is used and lived in; and to make the xvth century habitable today they have put in sash-windows everywhere.

One 'close', the Vicar's close, was nearly the best, it was so cloistered off (even from its quietest of streets): and so grey and green: for the local limestone has turned very sad with time, and has crannied, so that its angles are living with flowers of many sorts: and each of the 'cells' in this close has a little grass-plot between it and the common path down the centre: and on these plots poppies stood in groups like women at a garden party. There was sunshine over it, and a still air, so that all the essence of the place was drawn out and condensed about our heads. It was a college-like place, and looked good to live in: so for a while the camp waiting here for me became an ungrateful thought. Hogarth had written, hoping to get me back into the R.A.F. and the prospect of such happiness had made the Army nearly intolerable. However that's over, easily, for I was only hoping against the know-ledge that it wouldn't be possible.

Afterwards I trailed into the cathedral precinct, and lay there on the grass, and watched its huge west front, covered over with bad sculp-ture, but very correct and proper still, in the manner of the town. There is a remoteness about cathedrals now-a-days — : they are things I could not contribute to, if they were still a-building: and in front of Wells today there was a white-frocked child playing with a ball; the child was quite unconscious of the cathedral (feeling only the pleasure of smooth grass) but from my distance she was so small that she looked no more than a tumbling daisy at the tower-foot: I knew of course that she was animal: and I began in my hatred of animals to balance her against the cathedral: and knew then that I'd destroy the building to save her. That's as irrational as what happened on our coming here, when I swerved Snowy Wallis and myself at 60 m.p.h. on to the grass by the roadside, trying vainly to save a bird which dashed out its life against my side-car. And yet had the world been mine I'd have left out animal life upon it.

An old thing (it pleased me to call him Canon) doddered over and sat by me on the grass, and gave me a penny for my thoughts: and I told him (reading Huysmans lately) that I was pondering over the contrasts of English and French cathedrals. Ours set in closes so tree-bound and stately and primly-kept that they serve as a narthex to the shrine: a narthex at Wells grander and more religious than the building proper. Whereas French cathedrals have their feet in market places, and booths and chimneys and placards and noise hem them in: so that in France you step from your workshop into the aisle, and in England you cannot even enter till the lawns have swept the street-dust from your feet. The old clergyman gave me another penny to read him the riddle and I did it crab-wise, by a quote from du Bellay, and that Christchurch poem about Our Sovereign Lord the King. He was a book-worm too, and we talked Verhaeren and Melville and Lucretius together, with great pleasure on my part, and the vulgar relish that I was making a cockshy of his assurance that khaki covered nothing but primitive instincts.

He took me round the bishop's palace-garden, pumping me to learn how I endured camp life (living promiscuous seemed to his imagination horrible, and he by profession a shepherd of sheep!), and I hinted at the value of contrast which made all Wells crying-precious to me: and then we leaned over the wall and saw the fish in the moat, and it came upon me very hardly how excellent was their life. Fish are free of mankind you know, and are always perfectly suspended, without ache or activity of nerves, in their sheltering element.

We can get it, of course, when we earth-in our bodies, but it seems to me that we can only do that when they are worn out. It's a failure to kill them out of misery, for if there isn't any good or evil but only activity, and no pain or joy, only sensation: then we can't kill ourselves while we can yet feel. However I'd rather be the fish (did you ever read Rupert Brooke's 'And there shall be no earth in heaven', said fish)[1] or the little bird which had killed itself against me that morning.

There, my letters always end in tears! E.

[The following letter to Lord Wavell appears to me particularly important as an exposition of Lawrence's military ideas. The last sentence records his visit to Mecca in 1918 to choose his gold dagger.]

TO COLONEL A. P. WAVELL
(Later Field-Marshall Lord Wavell)

21. V. 23.

Dear Wavell, Many thanks for the book[2] (which has gone forward to its next) and for your long letter. It's exactly the sort of thing which I wanted to read.

No, I don't feel confident militarily. All the while we fought I felt like a conjuror trying an insufficiently-rehearsed trick — surprised when it came out right. A succession of such chances gave me the feeling I was apt at the business: that's all.

Chap. 35. The substance of this was boiled up for Guy Dawnay some years ago, when he started a thing called the *Army Quarterly*, & asked me for a contribution.[3] You will find it in the 1st number of the *Quarterly*. He liked it better than I did. Most people found it either recondite, or too smart.

I met your cousin once, at a push in London: had no proper talk of him.

As for the reply to raiding tactics. As you say, it's greater mobility than the attack. This needn't mean large drafts from the harrassed G.O.C. If the Turks had put machine guns on three or four of their touring cars, & driven them on weekly patrol over the admirable going of the desert E. of Amman & Maan they would have put an absolute stop to our camel-parties, & so to our rebellion. It wouldn't have cost them 20 men or £20,000 . . . *rightly applied.* They scraped

---

[1] 'And in that Heaven of all their wish, There shall be no more land, say fish'.
[2] A copy of the Oxford Text of *Seven Pillars of Wisdom*, which Wavell had returned.
[3] 'The Evolution of a Revolt', by T. E. Lawrence, *The Army Quarterly* No. 1, 1920.

up cavalry & armoured trains & camel corps & block-houses against us: because they didn't think hard enough.

I held the Rolls-Royce Armoured Cars in Akaba as a riposte if (or when) Turk cars came at us: for I couldn't imagine our being left free all the time: but we had only 5 R.R. and would have been on the defensive with them, quite unable to guard our raiding front. They would have sufficed only to cover Aba el Lissan—Tafileh, the Arab Regular Army front.

Well-destruction was possible only at Bair & Jefer, as our other waters were superficial: & we could have dispensed with B. & J. So that the Turks couldn't stop us with demolitions.

There is one other thing of which every rebellion is mortally afraid — treachery. If instead of counter-propaganda (never effective on the conservative side) the money had been put into buying the few venial men always to be found in a big movement, then they would have crippled us. We could only dare these intricate raids because we felt sure and safe. One well-informed traitor will spoil a national rising.

Bombing tribes is ineffective. I fancy that air-power may be effective against elaborate armies: but against irregulars it has no more than moral value. The Turks had plenty [of] machines, & used them freely against us — and never hurt us till the last phase, when we had brought 1000 of our regulars on the raid against Deraa. Guerrilla tactics are a complete muffing of air-force.

Jurgen I've read.[1] As you say V.G. Many thanks for offering me a copy: but in this atmosphere one reads very little.

As for writing more — to tell you the truth I'm sick of all manner of effort, & want never to do anything again. I've put my mind to sleep, coming here.

Yes, I've promised not to admit the Mecca jest. I did it because I wanted to choose my own gold dagger, & it was not serious for me. Hussein will never forgive it me.   .L.

TO MRS. THOMAS HARDY

21. V. 23.

. . . It sounds greedy, always to come when you ask me: but your house is so wonderfully unlike this noisy room that it is difficult to resist,

[1] *Jurgen*, by James Branch Cabell.

even for its own sake: and then there is Mr. Hardy, though you mustn't tell him so, for the thrill is too one-sided. He has seen so much of human-kind that he must be very tired of them: whereas for me he's Hardy, & I'd go a long way even to see the place where he had lived, let alone him living in it.

There, you will think me absurd: but still I'll arrive on Saturday!

Yours sincerely   T E SHAW

TO D. G. HOGARTH

13.VI.23

It's a difficult question you ask me. The Tanks are interesting, the company hardly tolerable, even to my stomach. There is an animal reek here which keeps me awake at night with horror that mankind should be like it: because I feel that we are the unnatural, & that Hut F.12 is the truth about human-kindness.

Contrast this with the R.A.F. (not Uxbridge: the exercise there was too severe for me) in which I was as contented as ever I had been: even my mind stopped working there: whereas here I lie awake nights on end, thinking about everything germane.

And why I enlisted? The security of it first: seven years existence guaranteed. I haven't any longer the mind to fight for sustenance. As you realize I've finished with the 'Lawrence' episode. I don't like what rumour makes of him — not the sort of man I'd like to be! and the life of politics wearied me out, by worrying me over-much. I've not got a coarse-fibred enough nature for them: and have too many scruples and an uneasy conscience. It's not good to see two sides of questions, when you have (officially) to follow one.

Exit politics (Irak candidates had no share in my disgust. Indeed I don't think I did badly, in sum.). There went most of my money value. Exit Lawrence: and there is most of the residue of my earning power gone. I haven't a trade to follow: and won't do the two or three things for which I'm qualified: hence I'm reduced to soldiering. You see, I'm 35 nearly: and that's too old to make a fresh start in a skilled business.

When I joined the R.A.F. it was in the hope that some day I'd write a book about the very excellent subject that it was. At that time I thought my Arab Revolt book very bad. Since then Shaw has turned my mind slowly to consider it good: and there's another ambition gone, for it was always in my hope to write a decent book: and if I've done it there seems little reason to do another. A pity, for my Uxbridge notes were good, & there was the making of a very good thing out of the life of a squadron. It will be a puzzle for my biographer (if I have one of those unprofitable things) to reconcile my joy in the R.A.F. with my disgust with the Army. The R.A.F. is utterly unlike this place: the men are so different, & their hopes & minds & talk. They weren't happy: it used to be said at Farnborough that I was the only happy man there . . . but they were essentially decent: and the going has been rather a jerk to me. I feel queerly homesick whenever I see a blue uniform in the street.

But for going back to the R.A.F. — there my hands are tied. Trenchard (in sacking me) offered me a commission. I said I couldn't take it: and begged to be left in: but he couldn't do it: asked me to take my discharge as final: and he's not a mind-changer, & I don't want to bother him with my personal whims. So I don't think there is any remedy.

You talk about Govt. money. I take it every week, so that I haven't any scruples: but I'm worth more than 3/- a day only in politics & Middle East, & there I don't play: and a temporary job at a high salary would only cart me worse than ever at the end. It's hard enough, now, to go poor again: and every year of money would make it far worse.

When I saw Amery he was thinking of coast-guard or lighthouse for me: and the latter felt to me like so complete a withdrawal from the world as to enable me to publish that book & get the job over.

Now that notion has gone of course, & I propose to let the book blush unseen. After all, so long as I can keep alive in other ways, why bother with the unpleasant way?

I took the All Souls' money this year, & have spent it on pictures. I felt nervous at the length of time my drawings were taking, & anxious to end them quickly; & I distrusted my power of earning enough in the Army or R.A.F. to pay for the six or seven yet required.

As a matter of fact I am earning a little — translating a French novel just now: and Cape, the publisher, has written suggesting I do Mardrus' *Arabian Nights* into English for him. I'm willing — if unsigned — and that would bring me in the price of some more drawings.

There, that's how I stand: and I see no way out of it. It's good that

A. has got that thing at the end.[1] He has wanted it persistently: &
therefore presumably deserves it. I agree with you about hellenistic
sculpture.   T E.

TO R. V. BUXTON

4.X.23

Dear Robin, Your idea of 120 copies at £25: it sounds V.G.

Lionel Curtis (whom R. Holland-Martin knows) was thinking of
something such. I've told him of your idea.

Also have written to the colour-printers to ask for a new estimate of
costs.

Will you put the enclosed in to your manager? Yours   T.E.

If the idea comes off I want to wangle enough to fill up my overdraft. It worries me rather, & yet is magnificent: for it has enabled me
to take a ruined cottage in a wood near camp, & this I'm fitting up
with the hope of having a warm solitary place to hide in sometimes on
winter evenings. This district is unusually desolate (of good company)
& I covet the idea of being sometimes by myself near a fire.

TO A. E. CHAMBERS

3.VIII.24.   *Clouds Hill Moreton Dorset*

... Wool is the Station, the cottage is alone in a dip in the moor,
very quiet, very lonely, very bare. A mile from camp. Furnished
with a bed, a bicycle, three chairs, 100 books, a gramophone of
parts, a table. Many windows, oak-trees, an ilex, birch, firs, rhodo-.
dendron, laurels, heather. Dorsetshire to look at. No food, except
what a grocer & the camp shops & canteens provide. Milk. Wood
fuel for the picking up. I don't sleep here, but come out 4.30 p.m. till
9 p.m. nearly every evening, & dream, or write or read by the fire, or

[1] His younger brother, A. W. Lawrence, had got a scholarship for travel and research
in Hellenistic sculpture.

play Beethoven & Mozart to myself on the box. Sometimes one or two Tank-Corps-slaves arrive & listen with me . . . but few of them care for abstract things. If you came you would be very much alone all day.

Nearly I came to look for you the over day. Wells (a novelist, H. G., nearly famous) asked me to his place at Dunmow for a weekend, & Duxford lay on my right as I returned by motor-bike. Only the poor beast wasn't running well, & I was in khaki & was ashamed. Ave

TES.
(ex J.H.R.
ex T.E.L.)

[On February 6th, 1925, Lawrence wrote to Trenchard: '. . . so for the third time of asking — Have I no chance of re-enlistment in the R.A.F., or transfer?'

By early May it became clear that his application had failed once more. He was not, however, prepared to accept this refusal tamely.]

TO JOHN BUCHAN

19.V.25   *Clouds Hill Moreton Dorset*

Dear Buchan, I don't know by what right I made that appeal to you on Sunday.[1] It happened on the spur of the moment. You see, for seven years it's been my ambition to get into the Air Force, (and for six months in 1922 I realized the ambition), and I can't get the longing for it out of my mind for an hour. Consequently I talk of it to most of the people I meet.

They often ask 'Why the R.A.F.?' and I don't know. Only I have tried it, & I liked it as much after trying it as I did before. The difference beween Army & Air is that between earth & air: no less. I only came into the army in the hope of earning my restoration to the R.A.F. and now the third year is running on, and I'm as far away as ever. It must be the ranks, for I'm afraid of being loose or independent. The rails, & rules & necessary subordination are so many comforts. Impossible is a long word in human dealings: but it feels to me impos-

---

[1] Lawrence had met Buchan in the street and had spoken of his longing to return to the R.A.F.

sible that I should ever assume responsibility or authority again. No doubt any great crisis would change my mind: but certainly the necessity of living won't. I'd rather be dead than hire out my wits to anyone importantly.

The Air Ministry have offered me jobs: a commission, & the writing of their history. These are refinements of cruelty: for my longing to be in the R.A.F. is a homesickness which attacks me at the most casual sight of their name in the papers, or their uniform in the street: & to spend years with them as officer or historian, knowing that I was debarring myself from ever being one of them, would be intolerable. Here in the Tank Corps I can at least cherish the hope that I may some day justify my return. Please understand (anyone here will confirm it) that the Battalion authorities are perfectly content with me. Nothing in my character or conduct makes me in any way unsuitable to the ranks: and I'm fitter & tougher than most people.

There, it's a shame to bother you with all this rant: but the business is vital to me: & if you can help to straighten it out, the profit to me will far outweigh, in my eyes, any inconvenience to which you put yourself!

I think this last sentence is the best one to end on, Yours sincerely

T E SHAW

TO EDWARD GARNETT

13.VI.25.

You asked me long ago how I was correcting the old text . . . since when I've had nothing convenient to send you. Here at last is a section (Book VI) ready for Pike, to whom please forward it when you have looked at it (if you want to trouble yourself still with the rake's progress of this deplorable work).

This, being the best written section, is less cut about than any yet: and has lost fewer lines: only a bare 15%: though a good many lines usually come out in the next stage (galley) and in the first page-proof which succeeds the galley. So not all that I have now left will survive to the end. My judgment gets furry, by dint of staring at the familiar pages.

What muck, irredeemable, irremediable, the whole thing is! How on earth can you have once thought it passable? My gloomy view of it deepens each time I have to wade through it. If you want to see how good situations, good characters, good material can be wickedly bungled, refer to any page, passim. There isn't a scribbler in Fleet Street who wouldn't have got more fire and colour into every paragraph.

Trenchard withdrew his objection to my rejoining the Air Force. I got seventh-heaven for two weeks: but then Sam Hoare came back from Mespot and refused to entertain the idea. That, and the closer acquaintance with the *Seven Pillars* (which I now know better than anyone ever will) have together convinced me that I'm no bloody good on earth. So I'm going to quit: but in my usual comic fashion I'm going to finish the reprint and square up with Cape before I hop it! There is nothing like deliberation, order and regularity in these things.

I shall bequeath you my notes on life in the recruits camp of the R.A.F. They will disappoint you. Yours.   T.E.S.

Post Office closed. So the stamps are put on at a venture.

[Edward Garnett was naturally much alarmed by this letter with its threat of suicide and wrote at once to Bernard Shaw who replied:

I saw the Prime Minister about it during his former term of office . . . I have now sent on your letter to Downing Street with a card to say that some decision should be made, as there is a possibility of an appalling scandal, especially after Lowell Thomas's book.   G.B.S.

John Buchan had also appealed to Mr. Baldwin on Lawrence's behalf and the Prime Minister humanely decided to intervene. The evidence for this is contained in letters to John Buchan. On December 26th, 1928, Lawrence wrote: 'I wanted you to know I'm making the best use I can of the gift you led Mr. Baldwin into giving me in 1925.']

TO JOHN BUCHAN

5. VII. 25   *Clouds Hill Moreton Dorset*

Dear Buchan, The oracle responded nobly. I was sent for by Trenchard on Wednesday last (horribly inconvenient, for my revolver course did not finish till Saturday, yesterday) and was told that I was acceptable as a recruit.

The immediate effect of this news was to put me lazily and smoothly asleep: and asleep I've been ever since. It's like a sudden port, after a voyage all out of reckoning.

I owe you the very deepest thanks. I've been hoping for this for so many years, and had my hopes turned down so regularly, that my patience was completely exhausted: and I'd begun wondering if it had ever been worth waiting and hoping for. Odd, that the Air Force should seem to me (after trial too!) as the only way of getting across middle age. I wish I could make you some sort of return.

Formalities will take some weeks: but I should change skins in September at latest.

Please inform your family that the bike (Boanerges is his name) did 108 miles an hour with me on Wednesday afternoon. I think the news of my transfer had gone to its heads: (Cylinder heads, of course).

More thanks, Yours ever   T E SHAW

[Approval of Lawrence's transfer from the Royal Tank Corps to the R.A.F. was signed by the Chief of the Air Staff on July 16th, 1925, and Lawrence was instructed to put in an application for transfer through his Commanding Officer.]

TO E. PALMER[1]

25.VIII.25.   *R.A.F. Cadets' College, Cranwell, Lincs.*

When I entered the R.A.F. station at West Drayton (a derelict misery-stricken unfinished factory-place) from its upper windows came 'The Lass of Richmond Hill', violently sung. At once I remembered Clouds Hill, and you, and H.H.B.[2] and I hung my kit-bag on a willow-tree and wept.

They set me sums: which I solved as fast as they brought them. A flight-sergeant came along, 'Hullo Ross!' . . . and a dynamo-switch-board-attendant behind him said 'Garn . . . that ain't Ross. I was at

[1] Private, Royal Tank Corps; nicknamed Posh.
[2] Sergeant Banbury.

Bovington when he came up, and he's Colonel Lawrence.' After that things got very complicated. Before lights out I was in charge of the recruits' hut.

Wednesday so passed. Thursday is a blank in my memory. On Friday early they sent me to a doctor. He said 'Have you ever had . . . . ?' 'No Sir' 'Have you ever had . . . . ?' 'No' (less confidently).

'Have you ever — broken any bones?' This was my chance: I poured over him a heap of fractured fibulae, radii, metatarsals, phalanges, costes, clavicles, scapulae, till he yelled to me to stop. So I stopped, and he made clumsy efforts to write them all down.

Anyway it was all over by noon on Friday. At two o'clock they put me in a tender, and sent me to Uxbridge in charge of a corporal, who was charged to get a receipt for my body. Everyone at Uxbridge was willing to take delivery: but none would sign for me. At last I was dragged into the Headquarters' Adjutant, the last hope. (All the world else being at the Wembley Tattoo). He glared 'What are you'? I very stilly replied 'Yesterday I was a Pte in the R.T.C.' He snorted 'Today?' 'I think I'm an A.C. twice in the R.A.F.' Snort second. 'Will you be in the Navy tomorrow?' 'Perhaps,' said I. 'I can't sign for you. I don't want you.' 'I don't want anyone to sign for me.' 'Damned silly . . . . who the hell are you?'

At this point my feeble patience broke. 'If your name was Buggins, and I called you Bill . . .' Then he yelled with joy, recognizing my names for him (as I might call you Posh when you are very old and rich and important) and gave me tea.

Friday night, 6 p.m. I am handed into the recruits' hut. Messenger arrives. A.C.II Shaw to report to Flight Office at once. 'Sergeant take this man to the Q.M. Stores, kit him at once, and put him into the first train for Cranwell. The Air Ministry have ordered his immediate posting.' Help: poor me: 8 p.m., two kit bags, a set of equipment, great coat, bayonet, like a plum tree too heavy with fruit. However 'last train gone'. Sergt. and self returned to recruits'. hut. I slept: very wet. On Saturday squared tailors and got my stuff altered: polished bayonet: scrubbed equipment.

Sunday blancoed equipment: polished bayonet. Walked round Uxbridge very new in blue. Monday 11 A.M. started for Cranwell. Finished up in a taxi. Reception-hut: hot and cold water laid on to hut: a bath. Heaven: sleep.

Tuesday, today. Reveille 7.30. Hot bath: Heaven: breakfast: H.Q.

office: M.O.Adjutant: S.-M. very curious questions. Posted as aircraft hand to B.Flight. Fatigues when the cadets are on holiday: pulling their machines in and out of the sheds, filling up, starting, cleaning etc. when they are here. Sixteen men in flight. Sergt. a speed-demon on a twin N.U.T.[1] Bath-furnace out of order. Cold: wet: not heaven.

Kit inspection once a month: hut inspection once a month: marching order parade once a month: no guards: church parade twice a month. Few other duties. Can do, I think. No P.T. Feel odd and strange: exhilarated: crazy sometimes. Is it going to meals does that? Haven't spent a shilling a day lately. Will you tell Clouds Hill that all is well so far? People who come to Cranwell often stay there for five years. I will go over to Nottingham on Saturday week, and try to see Brough, who has a 1926 S.S.110 waiting for me.[2] After that I'll get a room in some near village, and begin work. Meanwhile — got to scrub that equipment again.   T.E.S.

R.A.F. issue three towels: Also one pair plain light boots, and one pair marching boots. Slippers of normal Bovington type. No other changes to note. If there is a bunch of letters please insert in a fresh large envelope, and address as above. Willis has envelopes.

TO MRS. THOMAS HARDY

26. VIII. 25.   *R.A.F. Cadets' College, Cranwell, Lincs.*

Dear Mrs. Hardy, You see, it has happened! Quite suddenly at the end: so that I was spared a visit of farewell. It is best to go off abruptly, if at all.

I never expected the move to be so drastic. Cranwell is not really near anywhere (nor is it anything in itself): and the disorder of falling into a new station is yet upon me. The R.A.F. is a home to me: but it is puzzling to find the home all full of strangers who look upon me as strange. My known past always rouses curiosity in a new station. Probably in a few days things will be comfortable.

Alas for Clouds Hill, & the Heath, & the people I had learned in the two years of Dorset!

Please remember me to Mr. Hardy, who is no doubt wholly taken

[1] Motor bicycle.   [2] Motor bicycle.

up now in *Tess*. You have a good actress.[1] I hope it will seem fitting both to you & the public. It is hard to please two masters.

You said to me that I might see that work of yours again, some time. Please don't forget that: though I can't seem either to read or to write in this noise! Yours sincerely   T E SHAW

from THE MINT

[PART THREE] 9: FUNERAL

IT was an odd morning, that on which we heard Queen Alexandra was dead. The fog which collects here on most autumn mornings was so shallow. Across the ground it lay like a veil: but when we looked up we could see a sparkle, which hinted at a sun almost shining upon the eaves and mast-heads. When we parade in fog, our figures go flat. There is no thickness, no shadows, no high-light of polished buttons. Instead the fellows are as if cut out of grey cardboard, with a darker tint drawn round the edges where the shafts of refracted light slip round them.

We stood so, in our hollow square, this morning, while they hoisted colour, and played the daily salute for the King: but after the salute they held us at attention, ever so long in that dead shivering silence: for the air was very sharp. Then the ensign began to creep downward from the peak, while the massed drums of the band rolled. And they rolled and rolled all the minutes that the flag crept down. At half-mast the trumpets came out brazenly with the last post. We all swallowed our spittle, chokingly, while our eyes smarted against our wills. A man hates to be moved to folly by a noise.

They would not let us off the worst of it. There had to be a parade service the day she was buried. Our distrusted chaplain preached one of his questionable sermons. He spoke of the dead Queen as a Saint, a Paragon: not as an unfortunate, a long-suffering doll. With luscious mouth he enlarged upon her beauty, the beauty which God, in a marvel of loving-kindness, had let her keep until her dying.

My thoughts fled back sharply to Marlborough House. The yellow, scaling portal: the white-haired footmen and door-keepers, whiter than the powder of their hair: the hushed great barn-like halls:

---

[1] A dramatized version with Gwen Ffrangcon-Davies as Tess.

the deep carpet in which our feet dragged unwillingly to the ceiling-high fireplace which dwarfed the whispering Miss Knollys and Sir Dighton. She incredibly old, wasted, sallow: he a once huge man, whose palsied neck had let down the great head on the breast, where its gaping mouth wagged almost unseen and unheard in the thicket of beard which overgrew the waistcoat. Sir Dighton had won the first V.C. in the Crimea: and he was so old, and Miss Knollys so old that this seemed a cruel duty which kept them always on their feet. We whispered with them: everybody whispered in that charnel-house.

We had to wait, of course: that is the prerogative of Queens. When we reached the presence, and I saw the mummied thing, the bird-like head cocked on one side, not artfully but by disease, the red-rimmed eyes, the enamelled face, which the famous smile scissored across all angular and heart-rending: — then I nearly ran away in pity. The body should not be kept alive after the lamp of sense has gone out. There were the ghosts of all her lovely airs, the little graces, the once-effective sway and movement of the figure which had been her consolation. Her bony fingers, clashing in the tunnel of their rings, fiddled with albums, penholders, photographs, toys upon the table: and the heart-rending appeal played on us like a hose, more and more terribly. She soon dismissed us.

These memories lost me much of the sermon. I listened in again to hear the chaplain telling the story of Prince Albert Edward in the House of Lords warning Lord Granville he must miss part of his speech, because he had promised to take his daughter to the circus. 'This,' declaimed the padre, 'this was the domestic picture and example which the Prince and Princess of Wales set their adoring people.' 'Balls!' hissed someone, savagely, from behind me. In its thirty-second minute the sermon ended. More rolling of drums and last posts, now firmly resisted by all of us in our rage: and then back to dinner. 'Fall in at two for work!' shouted the Orderly Sergeant. 'Not even a half-holiday for the old girl,' grumbled Tug.

14: CLASSES

The Air Ministry recognizes a rightness in our worship of the technical engineer, by promoting sergeant or sergeant-pilot the best men from the ranks: those who have understanding of the souls of engines, and find their poetry in the smooth tick-over.

They form our aristocracy of merit. Against them, over them, stand the lords spiritual, the commissioned: whose dignity comes extrinsically, from some fancied laying-on of hands. When they are forceful souls, Tims or Taffys, one to a squad, all is well. The basic lesion of character in every enlisted man makes him ready to laugh or cry, always, like a child: but seldom leaves him sober. So the hand of a father seems neither incongruous nor disagreeable to us. We earn force, by our root-folly.

Our conscious inferiority excludes Tim from comparison or challenge: but there is rising up a second category of airman, the boy apprentice. They disrupt us now: for the men don't like the boys: but this inevitable phase is a passing phase. Soon the ex-boy will be the majority, and the R.A.F. I knew will be superseded and forgotten. Meanwhile there is jealousy and carping.

The boys come fresh from school, glib in theory, essay writers, with the bench-tricks of workmen: but they have never done the real job on a real kite: and reality, carrying responsibility, has a different look and feel from a school lesson. So they are put for a year to work with men. An old rigger, with years of service, whose trade is in his fingers, finds himself in charge of a boy-beginner with twice his pay. The kid is clever with words, and has passed out L.A.C. from school: the old hand can hardly spell, and will be for ever an A.C.2. He teaches his better ever so grumpily.

Nor do all the ex-boys make the job easier for those they are about to replace. As a class they are cocky. Remember how we, the enlisted men have all been cowed. Behind us, in our trial of civvy life, is the shadow of failure. Bitterly we know, of experience, that we are not as good as the men outside. So officers, sergeants and corporals may browbeat us, and we'll lie down to it: even fawn on them the more for it. That sense of inferiority may not save us from the smart of discipline (your bully will always find his way to be severe, if it's merely to put the fear of God in us) but it gives us the humility of house-dogs, under discipline.

The airmen of the future will not be so owned, body and soul, by their service. Rather will they be the service, maintaining it, and their rights in it, as one with the officers. Whereas we have had no rights, except on paper, and few there. In the old days men had weekly to strip off boots and socks, and expose their feet for an officer's inspection. An ex-boy'd kick you in the mouth, as you bent down to look. So with the bath-rolls, a certificate from your N.C.O. that you'd had a bath during the week. One bath! And with the kit inspections, the room inspections, and equipment inspections, all excuses for the dogmatists among the officers to blunder, and for the nosy-parkers to make beasts of themselves. Oh, you require the gentlest touch to interfere with a poor man's person, and not give offence.

The ex-boys are professionally in the R.A.F. as a privilege, making it their home. Soon, when they have made their style felt, officers will only enter their airmen's rooms accompanied, by invitation, guest-like and bare-headed, like us in an officers' mess. Officers will not be allowed to slough their uniform for social functions, while airmen walk about branded everywhere. The era of a real partnership in our very difficult achievement must come, if progress is to be lasting.

17: A THURSDAY NIGHT

The fire is a cooking fire, red between the stove-bars, all its flame and smoke burned off. Half-past eight. The other ten fellows are yarning in a blue haze of tobacco, two on the chairs, eight on the forms, waiting my return. After the clean night air their cigarette smoke gave me a coughing fit. Also the speed of my last whirling miles by lamplight (the severest test of riding) had unsteadied my legs, so that I staggered a little. 'Wo-ups, dearie' chortled Dusty. 'More split-arse work to-night?' It pleases them to imagine me wild on the road. To feed this flight-vanity I gladden them with details of my scrap against the Bif.

'Bring any grub?' at length inquires Nigger, whose pocket is too low, always, for canteen. I knew there was something lacking. The excitement of the final dash and my oncoming weariness had chased from my memory the stuffed panniers of the Brough. Out into the night again, steering across the black garage to the corner in which he is stabled by the fume of hot iron rising from his sturdy cylinders. Click, click, the bags are detached; and I pour out their contents before Dusty, the hut pantry-man. Tug brings out the frying pan, and has precedency. The fire is just right for it. A sizzle and a filling smell. I get ready my usual two slices of buttered toast.

Nigger turns over the possibilities. 'What are eggs?' he asks. I do a lightning calculation: penny ha'penny. Right: he chooses one egg. Rashers are a penny. Two of them and two dogs, at tuppence. He rolls me his sixpence along the gable. 'Keep the odd 'un for fat,' he murmurs. The others choose and pay. Selling the stuff is no trouble:

we have run this supper scandal among ourselves all the winter. The canteen food is dearer, though not dear; and much less tasteful than these fruits of our own fetching and cooking. And you have to queue up there, for ten minutes, to be pertly served.

Paddy, the last cooker of tonight, cleans the pan for tomorrow by wiping out its dripping on a huge doorstep of mess-deck bread. Later we'll see him put this bread to belly-use. 'Old grease-trap' Tug calls him, rallyingly. Meanwhile the gramophone plays jazz stuff to charm down the food. My brain is too dishevelled after a hard ride to be fit for string-music, its dope of a wet evening. For tonight I am drowsy-drunk on air. Lights' out finds us all willing for sleep. Tomorrow the golden eagle moults on us.

18: INTERLUDE

Service life in this way teaches a man to live largely on little. We belong to a big thing, which will exist for ever and ever in unnumbered generations of standard airmen, like ourselves. Our outward same-nesses of dress and type remind us of that. Also our segregation and concentration. The clusters of us widen out beyond Cadet College, beyond Whitewash Villas, beyond Depot, over hundreds of camps, over half the world. The habit of 'belonging to something or other' induces in us a sense of being one part of many things.

As we gain attachment, so we strip ourselves of personality. Mark the spiritual importance of such trifles as these overalls in which we shroud ourselves for work, like robots: to become drab shapes without comeliness or particularity, and careless, careless. The clothes for which a fellow has to pay are fetters to him, unless he is very rich and spendthrifty. This working dress provided us by the R.A.F. is not the least of our freedoms. When we put it on, oil, water, mud, paint, all such hazardous things, are instantly our friends.

A spell of warm weather has come back to us, as if summer feared to quit this bleak north. The wind keeps its bite; but our hangar shelters a calm crescent of tarmac and grass, and its open mouth is a veritable sun-trap. Through the afternoon eight of us lay there waiting for a kite which had gone away south, across country, and was overdue. Wonderful, to have it for our duty to do nothing but wait hour after hour in the warm sunshine, looking out southward.

We were too utterly content to speak, drugged with an absorption fathoms deeper than physical contentment. Just we lay there spread-eagled in a mesh of bodies, pillowed on one another and sighing in happy excess of relaxation. The sunlight poured from the sky and melted into our tissues. From the turf below our moist backs there came up a sister-heat which joined us to it. Our bones dissolved to become a part of this underlying indulgent earth, whose mysterious pulse throbbed in every tremor of our bodies. The scents of the thousand-acre drome mixed with the familiar oil-breath of our hangar, nature with art: while the pale sea of the grass bobbed in little waves before the wind raising a green surf which hissed and flowed by the slats of our heat-lidded eyes.

Such moments of absorption resolve the mail and plate of our personality back into the carbo-hydrate elements of being. They come to service men very often, because of our light surrender to the good or evil of the moment.

Airmen have no possessions, few ties, little daily care. For me, duty now orders only the brightness of these five buttons down my front.

And airmen are cared for as little as they care. Their simple eyes, out-turned; their natural living; the penurious imaginations which neither harrow nor reap their lowlands of mind: all these expose them, like fallows, to the processes of air. In the summer we are easily the sun's. In winter we struggle undefended along the roadway, and the rain and wind chivy us, till soon we are wind and rain. We race over in the first dawn to the College's translucent swimming pool, and dive into the elastic water which fits our bodies closely as a skin: — and we belong to that too. Everywhere a relationship: no loneliness any more.

[In the letter of June 21st, 1926, to Mrs. Hardy, Lawrence had announced that the R.A.F. authorities were sending him to India in the autumn and that he was glad he was going to be out of the country when *Revolt in the Desert* was published.

The voyage out in the troopship *Derbyshire* was, as far as Suez, an unpleasant ordeal. It is described in some pages of pencil manuscript found at Clouds Hill after Lawrence's death which appear to be notes for a final section of *The Mint*, to be called *Leaves In The Wind*.]

from LEAVES IN THE WIND

FINAL section *Leaves in the Wind*, snatches of life and letters, misarranged, from 2 lines to pages. M.Q.[1] sentry — the shabby haversack that denoted my office. The wash of the water, the *Derbyshire* swaying in a long slow swell, going over so far, swinging back: ever and again going further, with a muffled musical clash of crockery far away in her depths, oscillating back again — now and then an upward heave, and the slow sinking back. My eyes began to swim, and to see gassy clouds in the corridor, between the blobs of the dim safety lamps. They twinkled so electric blue. Wave upon wave of the smell of stabled humanity: the furtive creeping by rushes along the alleyway of the women to their latrine, fending themselves from wall to wall with the right arm, while the left held the loosened dress across their body. Belches of gas come back up my throat — hullo, I'll be sick if I stay here for ever — yet I promised the guard commander that I'd do two tricks: my poor little ex-apprentice relief got so bad down here after fifteen minutes that they had to help him up to the air. *Swish swish* the water goes against the walls of the ship — sounds nearer. Where on earth is that splashing. I tittup along the alley and peep into the lavatory space, at a moment when no woman is there. It's awash with a foul drainage. Tactless posting a sentry over the wives' defaecations, I think. Tactless and useless all our duties aboard. Hullo here's the O.O.[2] visiting. May as well tell him. The grimy-folded face, the hard jaw, toil-hardened hands, bowed and ungainly figure. An ex-naval warrant, I'll bet. No gentleman. He strides boldly to the latrine: 'Excuse me' unshyly to two shrinking women. 'God,' he jerked out, 'flooded with shit — where's the trap?' He pulled off his tunic and threw it at me to hold, and with a plumber's quick glance strode over to the far side, bent down, and ripped out a grating. Gazed for a moment, while the ordure rippled over his boots. Up his right sleeve, baring a forearm hairy as a mastiff's grey leg, knotted with veins, and a gnarled hand: thrust it deep in, groped, pulled out a moist white bundle. 'Open that port' and out it splashed into the night. 'You'd think they'd have had some other place for their sanitary towels. Bloody awful show, not having anything fixed up.' He shook his sleeve down as it was over his slowly-drying arm, and huddled on his tunic, while the released liquid gurgled contentedly down its re-opened drain.

[1] Married Quarters.   [2] Orderly Officer.

A REVIEW of *Novels by D. H. Lawrence*, published in *The Spectator*,
August 6th, 1927.

Martin Secker has been too careful in producing his cheap edition
of D. H. Lawrence's novels. In its clumsy type-panel the type looks
too big, and the reverse looms shadowly through the thin paper: also
the margins have been pared to the quick. This is a pity, for D. H.
Lawrence is a prodigious novelist, whose works need to be studied in
series (to learn their significance of growth) as well as to be re-read
frequently, each for itself, because of the rich depth and strangeness and
fine artistry of the author. These little volumes are likely to crack up
under the work booklovers will give them.

D. H. Lawrence has had a wonderful career, since the distant day
when *The White Peacock* took the breath of literary England with its
sudden independence and wealth of form. A young man's work this,
obviously, with its cadenced prose, beautiful in sound and mannered
in pattern. He was writing, then as now, for ear and eye together: but
he seemed to overvalue the classical tradition, to check his powers, in
too strict obedience to architectonic law. So with his next book, and
his next, *Sons and Lovers* being perhaps the prose culmination of this
first phase, which found itself, more transparently, in the poems:

> The sea in the stones is singing,
>   A woman binds her hair
> With yellow, frail sea-poppies
>   That shine as her fingers stir.
>
> While a naked man comes swiftly
>   Like a spurt of white foam, rent
> From the crest of a fallen breaker,
>   Over the poppies sent.

Do you see the doubled 's' in each first and last line? There is the young
Lawrence, his imagination playing lead to his mind. Appetite and
self-education rushed him into growth. Ideas leaped in flocks, full-
grown, into his work, too quickly to be always clear, too grown to
be always good company, one to the other. *The Rainbow* and *Women
in Love* and *Aaron's Rod* stutter and stammer with the heat of the
teacher who has felt something so exciting that he cannot delay to
think it into its fitting words. Words upon words, he pours them out
in a river.

Slowly the passion checked. It crystallized into conviction. In *Kangaroo* and the short stories we can see the molten stuff cooling, to grow hard and solid, yet plastic in the master's burning hands. Finally there came to us *The Plumed Serpent*, the 'magic' as *The Spectator* called it, a perfect achievement, the balance of mind and strength and spirit, a vivified independent creation of art.

What pains before *The Plumed Serpent* can be created! Book after book, each of them the hardest and honestest and best work of which his wits are capable, for nearly twenty years; and all the time growth, growth, growth. He never tries to please another judgment than his own, never walks in a made road, never re-treads the easy track of an earlier success. Every time he gives us, in both hands, all he can hold of himself. It is a pageant: novels, poems, scientific work — not good, this last. His pseudonymous Oxford history-book and his psychological treaties are unhappy: as though a maker, who could make live men and women, were bothering to model clay images of men and women. *Twilight in Italy*, too, was hard to read. It clung to the roof of the mouth, like an overkneaded suet pudding. But at his best he is an impeccable prose writer (which is not to say that he has all the virtues). Compare him with Brahms in music; and when the landscape painter in him feels the setting of a story, miracles follow. The Italian hill-villages in *The Lost Girl* are dizzy with their sense of height, and the supreme success of *The Plumed Serpent* is the lake, which becomes a major character in the book. However, there's no need to discuss *The Plumed Serpent*. It has arrived. It is more curious to see by what road it came.

In those early days, before the War, readers' hopes lay in Lawrence and Forster. These two heirs, through the Victorians, of the great tradition of the English novel were fortunate to have made good their footing before war came. Its bursting jarred them off their stride, indeed. Lawrence glances at the War twice or thrice, and wrote a haunting poem of a train-journey in uniform, but no more. Each man had tired of politics and action, and plunged into the dim forest of character in time to save himself from chaos. In imagination we used to make Forster and Lawrence joust with one another, on behalf of their different practices of novel-writing, as our fathers set Thackeray and Dickens at odds. Forster's world seemed a comedy, neatly layered and staged in a garden whose trim privet hedges were delicate with gossamer conventions. About its lawns he rolled thunderstorms in teacups, most lightly, beautifully. Lawrence painted hussies and bounders, unconscious of class, with the unabashed surety of genius, whether they were in their slippered kitchens or others' drawing-rooms. Forster's characters were typical. Lawrence's were individual. 'There have been enough stories about ordinary people', said he in self-defence: but it was easy for him to say that. Everybody in the world would be remarkable, if we used all our eyes to see them. Lawrence will call one eloquent, because his body curves interestingly when he stands still. Another is rich, because his dark silence means something. A third may thrill, once in the book, in voice. Some have interesting minds. Not many.

Forster may love a character, in a gentle, aloof irony of love, like a collector uncovering his pieces of price for a moment to a doubtful audience, as if he feared that an untaught eye might soil, by not comprehending, their fineness. Lawrence is a showman, trumpeting his stock, eager for us to make them ours — at his price. There is no comedy in him. He prods their ribs, prises open their jaws to show the false teeth. It is not very comfortable, on first reading. To be impassive spectators of the slave-market takes a training.

Forster is clever and subtle. Lawrence is not subtle, though he tries, sometimes, to convey emotional subtlety. In the big things his simplicity is shattering. His women browbeat us, as Juno browbeat the Gods at Jupiter's at-homes: but in the privacy of their dressing-rooms they jabber helplessly. Pages and pages are wasted in the effort to make the solar plexus talk English prose.

But Lawrence and Forster give their main parts to women whenever possible. This is their deliberate choice, for each can draw an admirable man. Look at the youths in the *Longest Journey*: or read what Lawrence has written about Maurice Magnus, or Cipriano, or that splendid Canadian soldier in *The Fox* (was it the 'Fox', or had the story one name in England and another in America?). But Lawrence never draws an average man or an average woman. He gets excited always over our strangenesses, and is the first thrall of his own puppets.

'If one could get over the feeling that one was looking at him through the glass of an aquarium', he says in *The Lost Girl*. So he himself feels the queerness of his creations. We see the poor fishy things writhing across his whirl of words, in the grip of emotion belonging to some other element than the every-day. They are not hard and strong. He is poet, and thinker, a man exquisitely a-tingle to every throb of blood, flexure of sinew, plane-modulation of the envelope of flesh. He feels, sees, and sings us instant and endless improvizations:

and there is weakness somewhere in it all. The excitements are some-times febrile: nor does he always play fair. Look at him dodging round his crowded characters, sniping at their back-parts (gutter-sniping almost) when they are most off-guard or distracted. What about that portrait of M.M., or of Hermione? Compare the shameless spite of *Look! We have Come Through* with the lambent raillery of the Queen Bee which signifies *Sea and Sardinia* into happiness. Then, after the long journey through all his works, return, in *The Plumed Serpent*, to Mexico and the accepted creed of a man who is at last sure of himself.

TO EDWARD GARNETT

15.3.28   *[Drigh Road, Karachi]*

Dear Garnett, I have today posted (as yesterday I finished) the R.A.F. notes.[1] They will come to you, round about through the parcel mail, in some ten days; I sent them by an official by-pass, for safety; as there is no copy, and the making this long manuscript has hurt my eyes exceedingly. I never want to write a thing again.

The notes eventually worked out at 70,000 words: the Uxbridge part was 50,000: and I added 20,000 on Cranwell, (built up out of con-temporary letters and scraps of writing which I'd hoarded against such a need) to redress the uniform darkness of the Depot picture. Cranwell was a happy place.

Will you let me hear of their safe arrival to your hand? If the first receiver does not put on stamps, and you have to pay, let me know that also. I have no English stamps here, and this is a gift to you: a very overdue gift. Was it 1923 I promised you the things? So very sorry.

This afternoon I am going out into the desert with some paraffin and the original draft, to make sure that no variant survives, to trouble me as those two editions of the *Seven Pillars* do. So before you get it your copy will be unique.

I think they fit their little book very tightly and well. I imagined the final size of them, from the draft, and had de Coverley bind me up the book, in the simplest blue morocco. It is the blue we wear, and you can imagine the tooling is our brass buttons. If I'd thought of it I've had had six buttons down the front, like me.

[1] *The Mint.*

Every word has been four times written: the original (bed-made) note: the pencil draft: a typed copy, to give me a clearer view: and then this inked version. So even if you do not like it, you will know that it is not because I have spared the pains to make it worth your acceptance.

I want it offered to Cape, for publication, in extenso, without one word excised or moderated. Can you, as his reader, arrange this? I'd rather no one read it but you (and David G. who feels rather like your second edition, revised and corrected by the author, but less spontaneous): and I want him to refuse it, so as to free me from the clause in his contract of the *Revolt in the Desert,* tying me to offer him another book. I hate being bound by even an imaginary obligation.

There: it's over. Six months hard correction and copying, all additional to my seven-hour R.A.F. day, and all done in barracks. Surely there should be actuality in its phrasing and feeling? Yours ever

T.E.S.

A REVIEW of *The Works of Walter Savage Landor.* Vols. I to III. Chapman & Hall. [This review was never published but was probably written in the spring of 1928.]

I think this is rather a wonderful effort, on the part of publishers and editor. It is probably the definitive edition of Landor, which includes everything he wrote, prose as well as verse, that any man could ever wish to read. When they talk about the complete works of authors they seldom mean more than this. Everybody has things like cheques and bills, and washing lists, that are indubitably his work, but which are not readable, in the particular sense.

Here is all Landor or all enough. It is magnificently printed, in a type of excellence, on good paper, in a size which is imposing, as Landor should be, without being unwieldy. I have carried its various volumes about with me, lately, trying to think out a review of them, and have not suffered either from their weight or size. The binding is apparently strong. A car wheel passed over Volume three, without its disintegrating.

The first, and I think most certain thing to say about this edition is that it can probably never be bettered. Those who purchase it (sixteen volumes, the publisher thinks, at 30s. each: a lot of money) are getting something final for their money. Not only does it include all the Landor hitherto collected, but there are extras of all sorts. Not the laundry bills and cheques and other ascripta which take up an appreciable time of everybody's pens, whether they are great authors or not, but the real writings of this strange and uncompromising man.

The second thing to be sure about with this edition, I think, though I say it only by guess, and have not collated Mr. Welby's texts with MSS or first collected editions . . . is that the editing is as final as the quantity of the texts. No quality but love for his author could have so subdued an editor to suppress himself. This is a definitive edition as easy and beautiful to read as an unscientific one. There are no disfiguring footnotes — or very few. No brackets, no apparatus of criticism, no impertinent explanations of what an author meant or did not mean. Mr. Welby has trusted Landor to say what he meant: — and magnificently did the old man mean it.

The old man; why do we think of Landor always as old? Other authors have grown old; why was Landor never young? why do we prefer to cherish the old man in our imaginations? I think I can, at times, love Landor but only as an old crotchet whose whims must be allowed to have their sway with me, for the sake of peace, while I am in his company. The risk, the loss, the expense, the disaster of quarrelling with Landor are too great to dare to face. They would for ever destroy one's pleasure in the work.

So we get an author to whom one must surrender if one is to enjoy him — a tyrannical writer.

Hence perhaps the smallness of his audience, at times, and the way in which ever so many people pick him up, cry 'glorious; I'll come back and have some more of this' and don't. We are so seldom in the yielding mood. Yield: — it's not yielding; it is complete abject laying aside one's own senses of values and standards, if one is to absorb Landor. He humiliates.

A great artist: he said his say beautifully. The cadences of his prose, the lambent smiling of the old thing, the ripeness of age, the prejudices and cock-sureness of too long a life, are all here, perfectly set down. His art was such another vehicle as the prose of George Moore: a vehicle which was so lovely itself that (for a long time) no one asks where it is going, or whether it is going anywhere. For a long time:— but for sixteen volumes? Not for me.

It's as lovely, and as remote, and as useless, as the sound that wind makes in the top of too close a grove of firs. A music of whispering, which steals down the cathedral-dark, pillared, yet starved trunks within the grove. It is good to listen there, once in a way. We may be sure that whenever we walk there, the music of the wind will be waiting there for us, as in a store: but it's a pleasure which, if made an end, wouldn't help us very much. It is too smooth, too sure, too un-faltering to hold much mind.

TO MRS. THOMAS HARDY

16.4.28   [*Karachi*]

Dear Mrs. Hardy, You should not have bothered to answer my letters: you know that these letters to the person left behind when someone dies are such vain, inadequate things.

One thing in your letter pleases me very much: you say you have failed him at every turn. Of course you did: everybody did. He was T.H. and if you'd met him or sufficed him at every turn you'd have been as good as T.H. which is absurd: though perhaps some people might think it should be put happier than that. But you know my feeling (worth something perhaps, because I've met so many thousands of what are estimated great men) that T.H. was above and beyond all men living, as a person. I used to go to Max Gate afraid, & half-unwillingly, for fear that perhaps it would no longer seem true to me: but always it was. Ordinary people like us can't hope (mustn't pre-sume to hope) that we could ever have been enough for T.H. You did everything you could: more than any other person did: surely that's not a bad effort? You thought him worth more: I agree: but life doesn't allow us an overdraft of service. We can give just all we've got.

The biography is a very difficult thing. They will trouble you very much about that. Do not let these troubles go in too far. What he told you, on November 28, that he'd done all he meant to do, absolves you from infinite toil. He will defend himself, very very completely, when people listen to him again. As you know, there will be a wave of detraction, and none of the highbrows will defend him, for quite a long time: and then the bright young critics will re-discover him, & it will be lawful for a person in the know to speak well of him: and all this nonsense will enrage me, because I'm small enough to care.

Whereas all that's needful is to forget the fuss for fifty years, and then wake up and see him no longer a battle-field, but part of the ordinary man's heritage.

You say something about giving me something that was his. You'll remember I have an inscribed *Dynasts*, which is suffering the Indian climate. After all, I am, too; and so must the book. I don't want to lock up a treasure against a day of enjoyment which may never come: but if you really have anything else, then please keep it for me, if you will be so good. It will be to fall back upon, if some white ant, or flood or accident robs me of this one which I have. Only I feel that his older friends have so much more right. I only came at the eleventh hour.

Please do not answer all this: it's just me talking to you, as I used to do in Max Gate, while we waited for him to come down. I wish I hadn't gone overseas: I was afraid, that last time, that it was the last.
Yours ever   T E SHAW

TO E. M. FORSTER

16 4 28   [*Karachi*]

Dear E.M.F., Forgive the pencil. I am inkless this afternoon.

Don't cut me off from anything you may write in future, because you've sent me one supremely good thing.[1] I've liked everything you've written: some of it very much, some of it less: but liked it all. I've tried to write, myself, and know that a man doesn't ever succeed in mating sound and sense and expectation. We land, always, other than we meant to land. That's presumably the fun as well as the vexation of writing. Your less-good work is very helpful to me, as an amateur of writing: for our minds are parallel enough for me to see your intention behind the expression, (or to flatter myself that I do partly and in some senses see it . . . oh shades of Henry James in this style of letter!) and just because it may not completely come off, so I may be able to see the works inside it more clearly.

And I don't expect you to be always at your best. Indeed I once said that it was the mark of a little writer to be very particular about his standard. The big men (of the Balzac, Tolstoi, Dostoevski, Dickens stamp) are incredibly careless, here & now. They seem to have said

[1] An unpublished story.

'well, it doesn't matter. If the readers can't see what I mean, they needn't'. There's a lavish ease about their stuff: and an agony of carefulness about the Henry James & George Moore & Flaubert class. These are two points of view. I like both lots. But don't, please, stand on ceremony with me. The most beautiful parts of all the best Greek statues are their mutilations.

What news of Posh? He is out of the service, I think, now. If you still hear of him, let me hear of his fortunes: even of his misfortunes. He must strike a smooth place, in living, soon: if he is to keep going at all.

Do not take my illnesses seriously. They are only indispositions: and may be partly due to my refusal to see that I'm too old to lead a boy's life much longer. They do not allow, in the Services, for grown ups . . . the whole treatment and regimen is designed for the immature: and physically I'm in decay, however half-baked my mind may be.

Here is a suggestion which I make with great diffidence and regret, for what may seem to you presumption. Long ago, at Uxbridge, I made some notes on life in the ranks. They are crude, unsparing, faithful stuff: very metallic and uncomfortable. Once I meant to make a book of them, by leaving them to sink down into my mind, & then reviving my memory by their aid, to distil something adequate to what is a very large subject: the enlisted-man-in-uniform.

Only the disappointment which the Arabia book's feebleness bred in me knocked all writing hopes on the head. So I told Edward Garnett, father of the David you know, that he should have the original notes, as a relic. My relics are hawked about, you see, and have a money value. Clouds Hill was floored and roofed out of the sale of my golden Mecca dagger![1]

Lately I sent Garnett his notes: not the originals, which I've just burnt, but a fair copy, rearranging, pointing, linking, dividing the notes. I've taken away, not one adjective, nor one word, nor one idea: but have lengthened by as much again what was almost a literary shorthand, into what I think is a palatable mess. Palatable? well, hardly: it's presumably oatmeal porridge sort-of-stuff: but a man might get through it, if he added the milk of time and the sugar of patience to its body.

David Garnett would probably lend it to you: but O Lord, it's no hospitality to offer to an esteemed friend. Don't choke yourself: don't try to, if porridge and dry bread & dough make you ill in advance.

[1] Bought by Lionel Curtis and now in the keeping of the Manciple, All Souls, Oxford.

Really to see it is no privilege, & to read it probably pain: but if you send me your imperfections (as I devoutly hope, for they seem to me more meaningful than other people's perfections) I should at least acknowledge to you the existence of writings of mine later & wiser than the *Seven Pillars*.

I want the existence of these notes kept dark; otherwise asses will want to print them, or read them. Mrs. Shaw: the two Garnetts: Trenchard (my sponsor in the R.A.F.) if he wishes to see them: you. I think that is all I care about. It would have been Hogarth too: but he has gone. He was like a parent who had never stopped growing.

TES.

TO EDWARD GARNETT

23. 4. 28. [*Karachi*]

Your telegram came this morning, most happily. I was on guard all yesterday and so felt pretty much in the dumps. It is a hateful, painful waste of time: everybody comes off guard throughly miserable: and all the day after feels wet. Besides, I'd had to make up my mind to get shifted from this place, as a precautionary measure. If I stay, there's a risk of trouble. So I've asked to be sent up country. It may be worse, or it may be better. I lose a lot of books, and music (only gramophone music, but the potted stuff is very well, for people away abroad), and the little conveniences I've arranged myself in the last fifteen months; and begin again. I'm stared at, a good deal, my first month in a new camp.

However the telegram was cheerful. It had my 'Ross' number on it, which excited the Orderly Room: for it was delivered as an official message. I don't know how you sent it. They presumed it was in code, and had a good try at it with their code books: then delivered it to me in despair, wondering if it was mine. I read it in a minute, and was delighted to know that the thing had brought up safely. It took so long to copy out, that I'd have grudged the Post Office its acquisition.

Also I'm delighted that the recipient likes his present. I am very deeply in your debt for advice, and experiences among books, & kindnesses: and I've been wanting for ever so long to make some return. Only being so nearly a pauper, by my own wish and will, I can't easily gratify a particular person. It is like making bricks out of thin air. So it was really kind of you to telegraph.

Do not let your enthusiasm for new notes in writing run away over *The Mint*. It is a new note, I fancy: I've never read any other book of exactly the same character. It is fragmentary, and has the dry baldness of notes: none the worse for that, for the *Seven Pillars* was prolix: and this *Mint* is not long-winded: or not often long-winded. Doubtless it would come down 20% with advantage; but in so short a book (is it 80,000 words?) the dozen pages more or less hardly matter: also it isn't a book. It's a note for your private eye: a swollen letter.

It is well-written, I fancy, as prose. The labour of the *Seven Pillars* taught me a good deal about writing: and I have worked very hard at other people's books and methods. So by now I must have acquired the rudiments at least of technique. I'd put *The Mint* a little higher than that: and say that its style well fitted its subject: our dull clothed selves; our humdrum, slightly oppressed, lives; our tight uniforms: the constriction, the limits, the artificial conduct, of our bodies and minds and spirits, in the great machine which the R.A.F. is becoming. I had to hold myself down, on each page, with both hands.

A painted or sentimental style, such as I used in the *Seven Pillars*, would have been out of place in *The Mint*, except in the landscape passages, where I have used it. But I doubt whether any un-versed reader would be able to connect the two books by any tricks of authorship.

The form of the book took a lot of settling. I worked pretty hard at the arrangement of the sections, and their order. Mainly, of course, it follows the course of our training, which was a course: but where I wanted monotony or emphasis, I ran two or three experiences together, and where I wanted variety I joggled 'em up and down. I got all the material out into a skeleton order, and placed it, so near as I could: then I fixed in my own mind the main curves of idea which seemed to arise out of the notes: and re-wrote them with this intention in the back of my mind. So I fancy there are probably hundreds of tiny touches (perhaps only an adjective or a comma) of a tendencious nature, which help to guide your intelligence to the ends I had in view. Only here again I was hampered, as in the *Seven Pillars*, by having true experiences to write about. I took liberties with names, and reduced the named characters of the squad from 50 odd to about 15: else there'd have been too many fellows in the book, and they'd have confused the picture. Otherwise it is exactly true.

Force — oh yes, I expect parts of it are forcible. That's the worst of feeling things as strongly as I do. Only I hope that some of my contentment and satisfaction in the R.A.F. appears, as well as the abuses I saw. So often we tend to take the sweets for granted. That's why I'm hoping that Trenchard won't ask to see it. He sees the R.A.F. from the top, and I see it from the bottom: and each of us, no doubt, thinks he sees straight enough: but I swear I'm as keen on it as he is: and I do all I can, down here, to make it run smoothly. It's only the little unimportant things in the R.A.F. that make airmen's lives sometimes a misery. I itch to tell him of them, and have 'em swept away. He is like a tank when he gets going.

However, it's no use going into all that. You like the booklet: which I made up to please you. Don't let the snare of ownership stifle your judgment. It is not a classic: but the précis of an (unwritten, and never to be written) book: and as it is not to be published, itself, you and I will never be able to check our judgments by public opinion. So: — regard it as a notebook of mine, given to you because you liked my *Seven Pillars*, and because I had no further room nor reason for it. I won't tell you it's rubbish: for I wouldn't have given you what I believe to be rubbish, but it's pretty second-rate, like me and my works: it's the end of my attempts to write, anyhow: but please believe that this inner conviction of the thing's not being good enough only increases the momentary pleasure which I obtain from having you praise it. I'd so like something of my creating to be very good: and I bask for the moment in the illusion of your praise. Very many thanks therefor.

T.E.S.

TO H. S. EDE

30.6.28   *Miranshah*

Well, I've moved from Karachi, and come up to the most remote R.A.F. Station in India: — and the smallest. We are only 26, all told, with 5 officers, and we sit with 700 India Scouts (half-regulars) in a brick and earth fort behind barbed wire complete with searchlights and machine guns. Round us, a few miles off, in a ring are low bare porcelain-coloured hills, with chipped edges and a broken-bottle skyline. Afghanistan is 10 miles off. The quietness of the place is un-canny — ominous, I was nearly saying: for the Scouts and ourselves live in different compartments of the fort, and never meet: and so there's no noise of men: and no birds or beasts — except a jackal concert for five minutes about 10 p.m. each night, when the searchlights start. The India sentries flicker the beams across the plain, hoping to make them flash in the animals' eyes. So sometimes we see them.

We are not allowed beyond the barbed wire by day, or outside the fort walls by night. So the only temptations of Miranshah are boredom and idleness. I hope to escape the first and enjoy the second: for, between ourselves, I did a lot of work at Karachi, and am dead tired. . . .

[Lawrence was once more to be the victim of his own legend. As early as July 23rd, 1928, an enterprising journalist had been trying to fasten a story on to his return to the East. Towards the end of the year the westernizing King of Afghanistan, Amanullah, had brought his unpopularity to a point where the conservative majority of his subjects rebelled, and the 'uncrowned King of Arabia at the head of the British Secret Service' on the borders of Afghanistan provided excellent copy for journalists all over the world, and a focus for the suspicions of English socialists and anti-Imperialists. Members of the English Labour Party became honestly convinced that the rebellion was due to the machinations of the Government of India and that Lawrence had been instrumental in bringing it about.

The *Daily Herald* and the *Daily News* took up the question of Lawrence's activities hotly.

In the circumstances, the decision of the Government of India to have Lawrence sent home immediately was natural and inevitable. Labour Members of Parliament would certainly not believe that Lawrence had been reorganizing the routine of engine overhaul at Karachi, even if they had been told so, or that he was using his leisure at Miranshah to translate Homer. Lawrence was therefore, to his great indignation, flown from Miranshah to Lahore on January 8th, 1929, and thence to Karachi on the 9th, where he was met by a senior officer of the R.A.F. who explained the matter. He left Bombay on January 12th on board S.S. *Rajputana*, with instructions to proceed to Tilbury and to report to the Air Ministry on arrival, unless he received orders to the contrary. Lawrence had to leave behind most of his possessions, including his gramophone and records, and was very indignant. The whole affair, conducted by the Air Ministry largely in secret cipher telegrams, which had to be specially locked away or hastily burned, was handled in quite the wrong way.

But though it may seem that the circumstances of Lawrence's return, and the publicity which followed it, were such as to increase his persecution mania and foster his eccentricity, they counted for little in the long run. For some weeks he was anxious, angry and sore; for some months he suffered intensely from the cold of the English winter. But Lawrence's return soon brought him renewed health, happiness in himself and in his work, and six years of comparative peace, during the last of which he was wrapped up in doing an important job.

All this was being brought to him by the officer who came alongside the *Rajputana* at Plymouth, and got him away without the reporters seeing him, and to whose squadron of Flying Boats at Cattewater Lawrence was now posted. Wing Commander Sydney Smith became not only Lawrence's Commanding Officer, but also a close personal friend who valued him as he deserved, and knew how to get the best work out of him in the interests of the Air Force.]

TO E. M. FORSTER

5/2/29   14 *Barton Street, Westminster, London, S.W.*1

Dear E.M.F., I am being hunted, and do not like it. When the cry dies down I'll come out of my hole and see people— unless of course the cry doesn't die down, and the catchers get my skin. I have a terrible fear of getting the sack from the R.A.F. and can't rest or sit still.

Some anonymous person or persons bought and sent me a very large and new and apolaustic Brough:[1] so if my life is saved out of the hands of the hunters, it will be a merry one: yet there's a fly in the jam. So large a present (valued at three years of my pay) pauperizes me a bit, in my own sight, for accepting it. Yours   T E S.

Of course, all Clouds Hill is yours, to take away. Are you ever in London?

[1] Mr. and Mrs. Bernard Shaw.

THE ROYAL AIR FORCE

TO ERNEST THURTLE, M.P.

9/2/29   14 *Barton Street, Westminster, London, S.W.*1.

Dear Mr. Thurtle, I doubt whether you properly observed the
street's name or the number of the house, the other night. Will you
hand it on, please, to whoever will return my books — and please
remind them to be uncommonly discreet over *The Mint*, the R.A.F.
book; for I have been told by the Powers that my visit to the House
was not approved: told very distinctly, I'm afraid.

It was very pleasant for me that you were so reasonable, that night.
You will realize that I can't spend an hour with everybody, explaining
that there is no mystery: and I'm delighted to have had the chance, by
lending you those two books, to give myself away to you completely.
If Mr. Maxton will read some of them, he'll never be nervous about
me, either, again. Yours sincerely   T E SHAW

CONFESSION OF FAITH

Not the conquest of the air, but our entry thither.
We come.
Our soiled overalls were the livery of that sunrise. The soilings of our
bodies in its service were prismatic with its light. Moody or broody.
From ground to air. First we are not earthbound.

In speed we hurl ourselves beyond the body.
Our bodies cannot scale the heavens except in a fume of petrol.
The concentration of our bodies in entering a loop. Bones, blood
flesh all pressed inward together.
Not the conquest of the air. Be plain, guts.
In speed we hurl ourselves beyond the body.

We enter it. We come.
Our bodies cannot scale heaven except in a fume of burnt petrol.
As lords that are expected. Yet there is a silent joy in our arrival.
Years and years.
Long arpeggios of chafing wires.
The concentration of one's body in entering a loop.

TO ERNEST THURTLE

26.IV.29   *Cattewater, Plymouth*

. . . I must put in a last word about my abnormality. Anyone who had gone up so fast as I went (remember that I was almost entirely self-made: my father had five sons, and only £300 a year) and had seen so much of the inside of the top of the world might well lose his aspirations, and get weary of the ordinary motives of action, which had moved him till he reached the top. I wasn't a King or Prime Minister, but I made 'em, or played with them, and after that there wasn't much more, in that direction, for me to do. So abnormal an experience ought to have queered me for good — unless my skin was as thick as a door-mat. What feels abnormal is my retirement from active life at 35 — instead of 75. So much the luckier, surely.

Here's a good little poem of F. L. Lucas, a Cambridge don and very subtle fellow, to cap my not very imaginative explanation. Yours

T E SHAW

> They laid Protesilaus to his sleep
>   Beside the Hellespont: there long ago,
> Out of his dust where now the peasants reap,
>   Twin elm-trees used to grow,
>
> Set by the nymphs, and taller in their pride
>   Than all the trees of Hellas. Day by day
> Their boughs climbed upward till their tops espied
>   The fields where once Troy lay —
>
> And straightway withered.

TO AN UNKNOWN CORRESPONDENT[1]

On the whole I believe that not doing is better than doing, and I believe mankind will reach its zenith when it determines to propagate

[1] This extract was copied by Colonel Isham from a letter of Lawrence's sold at the Anderson Galleries, New York. The word 'art' in line 3 was copied as 'and', which in my opinion makes nonsense. The most satisfactory reading would be to omit the word altogether.

art no more . . . I have done with politics, I have done with the Orient, and I have done with intellectuality. O Lord, I am so tired! I want so much to lie down and sleep and die. Die is best because there is no reveille. I want to forget my sins and the world's weariness.

13 years after Paris.[1]

TO R. V. BUXTON

[1930]   *Mount Batten, Plymouth*

Dear Robin, Yesterday a tall thin creature walked up to me in the Camp: grinned at me: afterwards I saw that it was my young brother, a queer creature, who is 30 and has a wife and one child. I thought he was in Spain, and said 'What on earth brings you here?' 'House-hunting' he replied: as if there were any houses at Plymouth. Absurd.

It seems they really do want a house. It must, they say, have one large room, to serve as a study (he writes real books, not trash): nothing else matters, I gather. Should be within economical distance of London or Oxford, for the library's sake. Which is why they went to Bodmin to-day, I suppose, to look at a reformed farm-house.

Suddenly I have remembered your cottage-farm: you said you had no tenant. Is that so? Do you want a queer vague definite creature living there? Would it fit an oddment, a spare part, a child-of-the-old-age of my two extraordinary parents? We got madder as the tale increased. I was only the second son, he the fifth. It ended then, God be praised.[2]

I picture you in pink, very mud-splashed and weary, late for your bath, & spoiling the dinner by keeping; all for inability to tear yourself away from my masterly depiction of life in the R.A.F. Only it isn't like that at all.

Lately a letter came to me from St. Andrews University (a minia-ture & charming place in Scotland) offering me an honorary degree as Doctor Of Laws. 'Ha Ha' said I 'some undergrad is pulling my leg.'

---

[1] Comparison of this with another letter leads me to believe it was written about June 1929, ten years after Paris.

[2] When A. W. Lawrence married, Lawrence wrote to him: 'If there is no insanity in the family there will soon be!'

I replied accordingly, and have had dignified remonstrances from John Buchan & Barrie: it seems Baldwin particularly put my name. Worst of all, in honest praise of St. Andrews I said that if it were mine I'd wrap a clean napkin round it & keep it on the side-table to gloat at, like a Stilton. Apparently they dislike Stilton. Barbares! Hoots mon: aweel.

T.E.S.

TO F. N. DOUBLEDAY

18.IX.30   *[On leave in Scotland]*

Effendim, Rotten pen and foul paper, but here on the North East edge of Scotland I've just heard that you are 'out of the wood'. So much to be thankful for, yet no more than is fitting. Understand, that yourself and illness do not go together! I think of you always as part pirate, like Kidd, part buccaneer like Morgan, with moments of legitimacy like Farragut. It is unthinkable to think of an Effendi incapable of bearing arms. So please recover quickly that we may laugh again. Meanwhile come on leave with me for ten days!

Come northward many miles above Aberdeen, and then strike towards the sea across the links, which are sand-tussocked desolations of charred heather and wiry weeds, harbouring grouse to whirr up alarmingly sideways from under-foot, and rabbits so lazy that they will hardly scuttle their snow-white little tail-flags from the path. Add a choir of larks and a thin high wind piping over the dunes or thrumming down the harsh stems of heather.

They are three miles wide, these links, and ever so desolate, till they end abruptly in a rough field whose far side is set on edge with a broken line of cottages. Behind their roofs seems to be pure sky, but when you near them it becomes sea — for the cottages had [been] built round all the crest of the grassy sea-cliff and down it too, cunningly wedging their places into its face wherever there was a flat of land as wide as two rooms. Almost to the beach the cottages fall. Beach, did I say? It is a creek of sand, cemented along one side in a grey quay-wall from which and from the opposing rocks up run the grass-grown cliffs in heart-comforting bastions to the houses fringed against the sky. The creek's a fishing port. You could find room to play a game of tennis in it, perhaps, if the tide went dry. So there are no bigger boats than dinghies and no room for any: nor heart for any with the jaws of greycold reefs champing white seas outside, all day and night.

Imagine whole systems of slate-like slabby rocks, flung flat-wise and acres square, thrusting out into the maddened North Sea which heaves and foams over them in deafening surges. The North-Easter, full of rain and so misted that our smarting eyes can peer only two or three hunched yards into it, is lifting the waves bodily into the air and smashing them upon the rocks. There is such sound and movement out there in the haze that our eyes keep staring into its blindness to see the white walls rolling in. The concealed sun makes all white things half-luminous, so that the gulls become silvered whenever they dip suddenly to turn a knife-edged cartwheel in the spray: and the thunder of the seas enforces a deafened silence on all other things, so that we feel as much as see the energy let loose. Each big wave makes the air quiver and sends a shading reverberation across the shore about our bodies.

That is the fighting of the sea against the land: and the sea's casualties have filled the port, around the elbow that the jetty makes. There the water is stifled and heaves sickly under a mat of sea-suds one foot thick. You know the creamed and bubbly foam that blows up a beach when the wind rises and the sea, together? Well, that flocculent stuff is all impounded in our bay, filling it so full that black water and jetty and steps and rocks and beach are all invisible, buried under it like a corpse in a blanket.

'Curse the fellow and his seascape, you are saying.' Am I paid to read his manuscript? Peace, Mrs. Doubleday will take it away and burn it, so soon as you roar in anger.

What are we doing here? Nothing, practically. There are 3 of us — Jimmy who used to work in Canada but came home in 1914 and was a gunner for four years in France: now he jobs horses in Aberdeen: — Jock, the roughest diamond of our Tank Corps hut in 1923; — and me. We have Mrs. Ross' cottage lent to us and reluctantly in turn sweep its floor and fetch the water and coal. For meals thrice a day we spread our coats to the wind and fly to the cliff-top, where the Mrs. Baker-and-Butcher feeds us in her parlour. Then heavy inside, we slide down hill to the cottage again in the cove: for ours is the nearest hovel to the high-tide mark. That is good in fair weather and exciting today. Great flocks of surf beat tattoos on the roof till the tide turned.

But what do we do? Why nothing, as I said. Jimmy has his horses to groom and feed and exercise. Sometimes we do the last for him.

Jock fishes: boys bring him mussels and he waves a pole from the quay at the wild wild waves. Once up came a codling from the yeasty deep, the poor orphan taking pity on him. He brought it us in silent manly pride, and we made him clean it. Scrape scrape his knife went, like a man cleaning a flower-pot. We helped him eat it, too.

Most of our food is fish, I remember. There is a local industry, called sperling. Cut open a round fish, flatten it, dry him bone-white for days on a rock of wire netting, smoke him, boil him in milk. Not bad, tasting like dull veal. The local people are lovers of sperling, though, and taste more in them than I do. Then there are baby soles, four-inch things too small for sale in the city with the adult soles. They are fried and delicious. Down with great soles henceforward.

The cottage has 3 rooms. Jock took the middle one with big bed and fire-place. Ours open from it and are cold. So we make his our sitting room, and have pushed the bed into the corner, farthest from the fire where I sit and think all day, while turning over the swimming suits to dry. Also I eat pounds of peppermints (pan-drops they call them: Aberdeen and excellent) or read H. G. Wells' *History* in a dollar edition lately produced, as you may have heard, by a young and pushing publisher in the States. I wish I had a dozen copies to give away: but only one ran the customs gauntlet to do Cassells out of his English rights. Believe me, it's a good book. 8/6d in England and a dollar in the almighty-dear States.

I tried to get Heinemann's elephant book *Novels Today* in Aberdeen but they had it not. Distribution faulty, for Lady Eleanor Smith and Strong are both first-class. The book-shop lady tried to work off on me a thing called *Angel Pavement*, also by Heinemann. She said everybody was buying it. 'Not quite everybody', I protested politely. 'This very man' she said 'wrote *Good Companions*'. 'Dreary artificial sobstuffed thing' I snorted, having luckily read *Good Companions*. 'You *are* hard to please' she grumbled, offering me *The Boy's Book of Colonel Lawrence* at a reduction, seeing I was in uniform and he now in the R.A.F. I told her I knew the fellow, and he was a wash-out: then I bought a *Daily Express* and escaped the shop. Alas, for I wanted to read *Dewar Rides*[1] again.

Effendi, what folly makes me want to talk rot to you when I hear you are ill? The whole man is a gladiator: who demands tall talk? Why babble when he is (temporarily) hurt? God knows. Ask Mrs. Doubleday to take the nasty thing away again.

[1] By L. A. G. Strong.

Our tea-time now. The winds have stopped, but the waves increase. They are so big that only two roll in to the minute now. I wish you could hear the constancy and fresh repetition of their thunder, and the sharpness and loneliness of the gulls questing through the spume. The poor gulls are hungry from the storm and beset our roof for the food-scraps we throw away. They have the saddest, most cold, disembodied voices in the world.

Evening now. I must go up the shop for oil for the lamp. The shop is the post office and I'll then send this off, before its length frightens me and makes me burn it.

Au revoir, Effendim, soon, let's hope.   T. E. S

P.S. for Mrs. D-D — make it London next summer too! and we *will* get to Kipling this time.

TO BRUCE ROGERS

31/1/31

Dear B.R., Forgive the typewriter: I write in office hours, and they mistake the yapping of this machine for my work.

Your letter is very re-assuring. Under such conditions the *Odyssey* can harm nobody and nothing. I am only doubtful if it will do anyone any good!

We must do our best to get the whole of the luxury edition placed before the date of publication: then the popular version will matter less.

As soon as the price is fixed I have several of my friends to inform about it. They will wish to subscribe to Walker's direct,[1] which benefits the firm to the extent of the booksellers' commission.

The arrangements you suggest for the U.S.A. edition sound admirable. Not many copies either of a Harvard or a Knopf edition would be brought into England, for there is no demand in England for more versions of the classics. I do not think the point demands any safe-guarding.

I return XVIII-XX, with some minor changes and the necessary em-

[1] Emery Walker published Lawrence's translation of the *Odyssey*.

bodying of the W.[1] corrections. Only I have refused to accept his championing of the ancient theory of hollow-bladed axes. The metaphor from ship-building seems as clear as daylight.

You may have thought me cavalier in preferring my own way to W.'s professional suggestions, sometimes: not his verbal suggestions, but his archaeology. Yet, actually, I'm in as strong a position vis-à-vis Homer as most of his translators. For years we were digging up a city of roughly the Odysseus period. I have handled the weapons, armour, utensils of those times, explored their houses, planned their cities. I have hunted wild boars and watched wild lions, sailed the Aegean (and sailed ships) bent bows, lived with pastoral peoples, woven textiles, built boats and killed many men. So I have odd knowledges that qualify me to understand the *Odyssey*, and odd experiences that interpret it to me. Therefore a certain headiness in rejecting help.

I have no more for you yet. My R.A.F. interruption is almost over, pro tem, and I hope to get XXI into shape before another week is passed.

The pleasurable memory of this *Odyssey* business will be our relations. I have found you the most considerate editor and producer imaginable, and it has been very enjoyable to work for you. The money will also be pleasurable, and alas also, too soon, a memory!

T.E.SHAW.

[On February 4th, 1931, an Iris III Flying Boat crashed near Plymouth. Lawrence was one of the rescue party and gave evidence at the inquest on February 18th. The following impression by Lawrence is written in pencil on the sheets of pencil manuscript headed *Leaves in the Wind*. It may refer to this crash.]

from 'LEAVES IN THE WIND'

IRIS crash — sea molten-visioned aluminium. Poor [*name omitted*] drunk with foolish laughter, like captive balloon whose gas wobbles it drunkenly as the strands that tether it to this earth are parting, one by one. Rest drawn, bleak grey-faced, tardily quarrelling amongst themselves. No joy but [*name omitted*] laughingly. We got on to him,

---

[1] W. was called in as an expert to give an opinion.

he promised betterment. Six of us crushed together in the crushed canister of the hull were bubbling out their lives. Great belches of air spewed up rose now and then, as another compartment of wing or hull gave way.

TO FLIGHT LIEUTENANT W. E. G. BEAUFORTE-
GREENWOOD

14.VII.31.   *Mount Batten*

Dear Flight Lieutenant Beauforte-Greenwood, Here is a final report, so far as present arrangements go, on the little surf-board target. It is very good for its proposed job, I think, the only difficulty being spotting, which is best done from the aircraft, the fixed base-line of 600 yards giving to the observer a good chance of guessing his shot's real position.

I had to give up towing it behind 159, as we did only 13 miles an hour with it, full out; and could only get out occasionally, the other two 35-footers being under top-overhaul for Schneider duty. So I hooked it onto the Biscayne Baby and ran it off its keel! The rough days (everybody said the wire would break in bad water) were great fun, the sea being much too bad for a Southampton upon our last occasion. Once I got it up to 35 m.p.h.: but 20-25 is really its fastest decent speed. For a fast target you would have to re-design, with flared bows and a flattened after-moulding, I think, to plane: with scoop-tubes like air intakes thrust through the floor amidships. You could make it weigh only half of this target's weight, I think.

This one slowed my light boat by about 3 miles an hour only, at its worst.

I think any quantity of reconditioned 5 cwt drogue cable is available, and its lightness and strength makes it ideal for this tow, if it is carefully handled. The art is to wind it regularly and so avoid kinks. If that is done, or if all kinks are cut and spliced, the wire will last indefinitely. The main reason for a power-driven drum is to be able to wind up smoothly, under load.

I'm afraid this photo should have been taken from behind the target, to show that its splash is much the same as my boat's. The 600 yards interval makes it look so remote and small. We have put the target back into station stores, now. It is a bit worn at its edges but still quite good. The Flying Boat very much enjoyed bombing at it.

The towing is dead easy: you can turn any way you please, as slow  or as fast as you like. I have doubled back like this within 50 yards of the target, with it proceeding blissfully in the former direction while I dashed by!

Yours sincerely

T. E. SHAW

Mount Batten is sad over the C.O.'s[1] posting to Manston on promotion. It is a great loss for flying boats and motor boats as he was keen on water work. Also he was a very good C.O. I wonder if Calshot have bust old 200 again!

[In March 1932 a monograph on the construction and handling of the 200 Class R.A.F. Seaplane Tender was stencilled and issued for the use of coxswains and mechanics employed as crew, or in servicing these boats.

It is a severely technical document but I have been allowed to quote from it and have chosen passages which illustrate Lawrence's capacity as a seaman, rather than as an engineer, as being more generally interesting.]

from THE 200 CLASS ROYAL AIR FORCE SEAPLANE TENDER

NOTES ON HANDLING

212. The 200 Class was designed to be as directionally stable as possible in all runs of sea and windage; and with that in view the after part of the hull has been kept high to balance the high forepart in side winds. Plenty of dihedral was also allowed to give side area or keel area, so that with very little draft they do not weathercock or blow sideways as readily as would otherwise have been the case.

213. The design is a compromise; and most of the resultants are on the side of advantage. The boats are not much wind-driven and yet draw so little as to escape tide effect. They have few bad manners and

[1] Wing Commander Sydney Smith.

no ugly tricks. In good trim of engines and hull they can be made to do anything their coxswain wants. They will run on one engine alone and steer against it, though difficulty will be experienced with a hard beam wind on the same side as the working engine. These handling notes are only provided because few R.A.F. coxswains have had much experience of handling hard-chined fast boats in a sea-way; and because such boats behave rather unlike the previous round-bottomed craft.

214. The primary purpose of the class is to save life or Service equipment from a crash at sea. Between emergencies they will serve for general duty; but they must always be kept in trim for high-speed work. Their coxswain's constant duty is to save the engines, by intelligent reading of the dashboard instruments and by moderation in use of the throttle. The engines are built to give 3000 revolutions at maximum; and to hold that speed throughout the boat's fuel endurance; but like all high-efficiency engines, they lose tune after much running at full throttle.

Approaching a Moving Object, or Crash

223. The approach to any moving object will naturally be made following its direction, so that steerage way can be kept on the boat. The universal rule is to drop speed a considerable way off the object, so as not to overshoot or call upon the engines to stop the boat. Only just enough advantage in speed over the object should be kept for choosing the time to come alongside it. A fast approach, with a sharp opening of the engines in reverse, will cause the boat's own wash to over-ride her and throw her off or against the object, depriving her of control for the critical moment — which is dangerous for the boat and uncomfortable for the passengers, besides looking and sounding clumsy.

225. In safe circumstances never approach a crash or tow from the weather or tide side, as it will drift away; but circle it, and come up bow to wind or tide, or both, or the best compromise. Keep away, if time permits, to see if the object or the boat is the faster down tide or wind. If the object is faster, make it travel past the bows.

226. If there is danger of fire or explosion in a crash, approach only from the weather side. It may be desirable to come in stern-on, to keep the forward efficiency of the engines and rudder for sudden get-away. Care should be taken to post a lookout aft, in such a case to warn the coxswain of any wreckage that might endanger the boat or foul the propellers. The methyl-bromide fire extinguishers will

extinguish any small quantity of burning petrol upon the water; but the danger of its re-lighting must be borne in mind.

Approaching a Stationary Object

228. As with a moving object, the universal rule applies. Drop speed so far away that no follow-up wash will complicate the come alongside. Gauge wind and tide. If they are helping the boat, then do not endanger her by driving close in; let wind or tide set her in. If they are contrary, near-steering is necessary. The boat will generally come in easily if the bow line is got away first and the outboard engine put into astern. With this design of boat and propeller there is no cast to the stern of the boat when starting or stopping, through propeller action.

229. At very low speeds the engine control is crisper than the rudder control; yet the rudder will govern the boat even when she is merely creeping on clutch drag, with both engines ticking-over in neutral. At 'SLOW AHEAD' on both engines, speed is about 7 miles an hour, which is altogether too fast for ordinary approaching. As a rule only one engine should be in gear, the other being kept waiting in neutral ready to engage reverse the moment it is required. Generally it is advisable to drive on the inboard engine, and approach slightly by the inboard bow, so that the astern action of the outboard engine will pull her in, parallel. At 'SLOW AHEAD' on one engine, in this fashion, the boat will be doing about 8 feet per second, which makes calculation of the time-lag of the gear control very easy. The engines may be allowed to run in neutral on clutch slip or drag, indefinitely.

Rough Water Driving

233. Rough water driving varies according to whether the sea is ahead, abeam or following; and the conditions may be divided into reasonably and unreasonably rough water. Reasonably rough water may be taken as a three to four foot sea maximum. In this the boat may be driven at cruising speed (or in the case of emergency full out) without any alarm on the score of safety. The naturing the boat into a head sea with wind ahead, or into a sea ahead with the wind astern, by the throttles is an art which must be practised, and which a good coxswain will quickly learn by experience. Except in emergency, the boat's forward rate should be made to suit the weather circumstances, remembering to keep her running at an efficient planing speed, to make her clean and steady.

234. Unreasonably rough water with the 200 class means any seas

above five feet in height. This can be encountered under two head-ings: — when the boat is put to sea deliberately and when it is caught at sea by the weather. The emergency which justifies the first, will justify the boat's being driven at full speed. She will stand the punish-ment to the limit of the coxswain. Her fore-part is boxed up and practically watertight. The after cockpit is self-draining and will not suffer from any water taken aboard. Here again the boat can be natured and handled to be sea-kindly, so suffering less risk of damage and reaching her objective quicker than by blind, forceful driving.

235. *Head Sea Conditions*. Remember the boat is most manoeuvrable. Ease her head away quickly to an on-coming sea. Having shouldered it straighten out to the course. Having ridden its head and started the dive down its back, prepare at once for helming away. According to the state of the sea, so this helming away or tacking becomes more stringent, until a stage may be reached in which it is advisable to helm away on an opposite tack. Fetching her about should invariably be done after riding the head of a sea. Never attempt it when climbing, and be careful to have the boat well in hand before sliding down the back of the sea. When coming about in such weather, if there are many aboard, get them to sit on whichever will be the weather side as she turns; begin the turn as described, and if in danger proceed (probably at greater speed) parallel with the sea until an opportunity of getting completely round presents itself. The turn can be helped by driving the weather engine wide open, to assist the rudder.

236. *Beam Sea*. During trials in a full gale (wind 60 m.p.h.) the trial boat was run parallel to the sea and kept there, being thrown sideways or chine-skidding down the lee side of big seas, by her speed. Engines both full open. The feeling was that the boat wanted to roll over; but the situation was repeated again and again, and she proved to have plenty of stability in reserve. The action to be taken in such case is helm hard down to steer the boat's nose into the trough of the wave; and open out both engines. This should correct the skid. If, on the other hand, the stern has already swung well down, helm hard the other way to drive the boat up the sea, where course may be regained. As a general rule any portable weight, including crew, should be moved to the weather side. In a beam sea any desired speed can be safely and comfortably maintained.

237. *Following Sea*. These boats with their very light bows are peculiarly easy to handle in a following sea, and quite safe. Some anticipatory instinct, quite impossible to describe but easily acquired

by practice, enables directional control to be maintained, against the boat's natural tendency to run off her course. The maxim should be to keep going fast, because the rudder is far more positive at speed than when going slow. The boat's contact with the sea, after running down one wave to meet another, should be eased with the throttles, to reduce her tendency to bury her nose in the water. Remember always to open throttle again as soon as the overtaken wave is shouldered. According to the state of the sea, the boat can be helped or eased by coming across the trough or head of the sea at an angle. This angle can only be found by practice each time with the run of sea encountered. It will be found that this type of boat is much less inclined to yaw, veer or fall off in a following sea than previous Service types. The deflection will be at the stern, and can be ruddered against before it develops. The coxswain will also find his ruddering to have a stabilizing effect, of considerable value. Anticipate the yaw for correction not only on the making of helm, but also on returning to midship position.

Impossible Weather

238. Should the weather become impossible, the boat must be slowed down to dead slow, and in heavy breaking seas kept head to sea. She will then ride with safety. If the engines break down the boat lies a little off the wind and sea, but has no tendency to broach to. A sea anchor or drogue would render her safe in almost any circumstances of sea.

251. These notes have been compiled from an experience of running the test boats of this class in almost every condition of weather to be found off the English South coast during two winters.

TO SIR EDWARD ELGAR

12. X. 32   *Mount Batten, Plymouth*

Dear Sir Edward, In the one week I have had letters from you and from W. B. Yeats — and it is a little difficult for an ordinary mortal to say the happy things when public monuments around him come suddenly to speech. I have liked most of your music — or most that I have heard — for many years: and your 2nd Symphony hits me between wind and water. It is exactly the mode that I most desire, and so it moves me more than anything else — of music — that I have heard. But thousands of people share my liking for your music, and with better reason for they know more about it than I do: so this doesn't justify the kindness of the Shaws in bringing me with them that afternoon. The chance of meeting you is just another of the benefits that have accrued to me from knowing G.B.S., who is a great adventure.

There are fleas of all grades; and so I have felt the awkward feeling of having smaller creatures than myself admiring me. I was so sorry to put you to that awkwardness: but it was inevitable. You have had a lifetime of achievement, and I was a flash in the pan. However I'm a very happy flash, and I am continually winning moments of great enjoyment. That Menuhin-Concerto is going to be a pleasure to me for years: and the news of your 3rd Symphony was like a week's sunlight. I do hope you will have enough enthusiasm left to finish it. There are crowds of us waiting to hear it again and again.

Probably it feels quaint to you to hear that the mere setting eyes upon you is a privilege: but by that standard I want to show you how good an afternoon it was for me, in your house. Yours sincerely,

T. E. SHAW

TO B. H. LIDDELL HART

26.vi.33

Dear L.H., You talk of a summing up to come. Will you (if you agree with my feeling) in it strike a blow for hard work and thinking? I was not an instinctive soldier, automatic with intuitions and happy ideas. When I took a decision, or adopted an alternative, it was after studying every relevant — and many an irrelevant — factor. Geography, tribal structure, religion, social customs, language, appetites, standards — all were at my finger-ends. The enemy I knew almost like my own side. I risked myself among them a hundred times, to *learn*.

The same with tactics. If I used a weapon well, it was because I could handle it. Rifles were easy. I put myself under instruction for

Lewis, Vickers, and Hotchkiss (Vickers in my O.T.C. days and rifles, and pistols). If you look at my article in *The Pickaxe*[1] you will see how much I learned about explosives, from my R.E. teachers, and how far I developed their methods. To use aircraft I learned to fly. To use armoured cars I learned to drive and fight them. I became a gunner at need, and could doctor and judge a camel.

The same with strategy. I have written only a few pages on the art of war — but in these I levy contribution from my predecessors of five languages. You are one of the few living Englishmen who can see the allusions and quotations, the conscious analogies, in all I say and do, militarily.

Do make it clear that generalship, at least in my case, came of understanding, of hard study and brain-work and concentration. Had it come easy to me I should not have done it so well.

If your book could persuade some of our new soldiers to read and mark and learn things outside drill manuals and tactical diagrams, it would do a good work. I feel a fundamental, crippling incuriousness about our officers. Too much body and too little head. The perfect general would know everything in heaven and earth.

So please, if you see me that way and agree with me, do use me as a text to preach for more study of books and history, a greater seriousness in military art. With 2,000 years of examples behind us we have no excuse, when fighting, for not fighting well.

I like your little book — wherever it does not repeat a told tale. It starts at Chap. II by the way, and goes on to page 335. That's what you've sent me. Yours   T.E.S.

REPORT ON TRIP OF R.A.F. BOAT NO. 200

[9. *June* 1934]

R.A.F. 200 left Southampton Water for Plymouth, her present station, on Saturday, June 6th, at ten minutes to eleven in the morning, carrying a special crew of five R.A.F. personnel, and nearly twice her

[1] The journal of the Royal Engineers.

normal capacity of petrol and stores. Wind S.W., freshening to 20 miles an hour. Tide contrary. Sea choppy.

Engines first set at 2300 to Hurst Castle at 11.40 a.m. There the sea became rougher, the wind and tide coming in together and raising a broken swell. Off the Needles the meeting of the cross-seas provided quite a rough twenty minutes, during which the boat was thrown about vigorously and took some heavy splashes of spray aboard. No rolling, and speed only temporarily reduced, as from Swanage onwards advantage was taken of the shelter of the Portland promontory to open her up to 2500, her best cruising speed, and run over the swell. From St. Aldhelm's Head onwards she was a perfectly dry boat, and this opportunity was taken to refuel her main tank from cans of petrol carried on deck, and from a temporary tank taken on board for the special run.

Portland Bill was reached at about two o'clock, and passed close inshore. The long seas at Lyme Bay gave further opportunity of keeping up her cruising speed economically, as the boat ran lightly over them, steadily and dryly. The tide was now ebbing in her favour. Course was set slightly to the N. of Start Point, and the Devon Coast sighted at 4 o'clock, a long and heavy rain storm making visibility very limited. Off Start Point more heavy and broken seas were met, and speed was again reduced for a time, past Prawle to Bolt Head off Salcombe. The wind then dropped off to half its former strength and the boat was opened up to 2300 revolutions and held cleanly on her course to Plymouth at twenty past six p.m. No water remained in her bilges upon arrival, thanks to the self-bailers arranged in each of the boat's compartments. No solid water was shipped during the run, and the main cabin remained perfectly dry and comfortable throughout.

The engines ran faultlessly. A little oil was added to them on the way, to maintain their pressures constant at 40 lbs.; except for this they were not touched or thought of. The water outlet temperature gauges stood constantly at 45° Cent. The oil put in amounted to 1 gallon, as noted. Before the run to Plymouth was started, the boat did two and a half hours of test and trial running in Southampton Water. The trip round took seven and a half hours; so that her total running on the day came to 10 hours. During this she used 90 gallons of petrol, and 30 gallons remained in tanks upon arrival at Plymouth.

The whole run was made at cruising speed, no attempts to save time or take the shortest course being made. The boat was slowed down whenever the sea conditions made it comfortable to do so.

TO ERIC KENNINGTON

6. VIII. 34   13 *Birmingham St., Southampton*

Oh yes, I take my time; indeed I take time to answer any letter. Why? Well, I think it is mainly laziness. There is my R.A.F. work which has to be done to schedule, willy nilly: so what is not compulsory is told to wait on the mood. And letter-writing, being difficult, is seldom the mood.

For it is very difficult to write a good letter. Mine don't pretend to be good . . . but they do actually try very hard to be good. I write them in great batches, on the days when at length (after months, often) the impulse towards them eventually comes. Each tries to direct itself as directly as it can towards my picture of the person I am writing to: and if it does not seem to me (as I write it) that it makes contact — why then I write no more that night.

Yet, as you would say if I was there to hear you, the letters as they actually depart from me are not worthy of this strained feeling. At the far end they appear ordinary. Yes, that is because I'm not writer enough to put enough of myself into any work. Or better, because there is not enough of myself to share out and go round. There has been, upon occasion. Both the *Seven Pillars* and *The Mint* (but *The Mint* especially) stink of personality. Where has it gone? Don't know. I'm always tired now, and I fritter myself away month after month on pursuits that I know to be petty, and yet must pursue, faute de mieux.

'What the hell's the matter with the chap' you'll be asking. You send me a sensible working-man of a letter, reporting progress — or at least continuity — and I burble back in this unconscionable way. I think it is in part because I am sorry to be dropping out. One of the sorest things in life is to come to realize that one is just not good enough. Better perhaps than some, than many, almost — but I do not care for relatives, for matching myself against my kind. There is an ideal standard somewhere and only that matters: and I cannot find it. Hence this aimlessness.

It is a pity, rather, that I took so many years teaching myself this and that and everything: for now that I'm full enough to weigh a lot, I've nowhere in which I want to use that weight. If I'd cared less about learning and more about doing things, the story would have been different. It's a common way in the world. The fuller the cask, the less active the damned thing seems to be.

Let's come down to earth. You still carve. I still build R.A.F. boats. On March 11th next that office comes to an end. Out I go. Clouds Hill awaits me, . . .

TO SIEGFRIED SASSOON

17. XII. 34   *Clouds Hill, Moreton, Dorset*

Dear S.S., Written, this is, from Bridlington: but I have been reading your *Vigils*, and I felt I could not write about them from the 'Ozone Hotel'. My cottage is where they should be read.

They have deeply moved me. They are so . . . gentle, I think I want to say. To be read slowly and in sequence. The rather conscious script helps them, by delaying the eye. These poems are like wood-violets and could easily be passed over by a man in a hurry. When I came to the war-poem I checked for a moment, sorry: but soon saw that it was right. Not if you had never written before; but here in its place among your poems it helps, by translating into quietude the fierce moods that held you for *Counter Attack* and the Satires. Every other one of the 22 looks forward. I can feel the solidity of the war-anger and the peace-bitterness under the feet, as it were, of these poems: they are all the better for it, but so far from it: so far above and beyond.

Sometimes, in a lyrical phrase or an adjective of accumulated beauty, I can link them to your earlier work: but only thus, externally, by a common ornament. Yeats has walked along something of the same path. His *Tower* poems are like the ash of poetry. People offended his taste by putting *Innisfree* into all the anthologies, because they liked it not for the poetry but for the green sap running through it. You are not ashamed of 'suddenly burst out singing' but growing shy of it. Just a word or two hint at happiness, and then your blotting paper comes down.

I will try to write you again about them when I have grown into them a little. They aren't like Shakespeare, at all. They are human and very careful and faint and solitary. Each seemed to me to shut one more door of your gigantic house. There are heaps more doors yet; and of course you might one day open one. By their implications

I date the first drafts of all of them from before that day at Christchurch, and I feel that you, yourself, have changed colour somewhat since the writing. You have more colour now, I think, and more colours too.

But these are exquisite poems, exquisite. First reading was like sitting under an autumn tree, and seeing its early leaves falling one by one. I shouldn't like you to go on writing *Vigils*, world without end. They are seasonal fruits, but lovely. You can dare them because of your past fighting: and those of us who have deserved a rest will feel them and be grateful to you.

That last little volume of political poems[1] had frightened me a little, for you seemed to look back. Here you go a full stride forward. Cheers, and long life to your pen. It is doing us good — and proud.

T E S.

I've read this through and see that I've forgotten to say that these things are streets ahead, in power and beauty and calmness, of anything of yours I've ever before seen. You presumably know that: but when, I ask you, are you going to reach your prime? Near fifty and still a growing poet. It's like T.H. isn't it? He grew till seventy. Don't answer this rot!

[The following note can be safely assigned to 1935.]

from LEAVES IN THE WIND

FEB. 6 wrote to Felix[2] saying. I must not try to sign on again in R.A.F. as in 12 years time I should be too old to be efficient. The wrench this is; I shall feel like a lost dog when I leave — or when it leaves me, rather, for the R.A.F. goes on. The strange attraction in the feel of the clothes, the work, the companionship. A direct touch with men, obtained no other way in my life.

[1] *The Road to Ruin*, by Siegfried Sassoon.   [2] R.A.F. Station, Felixstowe.

TO LORNA NORRINGTON[1]

24.2.35   *Bridlington*

Dear Lorna, I'm sorry to have been so slow in replying, but I've
been run nearly off my feet lately, writing letters to tell everybody
that I'm going away. I've had a lovely little card printed 'To tell you
that in future I shall write very few letters' and I'm going to tuck one
into each letter that I write for the next six months!

I was thinking of you today, when our dinghy was jumping over
the sea at the harbour mouth here. You would have loved it: the little
boat was going beautifully. Your father was looking on.

My cottage is waiting for me, and I'm hoping to like it very much.
I shall not get there for a couple of weeks, and will then go away
again . . . but I hope later on to settle down there a bit.

The address is Clouds Hill, Moreton, Dorset, so far as the Post
Office is concerned. Actually I'm not in Moreton parish, but the post-
man comes on to me from there, with his sidecar. When I'm away
he has a box, into which he dumps them!

As I'm only 40 miles from Hythe, it will be quite easy for me to
run over there on a bike and see you, when the weather is nice. I
shall enjoy a boat-ride, when that time comes. Yours   T E SHAW

TO ERNEST THURTLE

6. iii. 35

Dear E.T., My Dorset 'fastness' is beset, they tell me, by pressmen:
so I wander about London in a queer unrest, wondering if my main-
spring will ever have a tension in it again.

So I'm not cheerful, actually; but sad at losing my R.A.F. existence.
It was good, and I felt useful: also it was noticeably peaceful. I expect
there is a good deal to be said for the comfortable shadow of a 'bombing plane'[2] — now a term of abuse, but the only democratic weapon!

---

[1] Aged 15.
[2] Thurtle had written: 'Let the tanks and the bombing planes rust and rot. Much
good will they do us, poor mortals.'

Thank you for the book. I look forward to reading it when I get home . . . which is after the ink-slingers go to their homes. Theodore Powys, the brother of Llewellyn, is a rare person.

We must meet some day. In fact, I will again attempt Johnson's Court! Yours   T E SHAW

TO H. S. EDE

5.iv.35   *Clouds Hill, Moreton, Dorset*

Dear Ede, I have not been so long about answering as it has seemed. The Press have still been troublesome, and so I have spent this fine month almost wholly in wandering about the south-country. Very beautiful; all very beautiful. But I have wanted to settle here instead. Ungrateful creature, man!

Now I have persuaded the local police to patrol the place and during daylight hours I keep indoors. It works, so far: but soon I shall have used up my firewood, and then what? Perhaps the pressmen will tire soonest.

About your cheque. I have looked at it for two days, wanting to take it for your sake, but reluctant. You see, it is an experiment I am making . . . have I saved enough to live on in decency, or must I make more? The sooner I can find the answer to that, the better for me. If I take your £30,[1] that will carry me over in unexpected ease for twelve months, and next year I might feel the need of it.

As for the Brough, that is easy.[2] I have licensed it, and yesterday rode into Poole to buy some necessary fittings for the house. It goes like stink and is altogether a marvellous machine. But I should hesitate to call it necessary. A Rolls-Royce goes like . . . scent, shall we say? . . . and is a marvellous machine: but I am certain that a Rolls is not necessary to my pleasure. I want to find out if the Brough is. If it is, I shall have to save somewhere else, live below estimate, or make more, to be able to afford it. My earning power is potentially considerable: but I hate using it.

You will observe that the whole essay is deliberate, an endeavour to enjoy idleness. That is (by modern standards) not a very moral

[1] The cheque was found, after Lawrence's death, in a book at Clouds Hill.
[2] Till then he had been riding his push-bike.

aim. I do not care. I feel that I have worked throughout a reasonably long working life, given all I can to every cause which harnessed me, and earned a rest. My 'expectation' is less than 20 years, and the last few years of that 20 will be diminishingly pleasant, as infirmities increase. If I am to taste the delights of natural England, as has been my life's wish, I must do it before I grow really old. And I must do it on my own; not at others' expense.

I have no dependants, no sense of public spirit, or of duty to my neighbour. I like to live alone for 80% of my days, and to be let alone by 80% of my fellow-men and all my fellow-women below 60 years of age. The golden rule seems to direct me to live peacefully in my cottage.

I hope you will find me here some day: not yet, for all is sixes and sevens, as in a besieged town: but soon. The district is good for walking: and if I cannot put you up or feed you properly, why surely the neighbourhood can. What is Bournemouth for?

Your book.[1] I can't settle to it. These claims are distracting. So I send it back. Economics are like tides. We fail to harness them, yet they ebb and flow. The right thing would be to chart them, but nobody can distinguish their moon. Sorry to be unhelpful.

T.E.S.

TO GEORGE BROUGH

5. IV. 35   *Clouds Hill, Moreton, Dorset*

Dear G.B., Your two letters were sent on from Bridlington (I left the R.A.F. a month ago) and waited here for me, while I have been dodging about to avoid my enemies, the Press. This will now be my only and permanent address, I hope.

About your fan. Our propeller experiments were all marine, and they showed how little was known yet, even in that much exercised branch. Air propellers (of the suction type) have been, I am sure, very little studied. Large diameter of course means noise, as do broad tips. Four blades are quieter than three and as efficient. You can push an air-prop pitch up to great steepness, so long as the revs are not extravagant. But frankly I cannot help you. Our props had so different

---

[1] Maurice Colbourne's *Economic Nationalism*. Ede had asked Lawrence's opinion of the Douglas Credit Scheme.

an intention. The water is so solid an element. Have you considered Ethylene glycol for cooling? Or is the engine getting too hot for its oil? In the desert I ran a tiny condenser for our old Fords, and so boiled all day without using a pint of water, and with great thermal advantage. Later they doubled the Leader-tank, increased the pump output, and carried on without boiling. Petrol consumption then increased.

I have wondered of late how the new engine was shaping. You were going to make a new angle of inlet for the mixture. Now you are working on the timing gears! Please tell Mr. J.A.P.[1] for me that if I had his sized firm and couldn't get an aircooled twin right in 18 months, I'd eat my test-bench and wash it down with my flow meter!

Meanwhile I've only ridden the ancient-of-days twice this year. It goes like a shell, and seems as good as new. The push-bike is a reality, though. I came down here from Yorkshire on it and have toured much of the S. of England on it in the last three weeks. It is dull hard work when the wind is against: but in lanes, and sheltered places and in calms or before winds, wholly delightful. So quiet: one hears all the country noises. Cheap — very! not tiring, up to 60 or 70 miles a day, which is all that I achieve, with sightseeing: and very clean on a wet road.

The loss of my R.A.F. job halves my income, so that my motor cycling would have been much reduced for the future, even without this 30 m.p.h. limit idea. I had half-thoughts of a touring sidecar, for long jaunts, with the push-bike for leisured local trips, but we shall see. The old bike goes so well that I do not greatly long for its successor. If only I had not given up my stainless tank and panier bags and seen that rolling stand! But for those gadgets my old 'un would still be the best bike in the S. of England. Good luck with your fan! Yours

T E SHAW

TO FLIGHT LIEUTENANT H. NORRINGTON

20. IV. 35   *Clouds Hill, Moreton, Dorset*

Dear N., In retirement there are no ranks ... we are all 'have-beens' together: however you will not come to it for some years. For myself, I prefer work.

[1] Maker of J.A.P. engines.

The cottage has become quiet, now: except for a beastly tit, which flutters up and down one window-pane for six hours a day. First I thought he was a bird-pressman, trying to get a story: then a narcissist, admiring his figure in the glass. Now I think he is just mad, and know him to be a nuisance. If he goes on into next week I shall open the window some day and wring his silly neck.[1]

My time passes between swearing at him, cutting brushwood, and inventing odd jobs. No letter-writing any more, except under extreme need, and no duty. A queer lapse into uselessness, after that long-drawn series of jobs that made up my life.

Please remember me to Lorna and to Mrs N. I went to Hythe lately and scrounged a lot more screws. There was a dinghy for test, tell her! On Wednesday I hope to meet B.G.[2] there.

Bother that bird: he taps too regularly, and distracts me. Yours ever   T.E.S.

TO MRS. THOMAS HARDY

Easter Monday [22-4-35]   *Clouds Hill*

Dear Mrs. Hardy, I am sorry I missed you the day you came — as also at Max Gate, a week after, when I tried in turn to find you. The *Indiscretion*[3] proved charming. I like the appealing simplicity of the prose . . . like, and yet a very poor relation of, the sweeping sentences that make up *Jude*. I understand why he kept it unprinted, yet it is not a thing to be ashamed of. If only T.H. had found time and will to follow up *Jude* with yet one more work, it would have linked his prose, in power, with his poetry.

You have made a beautiful little book of it. I have enjoyed the reading, and enjoy the possession.

I am worried now about Mother and Bob in China. The troubles are touching their area. They are both longing to come home, now.

Clouds Hill is going to be all right as a living place, I fancy. The

---

[1] The bird continued this practice for some weeks until it was finally shot after Lawrence's accident. It had probably started nesting inside.

[2] Beauforte-Greenwood.

[3] *An Indiscretion in the Life of an Heiress*, by Thomas Hardy, which Mrs. Hardy had recently published.

last three weeks have been almost unbroken peace. I feel very indisposed to do anything more; and very tired.

Philpotts-Hardy, the rhododendron, is in good flower at the moment, leading his hillside by a month or two towards the promise of colour. I hope you will be able to see him, some day. Except for Wednesday (when I have to go to Hythe, to my old boat-yard) I shall be here continuously now, I hope . . . though in disorder, as the place is unfinished, and I potter with job after job. But please come, if you are in Dorset soon. Yours ever   T E SHAW

TO LADY ASTOR

8.v.35

No: wild mares would not at present take me away from Clouds Hill. It is an earthly paradise and I am staying here till I feel qualified for it. Also there is something broken in the works, as I told you: my will, I think. In this mood I would not take on any job at all. So do not commit yourself to advocating me, lest I prove a non-starter.

Am well, well-fed, full of company, laborious and innocent-customed. News from China — NIL. Their area now a centre of disturbance.   TES

[The following letter to the Keeper of the Department of Fine Art, Ashmolean Museum, seems to have been the last that T. E. Lawrence wrote.]

12.v.35   *Clouds Hill, Moreton, Dorset*

Dear Parker, I am delighted that your expert scrutiny has passed the John. To me it has always seemed a powerful and characteristic drawing: but ownership blinds the judgment, and then I liked both Hogarth and John as people. So I couldn't trust myself. However if it is a decent drawing, there is only one fit home for it, and that's in your place. Hogarth was so much the Ashmolean, for his last years.

In my letter to Leeds I asked that it should be classed as a drawing, not hung on the back-stairs among the former Keepers. This is in accordance with a wish of Mrs. Hogarth's. She dislikes it as a portrait — which is the side that most pleased me! I will also ask you to see that its label does not carry either my current or my obsolete name! That's a habit we had long ago, when Woolley and I were adding a hundred objects a year to the Collection. It looks all wrong to star oneself all over the cases and screens!

At present I'm sitting in my cottage and getting used to an empty life. When that spell is over and I begin to go about again, I shall see what John thinks of the Ashmolean as a home for some really joyful drawings . . . things done out of delight for himself Yours

T E SHAW

TO HENRY WILLIAMSON

[*Telegram; postmarked* 13 *May* 35]

Lunch Tuesday wet fine cottage one mile north Bovington Camp

SHAW

[Lawrence rode into Bovington Camp on his Brough motor-cycle and sent off this telegram to Henry Williamson and was fatally injured while riding back to Clouds Hill.]

INDEX

INDEX

INDEX

Arab Bulletin

The Mint

[not yet published(1951)]

OTHER EXCERPTS AND ARTICLES

The Letters

INDEX

ALPHABETICAL LIST OF RECIPIENTS OF LETTERS

The number given is that of the letter in the 1938 edition. In the chronological list above the letters are given in numerical order.

SELECTED PERSONAL NAMES, PLACE-NAMES AND SPECIAL TOPICS

Abbreviations: A.B. — *Arab Bulletin*; J.R.E. — *Journal of the Royal Engineers*; L. — *Letters*; M. — *The Mint*; L.W. — *Leaves in the Wind*; S.P. — *Seven Pillars of Wisdom*; E.R. — 'Evolution of a Revolt'; W.Z. — *Wilderness of Zin*.

INDEX

Fort at Geziret Faraun (Graye), 64-5 (W.Z.)

Gasim, 110-3 (S.P.), 124 (S.P.)
German-Kurd affair at Carchemish, 67-70 (L.)
Geziret Faraun (Graye), 64-5 (W.Z.)

Hamed the Moor, 96-7 (S.P.)
Harran, 52 (D.)
Hassan Shah, 154 (S.P.)
Hejaz, 80 (S.P.), 89-90 (A.B.), 93 (S.P.), 98-9 (S.P.), 118 (S.P.), 136-42 (A.B.), 153 (L.), 209 (J.R.E.)
Hogarth, D. G., 42 editorial note, 47 editorial note, 49-51 (L.), 80 editorial note, 179 (S.P.), 316-7 (L.)
Holdich, 77 (L.), 81 (S.P.)
Hussein, King, 80-1 (S.P.), 83 (S.P.), 87 (A.B.), 186 (S.P.), 260 (L.)

Ibn Rashid, 73 (L.)
Ibn Saud, 74 (L.)

Jemel Pasha, 152 (S.P.), 167 (S.P.)
Joyce, Colonel, 187 (S.P.)

Kethira, 130 (S.P.)

Lawrence family
    A. W., 31 (L.), 293 (L.)
    Father, 32 (L.), 240 (L.)
    Frank, 31 (L.), 240 (L.), 315 (L.)
    M. R. (Bob), 31 (L.), 36 (L.), 315 (L.)
    Will, 31-2 (L.), 76-7 editorial note
    (see also List of Letters, p. 324)
Lebanon, 199 (S.P.)
Lewis, 142-6 (S.P.), 148-9 (S.P.)
Lisieux, 42 (L.)

McMahon, 91 (S.P.), 117-8 (S.P.)
Mecca, 80 (S.P.), 187 (S.P.), 260 (L.)
Mesopotamia, 78-80 (L.), 117 (S.P.), 223 editorial note, 225-7
Middle East Department, 227 (L.), 231 (L.)
Military Tactics, 99-104 (S.P.), 214-20 (E.R.), 260 (L.)
Mint, The, 239 (L.), 266 (L.), 280-1 (L.), 285-6 (L.), 287 (L.), 290 (L.), 308 (L.) (see 'Classified List of Excerpts', p. 233)
Mohammed el Dheilan, 118 (S.P.), 123-4 (S.P.), 128 (S.P.)
Murray, Sir Archibald, 80-1 (S.P.), 92 (S.P.), 117 (S.P.), 134 (S.P.)

Nahi (Turkish Bey), 158-60 (S.P.)
Nasir, Sherif, 112-3 (S.P.), 116 (S.P.), 119-22 (A.B.), 123 (S.P.), 127 (S.P.), 129 (S.P.), 131 (S.P.), 194 (S.P.)
Nawaf Ibn Shaalan, 181-2 (S.P.)
Nesib (Nessib) Bey, 112-3 (S.P.), 117 (S.P.), 119-20 (A.B.), 123
Nuri Said, 187 (S.P.), 189 (S.P.), 193 (S.P.)
Nuri Shalaan, 118 (S.P.), 185-6 (S.P.), 189 (S.P.)

Odyssey, 397-8 (L.)

Parthenon, 42-3 (L.)
Petrie, Flinders, 57-8 (L.)

Rabegh, 84 (S.P.), 91 (S.P.)
R.A.F. (see Royal Air Force)
R.A.F. Seaplane tender, notes on handling of, 300-4, 306-7
Reading (books) at night, 40-1 (L.)
Recruitment in Army in 1922, 244-6 (M.) (see also Enlistment)
Retirement from R.A.F., 309 (L.), 310 (L.W.), 314 (L.)
Revolt in the Desert, 275 (L.)
Ross, J. H., 235-48, 267 (L.)
Royal Air Force, 235-317 passim (see also Enlistment, The Mint, Dismissal from R.A.F.)
Royal Air Force and Army life contrasted, 249-67 (L.)
Royal Tank Corps, 248 editorial note, 257 (L.), 261 (L.)
Rumm, 142-3 (S.P.), 166 (S.P.)

Sandstorm, description of, 104-5 (A.B.)
Sayidna (see Hussein)
Seven Pillars of Wisdom, 47 (L.), 202, 221 (L.), 238 (L.), 240 (L.), 241-2 (L.), 255 (L.), 263 (L.), 265-6 (L.), 287 (L.W.), 308 (L.) (see 'Classified List of Excerpts', p. 321)
Sex, comment on Forces attitude to, 252-3 (L.)
Shaw, T. E., 248 editorial note, 268 (L.); letters signed Shaw, 260-317
Sinai, complete map of, 73 (L.)
Stokes, 145-6 (S.P.), 148 (S.P.)
Storrs, Ronald, 81 (S.P.), 83 (S.P.), 84 (S.P.)
Sykes-Picot Treaty, 118 (S.P.)

Tafas, 84-5 (S.P.), 189-91 (S.P.)
Tallal, 157 (S.P.), 189-92 (S.P.)
Teras, 164 (S.P.)

327